Gardening for Pleasure

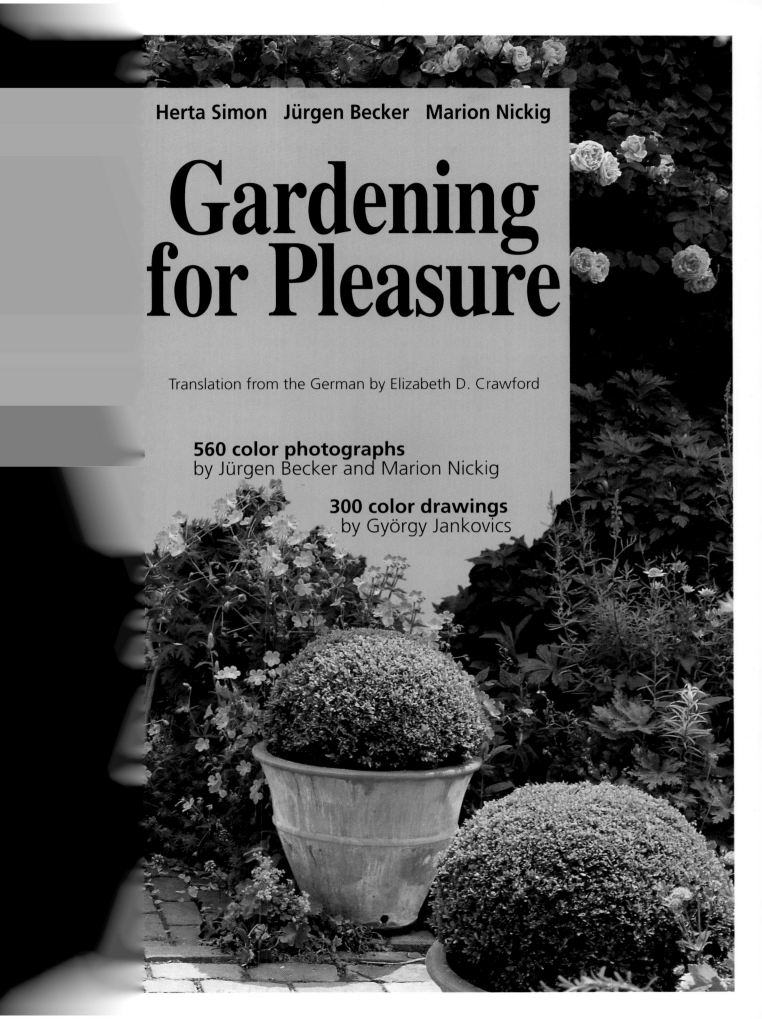

Herta Simon   Jürgen Becker   Marion Nickig

Gardening for Pleasure

Translation from the German by Elizabeth D. Crawford

560 color photographs
by Jürgen Becker and Marion Nickig

300 color drawings
by György Jankovics

GARDENING

INFORMATION   Pages 8–23

Small garden—all in fragrant white.

Clematis are enchanting climbing plants, usually foaming with an abundance of flowers. There's hardly a garden in which a spot can't be found for one.

GARDEN

IDEAS   Pages 24–143

GARDENING
PRACTICE   Pages 144–197

Flower bed in the complementary colors violet and yellow. White fits well into almost any color combination.

GARDEN
PLANTS   Pages 198–307

Foreword

A colorful display of flowers, the humming of bees, and the soft air of a warm summer day—every garden is a world of experience in itself and an encounter with nature. It is a place of leisure and relaxation, but it is also a challenge to creativity and the pleasure of design. Thus, there is hardly a garden that, in the eyes of its owner, cannot be made more beautiful and more meaningful. *Gardening for Pleasure* is a qualified helpful companion, a book with enchanting examples and ideas to feast on, and an adviser to consult, whose double-page spreads make much information available in an easily understood manner.

GARDENING INFORMATION. This first section gives answers to all the basic questions of gardeners: What is soil? How do plants live? What does climate mean? What legal problems can arise in the garden?

GARDEN IDEAS. Here all who want to recreate, change, or improve their gardens will find a wealth of exciting suggestions for design. Whether the establishment of paths or terraces, plant combinations, or original plantings of different garden sections— small garden situations are always described, which can be used as building blocks for construction designs for the large or small garden. Anyone who would like make a particular type of garden or has a very small garden will also find attractive examples here in words and pictures.

Lush summer bouquet of herbs from the garden—a pleasure for every sense.

GARDENING PRACTICE. This section gives the latest in gardening methods. Detailed, step-by-step drawings show the most important things to know about sowing, planting, care, and propagation. All can be easily followed, and the orientation is toward organic methods of gardening—for pest and disease control as well.

GARDEN PLANTS. The most beautiful ornamental and produce plants of our gardens are collected in this section. Photographs and plant descriptions make recognition easy and help in making choices.

Let yourself be seduced by the brilliant color photographs of the two renowned photographers and the delightful garden situations—and create your own garden paradise for yourself. The authors and editors wish you pleasure in all your gardening undertakings.

The Authors

Herta Simon, text author. A certified gardener with horticultural studies at Weihenstephan Technical University. For many years employed in international and national garden shows. Successful author of radio, television, and books, with a professional specialty in plant and garden themes.

Jürgen Becker, photographer. Studied painting. Has worked for many years as a freelance photographer for well-known book and calendar publishers as well as for international newspapers and magazines, with professional specialties in photography of gardens, plants, architecture, and landscapes.

Marion Nickig, photographer. Studied graphic design with Willy Fleckhause. For many years has worked for noted book and calendar publishers as well as for international newspapers and magazines, with professional specialties in garden and plant photography and still lifes.

Important: To maintain pleasure in your hobby, please note the information about working with plant pesticides on page 187 as well as the Warning and Note on page 319.

Childhood in the garden—a beautiful, imprinting experience that no one forgets.

Incomparable magic—roses and clematis might have been made for each other. Together they can create magnificent combinations when you choose plants that flower at the same time.

GARDENING
INFORMATION

Every garden is a green individual. Nevertheless, all the gardeners in this world must know and pay attention to the same things: their soil and the growing conditions of the plants, as well as the conditions in their gardens that are determined by climate and situation. You will find the basic information about these matters on the following pages.

Garden Dreams—Garden Styles

There is hardly a garden enthusiast who doesn't have dreams for his or her garden—how much these dreams can be translated into reality depends on the location, size, and condition of the area and not least on the gardener's own creativity. With some flair and careful planning, anyone can create his or her own garden paradise. Don't, however, try to turn your dream into reality at any price, but attune your plans to the conditions of your garden.

Wish List for the Garden

At first you should be clear and precise about what you want for the garden. Give yourself time for planning, because once basic designs have been carried out, they are only changed later at great cost.

Draw up a major list of your garden desires. Asking yourself the following questions can be helpful:

• Do you primarily want to relax in your garden? Do you want it as an emotional source of strength against stress? If so, you should strive for a design that is particularly easy to care for.

• Or would you rather be physically active in garden work and sport? If so, you can plan both care-intensive beds and hard-wearing lawns.

• Should your garden give you a better understanding of flora and fauna up close? If so, you can plan a garden that's close to nature.

• Do you prefer a garden of useful plants that will provide you with healthy fruit, vegetables, and herbs? If so, you should clear a correspondingly large place for these nourishing plants.

You must, by the way, also ask all these questions if you have your garden planned and laid out by a landscape architect. Then you should also take into consideration how your family circumstances may develop in the next few years. A garden can be so planned ahead of time that it is good for children to begin with and subsequently becomes "convertible" as soon as the children have left home. Measures such as the establishment of raised beds that are easier to work can be planned for when the garden may become too burdensome with the increasing age of the gardener. You should also weigh carefully how much work you are willing to do and are capable of, for the amount of care needed by a garden is not insignificant. The more "formal order" you want in your garden, the more intensively will you have to work at it. If, on the other hand, you keep to nature's order, you must only intervene now and then to control things. There is still time to listen to the birds, watch the butterflies, or read a book.

Elegant urban garden with different areas separated by hedges.

Centered layout, severely formal garden.

What Is Doable?

If you have now gathered all your desires and established the priorities, you can consider how doable your planned goals for your garden are. For this, you need to have certain information and the knowledge of the interrelation-

In the foreground, a natural area.

Garden paradise for many—enchanted garden plot.

ships in nature. Climatic conditions thus play an important role. Examine carefully what possibilities the plot offers, such as what are the light conditions, what construction might be necessary, what is reasonable under the given circumstances, and what costs would result.

Garden Styles and Types

The art of gardening, like that of architecture, has long been a part of cultural history. Almost all over the world, two style trends have prevailed until this day: the classic formal garden on the Italian and French models and the natural landscape garden according to the Chinese and English models. For centuries, gardens have been designed thus—in numerous modifications and countless variations: princely stately, large public, and small private. Today there are several style trends whose individual elements can be combined well. Above all, it is important that you tie the things together and harmonize them with one another. You will find suggestions and tips in this regard on pages 24–143, along with examples of special garden types, which will help you to develop a feeling for your own style. Below are characteristics of the arrangements of the most important garden types:

The formal garden (see pages 132–133) has an architectural organizational structure. Geometry, symmetry, and formal austerity characterize it. Pergolas, trellis walls, and hedges form and structure spaces. The produce areas are clearly separated. Austere enclosures and clipped hedges establish the impression. Pools, fountains, figures, and other decorative elements should be included.

The free-style garden offers the impression of artful nature. It is achieved with loose groups of trees and shrubs as well as irregularly arranged borders of perennials. The plants are the focus of interest. The constructed or formal elements, such as ponds or pools, and hedges as well, are subordinated to this idea. They can be geometric or free-form, with both side by side even a possibility.

The natural garden (see pages 134–135). Here the principal goal is to get as close as possible to the natural condition and to interfere as little as possible. The design bends itself to these demands. Ecological diversity has top priority. Just for this reason, such gardens have great charm. Along with the natural garden, the organic garden (see pages 136–137) is an expression of the greatly changed attitude toward nature in recent years.

Naturally there are also all kinds of possible mixes of these forms in which gardens can be shaped. An ornamental garden designed as a landscape, for example, harmonizes beautifully with a severely formal vegetable garden. The kitchen garden or potager (see pages 136–137) with its composed beds and the abundant planting represents such a mixed form. The photographs in this book also offer many examples of gardens with individual accents.

Climate and Location

Gardens are subject to the predominating climate in their surroundings. Along with the soil, climate determines how the plants thrive. In a given region during the course of the year, there are ever-recurring average values for precipitation, sunshine duration, wind conditions, and air and soil temperatures. Worldwide, differentiation is made on the basis of the particular climate zone, which often only supports a very specialized type of vegetation. Therefore, no general advice can be given about plant choice and use; ultimately the climatic conditions are always decisive.

The Climate

The length of thé growing season, the cumulative temperature, amount of precipitation, altitude, latitude, and proximity to a seaboard or lake—these factors and many more determine the overall climate of a region. Wherever you garden, select plants that will be comfortable in the prevailing climate, for successful, lower maintenance gardening.
Northeast region Characterized by temperate climate with warm, humid summers, cold winters, and on occasion, extreme cold or hot. Temperature fluctuates less near the Atlantic coast. Excellent gardening conditions.
Southeast region Relatively mild to warm winters, extremely warm to hot and humid summers, and a long growing season. Rainfall is usually generous as is sun.
Midwest, High Plains, and Western Mountain region Good gardening conditions but the winter and summer temperatures can be quite extreme with very cold, severe winters and hot, sometimes drought-prone summers. A fairly long

Fall mood in the morning. Every seasonal manifestation in the garden is

Cold Air on a Slope

Cold air is heavier than warm and flows down the slope. It collects in troughs and valleys and forms "cold pockets," and can thus cause frost injury to plants.

If you plant a hedge halfway up the slope—preferably one of free-growing shrubs—the flow of cold air is stopped. It can then form no "cold pockets" in the valley.

growing season with a shorter season in the higher altitudes of the Western Mountain region. Many ornamental shrubs and flowers need winter protection. Quite windy on the High Plains. Rainfall can be low; additional irrigation may be needed throughout the summer.
Southwest region Characterized by extreme heat, low humidity, low rainfall, and windy conditions. In higher altitudes in this region, colder temperatures, frost, and snow conditions occur. Water conservation and selecting garden plants that have low water needs take priority.
Pacific Northwest region Coastal conditions with high rainfall, mild winters, and warm to hot summers. Areas close to the Pacific coast are prone to foggy, cloudy conditions with brisk winds. Humidity can be high in some areas.

The Garden Climate

There are also variations in climate between city and open country: Houses store the warmth and protect from strong winds, so that less frost damage occurs.
Location. In a moderate climate, and on level ground, a north/south location offers ideal conditions for a favorable garden climate: The northeast side of the house blocks

ultimately determined by the climate.

Impermeable enclosures, such as walls, on the other hand, hinder the circulation of air in the garden. Air pockets develop very quickly and with them a drop of the cold air behind the wall. Within larger plots, vegetable beds can be protected by small hedges or trellises with beans and peas, but also by tall perennials and sunflowers.

Sun and rain. With every measure for wind protection, you should consider that behind the barrier there will be less light and precipitation reaching the surface. Houses, walls, trees, shrubs, and hedges cast shadows. This can be very comfortable for the garden user in the hot summer. But only shade-tolerant plants will flourish there. Diminished rainfall can be compensated for by watering.

Did You Know . . .

Phenology is concerned with the phenomena of life and development of the plant and animal worlds in relation to climate and weather. Plants can be charted every year, when and where they enter a particular developmental phase, such as blooming, leafing out, fruiting, change of leaf color, and leaf fall. Already variations of 2 to 3 weeks in apple tree flowering within one geographic region have been discovered. Usually spring moves at a speed of about 62 miles (100 km) in 4 days from the Southwest to the North. You can make such observations on your own and keep records in your own personal garden calendar. Thus, important dates can be discovered that are helpful for determining when to sow, plant, and harvest.

cold winds and protects terraces and gardens.

The south side of the house holds heat, and the garden receives lots of sun (see pages 38–39). Gardens on a slope can exhibit extremes of climatic conditions. Southern slopes are hot and dry; northern slopes shady and cool—the plantings must fit these conditions (see pages 140–141). Plots on hilltops are always subject to stronger winds.

Wind and frost protection. Protection from strong winds is frost protection at the same time, because plants usually don't freeze in winter—they dry out. The more severely wind and sun affect the plant, the greater its dehydration. Evergreens, in particular, which also transpire a great deal through their leaves even in winter, are affected this way. In addition, the water is retained in the ground with freezing and so is not available for the plants—they wilt. It is therefore important to water evergreen plants thoroughly once more before frost comes.

Artificial and natural barriers protect from cold and drafts (see drawing). Enclosures, therefore, have a material influence on the microclimate of the garden. Semipermeable elements such as hedges and fences favor it by allowing for air circulation but breaking the force of the wind.

Proper Wind Protection

Wind that encounters a massive obstacle—for example, a wall—flows over it and away or creates an eddy behind it. Plants that grow there should be robust; vegetables can be damaged.

An ideal wind protection should be about 50 percent permeable, as is the case with fences and hedges. They break the wind and so weaken its force that the plants that grow there are not affected by either air pockets or eddies.

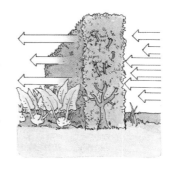

The Soil Factor

The soil forms the basis for plant life. Not only is it the medium in which the roots are anchored, but it also provides the plant with water and nutrients. It is a living organism, consisting of countless microorganisms, which through many transformation processes make available to plants nutrients from dead organic material and thus contribute to the fruitfulness of the soil. Its quality significantly influences plant growth. Therefore, gardeners should always concern themselves with the condition of the soil and promote the life of the soil through correct soil care.

Scientifically defined, the soil is the uppermost residual layer of the earth's crust. Physical and chemical weathering of firm parent rock first produces loose residual material that contains scarcely any organic substances. The soil slowly develops from this through biological and chemical processes as well as through the supply and decomposition of organic substances.

Schematic picture of the soil layers

① The surface layer is only a few centimeters deep.
② The humus layer is usually 4 to 12 in (10–30 cm) deep.
③ The mineral layer has less biological activity.
④ The subsoil usually consists solely of mineral elements.

Development of the Soil

If you dig a hole about 24 in (60 cm) deep in your garden, you can see the uppermost soil layers one on top of the other. They are usually clearly recognizable by their color. The soil can be roughly divided into 4 layers (see drawing):

The surface soil, only a few inches in depth, is the darkest. Its countless microorganisms convert organic material (such as remains of plants and dead organisms) into soil. This can be understood as similar to the process of digestion.

The humus layer is on average 4 to 12 in (10–30 cm) deep and is dark brown in color. This is where most plants root and likewise this is where countless soil organisms live—however, mainly different ones from those in the uppermost soil layer. Their task is to digest the substances predigested in the surface soil layer together with the mineral elements of the soil. This process produces the nutrients in a plant-accessible form, which can now be taken up by the roots. The surface layer and humus layer are together known as topsoil.

The mineral layer is less inhabited, but it is very rich in mineral nutrients, which must, however, first be released for the plants by the soil organisms. Here the substances coming down from above are stored, so it is also called the enrichment horizon.

The subsoil consists of stone that is undergoing a slow weathering process. However, no organic processes are taking place here.

Components of the Soil

About half of soil by volume consists of mineral components, 3% to 8% of organic substances, that is, primarily humus and soil organisms, and the remainer of hollow spaces, which are filled with air and water. The classification of soil types (see Table) is arranged according to the size of the soil's mineral components. A distinction is made among sand, loam, and clay soils.

Sand has a grain size of 2 to 0.063 mm.

Silt consists of mineral grains of the size 0.063 to 0.004 mm and is the chief component of loamy soil.

Clay is formed of components under 0.004 mm. Between the particles there are spaces, or pores, whose sizes differ according to the size of the particles. Large pores occur between the relatively coarse sand grains. Sandy soils are therefore well aerated, but they hold water poorly. Between the rather flat, tiny clay platelets there are only the tiniest capillaries. Soils of this type are therefore poorly aerated but can hold water well.

Soil water. The soil is provided with water by precipitation, groundwater, and humidity. This is the basic prerequisite for all the processes that occur in soil and the determining quantity for establishing plants. How much the plants are able to make use of the soil water is largely dependent on the pore volume: large pores drain off seeping water and so ensure that no water collection occurs. Small pores retain the water through the power of the capillaries and are thus the chief source of water provision for the plant.

Soil air exists in a reciprocal relationship to the water content of the soil: There is soil air in hollow spaces that are not filled with water. This serves the respiration of the roots and microorganisms. Therefore, the composition of soil air is also different from that of the atmospheric air: Because it contains abundant metabolic products, its carbon dioxide component is larger and its oxygen component is smaller.

Soil temperature influences numerous processes, for example, seed germination, the speed of growth of the plants, and the acceleration of soil development. When the temperatures sink to the freezing point, most biological processes rest.

The condition of the upper surface of the topsoil has a decided influence on the soil temperature: Bare soil warms faster (so remove layers of mulch in the spring); however, it also cools faster (therefore, mulch in the fall). Dark, humus soil warms best. The soil water works the same way: The wetter the soil, the more slowly it warms and also the more difficulty in cooling down again.

Humus is an extraordinarily important component of fertile soil. A distinction is made between nutrient humus, which by its decomposition provides the important nutrient elements of carbon, nitrogen, sulfur, and phosphorus, and permanent humus, which improves the character of the soil:

• It binds the nutrients to itself in such a way that they are available for the plants but do not become leached out.
• It has a stabilizing effect on the soil reactions and also on the acid-base ratio.
• It markedly increases water retention capability.
• It has a favorable influence on the formation of crumb structure.
• With its dark brown color it makes the soil more capable of storing heat.

Light Soil—Heavy Soil

Sandy soils are described as light soils. This term refers not to the weight, however, but to their workability.
• They have the following positive qualities: good aeration and water permeability, fast warming, good workability, and no clogging with mud.
• But they also have the following challenging qualities: They dry out quickly and are poor in nutrients. They also are deficient in living inhabitants because soil organisms find too little organic matter in them.

Clay soils present the other extreme and are described as heavy soils.
• They offer the following positive qualities: high water retention, and good nutrient supply because of the fast breakdown of minerals and minimal leaching out of nutrients.
• But they also have the following negative characteristics: poor aeration, poor water movement, poor warming capacity, difficult to work, and low biological activity because of little aeration.

Loamy soils possess qualities lying between clay and sandy soils, without having their extreme disadvantages. They usually come pretty close to being the ideal type of a good garden soil if they contain enough organic material or humus. They are rich in nutrients, permeable (well aerated and loose, without standing water), and fresh (retaining moisture).

Soil Life—Crumb Formation

The number and variety of soil organisms is simply unmeasurable. It is estimated that a gram of soil contains 2.5 billion bacteria, 700 million ray fungi, 400,000 fungi, 50,000 algae, and 30,000 protozoans (single-celled animal organisms). Furthermore, frolicking around in soil are eelworms, earthworms, pill bugs, spiders, mites, lice, bugs, ants, centipedes, snails, mice, rabbits, moles, and many more. They all ensure that the humus in the soil consists of plant and animal excretions, from which the plant nutrients are set free again. The loose crumb structure of the soil is based on clay-humus complexes, which for their part arise through the mixing of organic and mineral matter in the digestive tracts of soil organisms or so-called live synthesis. This denotes the conglutination of matter by living organisms—bacteria colonies, mycelia, and hair roots of plants. In any cultivation of the soil, an attempt should be made to retain the crumb structure and not to destroy the clay-humus complexes. Tips for soil testing and care are found on pages 148–151.

The Plant Organism

Without plants, no life on earth would be possible. They are the only organisms able to utilize the sun's energy directly (photosynthesis). Humans and animals depend on taking in through their food the carbohydrates like sugar, starch, and cellulose that have been synthesized by the plants. Furthermore, they need the oxygen produced by plants to carry on respiration.

The Structure of Plants

To a large extent, the seed plants are similar in their basic structure: They consist of roots, stem, leaf, flower, and fruit. Of course, these plant organs can appear very different—if one just compares the leaves of needle and foliage trees or the rose flower with that of the pine. However, these parts perform the same respective functions in growth and reproduction.

Roots. For one thing, roots anchor the plant in the soil, and for another, the root hairs provide the plant with water and nutrients. In a majority of plants, the roots enter into symbiosis (mycorrhiza) with fungi and exchange metabolic products with them.

Stem. It can be a thick, woody trunk, a herbacious stem, or a thin blade. It supports all the aboveground plant parts and provides stability for the plant. It also provides for the transport of water and nutrients from the underground roots to the leaves and the shoots by means of its interior conducting pathways. The speed of this transport varies from 39 in/hr (1 m/hr) in conifers to 328 ft/hr (100 m/hr) in vines.

Leaf. The green leaves are the primary locations for photosynthesis (see Tips and Tricks and drawing). As a rule, the leaf has a protective layer (cuticula) on its upper and undersides to prevent evaporation. Under the skin (epidermis) lie the cell layers in which photosynthesis takes place. In the cells of the green leaf tissue are found the chloroplasts—the bodies containing chlorophyll, the pigment active in photosynthesis. Numerous small openings (stomata) are found preponderantly on the undersides of the leaf; these serve in gas exchange.

Flower. It is mostly the goal of horticultural cultivation and can vary widely (see Table at right). As a rule, the flower consists of the following elements: the green sepals, the flower petals (usually colored), the stamens, the stigma and the pistil, as well as the ovaries with the seed store. Most plants have androgynous flowers; often they are self-pollinating. But there are also monoecious species, in

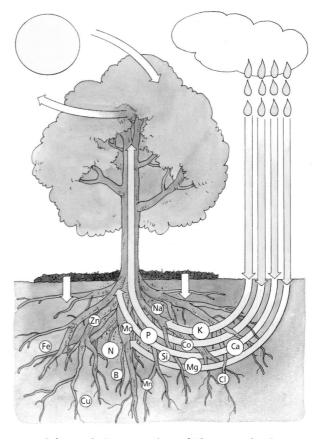

Schematic Presentation of Photosynthesis

which male and female flowers are separate on the same plant and dioecious ones, with individual plants that are entirely male or female.

Fruits. They are the result of successful fertilization and contain the seeds, which are to provide for spreading. But often the gardener removes the flowers immediately in order to hinder the strength-consuming process of seed development.

Growth Factors

The growth of a plant is controlled by many factors: light, warmth, water, carbon dioxide, oxygen, and mineral substances. It is important that each be present in the right quantities and that they be in the right proportion to each other. Too little or too much can lead to growth disturbances and finally to the death of a plant. In addition, the plant may have entirely different requirements depending on its origin. Desert plants such as cacti, because of their storage organs, need less water than plants that come from the humid rain forests.

Light. Sunlight is the critical energy source for the process of photosynthesis. Moreover, light also plays an important role in germination and flower development: There are light germinators and darkness germinators, plants that bloom when days are short and those that bloom when days are long—however, there are many that also behave neutrally.
• Too little light leads to bleaching of the plants; to soft, disease-prone tissue; and to long, thin stems that have poor stability. The horticulturalist calls this process "etiolation."
• Too much light, on the other hand, can even cause burning (sunburn). Plants in hot/dry regions or in light-intensive mountain regions protect themselves against strong irradiation and evaporation with thorns, hairs, or tough protective layers.

Temperature. In order to keep the course of metabolic processes on track, the temperatures appropriate for a particular plant species should not go over or under the optimum range. Great heat as well as cold can lead to damage.
• If it becomes too hot for plants, they can "sweat" and provide for a certain limit over transpiration itself for cooling off.
• With severe cold, some plants are also able to protect themselves a little, as rhododendrons do by curling their leaves.

Air. Plants need the gases carbon dioxide and oxygen contained in the air for life. They take them out of the air in the soil through the roots or out of the air through the foliage. Carbon dioxide is used in photosynthesis. All the vegetation on the earth annually consumes about 5% to 10% of the atmospheric carbon dioxide. Turning it around, at night, when no photosynthesis can take place, plants use oxygen for various metabolic processes.

Water. The plant mainly takes it up from the soil. Plants consist of 75% to 90% water. From this, it is evident how important this element is. The life processes in the plant are dependent on a certain degree of tissue tension (tonicity)—complete water withdrawal is fatal for them. Besides, this water serves to cool through evaporation. It is also the solvent for salts and gases as well as the transport medium for nutrients and all the products of metabolism. Hydrogen, which is produced by the breakdown of water during photosynthesis, is also a component of many organic substances.

The nutrients. These are mostly taken up through the roots and are categorized as principal nutrients (see page 157) and trace elements. This division is not made on the basis of their importance for the plant but according to the quantities necessary.

ABC of Flowers

Flower forms. There is a wide variety of them: For example, roses (*Rosa* species) exhibit a simple and symmetrical flower structure with their ring of quite regular petals. Also, the daisies (*Leucanthemum* species) appear at first glance to be similarly structured. But with closer study, it can be seen that in these flower heads there are many individual flowers crowded together. Daisies belong to the so-called composites, and small tubular flowers are crowded together in the yellow disk. Also the white petals around the edge are each individual ligulate flowers.
The leguminous flowers (for example, sweet peas, *Lathyrus odoratus*) have a completely different form. They consist of an upright standard, two side wings, and the carina. Labiate flowers, as in the sages (*Salvia* species) have a distinct upper and lower lip. Both lips can also be grown together in the Fumariaciae, which often—as in the corydalis (*Corydalis cava*)—still bear a spur.
Inflorescences. These denote the various possible arrangements of several flowers on one stem: The composites are already mentioned above. Also there are umbels, as in the primroses (*Primula* species), spikes, as in the mullein (*Verbascum* species), ears, as in the love-lies-bleeding (*Amaranthus caudatus*), racemes, as in the lupines (*Lupinus* hybrids), and panicles, as in the astilbes (*Astilbe* species).

• The chief nutrients include nitrogen (N), phosphorus (P), potassium (K), magnesium (Mg), calcium (Ca).
• Trace elements are: sulfur (S), iron (Fe), manganese (Mn), zinc (Zn), copper (Cu), chlorine (Cl), boron (B), and molybdenum (Mo). Furthermore, there are some so-called "useful elements"—they promote growth but are not necessary for life. Among them are sodium (Na), aluminum (Al), silicon (Si), and cobalt (Co).
Nitrogen is always listed first in the enumeration of the essential nutrients. This is because it is not sufficient or available for use of plants in most soils and thus must be added in comparatively large quantities. In addition, nitrogen is the element that is most easily leached out of the deeper layers of the soil and contaminates the groundwater. In contrast to phosphorus, potassium, and calcium, nitrogen is not released by the weathering process but is set free by the rotting of plant parts and the animal remains. Small animals and microorganisms take part in the functioning of this natural "nitrogen cycle." You will find suggestions for balanced fertilization of your plants on pages 156–159.

The Appearance and Growth Forms of Plants

The utter variety of vegetation is shown in the more than 250,000 different seed plants—especially in the temperate climate zones, where woody plants, perennials, annuals, and biennials constitute the plant cover. The woody plants, that is the trees and shrubs, are enduring forms and thus the important three-dimensional features in the garden. The majority of all other plants only attract attention at particular seasonal periods.

Woody Plants

Woody plants have a woody structure. Their leaf buds are located above the soil's surface. Their stature determines whether they are considered trees or shrubs. However, in poor locations, trees can grow like shrubs.

Trees are the most prominent forms in nature and in the garden. Large trees in full growth may be between 82 and 131 ft (25 and 40 m) tall. They are only rarely suitable for gardens, as opposed to the small and medium-size forms.

• Deciduous trees are plants with a usually continuous straight trunk (with a standard at least 6 ft [1.8 m] tall) and a bushy crown, which can vary greatly in form. The main boughs with their branches arise from the main stem, but they may also branch directly over the base and form a multistemmed crown, similar to a large shrub. They grow leaves that usually are shed in the fall.

But here there are also evergreens, which retain their foliage in winter.

• Likewise, conifers grow with single or multiple trunks. Instead of leaves, they have small needles or leaflike scales. In most cases, they are evergreen.

Shrubs normally have no central trunk but several equivalent woody stems, which can be several yards (meters) high.

Subshrubs stand between woody plants and perennials.

Growth Forms of Woody Plants

Woody plants frequently develop into particularly striking forms. The more interesting such forms are, the better they are suited to feature as a solitary planting or for a geometric formation such as a grove or an allée.

Pillars are especially suitable as focus points for spaces, or "rooms," and accents for level areas. They work like exclamation points. Clear lines can be formed with a row of pillars. Sometimes with age, they tend to spread sideways. There are pillar forms not only in the evergreens but also in the deciduous trees.

Cone shapes are a widespread and striking growth form among the conifers. Many of the large deciduous trees also develop broad, cone-shaped crowns.

Spheres are a growth form that is usually created by changes in the genotype and often these plants can only be propagated vegetatively. Spherical trees usually remain small-crowned and are thus well suited to small gardens. With them, as with pillars, entrances or axes can be emphasized.

Umbrella crowns most often appear as a mature form in large trees, especially if they can develop in a solitary location like the pine (*Pinus* species).

Weeping forms provide a feeling of picturesqueness and security. There are natural weeping forms with or without a pointed main shoot. Many weeping forms arise from a mutation and can only be reproduced vegetatively. The best known example is the weeping willow (*Salix alba* "Tristis").

Deciduous trees   *Conifers*   *Shrubs*   *Carpet*

Ground covers occur among the woody plants, but they also exist in the other plant groups. The thing they all have in common is that long shoots develop from their base and then cover the ground with a thick network of branches.

Climbing plants do not form a framework of shoots that can stand by itself but use trees and shrubs or artificial supports to reach the light. They have developed various climbing adaptations (see pages 216–221) acccording to their living conditions. But many can also creep along the ground as ground covers.

Perennials and Their Growth Forms

With perennials (see pages 232–247), the herbaceous aboveground parts die back after the first frost, at the latest, and the plants go dormant. But every spring, they put forth new growth from their sturdy rootstock and develop stems, flowers, fruits, and seeds. Perennials differ very greatly from each other in their growth habits. Many of them tend to die out at the center with increasing age. Therefore, they must always be redivided and planted anew.

Evergreen or wintergreen perennials such as purple rock-cress (*Aubrieta* hybrids) or Christmas rose (*Helleborus* hybrids) retain their shape and much of their foliage throughout the winter. They are often valuable ground covers, growing as creepers, cushions, or tufts.

Carpeting perennials develop on their shoots numerous new roots like the moneywort (*Lysimachia nummularia*)—they are, therefore, easily propagated. Underground creeping plants like the sweet woodruff (*Galium odoratum*) keep forming new sprouts at a distance from the mother plant.

Cushion-forming perennials like pinks (*Dianthus* species) and thrift (*Armeria maritima*) grow as low cushions, often in hemispherical form. Frequently they possess a taproot and are therefore difficult to propagate. Many alpine and rock garden plants belong to this group.

Rosette plants grow in circular or spiral form around a center. A typical representative is the hen-and-chickens

(*Sempervivum* species), but also primroses (*Primula* species) belong to this group.

Tuft-forming, upright perennials, out of whose center develop a great number of flowering shoots, are very numerous. Among them are the grasses with their typical tufts.

Bulbs and tubers are plants that form organs thickened for overwintering that, in contrast to the leaf buds of other perennials, which are situated aboveground or which lie on the surface of the soil, are located deep in the ground. These plants are often very slender in form; they can, however, also grow tufted and bushy like the dahlias (*Dahlia* species) (see pages 248–259).

Annuals

These plants flower, fruit, and seed themselves in the same year they are sown, then die completely if the plant is a true annual (see pages 262–263). In regions with mild winters they self-seed again.

Biennials

Biennial plants are sown in July/August and develop into young plants in the fall—usually in the form of a rosette—which then winter over. Flowers and seeds do not appear until the second year. Finally they die back, but often they sow themselves again. By cutting them back at the right time, you can sometimes make them continue to grow (see pages 268–269).

and cushion-forming perennials   *Clump-forming perennials*   *Grasses*   *Bulbs*   *Annuals*

Plant Environments

Plants all over the world in their natural habitats live together in quite particular associations. These plant communities form according to the dominant climate and soil conditions in their environment. Among them are both tolerant cosmopolitans that can thrive in many regions and also high-grade specialists that can only grow under very specific conditions. A plant's requirements as to soil, humidity, nutrient supply, acidity, light conditions, temperature, and cultivation can be very different. Often the appearance of a plant betrays something about its location: Plants that must protect themselves from heat and dryness often have a dense coat of hairs, with leaves that are small and gray or leathery hard. Shade plants, on the other hand, often have soft, deep green leaves in order to catch as many light rays as possible. In all cases, it is helpful to know the natural location of a species. This offers important hints as to its use in the garden and its care.

Environments in the Garden

With skillful design, many different environments can be created even in the small garden, which might not occur in such proximity in the wild. These areas are:

Woods and woods' edge. "Woods" means a woods-like situation, one often found in old, "mature" establishments.
• The shadow of the woods fosters development of typical forest plants such as the spring geophytes (see pages 250–251), hepaticas (*Hepatica* species), lungwort (*Pulmonaria* species), Solomon's-seal (*Polygonatum* species), and ferns and forest grasses (see pages 270–273). Almost all of them bloom before their leaves appear, so long as the light conditions are still good. However, only a few species thrive under conifers and birches; the stoneweed (*Buglossoides purpurocaerulea*) has proven itself reliable.
• Forestlike situations occur along a constantly shaded house wall as well as behind hedges and walls.
• However, only a few perennials can tolerate the constant root pressure of the woody plants. The fussy ones are excluded from this circle. Creeping, climbing, or wide-spreading plants such as cranesbill (*Geranium* species) are able to adapt to the changing light conditions during the year if they have enough room to spread. Some perennials also do not tolerate the dripping under the drip line of a tree either.
• The sunny, warm woods' edge—the usually humus area of transition to open garden space—offers optimal living conditions for many perennials (see pages 244–245). There are such marginal areas in almost every garden. For cultivation of smaller gardens, the most suitable of all are the wild perennials with bedding character like monkshood (*Aconitum* species), columbines (*Aquilegia* species and hybrids), foxglove (*Digitalis purpurea*), and primroses (*Primula* species).

Open space. This designation includes all open, warm, sunny surfaces without trees and shrubs. These areas have important ecological significance in the garden, for they create the principal basic food supply for bees and other insects. A broad spectrum of plants can thrive in this environment. It is divided according to soil requirements:

Woods　　　　　*Woods' edge*　　　　　*Open area*

• Prairie heaths form in warm, sunny, dry, and chalky locations. Typical plants are yarrows (*Achillea* species), sages *(Salvia* species), globe thistle (*Echinops bannaticus*), or mallow (*Lavatera thuringiaca*).

• Heaths form in sunny, warm, nutrient-poor, acid locations. Heath plants include the *Erica* and *Calluna* species.

• Meadows are moderately dry to fresh and damp. In these environments, the typical meadow plants thrive but also the wild perennials with the character of bedding perennials.

• Good conditions for warmth- and sun-loving plants exist in the backyard on the south side of the house, in front of walls and terraces. There is the place for all the gray-leaved and aromatically scented plants like lavender (*Lavandula angustifolia*), catmint (*Nepeta x faassenii*) and common rue (*Ruta graveolens*).

Water environments. These include deepwater, still water, running brooks, as well as banks with swamp and damp areas. These are areas close to nature in which a great many native plants thrive. The plant lover adds to them more with exotic species and hybrids. These environments are characterized by frequent overflows. Many plants tolerate changing water levels, living in damp or partially flooded ground (see pages 274–279).

However, marsh and water plants can also thrive in the backyard in artificial pools and in strictly architectonic environments. Then their function is primarily decorative and of little ecological importance.

Rock gardens. They can be arranged in a multitude of forms. Prerequisites are a sunny location and porous soil with a high content of gravel and pebbles—as is typical for the so-called alpine plants. The native plants here are without exception sensitive to wetness and need dry feet. The most important situations for these plants:

• Dry walls with only a little earth between the courses of stone and at the top of the wall. Similar conditions also exist in the stone courses at the edges of steps, terraces, and pathways. Among the plants that are comfortable in these situations are the colorful cushions of spring bloomers (see pages 242–243) that can attractively cover the walls. Also small ferns and grasses are effective between the stones.

• An alpine garden makes the highest demands for micro-climate, plant choice, and care. It is for experienced gardeners, rather than beginners.

• Rock gardens are also mainly gardens for collectors and fanciers. Regular care is unavoidable in order to maintain the balance between vigorous and weakly growing plants. Old rock gardens often consist only of woody plants and some vigorous cushion plants like candytuft (*Iberis sempervirens*).

Beds. These are artificial environments that are only encountered in the garden. Here is the proper place for all demanding, showy perennials. But wild perennials, bulbs, and tubers, as well as annuals and biennials also find good conditions here. There are plants with entirely different requirements, which need the appropriate care. The soil should be kept free of undergrowth in order to make care easier and not to let any strong root competition occur. Certain orders of dominance are maintained in the beds: the lead plants set the tone, which is amplified by the groups of perennials and the companion plants (see pages 74–77).

Bedding perennials are planted at the widest possible intervals in order to guarantee adequate room for growth. Good hole fillers for the early years are the annual summer flowers (see pages 262–265). The picture of such a border alters constantly because the plants change at varying speeds, their growth slows or their need to spread takes over. Therefore, they must be divided from time to time and replanted. This environment is subject to the sharpest and fastest change, but it can also be the easiest to correct again.

Pond   Marsh zone   Rock garden   Bed

Law in the Garden

The peaceful tasks of the gardener appear to have nothing at all to do with statutes and legal arguments. But that's very wrong, for all kinds of complications can also occur here. In order to avoid them, you should make yourself familiar with the subject ahead of time.

Legal Precautions

Unfortunately one cannot simply look up somewhere to find out what rights and duties garden owners have, for there is no special "garden law." Frequently, for example, fencing, erection of gazebos or summerhouses, setting out of trash cans, planting distance from the neighbors, and, in some cases, even the choice of plants are subject to various laws, ordinances, and regulations. These can vary from state to state and even from community to community.

Important: Your city or local government, especially the building inspector's office or zoning board, can inform you of your local building regulations.

Building Permits

The building ordinances in each community contain not only regulations about building houses but sometimes for the establishment of a garden: If you put in a pond that is deeper, or a hill that is higher, than local regulations, you need a building permit. The same may go for see-through fences (wire netting fences) over 6 ft (1.8 m) high, solid fences (walls, board fences) from 5 ft (1.5 m) high, as well as wooden arbors and summerhouses of more than 100 sq ft (9 sq m). They may also be required to be a minimum distance from the property line. In recent years, also, more importance has been attributed to protection of groundwater. So in some communities there are limits on fertilizer-dependent plants.

A look over the fence is still allowed—but what if the neighbor's

Design Regulations

As a rule, construction and planting in the gardener's own garden can be according to the owner's own taste, but there are also exceptions. In some communities, the external appearance of the developed lot is controlled by regulations, where there may be rules about the materials used and the maximum height of any fencing. It can be required that walls be built as dry walls or cement walls faced with natural stone, or only planted with appropriate or "fireproof" shrubs. Some communities also forbid the establishment of parking places for cars in the front yard.

Tree Protection Regulations

These are part of conservation laws and regulate the conservation of particular tree species of a certain trunk diameter. Accordingly, old trees that are entered by the city on a development plan as worthy of protection can only be felled with a permit. This is only granted for sick trees, however, with the condition that just as many young trees must be planted as a replacement.

Law of Neighbors

The trees in the neighbor's garden are often the cause of disagreements: Their roots and branches don't take account of property lines, their leaves stop up the gutters, or their flowers and seeds make a mess. But when it is a matter of the overhanging fruit, they can also evoke great joy in neighbors. Courts decide on a case-by-case basis, for it is not easy to establish, for example, what represents an encroachment on a neighbor's property. Much better than to insist on one's rights with a civil complaint is to cultivate a good understanding with the neighbor. In general, the following holds true:

cat decides your garden is its territory?

• Often there are quarrels about fences and walls because of money: On your land, you must maintain them in good repair at your own expense; for property-line fences, both neighbors should be responsible for maintenance.

Distance from the Line

If you don't abide by the regulations, you put into play your good understanding with your neighbors and risk having to dig out the plants you have planted after a few years. Therefore, find out ahead of time, before planting trees and shrubs, what the legally prescribed minimum distance from the property line is. Entirely different regulations are in effect in different localities. If you fall short of the minimum distance, the neighbor can require the removal of the planting. This demand need not be put into effect right away, however. You can also agree on special rules with the neighbors, but these should be declared in writing. Check with your local community about regulations relating to line of sight at intersections if you have a corner property.

Noise and Odor Nuisances

The noise level of motor-driven garden equipment, especially leaf blowers, is frequently the cause of bad feelings between neighbors. Therefore, to be a considerate neighbor, these garden helpers should not be used on weekdays in the period from 7 P.M. to 7 A.M. and not on Sundays and holidays, if possible.

Composting is practical, but some neighbors are disturbed by the sight of a compost heap and are afraid of disagreeable odors. A properly constructed, well aerated compost heap will not be offensive. Nevertheless, preferably you should not establish your compost heap right next to the neighbor's terrace. Your local municipality or extension service generally has brochures showing the proper way to start and maintain a compost heap. Grass clippings should be mulched and left on the lawn.

• If branches or roots grow into the neighbor's property, the neighbor may request their removal within a given time, if they severely encroach on his use of his yard—for example, his vegetable garden. If you allow the time period to lapse without taking any action, he may professionally prune both himself.

• Leaf and flower drop along the property line is not usually classified as an encroachment by the courts. But if necessary, the owner of the tree may be required to have it removed or make good the cost of having it done.

• The flight of seeds from weeds from the neighbor's garden cannot be prevented by complaint, even if dandelions in a carefully groomed lawn are so unsightly. There is no requirement in any state that a garden owner must keep his property free of weeds.

• Fruit that falls from a tree into a neighbor's yard may be collected by the neighbor and kept. The owner of the tree may also harvest the fruit that hangs on the tree in the neighbor's air space—a picker with a long handle is helpful for that.

GARDEN IDEAS

Garden design is dictated
when you want something for
your garden—be it a place to
sit for parties, a fragrant rose
arbor, colorful flower beds,
or even a pond of your own.
The following pages present
you with a wealth of ideas for
construction plans, plant
combinations, and garden
types.

Old Gardens—New Gardens

Not everyone can call one's garden a paradise at the outset: a charming, well-established garden with clumps of old trees, weathered stones, and materials that have developed a patina over the decades. In case you have such a garden, after a certain time you can't get out of making some modifications if you want to maintain it in its most beautiful form. On the other hand, anyone who is starting a garden from scratch has a chance, with planning ahead and a good concept, to lay the foundation for a dream garden.

Changing Old Gardens

If a garden has reached the highpoint of its development and a stable plant community has formed that is mutually protecting and supporting, only a few interventions are still necessary. A further advantage: A cared-for, well-established garden possesses a profoundly lively, humus soil. This thick humus layer offers the best conditions for the thriving of certain plants, like roses and showy perennials, such as delphinium (*Delphinium* hybrids), phlox (*Phlox* species/varieties), and peonies (*Paeonia* species/varieties). However, these all need enough light. Therefore, even an old garden must be changed somewhat now and then and planted anew—and of course for many reasons.

Old, established gardens have special charm—usually with large

What to do with too much shade?
Dense, high shrubbery is the chief characteristic of an old garden. The large woody plants are just the ones that need decades to reach their typical habit, often with picturesque, trailing forms. For all its beauty, the growth increase linked to age has certain drawbacks. A tree that is 10 or 20 years old can cast large shadows, and the ground also remains relatively dry in summer under its thick cover of leaves. Its roots force the other plants to compete for water and nutrients. Over time, the shrubs and perennials planted there can no longer thrive. The places grow bare and must be replanted—with shade-tolerant plants. Fortunately there is a whole list of plants that do particularly well in the shade of large deciduous trees: the small spring bloomers (see pages 250–251) like squill (*Scilla* species), snowdrops (*Galanthus* species), as well as perennials for the edge of the woods (see pages 244–245) or ground covers (see pages 246–247). They multiply from year to year and make up the charm of old gardens.

For new (sun-loving) plants, you can again create light and air by thinning out the stands of trees and shrubs. Thus,

prospects and sightlines are produced again.

Old stands of trees are of priceless value, both on aesthetic as well as ecological grounds, but they can also severely limit a large reorganization of the garden. It is important to check with your utility company to be sure that felling the tree won't damage electric, water, and sewage lines (see pages 22–23).

What to do with sections of the garden that have gone wild?
Wild garden areas—aside from their picturesque aspect—have an important ecological significance and should be retained, at least on a small scale. Besides the vegetation that can spontaneously appear there, small mammals, amphibians, reptiles, insects, and birds can also find diverse living spaces. However, you should inspect regularly to make sure that the plants don't run over into other garden areas. You should especially remove the seedlings of trees, or the garden will turn into a regular jungle.

What do you do when your wishes or needs change?
Usually after 10 to 20 years, the family circumstances change and with it the wants for the garden. When the

---

GARDEN
TIPS AND TRICKS

Protection for Old Trees
If it is necessary to do any building in an old garden, fence the tree along the circumference of the crown (the drip line) so that the roots of the tree will be protected. If the tree roots get damaged in spite of this, you can restore the balance by pruning out the crown.

...shaded areas in which only special plants will still thrive.

New Gardens

To turn a building lot into a beautiful garden, you need instinct and patience. You will find out the step-by-step order to proceed in on pages 38–39. Above all, have patience: There is scarcely a garden that is laid out perfectly and correctly from the very beginning. In addition, every garden lover keeps wanting to try out new ideas. Here are some tips for a start:

<u>If the trees are still small.</u> The shade necessary for the survival of many plants can also be artificially created at first: perhaps with twining elements that are planted with trellises and annual vines. Also, various light conditions can be created with fast-growing filler plants, bushes, perennials, or annuals, so that variegated-leaved plants and ground covers find the optimal conditions relatively quickly.

<u>Small spring-flowering plants.</u> You should establish bulbs under a hedge or a group of trees early on, for they take years to seed themselves or to increase by division. Let the leaves stay on them in the fall and also mulch them for the rest of the year.

<u>Regular soil care in the beds.</u> The soil must consistently be provided with compost and organic fertilizer, for only then does it form the conditions for long-term healthy growth. Green fertilizers and mulchs (see pages 150–151) help with this.

<u>Incorporating old trees.</u> If your lot contains overaged or died-back trees, include these in your design concept, perhaps through entwining with clematis (see pages 218–219), roses (see pages 224–225), fallopia (*Fallopia aubertii*), or climbing hydrangea (*Hydrangea petiolaris*, see pages 220–221). A newly planted tree can grow in the vicinity of an old one in order to replace it in time.

<u>Choosing the right tree.</u> For small to medium-size gardens, trees with small crowns or that will grow to medium size or shrubs should be considered (see pages 204–215). The important thing is to plan with foresight and to lay the foundation for the future with the proper choice of the plant framing and skeleton. For this, the deciduous trees are best. Evergreens (see pages 212–213), such as yew (*Taxus* species), common boxwood (*Buxus sempervirens*), and holly (*Ilex* species/varieties) are shade tolerant and thus thrive very well as underplantings with large, spreading trees. Ornamental shrubs (see pages 208–211), climbing plants (see pages 216–221), perennials (see pages 232–247), and bulbs (see pages 248–250) as well as grasses (see pages 270–271) and ferns (see page 272–273) round out the garden picture. With such a planting, you form the foundation for a many-sided and multispecies development over decades.

children are out of the house, you can change the play areas and a portion of the vegetable garden into decorative plantings with roses or perennials or into an environment, like a garden pond or a flower meadow. And even the ardent gardener who is slowly getting along in years will have increasing interest in making the garden easy to care for: perhaps with easier-to-work raised beds (see pages 84–85) or plantings of ground covers or native plants that demand little care.

<u>What to do if the garden is laid out unattractively and is fundamentally wrong?</u> When gardens are laid out wrong and there is no fundamental underlying concept, neither age nor beauty will help. If, for example, it is dominated by conifers, under whose needle drop no fertile soil develops as it does with deciduous trees, you should remove individual trees from the stands in order to create light. You can improve the soil gradually by adding mulch (see pages 160–161) and compost (see pages 150–151). Then, plant shrubs and perennials.

Tone-on-tone—dark red original garden sculpture between roses of the same color.

BASIC COURSE IN DESIGN

It's the same if the garden you call your own is one that is already laid out or you have the chance to turn a new piece of ground into a garden—every gardening activity should take account of design principles. Beginners regret nothing more than if they plunge forward recklessly at the start.

You only achieve a garden paradise step by step. This means not only doing things in the proper order but also recognizing the basic design principles that apply to pictorial art and architecture as well as to laying out a garden. This requires taking into account that the garden fits with the house and the surroundings, that it is not conceived as a flat surface but is divided into areas by shaping and vertical elements like trees, shrubs, hedges, pergolas, and much more. And thus, already, you have numerous opportunities for creating surprise visual angles, cozy corners, or garden rooms entirely according to your needs. After that there is still the exciting task of planting this garden area interestingly, an extremely creative play with growth forms, leaves, and especially the color of the plants. What we regard as beautiful can be translated into actuality, for very definite laws underlie aesthetics. You will gain the foundations in the following short design and color lesson—a guideline for everyone who would like to design or redo his or her garden. So don't hesitate to translate your garden dreams into reality!

*Enchanting example of designing with color.
A single red flower in front of an appropriate
background establishes a strong accent.
Here, the effect rests on the contrast of the two
complementary colors: red and green.*

The Garden and Its Surroundings

How you design your garden depends on the environment in which your plot lies: in the country, it's a question of making the plot fit into the landscape; in the city, architecture and the surrounding buildings influence your planning. Moreover, the layout of the garden and its planting can lend individuality to the most uniform house.

Tying In—But How?

Incorporate the natural factors into the design of your garden: a clump of trees, a projecting rock, a marshy pool, or a spring are nature-given possibilities that you should use. You can emphasize a beautiful view by creating a frame for it with trees. House and garden should, if possible, be in harmony with the topography of the country. Crucial for the livability and practicality of a garden are what part the house occupies and how it is oriented: light, shadow, and wind conditions influence occupants as well as plants. The best use of space and light occurs when the house is located in the northeastern area of the plot. The bigger the lot, the freer you are in your design opportunities.

Country—or City?

How you shape your garden, what structural elements you use, and what style you establish, even the choice of plants, should all take place in view of the adjoining area and should harmonize with it.

A lot in the country. Houses standing alone are, with their gardens, often already a part of the landscape. Here the transition from the lot and the open country should be flowingly designed, so that the garden leads into the natural surroundings. If possible, when choosing your

Asymmetrically laid-out garden with sight lines running diagonally into the open countryside. Trees and shrubs at the edges frame the view.

Symmetrically laid-out garden with central sight line into the countryside. The natural open space is a focal point behind and over the foliage.

plants, orient yourself toward choosing native vegetation, choose building materials that appear in the region, and keep the view from the garden into the surroundings open. If the lot is small, provide low plantings and fences for optical breadth and establish the connection to the landscape.

A lot in the city. The design of a garden in an urban situation should take its orientation from the architecture of the house and the neighborhood. The more strongly a garden area is closed to the outside or has the character of a courtyard, the less the neighboring buildings need to be taken into consideration. Here you have the opportunity to create a garden world for yourself that only takes its connection from your own house. You can also choose striking exotic plants—like trees with round and weeping forms or plants

needing warmth, which thrive well in the protected microclimates between houses. In urban gardens, foreign style elements can also be introduced without being felt as disturbing, perhaps playful or futuristic pavilions—or even elements of Japanese high garden culture. Row house developments with small gardens, which all too often are arranged according to a uniform unit plan, deserve special consideration. Here garden owners should come to an agreement at the beginning, for common planning can be advantageous. Anyone who uses shade in common, for instance, gains valuable space. The avoidance of a separating fence as well as

Climbing plants link house and garden in time-honored fashion.

agreeing on the design and choice of plants lets the gardens appear larger.

Important: The more rural the surroundings are and the more open a plot of land is, the more important it is to integrate the garden into the landscape by picking up the elements and plants of this landscape. But even here, the narrow area close by the house can be designed to be emphatically "gardenerish." The more strongly urban and architectural the surroundings are and the more tightly the garden is enclosed, the freer and more various the design possibilities.

Creating and Designing Spaces

A garden is more than a planted area that is surrounded by a fence. The art of design lies in bordering it beautifully and meaningfully so that it becomes a space with varied aesthetic experiences for its user, where the proportions work together and the plants can unfold to their full effect.

How Is a Spatial Effect Created?

The garden is a place in which we seek relaxation and healing, a green oasis in which we separate ourselves from the everyday. It's obvious that from this, for many, grows the wish for a closed-off garden space, a protected private sphere. And this results in boundaries being drawn around to keep out everything from the outside. Thus, the complex garden space arises from these vertical barriers. Of course, you shouldn't stop there but should also structure your garden internally.

Enclosing the Garden Spaces

For this, construction materials like fencing (see pages 42–43) or walls (see pages 50–51) are suitable, but also plants like trees and shrubs, especially in the form of hedges (see pages 80–83).

Before you decide on the type of garden enclosure you want, consider the following:

• The framing need not be severely closed with high walls or thick hedges to create a feeling of space. You can also achieve a spatial effect with see-through fences, twining elements, low hedges, or a loose planting.

• But a severely closed frame can also be broken in one or two places in order to create sight lines from a "room" out to the garden at large. Nevertheless, the intimacy in the rest of the garden is maintained.

• The garden space is also determined by the relationship of free surface and the height of the boundary. A small garden will, for instance, appear even smaller if it is surrounded by a high hedge or wall. In the same way, the frame in the form of large trees can also lie outside one's own boundary line.

The direction and paving of the path structure this formal garden.

Shrubs and plants here create a frame for the lawn and pond.

Creating Spaces Within the Garden

Small gardens are occasionally laid out without further subdivision (see photo, page 124 top). Usually, however, there is already a division of the garden space according to the various practical needs of the owner. Don't miss a chance to subdivide, for it provides enchanting possibilities, which make the garden more complex and exciting.

First consider any wishes you have for a produce garden and establish the areas for that. Only then consider the design options.

• Vegetable gardens should be in full sun.

• Play areas for small children should be set up within sight from the house.

• Rest areas can also be created in secluded parts of the garden.

• Grass areas should be one or two thirds of the garden for good proportioning.

• Small gardens must be laid out in small parts, larger plots in larger areas.

• The individual surfaces and spaces should be of varying sizes; this creates excitement.

GARDEN
TIPS AND TRICKS

Small, Long-and-Narrow Gardens
are best divided several times straight across the length. Under no circumstances emphasize the narrowness of the space with high walls, fences, hedges, or trees along the narrow side!

The imposing pergola divides the garden into two rooms—into a formal one (foreground) and a free-form one (rear).

How You Form Rooms in the Garden

You can frame and separate the individual rooms of your garden strongly with solid elements or you can merely indicate them through structuring of the garden surfaces.

Room dividers, like walls, hedges, planted pergolas, trellises, and pavilions provide a strong spatial division. For marking off very small spaces, however, they are too high.

Small shrubs, perennials, and grasses up to 6 ft (1.8 m) high are good for loose boundaries and as backdrops for small surface areas.

Single plantings, found objects, and decorative objects are focal points and, therefore, already signal a stop for the eye. Because they emphasize the vertical, they can be well employed to accentuate different structured surfaces.

Ground covers, flat flower beds, and lawns possess different textures, which stand out from one another as well as from other garden situations and, thus, create the impression of another space.

Ponds, with their reflecting water surfaces, have the same effect.

Walks and pathways also separate the garden planes. Depending on how you design their course or their form but also on what paving you choose, you can provide a streak of visual contrast or a harmonious underlining of the garden surface.

Soil molding and terraces are also suitable to enliven garden spaces and bring about separation into areas. Even small humps, gentle curves, a low wall, or a sunken place to sit serve to make the garden appear larger.

The sunken garden is the most outstanding form of this type of modeling with its deeply depressed central surface—which can be taken up by a pool—and the plant surfaces rising on all sides.

Views from the house. Don't forget the view into the garden. You can make it appear roomier from the house by emphasizing the foreground with a vertical line, for instance with a single tree or a decorative element. The background should be quiet, for example, a lawn or a low-growing bed.

Designing with Growth Forms and Leaves

Our eyes usually perceive the variety of the plant world only as a whole. Try sometime to see the plants with the eye of a painter or a photographer, and you can discover a new, fascinating world of forms. The eye for detail helps to set the shapes of the plants in the garden effectively.

Lime green filigreed leaves with blue-green round-oval ones.

Combination of narrow lanceolate and round leaf shapes.

Deeply toothed leaves next to closed round forms.

Designing with Different Growth Forms

What gardener has not tried to think of the design and planting of his or her garden primarily on the basis of the beautiful color combinations of the flowers? But the blooming period of the plant is often the shortest phase of its life. Plants usually retain their growth form much longer (see pages 18–19). Therefore, consider the habit (growth character) of the plant in your design concept, for it will stamp the picture of your garden longer than the flower combinations.

You can design with the growth forms of plants, for example:
• Forming garden rooms. The garden can be framed and subdivided with tall plants and hedges.
• Creating focal points. Tall and striking plants (see Specimens, pages 78–79) establish accents.
• Making backdrops. Trees, tall grasses, and perennials bring height and depth to the garden.
• Producing contrast and interest by grouping contrasting growth forms.
• Creating quiet, harmonious areas by planting similar growth forms together (see ground-covering perennials, pages 246–247)

Woody plants, with their long period of growth, create an impressive structure of any garden. Primarily it is their contours that characterize the garden space.

Conifers, with their architectural dark forms, have a stronger effect than deciduous trees. With deciduous trees and shrubs, it pays to consider how they will look when they are leafless. For that is how they will determine the structure of the garden for almost half the year. Among them there are examples that unfold their beauty at just that time such as the corkscrew hazel (*Corylus avellana* "Contorta") or the dragon-claw willow (*Salix matsudana* "Tortuosa") with their twisted branches.

Perennials are herbaceous plants that put out new growth from an enduring rootstock year after year and, thus, grow and decline before our eyes in the course of a garden year. The appearance and duration of this time vary from plant to plant (see pages 18–19). For single plantings, suitable plants are imposing perennials like donkey thistle (*Onopordum tauricum*), willow-leaf sunflower (*Helianthus salcifolius*), the artichoke (*Cynara scolymus*), or rodgersia (*Rodgersia* species/varieties). Suitable lead plants in a bed are dominating plants like peonies (*Paeonia lactiflora* hybrids) or delphiniums (*Delphinium* hybrids). Grasses and ferns and cushion and rosette plants form especially beautiful, striking, and long-lived forms.

Plants whose foliage (and growth form) passes quickly, such as tulips and narcissi, should, therefore, not be planted in the foreground of a bed, if possible, so that no "holes" occur there.

Designing with growth forms—the easy going, bushy hostas are seen through slender, tall grasses.

Designing with Leaves

Leaves can determine the expression of a planting in a striking manner, be it through their color, their form, or their surface texture. Large, broad leaves increase the volume of the plants, so that they appear massive and lush, for example the ornamental ligularia (*Ligularia* species/varieties). Filigreed, feathery foliage, on the other hand, allows even imposing plant forms to seem loose, soft, and delicate, for example, fennel (*Foeniculum vulgare*). It is also of great importance whether the leaf venation is fine or coarse or whether the surfaces look smooth, hairy, frosted, glossy, or dull.

The beauty of the leaves becomes especially intriguing in plantings for effect that are kept in tones of green. Many grasses (see pages 270–271) and ferns (see pages 272–273) as well as ornamental-leaved plants are perfect for shady situations (see pages 000–000) in which flowers are rare. Here they show to their best effect. The combination of sturdy, large, round, and narrow grasslike leaf forms goes best with water and bank's edge areas—this corresponds to their natural character.

Design Tips

• If you would like to use large shrubs to create a background (backdrop) or the framework of the garden, don't choose too many different growth forms or the design will become busy.

• In a small garden, limit yourself to a few large shrubs, and don't choose too many coarse and broad-leaved forms or lushly growing plants.

• Strongly contrasting growth forms need a quiet background, for example, clipped hedges.

• Colorful plantings can be separated and structured with grasses.

• Spherical and pillar forms draw the eye and are suitable for row plantings, for marking, as well as for formally architectural gardens (see pages 132–133).

• Only use umbrella-like, broadly spreading growth forms—especially trailing ones—as specimen plantings and plant them in front of a quiet background.

• Plants with delicate foliage are well suited for placement above low plantings.

• Large-leaved plants with coarse structures work better in large gardens.

Designing with Color

The form of a plant is due to its basic function throughout the change of the seasons, but highlights and atmosphere are created with the color. Colors have precisely defined optic characteristics, but they are perceived subjectively by human beings.

In addition, their effect depends on the light conditions as well as on the surfaces and structure of the flowers and leaves.

• Intense colors are even stronger in the sun.
• Dark colors appear dull and flat without sun.
• Light colors (white, cream, yellow, silver-gray), on the other hand, appear lighter in twilight, cloudy light, or half-light.
• Shiny leaves and flowers reflect the light and thus appear brighter and more radiant.
• Dull leaves and flowers swallow the light and thus appear darker.

Composing with the Color Wheel

As with individual tones in music, harmonic chords can be formed with colors. The color wheel with the colors of the spectrum (see drawings at right) can be helpful in this because it shows the contrasts and similarities of the colors.

Primary colors are red, yellow, and blue. These are also called pure colors because they cannot be made by mixing two colors.

Secondary colors are orange, green, and violet. They are created by mixing together primary colors.

Warm colors are yellow, orange, and red, which are located on one side of the color wheel.

Cool colors are blue, violet, and green. They are on the opposite side of the color wheel.

Neutral colors are white and black. Theoretically, you can mix all colors with them. This is how the shades are derived. If you mix them with each other, gray results.

Pastel color is created when a color is mixed with white.

Adumbration occurs through mixing the colors of the color wheel with black.

Possible combinations

Using the color wheel makes it possible to create a variety of combinations (see drawing, page 73):
• colors that clearly contrast with each other;
• runs of color that blend softly into the next one;
• tone-on-tone combinations in differing degrees of brightness of a color; the effect is particularly quiet and elegant;
• strongly contrasting hues; such combinations can be toned down by the addition of a neutral color like white or green.

Color Design in the Garden

With permanent plantings—whether perennials, roses, or other flowering shrubs—you should plan the play of color beforehand. On the other hand, with beds of bulbs or annuals only, you can try out something new every year. It is always important how you distribute the colors and place them with one another. Nature itself, with its main colors of green, gray, brown, white, and sky blue, provides quiet shades—a backdrop or underlayer, in front or on top of which the colored flowers can completely unfold their effect.

Pay attention to the surroundings. In choosing colors, take into account also the area around the planting, for example, the material of the paths and the terraces. Garden furniture and decorative elements can also provide color accents, with which the plantings should be in harmony. In general, the following hold true:
• In smaller gardens, use fewer colors.
• In large gardens and enclosed urban lots, you can usually get away with more liberal use of color.
• In country-oriented gardens, which should fit into the surrounding countryside, be cautious with installing red-leaved and variegated shrubbery.
• However, a country garden can be gay and colorful in the manner of the kitchen garden (potager).
• Color-intensive plantings are always suitable in entry areas and close to the house.

Properly balanced color proportions. When the lead color is determined, the companion colors can be chosen in balanced proportion to them. The effect of a color is increased considerably by putting it next to one or several others. Be careful to have the lead color dominate, for same-size planes of color next to each other are usually boring.

Allow for the neutral color of green. In nature, colors rarely appear concentrated; they usually appear as dots of color in their surroundings. So the leaf color green as a basic color of the summer garden is especially important. With its wealth of nuances, it forms the backdrop (of trees, shrubs, and grass) for the variously colored leaves and flowers as they appear during the course of the seasons.

The Most Important Color Combinations

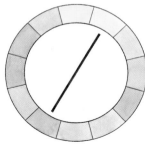

Complementary Colors
The colors situated opposite each other on the color wheel are termed complementary colors. Combined with one another, they look very exciting. If the tones (for instance blue-orange) are not pure but are lightened with white or darkened with black, the sharpness of the contrast is diminished.

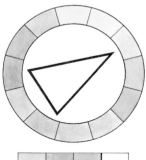

Color Triads
The color wheel permits establishment of equilateral or different isosceles triangles whose points always create new color triads with turning of the triangle. The sharpest color combinations (for example, red-blue-yellow) are always created with equilateral triangles, but these can work together very harmoniously in lightened or darkened form.

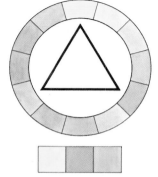

Color Quartet
Be careful of too many colors. However, a combination of four colors always works well if you combine a color triad with a neutral color like white or green. You can determine possible triads as above, by turning an equilateral or isosceles triangle.

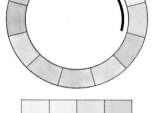

Color Run
The neighboring colors of a wheel segment always result in beautiful, harmonious color combinations: However, you should separate cool and warm colors. If you carefully include one or two contrasting colors with it, the composition looks livelier.

The green is often so interesting that it doesn't need many color accents. The more colorful the foreground, the quieter the green surroundings and the background should be kept. The more green parts a plant has, the more natural its effect, the more contrasting color shades it tolerates. It works the other way around too: The more color tones you choose and the stronger they are, the larger must be the portion of neutral colors. There are many more moderating colors in nature besides green and white, for instance the blue-green, silver-green, bronze, gold, and copper of leaves and grasses. Put pastel-colored plants in the foreground. Pastel tones, like quiet colors, don't have much effect at a distance. Plan colorful beds. Multicolored beds also need to be planned. Above all, it is important that the extended surface of plants is interspersed with healthy, long-lasting leaves. For if, during the summer, some of the flowering plants are cut back or become unsightly, the green of these leaves will remain and fill in the holes that occur.

Plan a play of color for the entire year. The plant community changes constantly during the growing season and with it also the play of color in the entire garden or in the single bed. With good planning, you can maintain the same color play throughout with different plants or—according to the season—provide for continual new color displays, for example:

• in spring: Red-orange-yellow (color run) with tulips, fritillaria, and narcissi; rose-blue-white through pink- and-white flowering ornamental cherries and crab apples, with matching tulips in tone-on-tone and blue grape hyacinths and bluebells; or monochrome white with snowdrops, crocus, anemones, tulips, and narcissi.

• in early summer: Rose-light blue-white (pastel triad) with roses, catmint, and delphinium or with marguerites (daisies), iris, and fleabane.

• in high summer: White-pink-violet (tone-on-tone) with phlox and bee balm or yellow tones with varieties of daylilies.

• in late summer: Yellow-orange (color run) with heliopsis, sneezewort (*Helenium autumnale*), rudbeckias, and grasses or white-rose-violet with astilbes.

• in fall: Violet-rose-white (tone-on-tone) with tall and low asters or yellow-violet with sunflowers, inula, violet asters, and different foliage colors.

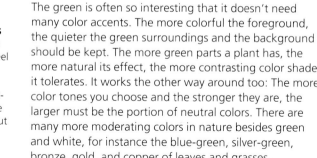

GARDEN
TIPS AND TRICKS

Intense Colors
You can bring the garden background forward visually with these. Vivid red-flowered rhododendron or bright yellow forsythia far back in the garden form brilliant spots with a signal effect.

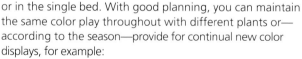

Step-by-Step Garden Planning

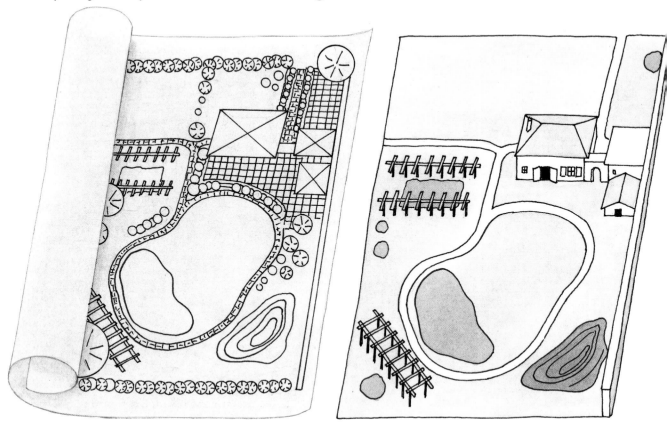

The basis of planning is a site plan of the property in a scale of 1:100 or 1:50. Entrances, windows, and outside steps must be shown for the planning of the garden. Copy the ground plan onto transparent paper, so you can always make new drafts.

In this phase, plan the terrain. Then have ponds, paths, sandboxes, holes for trees, and so forth dug out. Use the dug-out soil, together with that excavated for the house, for shaping (for instance, for privacy walls or rock gardens). Establish all constructed elements like pergolas, terraces, or summerhouses now.

Planning

If the garden is planned at the same time as the house, you are best able to realize unity inside and outside. Get the advice of a landscape architect. In this phase, the concerns are:
• division into various areas according to function,
• establishment of paths, sitting area, terrace, pergola, rock garden, pond, sandbox, vegetable garden:
• conclusions about the type of enclosure (fence, hedge, wall);
• decisions about all installations such as wiring for lights and water pipes.
Important: In all these determinations, you must take into consideration the compass points and the shadows cast by the summer and winter sun as well as the trees already present—for the trees also cast their shadows on your lot. Furthermore, include in the plan the environment surrounding the house and the garden and get advice on questions of material, technology, and planting. Inform yourself thoroughly beforehand on all possible applicable rules about building and planting.

Plot Development

It is advisable to entrust a landscaping firm with the new installation of a garden. Professionals understand how to transfer a plan to the plot dimensions, to properly lay out spatial elements, heights, and slopes. Now is the phase for all excavation and building work. First of all, the topsoil must be carefully removed and properly stored. This is best accomplished in the form of an earth stack that may be 6.5 to 9 ft (2–2.7 m) wide at the base and up to 5 ft (1.5 m) high maximal; otherwise the soil organisms are endangered. The stack can be as long as necessary, but in any case it should be covered to prevent drying out and erosion. For long storage, seeding with green manure plants (see pages 160–161) or nasturtium is recommended. In this phase, paths, sitting areas, walls, and fences are also laid out. If, however, machinery is going to need to be used in the garden later, the paths should not be finished but only the preliminary substructure established. Only erect fences after the heaviest work has been done.

Have the garden soil rototilled to about 2 spade lengths deep. Plant larger woody plants (ornamental trees and such) and hedges. Along with this, pave entrance, paths, terraces, and sitting areas (gravel, cement, flags); line the pond with plastic sheeting; if necessary, lay path edging that can be walked on.

Fill the pond and plant it. Enrich the topsoil of beds and lawn with compost or other aids and loosen thoroughly once again while doing so. Rake beds smooth and plant or sow.

Soil Preparation

The soil is usually severely compacted by the construction work. For plants to be able to thrive later, the subsoil must be thoroughly aerated. It isn't enough simply to apply the stored topsoil. After a very few years, the symptoms of soil compaction will appear: Plants fail to thrive; water stays on the lawns for a long time; moss forms. If not enough top-soil is available, you can buy some more humus.

For lawn areas, add humus to a depth of about 8 in (20 cm).

For plant areas, spread topsoil/humus to a depth of about 12 to 16 in (30–40 cm).

Holes for large trees should be dug about 2.5 to 3 ft (76–91 cm) deep and filled with humus.

First, have the large quantities of soil distributed by an excavator with a long bucket arm. Then spread it with a rake, working from back to front so that the finished area will be walked on as little as possible. Paths and terrace areas should have a slight slope (2% to 3%), so that the water will run off.

Soil Improvement, Planting

When all the large structural improvements are done as well as the enclosure (hedge, fence, wall) and the framing planting of the garden is completed, the ground for the other beds can be prepared. It is advantageous to apply a green manure (pages 160–161) before planting—especially with heavily compacted soil.

Before planting, loosen the topsoil deeply once more, but don't mix up the layers. Remove stones and rubbish, and rake the surface smooth.

When planting, always place trees and shrubs first, then follow with other plants. Spread out boards, which distribute your weight and so prevent recompacting the soil. The best planting time is spring or fall. Many shrubs and perennials are sold in containers, however, and can be planted all year-round—except when the ground is frozen.

After planting, loosen the soil once more and mulch between the shrubs (see page 161).

A wealth of construction elements such as path, gateway, and steps. Terra-cotta pots with boxwood establish accents at junction of paths.

DESIGN ELEMENTS

Design elements shape the basic character of your garden—usually for a long time. Take inspiration from the pages that follow. They offer a representative choice of the most important examples in different styles.

With the structural elements—such as fences, paths, steps, terraces, ponds, pavilions—you divide and enclose the garden space. You should consider these primarily architectural installations very carefully before you undertake them, for their construction usually involves the expenditure of much energy and money. Three things are important in construction and design:

• that you choose the right location. You can thus place accents and surprise eyecatchers but also provide for coziness and relaxation. Just think of the restorative value of a bench by a pond,

• that you choose appropriate form and style. With the style of the entry and fence, pergola, terrace, sitting areas, or pavilion, you establish whether your garden is going to have an elegant or, rather, a country-natural effect. Through skillful direction of paths or walls or steps, you can visually enlarge or shrink, create various garden rooms, and so make the space many-sided and varied.

• that you choose the proper materials. This way you can, for example, produce a unity of house and garden but also of the garden and its larger environment.

• Among the movable elements are furniture for terraces and gardens, containers, art objects, and all the other decorative objects that lend a garden aesthetic charm. They are very often the dot on the i and the crowning achievement of a successful garden design.

With beautiful containers, decorative elements, and garden sculpture, you can create incomparable moods in the garden—according to the light and the season.

Fences in Variation

Whether simple, rustic, solid, or elegant, the possible variations of fences are almost boundless. Aside from your personal taste, there is a list of criteria that should make choice easier for you:

Purpose. A fence is more than just a boundary of a plot of land. It protects from view four-legged intruders, dust, noise, and wind. If you regard your fencing as more a visual border than as a protection, you can choose a low, see-through fence. Moreover, a simpler version on the street side is often enough, which limits your costs. There the fence should allow small animals through and should ensure that air can circulate.

Surroundings. The fence should fit harmoniously into the surrounding picture in terms of type, color, material, and height. Therefore, take the following into consideration: Is your property in the city or the country, in a development or in an estate area? Be guided by regional characteristics as well as the architecture of your house.

Design plans. A fence on the street front has a represen-tative function. In planning, consider local building ordinances. As always—you can also give your fence an individual character with plants.

Materials and Forms

Wood and metals are most suitable for fencing materials. Which you decide on depends on what purpose the fence is to fulfill. Both variants need regular care.

Metal fences. The spectrum runs from chicken wire to artfully formed wrought iron. Wire mesh is the most convenient solution and is thus recommended if you

White-painted, slightly undulating fence.

Rustic ranch fence.

choose a planting, perhaps a hedge (see pages 80–81 and 82–83), as an additional enclosure. It offers protection until the planting is high enough. The fencing is fastened to posts, which are placed at intervals of 6.5 to 8 ft (2–2.5 m) and is supported by 2 to 3 wires stretched horizontally. Corners, ends, and about every 10 posts need braces. The fencing should have about 2 in (5 cm) ground clearance (see drawing at left).

Railings are more stable than wire fencing, just as transpar-ent, and ideal for covering with vines. You can buy them as plastic-coated or galvanized elements, which are easily installed. Metal railings are usually sold as sections forged in a box angle or tubular framework. They are very durable and fit well with different styles, but they must be painted now and then. Wrought iron is aristocratic; it can be simply worked but also decoratively and the effect is very elegant.

Wire Mesh Fence
Place posts at intervals of 7 to 8 ft (2–2.5 m), 2 ft (0.6 cm) deep. Brace every tenth post. Fasten wire mesh with 2 to 3 tension wires running horizontally.

Anchoring
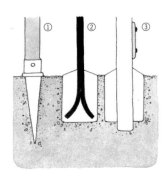
① Wooden post in metal shoe.
② Metal post with anchor in cement foundation.
③ Wood or cement post in cement.

Almost indestructible and elegant—massive wrought iron fence.

Dainty, charming painted wrought iron fence.

Blue picket fence with diamond-shaped cutouts.

Modern, artistically designed iron fence.

<u>Wooden fences.</u> Wood offers numerous, outstanding design possibilities. Moreover, wooden fences can be seen through, but—in contrast to metal fences—can also be completely enclosing and thus offer optimal privacy. You get suitable closed fencing as vertical or horizontally woven or layered boards in ready-made modules with framing from fence dealers. The life of a wooden fence depends on the kind of wood (usually available are various native soft- and hardwoods). Regardless of the kind of wood, all fence parts must be pressure treated and painted regularly (with environmentally safe sealer or paint). The most widely available type of wooden fence is the picket or board fence. Here the individual elements are of rectangular or half-round pickets arranged vertically or horizontally side by side. The space between the pickets should amount to one third, but at the most one half, of the width of the picket.

Wall-Fence Combination

Very beautiful enclosures are created by the combination of wall and fence elements. This involves anchoring individual fence sections (framed wood, simple metal, or elegant wrought iron grills) between masonry posts. The wall foundation should be dug below the frost line (32 to 39 in [81–100 cm] deep). Posts and wall can be of natural stone, of (plastered) brickwork, or cement faced with natural stone. The construction looks appreciably lighter than a real wall. The higher the base wall of the fence, the more protection it offers: protection against splashes from the road, dogs and cats and wind or people looking in.

DESIGN ELEMENTS
Entrances and Entry Areas

The entrance to a property has special importance; it is something like the visiting card of the house and its owner. Gate and door, as well as the bordering area, offer visitors a first impression. Gates and doors form the transition from the outside to the inside, from public to private. A door or a gate can have a repelling or an inviting effect. Those who wish to prevent others from looking in must, however, consider that they also then no longer can look out. Entry gates and gateways should form an optical unity with the area around them and fit with the character and style of the house. Also, for the rather monontonous building styles of today there are numerous individual solutions: not only the choice of gateway but also the design of the entire entrance and the planting contribute to creating a personal note.

Practical Considerations
A whole list of points can help you make a decision about your entrance.

Purpose. First you should ask yourself what purpose the gate has: Is it purely for decoration or does it also serve for security of your property? May it allow looks in or must it screen them out? Because entrances and exits are used constantly, they must also satisfy certain practical requirements.

Stability. Gates and gateways must be sufficiently reinforced, because they—more than a fence—suffer severe stress with the constant opening and closing. Masonry columns of natural stone, brick, or cement block are suitable supports for the gates, as are posts of steel and wood. It is important that they be strong enough on the one hand, but on the other they should not be too massive.

Security. For child security, a lock or a bolt that makes the gate more difficult to open is recommended; the mechanics should naturally always function well. Gates that open electrically from the door of the house are very practical. It's preferable to have the wiring for that installed with an outside light and the doorbell. If the entrance to the garden and the house are far from the front door of the house, it is recommended to install an intercom at the garden gate in addition.

Protective function. Openwork gates, like some fences, let cats and dogs slip through, for example. It is advisable to think of this ahead of time, for gates with wire strung across them later don't look very attractive.

Large, wrought iron gates between brick posts. The classic stone vases

Old, wrought iron gate.

Garden gate with beech arch.

The photos above show different solutions for the design of gates, fences, and plantings. Left, the historical example of a wrought iron gate, set into a massive stone wall. A striking contrast of stone and metal. Right next to it, an austere and integrated beech hedge arches to frame a white wooden gate.

Gate with a dovecote.

...dd charm.

Wooden gate with stone posts.

Individually designed white metal fence with entrance gate.

This fence-gate treatment is not marked by contrast but by the decided attention to unity of material, style, and color. The exciting relationship here derives from the strongly stylized fence-gate construction and the living green of the garden plants.

<u>Sufficient width.</u> The gateway should be wide enough so that quite large objects, for instance furniture or garden equipment, can be moved through it. A width of 4 to 5 ft (1.2–1.5 m) is enough to comfortably allow two people or one with a bicycle to pass through. If a second gate exists, perhaps at a garage entry, a small garden gate is sufficient, which can be thickly planted at the sides. However, the space in front of and behind the gate should be laid out as generously as possible. <u>Regulations.</u> Make sure that the entry gates and gateways as well as fences are in conformity with legal requirements, which can vary from locality to locality.

Ideas for Gates and Gateways

There are gates of various materials and designs: of artfully worked, elegant wrought iron, of simple or imaginatively assembled wooden pickets.

The effect is very spacious when the garden gateway and the surrounding fencing are "cut from the same wood." But, with the utmost stylistic harmony, you should also make sure that the gate and gateway are clearly distinguishable from the fencing so that they are clearly visible from the street and the visitor can easily find them. There are countless possibilities to make an entrance gate optically prominent without interrupting the stylistic unity.

For instance, an entrance gate can be emphasized by making its posts or columns higher or stronger than the rest of the fence. Also portals and arch constructions look very attractive; however, they do not fit into every situation. If the enclosure is of thick, high hedge or walls, there are two solutions: an openwork gate allows looking inside; a solid, closed gate, on the other hand, maintains privacy. Plants can make a special focal point out of the entrance. They lend fencing and entrances a living and aesthetic structure. Also, here there are numerous possibilities for variation: starting with an ornamental tree (see pages 78–79) that spreads its crown over the entrance gate, to the blooming and fragrant shrubs that border not only the entrance but the entire pathway to the house. Climbing plants and clipped evergreen shrubbery that symmetrically flank the entrance are also outstandingly suitable. A planting in front of the gateway, outside the garden area, has a particularly inviting effect but is not permitted in some areas.

In the new installation of entrances and front yards (see pages 122–123), storage places for garbage cans and bicycles must be taken into consideration. Also mailboxes, house numbers, nameplates, doorbells, and lighting should be worked into the plan.

Garden Paths

Paths not only have a practical function inside the garden, they are also an important design element and serve to delineate areas of the garden. In formal gardens, they form the symmetrical axes; in natural gardens, their course points to the landscape and picks up the lines of the house or plantings. If possible, lay out the pathways when you are planning the garden, as connecting elements to sitting and play areas, ponds, or the vegetable garden, even if you only gradually create these places. When planning, consider where the gaze of the viewer should be directed. By means of a pathway, the gaze can be directed toward a point, but it can also offer a moment of surprise if the path disappears around a bend. In this way, the sense of distance is created. In a small garden, too lively a network of pathways creates unrest.

Paths and Materials

Pathways should be comfortably maneuverable, not require too much care, and, on top of it all, also be environmentally correct. For two people, figure a width of 4 to 5 ft (1.2–1.5 m), for one person 2 to 2.5 ft (60–76 cm) is enough. There are a number of design ways to tie the path harmoniously into the garden picture.

Paths in the entrance area and in the vicinity of the house as well as much-used and sloping surfaces must be more firmly fixed because they are heavily traveled and exposed to all kinds of weather. The first materials to consider here are flagstones, paving blocks, or pebbles.

This path is beautifully lined by plantings of perennials left and right,

Path with Curbing

Mark out path width plus 8 in (20 cm) of working space to left and right. Dig out the path to 12 in (30 cm) deep. Set curbing stones (2 to 3 in [5–8 cm] wide) in a lean concrete foundation 12 to 16 in (30–40 cm) deep. The curbing can stick up 2 in (5 cm) at most.

Substructure: 8 in (20 cm) coarse gravel, 2 in (5 cm) crushed stone, 2 in (5 cm) pebbles. Set beds 0.5 in (1 cm) deeper than the path curbing so that the earth from the garden won't flood out onto the path.

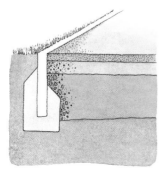

Gravel Path Level with a Lawn

Mowing is easier if the path edge is level with the lawn. A line of paving stones can also be set in mortar for an edging. Substructure as above. Important: Slope the concrete foundation slightly higher toward the lawn or bed surface so that the curbing won't tip.

Path in a mix of materials.

Path of natural stone slabs.

Materials of natural stone, like gravel or flagstones, go particularly well in gardens with a natural character. At the left, a path of large river gravel in conjunction with concrete blocks. The natural impression is retained because the gravel dominates; the concrete blocks function as edging stones to the right and left of the path as well as interruptions in the path's run and, thus, shorten its length.

giving a natural feeling.

Driveways or parking places are good left green. Lawn checker brick, perforated clinker brick, or paving with broad grass joints offers room for vegetation and creates a natural picture. These pavings are ecologically very valuable, for they allow even evaporation of water.
Simple garden paths can also consist of a (not too narrow) grass strip. In country gardens, they are also often made of wood and bark. However, wooden paving can become very slippery in shady areas and in rain; bark mulch scatters easily into neighboring plantings, where it can cause damage, at least to herbaceous plants (see Mulches, pages 160–161). For paths with bark surface, a foundation drainage layer is recommended.
Between plantings, stepping stones are enough; in vegetable gardens, for instance, duckboards permit comfortable working around plants and harvesting.

Tips on Making Pathways

The type of foundation depends on the climate, the condition of the soil (porous or water-retaining), the type of pathway covering, and the amount of traffic the pathway is exposed to. There are basic differences between simple garden paths and paths in areas subject to more traffic. Depending on the climate, drainage below frost level can be up to 2 ft (60 cm) deep. Above all, make sure that each layer of the foundation is well compacted (see Walls, pages 50–51).

Cement slabs and bricks.

Flagstone path in the grass.

A band exclusively of large square or rectangular slabs often can make paths and surfaces appear boring. The surfaces loosen and become interesting with combination of the slabs with other materials and other shapes. With the slabs set into the lawn, the strips of lawn between them take over this function.

Slab Path

Lay the edging (see drawing, page 46). Excavate 12 in (30 cm) deep.
Substructure: 8 in (20 cm) coarse gravel, 2 in (5 cm) fine gravel, 2 in (5 cm) bed of sand or broken stone in which the slabs are laid. Pretty: Planted holes in the path or in spaces between stones. With slab paths, the edging with curbing can also be omitted.

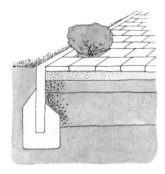

Lawn Checker Bricks

Parking places, paths, and depositing areas can be made beautifully green with lawn checker bricks. Dig out the area 16 in (40 cm) deep.
Substructure: Fill in with 8 in (20 cm) coarse gravel and 2 in (5 cm) fine gravel and shake it firm. Lay pierced bricks or lawn checker bricks (height about 4 in [10 cm]) close together. Fill the holes with earth and sow grass.

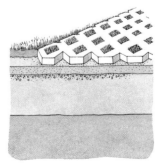

Stairs, Steps, Ramps

Stairs, of course, fulfill a primary purpose: to ease the negotiation of differences in levels. On top of that, you can achieve exciting effects with stairs. By means of specific direction of paths and stairs, the garden can be seen from ever new visual angles. Important in the design of stairs and steps is that you choose materials that fit into the surroundings—perhaps with pathways, terraces, and walls—and link the steps harmoniously to the garden as a whole, for example, with plantings.

Basic Considerations

In general, one begins with the idea that steps are necessary for any slope over 8%. However, this is only an approximate value. Consider in your planning that even less strongly sloped surfaces create dangers in wet weather and in winter. How the stairs run depends on the field conditions in your garden. You can choose among linear, curving, or circular courses. The shallower the steps, the more inviting and elegant the stairs appear. A step height of 5 to 6 in (13–15 cm) has proved successful for the garden. Preferably you should place at least three steps in succession on a path; a single step easily becomes a stumbling block.

With long sets of stairs, you should incorporate landings. They serve as visual interruptions of the course of steps but also for resting. A succession of steps with a landing every so often results in an extended set of stairs. The length of such landings should (just like the steps) be determined by the length of a footstep. For a long run of stairs, there should be one footstep to each landing. The footstep

Natural stone steps with a supporting wall at one side.

Laid Steps

Set 2- to 4-inch- (5–10 cm) thick stone slabs on a foundation of stones, which may be faced. The slabs should overhang somewhat. Choose different thicknesses for slabs and foundation stones, about one-third slab to two-thirds foundation or vice versa, so you will achieve a good visual effect.

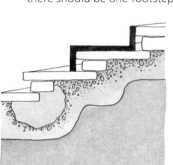

Block Steps

Block steps are all in one piece; they are made of natural stone or concrete, usually 5 to 6 in (13–15 cm) high, and available in different widths. The bottom step should be sturdier or be set in lean concrete. Each step covers the one under it by 1 to 2 in (2.5–5 cm).

of 25 to 26 in (63.5–66 cm) is arrived at by doubling the height of the step and adding the tread depth of the step. The formula for depth of an intermediate landing is: number of steps times the 25-in [63.5-cm] footstep length plus the tread-depth of the step. Each step should have a slope of 1% to 2% so that rainwater can flow off, and landings of 2% to 3%. That way the danger of icing in winter is avoided.

For small sets of stairs in the garden, it's enough to have a foundation of well tamped-in pebbles (12 in [30 cm]), with a layer of sand 1 to 2 in (2.5–5 cm) thick on top of that, on which the steps, flags, or paving stones are laid (see Paths, pages 46–47). For more heavily used stairs, you should put in, at least for the bottom step, a foundation of premixed lean concrete 12 to 16 in (30–40 cm) deep (see drawing, top left). Steps can be very quickly and easily built with cement blocks, and a foundation is also unnecessary. Often a ramp beside the steps is practical; for example, it makes the movement of garden equipment easier, and people in wheelchairs can pass more easily.

Original stepping stones of concrete rings with paved treads.

Shallowly ascending steps with wide treads.

Stair Design

Stairs can be tied into the overall garden design in numerous ways. Stairs that are framed left and right by walls or have landings have a very stiff effect. On the other hand, a staircase bordered by a little wall on one side is very charming. If the steps can run into the ground on both sides, there are numerous design possibilities. For example, you can define the steps with small, low shrubs, perennials, and cushion plants; that way they will look more lively and natural. Block steps, which, if you leave out their weight, are relatively easy to install, are most suitable for this. The addition of soil at the sides results in the line of the slope leaving a portion of the step clear: Then at the front end of each step, there is a triangle of soil. If this triangle is visible—perhaps if there is lawn right next to it—the step should be cut here to correspond to it visually. But you can also conceal the transition with plants.

With laid steps and fixed steps the sides are usually filled in with earth, so they get dirty more easily and it takes longer until the plants anchor the soil.

Fixed Stone Steps

Set cement or natural stone slabs, curbstones, or stacks of bricks vertically in a bed of mortar (about 12 to 16 in [30–40 cm] deep), or sink up to one half or one third of the slab in the ground. Tamp the treads firm and either fill in with gravel or pave to keep from washing out.

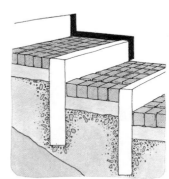

Fixed Wooden Steps

Drive 20- to 24-in- (50–60 cm) wooden posts into the undisturbed soil at the left and right ends of the steps. Behind the posts (overhang about 6 in [15 cm]) nail wooden sticks or boards. Fill the treads with coarse gravel, compress, and cover with bark mulch.

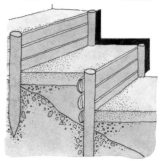

Walls and Palisades

Walls and palisades are massive and compact alternatives to fences, for you can enclose your property with them. But primarily they are appropriate where you want to adjust differences in level, interrupt slopes, or prop up steep grades. Walls have especially high aesthetic interest and a long tradition: Just get some inspiration from books or a vacation in southern Europe, or copy the example of walls from a city area! However, don't fail to check the local building regulations and try to make the construction fit in with the surroundings. You can errect a wall up to a height of 31.5 in (80 cm) by yourself without any problem, perhaps a dry wall (see drawing, page 51), which is made without cement and mortar. For building higher freestanding walls or supporting walls, you should hire a wall-building specialist, so that the necesssary stability is guaranteed by a professional. The same goes for palisades: experts must be employed here if the height goes over 31.5 to 39 in (80–99 cm).

Materials
You can use various construction materials to erect walls. Besides a variety of natural stones, for instance hard rock like granite or sedimentary rock like sandstone, especially suitable are clinker bricks, but also bricks, which can be plastered or painted white. Such walls can have a topping, for example, of roof tiles.

Concrete is very popular and extremely reasonable. It is also used in the form of L- or U-stones; they are easy to handle and up to 39 in (99 cm) in height and they need no frostproof foundation, only an about 4-in- (10-cm-) deep bed of compressed pebbles or lean concrete. Concrete walls can be treated in many ways: simply painted, as using a broadcast method with an outer surface of pebbles, or with textures that are produced through forms and special treatments.

Palisades are most often made of treated round or rectangular stakes (see drawing at right); you can, however, also erect cement posts, which last longer than wood.

Designing with Walls and Palisades
Walls and palisades can be designed and integrated into the garden scene in numerous ways.

Freestanding walls. Walls work most beautifully when they imitate the architecture of the house in their form and fit in with its character. For instance, wall sections are wonderful as sight and wind protection on terraces or for separation of properties of row houses or attached houses. It is important that the proportions match: for small properties, high walls are too massive; on the contrary, low sitting walls (see photo, page 53 top), perhaps in the area of the terrace or as the enclosure for a depressed sitting area in the garden, can be integrated easily. Here palisades are also suitable (see photo, page 53 bottom), because their effect is lighter.

Medium-high curving wall of clinker bricks in combination with a few st[e]

Palisades
They support slopes. Pressure-treated round logs or concrete posts are suitable for the purpose. They should show above ground by about one third to one half. Dig out a trench 24 to 32 in (60–81 cm) deep. First lay a layer of gravel 8 in (20 cm) deep to act as a water conduit so that the wood doesn't rot. Set the palisades next to one another, and fix with lean concrete about 16 in (40 cm) deep. Fasten at the tops with wire so that they don't slide. Line with roofing paper or insulation at the back side so that rain won't wash soil through between the posts. Fill in with soil and tread firm.

Dry walls. The traditional dry wall is enjoying a renaissance in modern natural garden layouts. It not only creates a very attractive effect, but also, because it is erected without any mortar, it is environmentally sound: With its open courses it offers the small creatures like warmth-loving lizards, toads, crickets, bumblebees, and wild bees plenty of places to live. Flowers and herbs often seed between the stones on their own, but they can also be planted when the stones are set.

Support walls. The job of a supporting wall is to support earth or a terrace against slippage. Steeper slopes can be worked and planted more comfortably if they are terraced, because flat surfaces are created by making steps in the slope. In addition, soil erosion is prevented (see Gardens on a Slope, pages 140–141).

Important: You should make sure with created slopes that the ground has first been very well compacted. Even so, especially stable support walls are required here, as well as a below-the-frost line foundation at least 31.5 in (80 cm) deep, in order to support the terracing. With non-porous soil, a drainage pipe must be inserted at the back of the foundation after excavation.

pretty solution for a garden with different levels.

Planting a Dry Wall

A dry wall is best planted while the stones are being placed. Choose rock garden plants (see pages 106–107 and 242–243) for sunny or shady locations depending how your wall is situated. Where you don't intend to plant, soil is only placed between the stones so that wild plants can seed there. Set the stones as horizontally and flat as possible. At least one third of all the stones should be the same depth as that of the wall (binders). For stability, avoid crevices that cross. The crevices can be protected with crowning stones (a layer of thick stones).

Dry Wall As a Supporting Wall

Dry walls are based on a gravel layer about 8 to 16 in (20–40 cm) deep. With porous soil, a row of large stones is enough foundation for a wall if they are set half-way into the ground. The breadth of the base of the wall should correspond to one third of the height, but it should be at least 12 in (30 cm) thick. With very loose or heavy soils, a foundation 16 in (40 cm) deep and 16 in (40 cm) wide of ready-mixed concrete is advisable. The stones are set with a 10% to 15% lean toward the slope so that water can run off. After construction, fill in behind the wall with gravel and crushed stone.

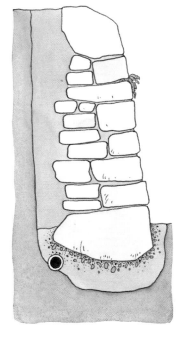

DESIGN ELEMENTS

Terraces—Position and Layout

The terrace is an important connecting element between the house and the garden. In drawing up a design, it is important to respect the character of the lot and to attune the inside and outside through use of materials that are harmonious with each other.

To make a terrace livable and also usable despite the weather, it must be somewhat protected: perhaps at the side by a wall or a house wall as sight, wind, or noise protection, overhead by a roof projection or a projecting balcony. Also important is the paving medium: It should fit the style of the house, be environmentally and user friendly as well as frost resistant and level, but have a nonslip surface and dry off quickly after a rain. See that you have a slope of 2% away from the house. For terraces that do not have a roof, a sill between the living area and the terrace is recommended to prevent the entry of snow or water into the house.

Location of the Terrace

Ideally, the living spaces, terrace, and garden lie on the same level, for then the lawn can be used too. However, there are also good solutions for other spatial conditions. For example, if the house is situated high over the garden, it is advisable to bank up the land (see Gardens on a Slope, pages 140–141), in order to broaden the terrace. Thus you can include at least a piece of the garden in the living area. Walls or palisades (see pages 50–51) support the soil, and the remainder of the grounds are reached by steps (see pages 48–49). If the garden lies above the house, you should still provide a large, even surface for the terrace if possible.

Walls low enough for sitting are also good to separate a terrace from a slope. If the ground falls away gently, you can model the grade (in a ratio of 1:3 or 1:4, which means that the land slopes 3 or 4 yards [meters] for every 1 yard [meter]) so that the grass is reachable directly from the terrace, at least on one side.

Paving

The choice of pavings for firm surfaces is enormous. Be guided in the choice by the landscape itself and regional building style.

Natural stone from local sources always fits into the picture and the costs of transportation are limited. There are pavings of natural stone flags or slabs, which are especially symmetrical; however, in wet conditions— depending on the kind of stone—they can easily become slippery.

Brick, paving, or concrete squared stones (ashlars) almost always integrate well. Concrete ashlars are available in various colors and with variously structured surfaces;

Ground-level terrace with clinker bricks laid in a circular pattern.

Terrace of wooden planking enclosed with timbers.

Natural Stone Paving

Natural stone slabs can be of hard stone like granite or of soft stone like sandstone. They are often laid in a so-called Roman pattern. In this pattern, the different-sized stones are laid at right angles to one another so that no crossing cracks occur.

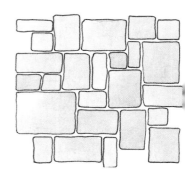

Cement Slab and Cobble Paving

Mixed materials are good for loosening up large surfaces. A charming pattern is created when small cobbles (about 2.75 in [7 cm] square) of gray granite or red porphyry are laid in ribbons of edging between the uniform cement slabs.

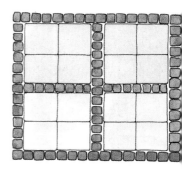

Terrace and gravel surface enclosed with a low wall.

Ground-level terrace with paving of mixed materials.

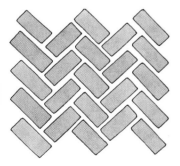

Brick and Clinker Brick Paving

Bricks and clinker bricks can be laid lengthwise or crosswise and in different rectangular patterns. Also charming are herringbone patterns, which are good for paths. Combinations of natural stone or cement slabs are pretty. Use hard-burned brick.

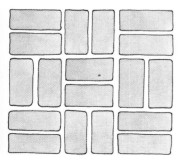

Ceramic and Clay-Tile Paving

These can be laid in special patterns like brick—often two and two as squares and then turned 90°. Glazed tiles are easy to care for but they are slippery when wet. Make sure with unglazed tiles that they will withstand frost.

some kinds almost look like natural stone. There are also those with a facing of real natural stone—an inexpensive alternative to real natural stone. With bricks, you should be careful to get ones that are fired to be frost hard. They can be laid in any number of possible patterns.

Wood in the form of paneling or paving is best suited for sunny areas, because it is slippery when wet. Again, be guided in the design of your terrace by the materials that are used in the rest of your property. You will thus create visual calm and the impression of spaciousness.

Combinations of various materials can, on the other hand, help to enliven structures and upgrade the grounds. Especially with sizable terraces, a mixture of materials serves wonderfully to break up the large surface, for example, large natural or cast stone blocks, which are worked in with small mosaics of paving or bricks. Also, a combination of stone and pebbles or wood works very well. You gain charming effects when you put some rock garden plants or slow-growing herbs along the edges of the terrace or in the spaces between the paving stones. Pavings of mixed materials are, however, less even. Therefore, you should choose paving that is uniform for the surfaces on which you want to place your chairs.

Not only the material and the way it is worked are important in paving, but also the various patterns of paving, which lend each area its own special note (see drawing at left).

Irregularly laid natural stone slabs with spaces for planting rock garden plants.

Important: Terraces, like paths (see page 46–47) require a foundation. However, with the terrace, you must also take into consideration that it can settle after some years if the soil beneath it was added during building. Therefore, it is recommended not to cement in the flags or pavement but only lay them in a sand bed about 1 in. (2.5 cm) high. Corrections can then be made easily at any time.

Terraces Designed for Livability

On warm days, the terrace becomes a living room surrounded by greenery. There are a wealth of possibilities for making it a place of complete comfort and atmosphere. Here are some of the most beautiful design ideas.

Division of Space

The design of a terrace is dependent on the conditions of the place but also on the direction in which it faces. Large terraces of from 300 to 500 sq ft (30–50 m²) or more require subdividing so that they appear cozy. They offer room for spacious sitting areas; plants in handsome containers add to livability. So that the terrace retains its structure over the winter months when furniture and plants are missing, it is advisable to erect a permanent framework, perhaps with a fireplace, pond, raised beds, or plant islands. Walls of sitting height can serve as frames, as does a pergola, which offers protection from sun, wind, and the eyes of the neighbors. Also, furniture and other objects that are used in the garden can be stored in the pergola. In this case, however, a roof that is at least partially closed is needed. If you want to "green" the pergola, choose plants that don't drop too much when withering or lose their leaves early, as is the case with wisteria (*Wisteria sinensis*), for example.

Important: Remember light and power sources as well as a water supply so that you can water the plants and keep the terrace clean without a great deal of effort.

Two garden rooms side by side—broad terrace and bewitching water lily

Strawberry jars are charming multipocketed plant containers for small terraces.

Furnishing

For how much space to allow for an eating area, use the following rule of thumb: length of the table + 5 ft (1.5 m) (for chair and working space). Round tables need more space than rectangular ones. For 6 people you need about 108 sq. ft. (10 m²), even more with voluminous furniture. Also, the shape of the terrace is an important factor: Long, narrow, or round spaces are harder to arrange.

The choice of garden furniture is enormous. It's important that it correspond to the character of the sitting area. Beyond that there is a list of criteria that are crucial to the decision: If the furniture is to be outdoors all year-round, it must be weatherproof. It should also be appropriate in size. Heavy, bulky furniture should only be installed where there is enough space, for it is hard to move. Garden furniture should not only look nice but also be comfortable; therefore provide cushions or upholstered pads. It is advisable to choose material, color, and pattern so that the cushions are both easy to care for and not too dominating visually, so they don't steal the show from the garden flowers. If you have a storage space (chest) nearby, you always have the pads readily available.

Garden furniture is available in different colors and materials:

Wooden furniture. Wooden furniture goes almost anywhere; it harmonizes with all kinds of paving and has a warm sitting surface. Simple variants of softwood (spruce, pine) are treated but must be retreated with preservative every 2 years.

Superior executions in hardwood (birch, locust, plantation teak, redwood) have a long life without any treatment.

Metal. Metal or wrought iron furniture is stable and weather resistant, but it has its price. The graceful forms, depending on the style, fit as well in the romantic garden as in the classic or modern one. There are also those with (warmer) wooden seats.

ond. See below for important aspects.

Small livable terrace with wicker furniture and plants in containers.

About the large photo above
*Garden ponds usually end at terraces with a steep bank. There,
a wall is erected at the installation of the pond, over which protecting insulation and plastic pond sheeting (see pages 62–65)
are then placed. Insulation and sheeting are fastened under the
terrace planking over a horizontally placed timber. The wooden
planking extends over the pond somewhat.*

Stone. Natural and artificial stone are suitable for permanent installations because of their weight. Such benches,
perches, and walls always need a warming overlay such as
cushions or wooden grates.

Wicker. Wicker furniture belongs to classic conservatory
furniture. Its natural style and lightness of handling make
it ideal for seating on the terrace. However, it should be
protected from the elements.

Plastic. Plastic furniture is easy to move, easy to care for,
and survives almost any weather.

Color. Materials left natural as well as gray, green, and
brown tones fit best into the garden scene. Also broken
color tones like light gray or beige fit in well. Hard white,
on the other hand, is dominant and makes an object,
such as a bench in front of a dark background, automatically a focal point. Strongly colored furniture can be
installed as a style vehicle and decoration, perhaps to
underline a planting. You can also paint wood and metal
furniture any color you like; but then it needs regular care.

Terrace Plantings

Finally, for a comfortable atmosphere on the terrace,
provide plants. A focal point at the side of the terrace or
in the foreground stops the eye. Vines on the pergola and
perennials in the spaces between paving stones lend charm
to a sitting area. Beautiful containers with perennials,
hanging or tub plantings on the terrace, and bed edgings
round out the picture as does an ornamental tree (see
Specimens, pages 78–79), which produces the reference
between house and garden. Especially pretty and fragrant
plants belong on the terrace and around its borders. Thus,
you can also enjoy flowers in winter and spring, such as
the witch hazel (*Hamamelis* species/varieties), winter
jasmine (*Jasminum nudiflorum*), or the fragrance of the
winter flowering snowball (*Viburnum farreri*). Smaller evergreens and shrubs near the terrace also provide a pretty
frame for the view out of the living spaces in winter. From
spring to fall you experience the flowers of bulbs, roses,
and perennials. With butterfly bushes (*Buddleia davidii*
hybrids), you can induce butterflies and observe them.
Sunny, protected terraces are also ideal for an herb corner.
On a semishady terrace, on the other hand, you can provide your houseplants with a summer vacation.

DESIGN ELEMENTS

Sitting Areas As Exciting Spaces

Several sitting areas in a garden make possible different views and create exciting spaces. Why not view the house and the terrace from the garden once in awhile? In addition, you can take advantage of light conditions at different seats at all times of day and in all seasons.

Sitting Area Variations

The large terrace at the house (see Terraces, pages 52–55), open to the south and west, protected by warmth-storing walls and a roof, is of course ideal. But in summer, it has its disadvantages: It can become intolerably hot under an awning or a pergola. In this case, it pays to establish a shady spot where two people can sit.

The shady side of the house. If your house offers the opportunity to lay out several terraces on different sides of the building, take advantage of it. Then you can enjoy light and shadow depending on the direction and requirements. In sloping situations, these sitting areas are often at different levels, with charming garden views.

The shady seat from which to contemplate the whole garden. When the spaces around the house are too confined or the land falls away steeply, a seat in the garden, away from the house, is the better solution. It can be situated under a tree, in a pergola, under a sun shade, in an arbor, or in a pavilion. Protection from the wind and rain is always good. This sitting area can form a counterpoint to the terrace and looking from it can embrace an idyllic ensemble of trees and flowers.

The secluded place in the garden. Even more than the seat that overlooks the whole garden, the sitting area that is screened, entirely hidden in the green of the garden, fulfills our requirement for relaxation and immersion in nature. Such places for reading and dreaming are best located in a private corner of the garden. Especially relaxing are seats that are situated by a pond. But also important here is shade.

Place for sitting in a rose arbor in the middle of the garden.

Spot for sitting on the lawn under a flowering cherry tree.

The large terrace at the house (see Terraces, pages 52–55)

Practical Considerations

The sitting area can be situated on flat ground—tied in with the garden plantings—but also somewhat raised, with a free view, or sunken-in level. Often no special construction measures at all are required for a grass surface or meadow, a wooden plank or path already offers the best precondition for a sitting area. Sometimes it's enough to pave the ground with a few flags or wooden planks. Furthermore, all materials that are suitable for building paths and terraces can be used here. The paving material should always be the same as that of the terrace or path. The smaller the garden, the more important the dictum that mixed materials structure and make smaller; homogeneous materials produce spaciousness. You should also follow this principle with the furniture (see page 54).

For a ground-level sitting area that is rarely used, a natural paving is enough, perhaps gravel, paving blocks, or bricks with wide joints, lawn checker bricks, or perforated bricks (see page 47), which allow enough free space for all the vegetation. With gravel, the edge grows slowly inward, and the place then only shows traces where it is heavily used. This solutions looks particularly natural.

A sunken sitting area possesses a particularly homey and protected feeling, but it requires more extensive construction: A depression must be dug out, the side walls must be reinforced with walls or palisades (see pages 50–51). For the ground a stone or wood paving is best. Such protected sitting areas are wonderful spots for a barbecue. For this purpose, however, you should avoid a wooden flooring, at least in the area of the grill.

White garden furniture immediately attracts the eye. Circular benches permit enjoyment of differing views and light conditions.

The softer the ground, the more solid the furniture must be. If you value somewhat more comfort, have a garden outlet installed; then you can enjoy light and heat far from the house.

Plantings at a Sitting Area

For designing a sitting area with plants, the same criteria as for terraces apply: Important factors are fragrance, beauty of the flowers, and the possibility of being able to observe butterflies and other flower seekers close up. In contrast to the terrace, whose plantings should be enchanting all year-round, in a garden sitting area it is primarily a question of an attractive summer planting. Always be guided in your choice of plants by light and soil conditions. Tub plants or prettily planted stone troughs are pleasant; therefore, a water connection in the area is an advantage.

Deck chair by a small pond.

Wooden bench in a natural garden.

You can best enjoy the features of your garden with various sitting places; you can spontaneously seek out the places where something is blooming and fragrant at that time. With movable seats, you also have the opportunity to follow the appearance of light or shadow in your garden.

Pergolas, Arbors, and Trellises

Pergolas, arbors, and trellises are architectural elements that visually separate parts of the garden or tie them together. Even as unplanted frameworks of wood or metal, they form a visual focus. But they produce the most beautiful effects when entwined with leaves and flowers.

A Little Basic Information

Pergolas are leafy passages that arch over an entire path. They consist of many archways linked together. But the elements can also be set up singly very effectively: as arches at an entry entwined with roses, as a one-sided companion to a garden pathway with vines growing over it, or as a frame for a beautiful view. A pergola can tie a house and garden together if it covers the terrace extensively; it can subdivide the facade of the house and create new spaces, perhaps as the roofing for a seating area (see pages 56–57).

A simple arbor can be erected by adding trellises and latticework walls to the vertical posts of a pergola frame, which with light vining offers protection from the sun and wind with back covering as well as at the sides and top, but still remains permeable. The growth on it should be appropriate, whether the trellis or the vine wall is simple or luxurious. Vigorously growing vines like wisteria (*Wisteria sinensis*) or fallopia (*Fallopia aubertii*) offer protection, but they entirely cover artistic trellising. Wisteria will also crush to death anything less than very sturdy after relatively few years. For particularly handsome frames, which ought to remain partly visible, roses and clematis are preferable.

Here, a single-sparred pergola stretches across the garden as a large-scale s...

Building a Pergola

The steps: ① Install 5- to 6-in (13–15 cm) well-waterproofed wooden posts no farther apart from one another than 10 ft (3 m) so that they won't bend under the cross beams ② (purlins, bearers) laid over them. The supports should be at least 7 to 7.5 ft (2–2.3 m) high. The covering timbers ③ (riders, rafters) rest on the supporting construction at intervals of 16 to 24 in (40–60 cm). Anchor the supports with a metal shoe ④ in a concrete foundation (see drawing page 42).

Homemade rustic arbor of wood.

Pergolas are wonderful design elements and give a garden a very special flair. Depending on whether you want to connect two construction elements with one another or reduce a large garden to managable dimensions, pergolas can be unifying or dividing elements. However, a pergola derives its glory from appropriate vining. Be careful: Vigorously growing plants get heavy!

...er and supports climbing roses for a glory of bloom at a lofty height.

The shade provided by a pergola depends on the density of the planting— but also how the top parts, "the roof," are constructed and the distance between them.

Tips for Building Pergolas and Arbors

As with all design elements, you should also make sure that the pergola or arbor fits harmoniously into your garden. For smaller gardens, suitable construction materials can be worked narrowly and, thus, suggest lightness like wood, steel, or concrete. Larger garden layouts also tolerate columns of brick and natural stone.

<u>Wood.</u> Usually rectangular or round sticks of resinous evergreen are used. Softwoods gain a certain amount of permanence with pressure treating. Trellises should be painted or stained.

<u>Metal.</u> Steel mesh, steel grill, or pipe constructions are especially good for arches and arbors, because they are stable but still graceful.

<u>Stone.</u> Supports and columns may be made of natural stone, concrete, or brick. There is also the possibility of covering a less attractive concrete core with natural stone or bricks. The riders (see drawing) are made of wood or metal. A pergola on the terrace usually leads directly toward the house and therefore picks up the horizontal lines of windows, doors, or the roof. It can be closed on one side with a wall or a wall of vines, with which you achieve good privacy and wind protection.

Modern asymmetrical arbor of metal.

Arbors can be achieved with few construction elements. Individual and unusual solutions are also possible, as the photo above shows. Here, the arbor looks like a large garden sculpture. Anyone who has in mind a completely overgrown arbor should try Dutchman's pipe vine (Aristolochia macrophylla) or Virginia creeper (Parthenocissus quinquefolia).

Simple Pergola

Double-sparred pergolas in gate form, to which additional trellises and lattice walls are attached, can act as dividers, privacy walls, or boundaries. Even simpler is the single-sparred pergola, which consists of 2 supports, a linking cross beam, and several rafters across the top.

Pergolas of 2 Materials

Pergolas and arbors with masonry pillars or stone supports fit in large gardens. Cross beams and rafters are usually of wood. Such constructions need a stable foundation and should only be erected by experts. Make sure that the proportions go together: The pergola should always be somewhat higher than it is wide.

Gazebos and Summerhouses

A gazebo in one's own garden—who wouldn't like that? Today this dream has come within reach. The once-so-popular garden gazebo has been rediscovered and can be admired in various executions in gardens. Expensive imitations of baroque or Victorian gazebos are at your disposal as well as artistic handcrafted fantastic creations or rustic wooden pavilions, which often are available ready for assembly. The spectrum extends to modern conservatory glass house construction. The only thing that is important is what type suits your garden and your house. In renaissance or baroque gardens, pavilions often formed the center spot of the garden space. The austerely laid-out axes of paths joined under its roof, so to speak. If one looked out through the openings in its sides walls, the individual sections of the garden appeared in a picture frame, and they were visually separated from one another. An alternative to that was the pavilion as a focal point at the end of a path axis—there often as a cover for a work of art—or as a "lookout" at the edges of the property.

In modern gardens, pavilions are no longer used exclusively as architectural points of style. As intimate small spaces, they offer the chance for withdrawal, meditation, and rest. If the gazebo is to have a decorative function as its primary purpose, it belongs in a highly visible spot in the garden. However, a corner in an out-of-the-way part of the garden, perhaps where you have a pretty view of the house and garden, is also a suitable spot.

Pavilions in Many Forms

The boundary between the concepts *pavilion, arbor,* and *summerhouse* is often blurred. As opposed to arbors (see pages 58–59), a garden pavilion or gazebo has a solid roof. It can, like an arbor, be open on one or several sides. If it is closable on all sides, it is considered a small summerhouse. The footprint of a pavilion is usually round, square, hexagonal, or octagonal. Form and roof construction often are reminiscent of small temples.

Pavilion. The garden pavilion represents a real alternative to the protected house terrace (see pages 58–59). Like a thickly vine-covered arbor, its closed roof offers a feeling of security, and the garden can be experienced more directly than from the terrace. Gazebos and dense arbors offer the best protection from the wind, rain, and sun—here you can also enjoy your garden in inclement weather. It's optimal, of course, if you can have both: a typical open terrace at the house and in addition a pavilion in the garden into which you can withdraw.

Summerhouse or garden house. In contrast to a gazebo, a little garden house has solid walls all around, as well as windows and doors that can be closed. It usually houses a small, comfortable garden room. Some also have a small veranda or folding doors, which can be opened wide. However, garden houses are often built less to aesthetic

Hexagonal garden house with French doors.

criteria and much more according to practical considerations and also often serve for storage of garden equipment or quarters for wintering over tub plants.

Materials

Pavilions, garden houses, and arbors can be made of many different materials and adapted to many types of styles. Depending on the kind of material, cleaning and maintenance are more or less expensive.

Wood. Many a garden refuge consists in large part of wood; but they can also have a frame of brick or stone that is combined with wooden sections. There are rustic expressions but also very elegant ones. White-painted pavilions of wood look especially inviting. They are a clear focal point in the garden. Natural-colored pavilions, on the other hand, are less noticeable in the garden scene. Especially when they are covered with vines, they become a constituent part of the garden.

Pavilions are often as transparent and airy as arbors. Constructions of trellis (wooden latticework) are especially

Pavilion with white wooden trellises for climbing plants.

Homebuilt movable pavilion.

Pavilion of wickerwork wound around with clematis.

charming. These variants go back to the time of the Renaissance. The tradition is primarily distributed throughout the Northern European countries, but today it is enjoying a generally increasing popularity. These lattice elements are wonderfully suitable for the greening of walls, arbors, and pavilions, because plants can find opportunities to attach and twine. However, choose the vines intended for them very carefully; trellises should not be too heavily overgrown or their beautiful architectural effect is obscured.

Metal. Pavilions of metal or wrought iron can also be very charming. They look especially transparent and light and are best suited for vining. You can paint them in various colors and so achieve very charming effects.

Glass. Glass pavilions, as a rule based on a metal or wooden framing, are also suitable for attractive greenhouses. Special plant collections are set off very beautifully in this way. Because they, like conservatories and greenhouses, can be very hot in summer, good ventilation arrangements and provisions for shading are very important. For overwintering of tub plants, they must be heatable.

Tips for Construction

If you live in a colder climate, every kind of pavilion or garden house needs a below frostline foundation (therefore, a strip foundation at least 31.5 in [80 cm] deep of concrete or crushed stone and gravel). With light constructions, just a concrete foundation under the posts (see Fences, pages 42–43) is enough. More solid constructions require correspondingly more expensive foundations. Some kinds of pavilions are available in the trade as prefabricated elements and parts. Otherwise, you should get advice from a professional for safety's sake. You should refer to your landscape architect for individual solutions.

Octagonal wooden pavilion with glass windows.

Modern steel and glass construction.

A Lively Natural Pond

Ponds make a garden especially lively, for they offer living space to many animals and plants. If you are concerned about conservation, you can make a contribution to it with a pond. Ideally, your garden should be at least 5,000 sq ft (500 to 1000 m²) or more. To make the installation appropriate ecologically and functional over the long term, you need to observe certain criteria.

Basics

A healthy natural pond is demonstrated through a stable biological equilibrium. The natural chemical cycles can only continue unhindered if the proportions among plants, animals, and the microorganisms in the water are correct. In this sensitive moist biotope, the tiniest changes can lead to "tilting" of the water (eutrophication). Small ponds can regenerate themselves less easily and therefore are particularly labile. Here regulatory measures are often necessary. Above all, the water of a pond should not be too rich in nutrients. Underwater plants should guarantee that enough oxygen is produced. It's better not to introduce any fish at all, and if you do, then only in a pond with a size of at least 215 sq ft (21.5 m²) because these severely reduce the other animal life. The appropriate location for a garden pond is a bright but not constantly sunny spot. Therefore, provide for shading to the south so that the water doesn't get too hot in summer; this will lead to the growth of algae and lack of oxygen.

However, don't locate the pond under large deciduous trees. The roots of the trees can be injured in the excavation, or the seal of the pond can be endangered by root growth. A tree crown casts too much shadow over it and covers the pond with its leaves in fall. Also, too much organic material sets the rotting process in motion, which ultimately disturbs the biological equilibrium.

The pond should lie protected, if possible not in a cold air lane. It works best in the deepest part of the property, where water will collect naturally. In a sequestered area, flora and fauna can develop undisturbed; but there you can't observe the pond from a nearby area. If the pond is near the house, you can pipe in rainwater from the roof, and besides, electrical and water connections are comfortably accessible.

The Pond As Environment

The size and depth are decisive for the stability of the biological equilibrium of a pond. A water surface of at least 215 sq ft (21.5 m²) is required for an installation that will be viable over the long term. The extent naturally depends to begin with on the space conditions in your garden. Water and bank areas should blend as smoothly as possible into the surrounding areas. Marsh and silting areas enrich the environment in addition and offer protection to a multitude of animals.

Densely and diversely planted natural pond with shallow-water and

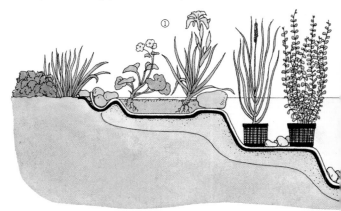

Diagram of a Pond Lined with Plastic Sheeting

For detailed instructions on building, see pages 64–65. Shape natural ponds with banks sloping as gently as possible. Three to four levels are pleasing.

① The marshy area on the edge of the bank. Soil height 8 to 10 in (20–25 cm), water level 0 to 6 in (0–15 cm). To keep the soil from washing down to the next level, the area is sealed off from the open pond with stones.

② The shallow-water area reaches about 12 to 16 in (30–40 cm) in depth.

Natural pond with summer planting.

marsh areas (left).

Fall impressions at the same pond.

③ The deep-water area. Water height 20 in (50 cm) and optionally more for floating-leaved plants (see pages 276–277).
Tips for construction: Add a layer of 2 to 4 in (5–10 cm) of sand to the excavated hole, then a layer of plastic insulation, and then the plastic pond sheeting on top of that. With a bank formation that drops off gently, the capillary block (see left bank) is important. The edge of the sheeting is pulled up vertically so that it sticks up above the water level. This keeps the soil around the edge of the pond from continually drawing up water. The right side of the pond can be walked on. Such places can also be arranged with natural ponds.

Natural ponds should be at least about 3 ft (1 m) deep per surface area of 10 sq ft (1 m²). Also, in the coldest winter, the pond will not freeze to this depth. This frost-free zone guarantees overwintering for the fish, too. Besides, deep pond installations equalize temperature fluctuations better, which has an effect on the quality of the water. Also, some plants, particularly the large water lilies, require a higher water level. So that many plants and animals feel good in this habitat, you must provide for differing water depths and shallow water areas. There are plants that are particularly suited for each of these zones (see pages 274–279). If the pond contour is arranged with three or four steps, the planting medium or plant containers won't slide so easily, and the water inhabitants can easily get into the water and out again. Also such a stepped layout offers a certain protection for children and animals. Steep bank areas are extraordinarily dangerous for them (see Child Security, page 66).

The Ornamental Pond

Do you want a pond with goldfish, a fountain, or spring stones? Then you have an ornamental pond or pool in mind, irregularly or geometrically shaped, with slanting or vertical walls. The planting will look less lush but rather more decorative. With ornamental ponds, the aesthetic charm is in the foreground; in contrast to natural ponds, they are usually too small to be able to regulate themselves biologically. The closer the ornamental pond is to the house, the more austere and distinct its form should be.

A Pond Lined with Plastic Sheeting
Whether for a natural or an ornamental pond, the installation of a pond lined with plastic sheeting is always the same.

Substructure. When the location is determined (see pages 62–63), the form of the pond is marked out with pegs and string. As to the size of the pond: A decorative pond with fish or water lilies should be frostproof and thus at least 39 in (1 m) deep. Begin the excavation with a ditch of at least 10 sq ft (1 m²) for the deepest place. Figure in work space and space for the lining. In addition, mark the different water levels and dig out the steps accordingly. These steps form habitats for plants and animals. Also a marshy and silting area (see drawing pages 62–63) should be taken into consideration at the beginning. Check with the help of a level tool whether the edge of the pond is level. Then, clear the bottom carefully of rubbish, stones, and roots, smooth the soil, and stamp it firm. With a particularly stony subsoil, an extra layer of about 2 in (5 cm) of fine sand is recommended. You can lay wire mesh under it as a protection against voles, but in any case you should line the pond hole with a lining protector. Only then add the plastic sheeting.

Pond lining. It must consist of all one piece (available from the supplier). Don't save on plastic sheeting: Only quality, high-value products hold up to stress over time. The larger the pond, the thicker the sheeting should be. It comes in thicknesses of 0.8 to 1.5 mm.

As soon as the plastic is installed, the water must be run in. Let the level rise slowly, so that the sheeting can press firmly against the soil. Folds won't matter. Wait for about 10 days until the pond bottom has set. Only then should you undertake the edge formations and cut away the extra sheeting.

Spillover. A spillover is also important. The best thing is to simply make a drainage ditch beside the pond, which is joined to the pond with a pipe.

Building the edge. When building the edge, make sure that the firm curbing or walkway around the edge is solidly supported. A foundation of premixed concrete or an underlayer of gravel and stones guarantees the necessary stability here.

The sheeting is also more easily concealed than with a natural bank. It's best anchored between the wooden planks or under the flags with which the pond is ringed. If you allow this edging to extend on the inside for about 2 in (5 cm), all the unattractive edges of the sheeting—also those of a plastic pool—are invisible. In a natural-type pond, the edge can be very well concealed with gravel and large found objects as well as appropriate planting.

With such level-edged ponds, there is the danger that the surrounding soil will draw water out (capillary or wicking effect) and you must constantly replenish the water. You can remedy this if you pull the sheeting up vertically, with a small "lip" of excess sheeting anchored between stones and plants along the edge (see drawing, pages 62–63).

Installing a Ready-made Pond
If you opt for a ready-made pool you must mark out the shape according to the shape of the insert and add at least 4 to 6 in (10–15 cm) around it. This space is important as working space and for the underlining of the pool form with sand. At first, dig out the deepest part of the pond—corresponding to the deepest setback of the pool form—then firm the ground. Cover the soil with a 2-to-4-in- (5–10-cm-) thick layer of sand, put in the pool form, and carefully fill in with sand on all sides. It is important that the form be straight (water level!) and also that it cannot tilt later. You can prevent this by letting the water run in slowly immediately. Ready-made ponds also need an overflow with a provision for runoff. Very pretty also are ornamental pools that are set into a terrace. In places where there is too much rock underneath, you can leave a pool form freestanding and cover the sides with wood, tiles, or natural stone. With an edging comfortable for sitting, you can enjoy this pool entirely relaxed.

Ornamental Pools with Vertical Walls
Pools of this type used to be quite common. Their walls were masonry or concrete and made watertight with a special paint. However, they are particularly dangerous for children and small animals. In winter, these pools must be emptied so that the water can't freeze and produce cracks in the pool with the increase in volume.

Ornamental pond with square masonry pool—ideal for small gardens.

This danger does not occur with pools with slanting walls or banks that are shallowly graded. Vertical or steep walls can be well planted with the aid of jute pockets. At the same time, the edge of the pool can have plants trailing over it.

Fish in Ponds and Pools

The small, exotically colored goldfish are primarily suitable for small ornamental pools from about 30 sq ft (3 m²). The larger, more expensive koi need at least 100 or more sq ft (10–15 m²) of water surface and also greater depth. You need to change the water regularly with a pond with fish. Also an oxidator is required for the air intake and a filter system for circulation, for clean, oxygenated water creates the favorable living conditions for all ornamental fish. There are particular reagents and test strips for checking the water quality that are available in a pet store. Goldfish tend to "burrow," that is, they root around in the bottom of the pond. Preferably, to prevent cloudiness of the water, you should only keep plants in baskets and cover the soil with insulation or stones. If the pond isn't deep enough—that is, not frostproof—the fish must be wintered over in

Modern ornamental pond linked with the architecture of the house.

an aquarium. On the other hand, with a depth of 39 in (1 m) you can let the fish winter over in the pond; however, the pond must be kept ice-free at one spot (purchase an ice-melter at the pet store). In any case, it is best to get advice at the pet store before you install fish.

Ideas for Around Water

Water is one of the most fascinating design elements in the garden, which allows itself to be used in numerous ways: As still water, it is the basis for abundant plant and animal life. As a brook, a waterfall, or splashing fountains, it creates effects through movement and the sound it makes, at the same time giving off coolness and oxygen-rich humid air for people, animals, and plants.

Water Play

There are a number of possibilities to use water as a design feature in the garden. A little water play can be integrated into any garden, and there are no limits to your imagination as to how.

<u>Spring stones.</u> Suitable for this are not only costly millstones, but also found objects, which you can have bored.

<u>Springs and wells.</u> An old trough, a bucket, an artistically designed well, or a water sprayer at the edge of a pool lend a special flair to the garden.

<u>Birdbaths.</u> There are countless forms, usually made of stone or terra-cotta.

<u>Waterfalls.</u> The individual elements consist of natural stone slabs or concrete ready-made pieces arranged on top of each other like steps, with each projecting over somewhat. The water falls free like a veil over this overhang.

<u>Fountains</u> offer the viewer a charming picture. In addition, they enrich the standing water with oxygen. Water lilies and other plants prefer quiet water, however. If you want to combine both, you should provide enough distance or mount only a small bubbler or water bell, which have an effect similar to a fountain's but disturb the water surface less.

These water players are also less dangerous for small children than a pond or a pool.

<u>Paddling and swimming pools</u> naturally have a special charm for children and with proper planning can later be turned into a decorative pool or a pond. Consider ahead of time what is going to become of the pool once the children no longer use it and take this into account in the choice of location and shape.

A spacious variant is the combination of bathing and plant pool and a brook. The water runs out of the bathing pool into a planted pool, is filtered there, and enriched with oxygen in the brook.

Oasis in the garden with a bubbling stone spring.

Murmuring water steps of natural stone.

Water Technology

If water has to be in motion, technology is involved. There are water pumps with various capacities for pumping out, for circulation, and as drive mechanisms for fountains. Get advice from a dealer as to which pump with which capacity is the right one for your purposes. For example, with a brook, the delivery capacity of the pump needed depends on the height of the incline and the quantity of water that is to be moved. Here, instead of a special pump, a pond filter with an integrated pump may also be used. Over the winter, the brook is quiet and the apparatus is removed. Underwater lights, spotlights, and floating lights (see photo, page 143) are pretty technical toys with which ponds or ornamental pools can be effectively lighted in the evenings. But consider that animals and plants also need their rest. Therefore, only make use of this technology for hours at a time.

Important: All installations with water and electricity must be made by electricians for safety reasons.

GARDEN
TIPS AND TRICKS

Child Security
If there are small children in the house, you should secure the pond or fountain with a 24-in (60-cm) high wooden fence or by a protective grating about 10 cm under the water surface. Pile up bricks at several points in the pond and put a structural-steel grid on top of it (photo, page 142).

A Brook Course

A brook in the garden is a wonderful expansion of an already existing pond, for it filters the water and enriches it with oxygen. But it can also work without a pond; in this case the brook simply seeps away in a marsh bed. The models for garden brooks—as with the pond—are found in nature. Unlike the pond, however, here it cannot work without technology.

Depending on the lay of the land, the course of the brook between source and outflow may run slightly winding and smooth, perhaps as slow flowing water through a meadow or along the edge of a property—an incline of 1% to 2% is enough. On sloping land, it can rush over stones, collect in pools in certain places—through which the rush of water is slowed again—to then flow more smoothly at the end. Great differences in height may be bridged by a waterfall. However, it should not be made too high. Its steps should be set steeper at the beginning, then flatter and more irregular. The water can exit at the source very naturally between stones or out of a bubbler. If there is no pond present, an underground catch basin (see Filter Ponds above) must be installed in the area of the outflow, from which the water is again pumped to the source. Dig the course of the brook alternatingly wide and deep; like a pond, cover it first with sand, then with film (see pages 64–65), and spread it with stone fragments or in flat places, with gravel and sand as naturally as possible. Distribute large and small stones irregularly over the streambed.

Brook course with small waterfalls.

Filter Ponds

With filter ponds, the pond or brook water can be cleaned in a biological way; they represent a natural botanical purification plant. They consist, like other pond containers of plastic, and various sizes can be bought. The container for a filter pond is sunk into the ground. Through attractive planting, you can tie it harmoniously into the environment. If there is no pond present, it serves the brook as a catchment. If the brook drains into a pond, the water is pumped from there out into the filter pond through a hose connection (only minimal pumping capacity is required here). The water that is filled with algae and suspended matter is then impelled from the bottom to the top of the filter pond through a layer of coarse and fine gravel. This catches the suspended material and the microorganisms are broken down. Also, the roots of the marsh plants have a filtering effect, by means of which the plants withdraw superfluous nutrients from the water. The purified water is finally returned directly to the pond or brook again.

Installing a Brook

A brook course is best laid out with string or a line of sand. Dig out and make the edges as for a pond (see pages 64–65). The brook should be at least 12 in (30 cm) wide and 10 in (25 cm) deep. At the mouth (in a pond or catch basin), install a pump ①. The pump must not be too powerful or the water will flow too fast, which is not good for plants and animals. An underground line ② pumps the water to the head ③. The water loss is replaced by a supply ④ from the main water system.

DESIGN ELEMENTS

Classic Garden Ornaments

Even in antiquity, statues and vases decorated the gardens of villas—thus, objects as garden ornaments have a long tradition. These models inspired the garden artists when the first large European park creations arose in Italy during the Renaissance. First, it was primarily figures and vases with which allées, plazas, and hedge backdrops were decorated. But in time, a number of other decorative elements developed, such as the pinecones of stone and terra-cotta derived from nature. In baroque Versailles, this garden art reached its zenith. A whole line of decorative elements go back to this period, for example, the square white planters that are so very much in fashion today. Only when the English collected plants from all over the world were the gardens filled with ever more abundant and colorful vegetation, and the plants moved more strongly into the foreground.

However, ornamental elements still remain very important vehicles of horticultural art. Combined with plants and water, they have decorated European parks and gardens for centuries. In the 19th century, there arose true mass production of figures and containers of cast iron and artificial stone.

Which Ornament for Which Garden?

A garden is more than just a collection of pretty plants. Garden ornaments are not only effective in great parks, but small gardens can also profit from inclusion of such elements.

Style. It is crucial that these objects fit with the style of the house and garden. The smaller the property, the more important it is to maintain a particular style orientation in the choice of single elements. With carefully chosen decorative pieces, you can make your property into a harmonious whole. Statues of antique gods or lions and hunting dogs don't fit very well into a municipal garden. Simple classical references and modern garden sculpture, on the other hand, are very appropriate for the small modern garden. With some luck, you may acquire an original; otherwise, there are also superior and attractive reproductions available in the trade. Give yourself time to choose, and don't buy too much: In a garden in which everything is small and visible at a glance, one or two such accents is enough.

Focal point. The focal point is a traditional vehicle of style in garden art. It plays an especially important role in the strictly formal Italian and French gardens of the Renaissance. The spaciousness of the huge parks was particularly emphasized by objects, which were installed as focal points at the end of an allée or an axis of paths.

But decorative elements don't just belong in classical gardens and landscape parks; they can also be installed effectively in modern gardens. Thus, small, narrow, and close garden spaces gain visual breath through such

The closed form of a terra-cotta vase here becomes a focal point in a

Distinct forms—pinecone . . .   . . . and stone sphere.

A beautiful container need not be planted but like a sculpture can create a pretty contrast with the living structures of the vegetation. Simple classical forms are the most effective this way. Make sure that the clay wares are fired hard enough to withstand frost. In winter, open containers should be tipped over or closed for safety's sake.

Terra-cotta column, fruit baskets.

diverse perennial planting.

Baroque column and cherub.

Terra-cotta jugs as part of a still life with plants.

Even playful arrangements can lend a garden additional atmosphere or provide moments of surprise in particular nooks and corners when small stone figures suddenly pop up from the green jungle between ground covers and decorative-leaved plants or are discovered at the end of a path in front of a shrubbery backdrop.

accents. An eye-catcher allows a spacious feeling to develop; the proportions of a garden can be visually changed through them.

The principles of garden art—the design tricks and visual ploys—work for large and small gardens alike. Decorative objects as focal points stand out, draw the eye to certain beauties, enliven monotonous spots, and bring serenity and permanence to the garden scene, which is otherwise marked by the growing and withering of the plant world.

Placing Decorative Elements

It is important that the decorative element be stylistically appropriate for the house and garden. But the location is also crucial for the effect that the object produces. It should fit as naturally as possible into its surroundings. For it to become an integral part of the garden, it must be tied into the current situation. The object can stand alone on the lawn or in front of a colorfully agreeing background. With light objects, you can change the location once in awhile. On the other hand, with a heavy one, it's necessary to find the best location at the beginning. Take time for it, consider different spots in the garden, and observe them at different times of day and seasons. It's best if you test the effect of an object with help of a dummy or an especially easily transportable piece. This method has also shown to be helpful if an already present piece has to be integrated into the garden picture. In a large garden, it's best to place decorative elements so that only one, or at most two, is ever in the field of vision at one time.

When you busy yourself longer with the question of location, your eye for details in your garden will be sharpened. This helps you also with other design questions and with the placement of plants. Specimen plantings (pages 78–79) produce charming effects in combination with decorative elements, perhaps if a small tree, an ornamental cherry (*Prunus* species/varieties) or a Japanese maple (*Acer* species) is spreading its branches picturesquely over a figure.

The purposeful placement of a garden sculpture is like staging a theatrical production: An entirely specific place is assigned to a special walk-on. It is simplest when you buy the ornament for its specific purpose and for the place in the garden that you sought it for in the first place. Then you can best reconcile the broad proportions to one another. It is more difficult when something you already have must be correctly incorporated.

Contemporary Garden Ornaments

The garden art form offers wonderful possibilities to work with decorative accessories. For centuries, decorative elements have been constituent parts of gardens. Not only ancient Greece and Rome have influenced this tradition, but forms from East Asia have also entered into European garden architecture.

The spectrum of variations has never been so broad as it is today: from kitsch to arts and crafts to modern sculptures of great artistic quality. The boundaries are fluid, and every garden owner may find something according to his or her taste.

Art Objects and Collectors' Items

Make sure that the desired object finds not only the right location in your garden but also the right frame. As antique goes with modern in furnishing a house, so in the designing of a garden, beautiful effects can be achieved by the combination of natural with strictly formal, wild with classical.

The form of a piece of art shows to very good effect in front of a quiet background. However, this does not mean that it will not also work in front of a contrasting backdrop. You can use modern, playful garden art entirely unconventionally. The objects that enrich the garden beyond the planting designs also give information about the preferences of the owner. It can be typical art objects, but also entirely ordinary trifles, collectors' items, souvenirs, homemade goods; however, the objects should always have a certain style, for they, thus, stamp the character of the garden. Don't put too many of them in the garden, which creates unrest and lessens their effect.

Decorative Elements and Their Effect

There are countless possibilities to include decorative elements in the garden. They can serve as a focal point, make a small garden interesting, and catch the eye in a large one. It is important that the ornaments harmonize with the plants, which provide the frame and the backdrop for them.

• Large sculptures can break up and loosen straight horizontal lines—hedges, for instance. A pavilion can also perform this function and become a decorative object.

• Smaller objects bring certain parts of the garden into the visual field; also, pairs flanking paths, steps, and entrances appear very stylish.

• Light objects bring light and variation into dark areas of the garden where the design possibilities with plants are limited because of the light conditions.

• Colored objects can enliven a uniformly green hedge or even provide color in the garden at times when little is in flower.

Gaily painted wooden birds enliven this green backdrop of hedge.

Cherub in its plant kingdom.

Witty animal sculpture in the perennial bed.

• Obelisks and vine supports become green sculptures through planting with climbing and twining plants. With their vertical lines, they emphasize spaciousness, in flat beds, for example.

Cheerfully colorful "garden spirits" turn this enchanting garden into a gallery.

Cat of papier-mâché.

Beautifully shaped stonework.

• Columns and pedestals lift smaller objects over the other planting and, thus, bring them to attention.

• Sundials and fountains, once useful items, can today serve as ornamental elements to draw attention in the center of the garden.

• Glass balls on shafts bring color and reflective effects into the garden.

• Also, especially beautiful found objects or remarkable roots can become ornamental objects in suitable spots.

• A skillful lighting concept can help bring out attractive plants and decorative elements to advantage even in the dark or at dusk. Very distinctive are floating lights for the garden pond (see photo, page 143).

• Decorative containers can be set in the garden in several places to provide accents. Planted, they bring color and structure into less attractive garden areas. However, they also retain their aesthetic interest when the glory of their plantings is long gone.

Designing with growth forms. Upright ornamental grass in fall coloring in front of sedum with hoarfrost.

DESIGNING WITH PLANTS

Plants naturally play a large role in the garden. On the following pages, you will learn how many different ways they can be used in the garden. Besides attractive combinations for every season and plant recommendations for the various garden areas, you will of course also find important tips for the proper planting of a flower bed. Among these are how to group plants skillfully, how to construct the bed with various graduations in size for visual effect, and—what everyone always wants to know—how to do it so that there is something flowering in the bed all year-round. Brilliant color photographs and descriptions provide you with a wealth of examples of designs.

With high-growing plants like trees, shrubs, hedges, and tall perennials, you can create frames and backdrops but also use them as focal points, emphasizing them by placing them as specimens.

With low-growing plants, you can weave thick or loose carpets in all colors, create encirclings and bands, or underplant high plants.

With flowering plants, you have the opportunity to provide ever new color combinations with the changing seasons.

Ornamental-leaved plants, shrubs, grasses, ferns, vegetables, and herbs offer you a gigantic field for creative play with growth forms as well as leaf forms and colors. Designing with plants can be the highest artistic perfection—no wonder that painters like Claude Monet or Pierre-Auguste Renoir not only addressed this theme with brush and paint, but also, as gardeners, they prized above all the various dimensions of a magnificant garden planting.

Designing with color in contrasts of the complementary colors yellow–violet. The enchanting yarrow "Feuerland" (Achillea hybrids) in front of the violet-blue Michaelmas daisy "Mönch" (Aster x frikartii).

Tips for Using Plants

For plants to create their full effect, they need the proper environment and neighbors that fit with them. Not only the garden as a whole requires careful planning, but individual beds need to be designed as well. And this is an extraordinarily creative as well as a many-faceted task.

Basics of Planting

Only when you choose herbaceous plants that fit together will you have long-lasting pleasure in your garden. Plants—like all living things—have entirely individual personality traits. There are loners that work best as specimen plantings but lose their effect in group plantings, as for instance the palm lily (*Yucca filamentosa*). Others, on the other hand, are really social. They need their own kind in order to be able to show to advantage. Alone they have no effect at all; but that much more as a group. Among these are phlox (*Phlox paniculata* hybrids) and lilies (*Lilium* species and hybrids). In addition, there are noticeable differences in growth habits of plants: Some are robust and vigorous growers; others are sensitive and tender. If these two different plants are put next to each other in a bed, the vigorously growing one will quickly overrun its weak-growing neighbor if the controlling hand of the gardener does not keep them regularly in check. Interestingly creative and horticulturally peaceful plantings develop when you observe the following criteria:

Flowering time of the plants: Choose the plants so that there will be a succession of blooming times in the bed.

Flower colors and forms. You can have your planting monochrome, tone-on-tone, in complementary contrasts, in three-color or four-color harmonies, as well as in color shadings (see pages 36–37).

Growth forms. Also consider whether the plant grows stiff upright, overhanging, as a cushion, or forms a carpet (see pages 18–19 and 34–35). The height is also important for good combinations.

Leaf forms and structures. In color-poor gardens or shady locations, in which only a few flowering perennials thrive, the form of the leaves, their surface, and their color takes on great importance (see pages 34–35 and 104–105).

Growth characteristics. Find out about the growth habit of the plant. Anyone who puts vigorous and delicate plants next to each other must freqently intervene horticulturally.

GARDEN TIPS AND TRICKS

Flowering Shrubs

They need more sun than woody plants, where the focus is on the foliage. In contrast to wild shrubs, they also need more feeding. Depending on the soil, an addition of compost in the spring should be enough.

Pattern for a Planted Bed

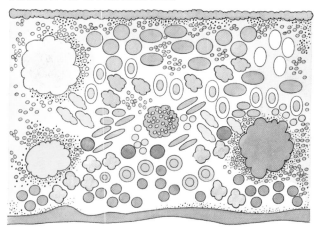

Shrubs and lead plants form the structure. Tall and low perennials are grouped in such a way that something is always in bloom.

Shrubs

①   Viburnums (*Viburnum farreri*)

②   Yellow shrub rose "Lichtkönigen Lucia"

③   Boxwood (*Buxus sempervirens*)

Perennials and bulbs

Peony (*Paeonia lactiflora*) hybrids

Yarrow (*Achillea*) species/varieties

Tall Michaelmas daisies (*Aster novi belgii*) varieties

Cushion asters (*Aster dumosus*) varieties

Shasta daisies (*Leucanthemum maximum*) hybrids

October daisies (*Leucanthemella serotina*)

Delphiniums (*Delphinium*) hybrids

Bearded iris (*Iris germanica barbata*) groups

Oriental poppy (*Papaver orientale*) varieties

Phlox (*Phlox paniculata*) hybrids

Summer sage (*Salvia nemorosa*) varieties

Sedum (*Sedum telephium*) varieties

Rudbeckia (*Rudbeckia fulgida*)

Rose fountain grass (*Pennisetum alopecuroides*)

Spring-flowering bulbs (*Narcissus, Tulipa, Fritillaria*)

Small spring-flowering bulbs (*Galanthus, Eranthis, Scilla*)

Early-spring-flowering small perennials (*Doronicum orientale, Brunnera macrophylla*)

A Bed Planted According to Phases of Bloom

Winter

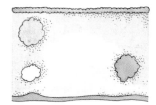

A few shrubs also contribute to keeping the area of the flower bed interesting in the winter months by retaining structure. Choose shrubs with different flowering times and colors as well as those that are green only in summer and are evergreen. Clumps of grasses are also very pretty in this season.

February–April

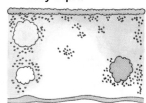

Plant the first small messengers of spring (see pages 250–251) in the perimeter of shrubs and trees. Tulips and narcissi are always planted in the middle and back areas of the bed, so that later their yellowing foliage can be concealed.

May–June

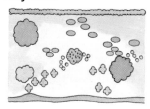

First climax of bloom in the perennial garden. Peonies and delphiniums take over the function as leaders in the bed; they are accompanied by poppies, iris, and sage. The early fading early-summer perennials are overgrown by the succeeding grasses and fall bloomers.

July–August

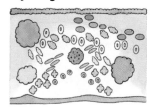

The grasses with their green clumps form a pretty contrast to blue sage and to the yellow yarrow. These tireless bloomers are placed in the foremost third of the garden, whereas in the background the tall phlox take over the role of the delphinums.

September–October

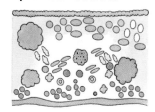

Tall and low asters balance the flowering grasses in the middle area. Plant the low cushion asters in the foreground. In the background, the repeat-flowering delphiniums and the white October daisies provide brilliant accents.

Elements of Bed Planting

You arrive at a planting that lasts for several years by a combination of shrubs with perennials.

Shrubs. In the form of a hedge, they can form the frame on which the perennial bed depends. If there is going to be a planting of a larger bed that does not adjoin a shrub area but is out in the open or is located in front of a wall, it is advisable to establish a few bushes in the bed to improve the structure. These may not be too large and spreading or too small. High and low deciduous and evergreen shrubs can also expand.

Evergreens like boxwood (*Buxus sempervirens*) or the darker yew (*Taxus* species/varieties) are very suitable here because later they can be pruned if the planting becomes thick. But as shaped shrubs, they create a pretty contrast in a loosely constructed bed even at the very beginning. Shrub roses also can be used well in a perennial border. They have the potential to bloom for several months and thus lend continuity to the border. With blooming shrubs, you should, of course, match the color of the flowers to other plants. Keep in mind the time and the length of flowering. For this reason, white-flowering shrubs are always uncomplicated.

Lead plants. Among these are compact and tall-growing flowering perennials, but strong plants with long-lasting, beautiful foliage can also take on this job, as can grasses. Lead plants stamp the character of a border. The choice of the other plants should be guided by their growth form and flower color. They can be planted singly or in small groups.

Companion plants should be of medium to low height and be placed in a somewhat larger number than the lead plant—the taller in clusters, the lower ones rather spread out. They should first of all increase the effect of the lead plants and fill out the periods before or after the main flowering of these with foliage or flowers.

Filler plants. They are put on all the leftover surfaces in the foreground or background. Suitable for this purpose are bulbs and corms (see pages 248–259), which mostly only bloom for a short time, but above all annuals, which mostly last from June to the first frost. With these, you can either place colorful accents or bring quiet to the planting.

Ground covers. For plantings that remain low, perennial ground covers that can develop into thick carpets are suitable. So, for instance, you can shape border edges in shady areas with surface-hugging ground covers (see pages 246–247), or those in a sunny situation with cushion plants from the rock garden (see pages 242–243).

Bed Construction and Design

A well-planned bed has a spacious effect that is achieved with framing plants, groupings, and backdrops. The plant areas work especially naturally when the structural plants are placed irregularly. Striking plant forms that are placed individually as specimens create focal points.

Design Principles of Bed Design

There are no firm rules for laying out a bed, only general basic principles. You can, for instance, use the tall-growing delphinium as the lead plant in a bed or as a group plant. This is entirely left to your own design intention.

Steplike gradation. If the bed is against a hedge or a wall, the higher plants are placed in the background so that the effect of the bed rises toward the back. This steplike gradation is the construction of the classic border. The border is only seen from one side. In front of a quiet background, contrasting flower colors work very well, and tall, upright plants are best situated here.

Pyramidal gradations. For a bed that stands in the open, a pyramidal construction is recommended. With this, the middle of the border is emphasized with the tallest plants, whereas the other plants form the contour, falling away steeply on all sides. The tall plants are surrounded by the low-growing companion plants, which are grouped around them. Beds of this kind are usually viewed from all or at least several sides.

Undulating contours. Make sure that the gradated bed structure does not lead to a choppy, steplike arrangement but achieves flowing, sweeping contours. The growth forms of the individual plants also show to the best advantage then.

Rhythmization. This principle applies primarily to large bed areas. For small beds, it often cannot be put into practice. It says, distribute plant groups of lead plants and companion plants in rhythmic repetition over the entire bed. This means that the lead plants are repeated at intervals, as are the companion plants.

Irregularity. Intervals, numbers of plants, and distribution of plant groups should be irregular. This gives tension/suspense and movement to the planting.

Accenting. Wonderful contrast effects can be achieved with color and/or growth forms. Individual plants or plant groups of different heights that rise out of flat groups or mark a dark background lend the planting a spacious character. Primarily suitable for this are architectonic plants like allium (*Allium aflatunense, A. giganteum*), mullein (*Verbascum* species), palm lily (*Yucca filamentosa*), and tall grasses (see pages 270–271). This principle is very helpful in designing beds in small gardens.

Tall over short. You create an especially natural looking garden scene when you place loose-growing, tall plants over a bed of predominantly low plants—sometimes

Classic perennial border with ascending heights.

Pyramidal bed construction with ornamental grass as the high point.

Ascending Arrangement
Low cushion or creeping plants enclose the bed or provide an edging along a path or lawn. Vigorous and tall plants form the background, with the mediating role being taken over by the plants in between.

Pyramidal Arrangement
Beds located in the open garden should be able to be viewed from all sides. Arrange the plants so that the bed looks like a pyramid or a cone on several sides. Some of the tallest plants will then be found in the center of the bed.

dense or sometimes loose. Good for this are narrow, tall annuals like verbena (*Verbena bonariensis*) and cosmos (*Cosmos bipinnatus*), which is best started in early spring indoors (see page 152) and planted out in the garden in May.

Grouping. The plants should be variously grouped according to their size and after that according to their location value.

• Plant framework plants singly or in small, uneven numbers (1, 3, or 5). As a standard measure: 3 plants per 10 sq ft (1 m²). These groupings should turn up several times in large beds.

• With the companion plants, one differentiates between large- and small-group plants. With large-group plants, which grow taller and thus need a larger space around them, figure on 3 to 5 plants per 10 sq ft (1 m²). For small-group plants, set them 6 to 9 plants per 10 sq ft (1 m²).

Important: The smaller the plants and flowers, the more of them you should plant. Thus you should plant at least 10 to 20 of small-group plants in order to create a balance for the framework plants. Then the proportions in the border will balance.

Checklist for Plant Choice

• Is the plant in its right location? This means, do soil, climate, and light conditions in the proposed location meet its requirements?

• Do the existing conditions in the location cover the growing requirements of the plant?

• What plants are suitable for the creation of a permanent structure? What colors are their flowers?

• What plants are suitable for lead plants in the particular seasons?

• What plants can be considered for companion and filler plants in the particular season?

• How will I group the individual lead and companion plants over the year?

• How often can I repeat the individual groups?

• What plants are suitable for framing and planting in front and below?

Tips for Planting

First draw up a planting plan. Then set out the plants in their appropriate hierarchy in the border. In this way, the rhythm of the planting can be judged and you can already imagine the later picture—and can still correct it if necessary. In larger borders, it's a good idea to spread sand in a grid of 10 sq ft (1m²) in order to be able to carry out your planting plan as exactly as possible.

Undulating lines in staggered planting.

Ornamental alliums rising over a low planting.

Undulating Contours

Arrange the plants so that each forms a unit by itself, which differs from the ones around it in height and spread. Plant these groups in staggered lines so that undulating lines occur like those in a hilly landscape.

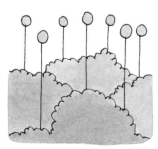

Accenting Differences in Height

With special accents, for example, with specimens in the foreground or several single plants in little groups, you can raise them over a low planting in a loose arrangement that increases the feeling of space in the bed.

DESIGNING WITH PLANTS
Specimens, Ornamental Trees

As with decorative elements (see pages 68–71), you can create focal points in your garden with specimen plants. Large specimens are most effective when situated in front of hedges or in entrance areas, at the foot of a set of stairs, or beside a pool or terrace. An ornamental tree can make a bare corner of the house or a wall look attractive. In low beds or rock gardens, specimens provide for spaciousness, because they stick up out of the low carpet of plants. Charming chairs can be situated under a tall, freestanding fruit tree in the lawn (see photo, page 56). Spreading specimen trees near the house—perhaps at the terrace—are excellent shade providers. Multi-trunk woody trees and shrubs have special beauty. For a tree next to the house, you should always use a deciduous one (see pages 204–207 and 282–285), so that the sunlight can come into the living areas during the winter time. Conifers are better in front of a windowless wall and should not be placed too close to the house.

Heavily flowering ornamental cherry as a tree near the house.

What Makes a Plant a Specimen?

Suitable specimens can be annuals, tall grasses, and perennials, but primarily shrubs like roses, beautiful flowering shrubs, and small trees. You can decide what is going to become a specimen plant according to the design of your garden. Nurseries offer certain woody plants under this designation. They are plants that are striking because of their elegant or bizarre growth form or showy because of their especially beautiful flowers or coloring. But also simple shrubs can be specimens if planted in small groups of three. Any other tree, shrub, tall grass, or imposing perennial can, however, take over the function of a specimen. For in its freestanding location, the plant develops its full beauty. Its growth form (habitus) is naturally determined by the species, but the location, climate, and soil cause it to develop an entirely individual character. You can increase the effectiveness of the plant even more if you place it near a decorative element, for example, stone pillars, pools, or found objects. But make sure then that the specimen has enough distance from plants around it so that they don't compete with it to any great degree.

Shrubs that bloom very early or very late or have exquisite fragrance offer special garden pleasure. Have these near the house in order to be able to enjoy their advantages best. Set plants in view so that they can be

Viburnum plicatum—flowers abundantly and has fall color.

Brilliant fall red—Japanese maple (Acer palmatum) "Atropurpureum."

seen from a window, or at the entrance so that you see them when entering or leaving the house.

The bigger the garden, the more specimen plantings it can tolerate. Here smokebush, conifers, and golden elm in a single planting.

Specimens for Every Season

In spring and summer, it is primarily the flowers that are noticeable in a plant; in fall, the attractiveness consists of colorful foliage and fruits. With the right choices, you can enjoy splendid specimen plantings all year long.

Winter/spring. Rarities are witch hazel (*Hamamelis* species, see photo, page 208) and viburnums (*Viburnum x bodnantense* and *V. farreri*). Their flowers open even in the middle of winter, though they remain closed in snow and frost. The witch hazel should stand all by itself; its growth habit is bizarre and wide spreading. In fall, its foliage is orange-yellow. A charming spring bloomer, especially over a carpet of Siberian scilla (*Scilla siberica*) and pink-flowering snow heather (*Erica carnea*), is the buttercup witch hazel (*Corylopsis pauciflora*, see page 209), which only grows about 39 in (1 m) tall. Magnolias (*Magnolia* species, see page 204) are among the most valuable specimen plants, but they only reach their full beauty with age and need a mild climate as well as a frost-free location. Ornamental cherries (*Prunus* species/varieties) and flowering crab apples (*Malus* species/varieties) thrive almost anywhere.

Summer. The transition from spring to summer is provided by the flowers of beauty bush (*Kolkwitzia amabilis*) and weigelia (*Weigelia* hybrids). Beauty bushes, especially, have a graceful, overhanging growth habit. Both shrubs are undemanding and also fit well in large shrub borders. On the other hand, rarities are the dogwood (*Cornus florida* and *C. kousa*). With their picturesque growth habit and the colored bracts, they have a very exotic effect. However, they need humus, acid soil. Later in summer, there are summer lilacs or butterfly bushes (*Buddleia davidii* hybrids), rose of Sharon (*Hibiscus syriacus*), and various hydrangeas (*Hydrangea* species, see page 211), which are suitable for specimens.

Fall. Now the shrubs with outstanding colored foliage and fruits are especially effective. It is time for the different Japanese maple species (*Acer* species, see photos, pages 202–203), but also the winged euonymus or burning bush (*Euonymus alata*), with its fire red foliage, as well as the green- and red-leaved smoke bush (*Cotinus coggygria*, see photo above and page 211), and the beauty berry (*Callicarpa bodinieri* var. *giraldii*), with its little violet pearl fruits, now draw a great deal of attention to themselves.

DESIGNING WITH PLANTS
Clipped Hedges

Clipped hedges are living architecture, with which you can shape your garden. Hedges structure the garden and perform the function of walls and fences, but they are usually more ecologically valuable and often are more pleasing than these. However, they require care, and it takes time until they are large enough to be able to function as "green walls."

Hedges serve as protection against wind, dust, sight, and noise and are suitable for charming backdrops for solitary plantings, colored flowers, and decorative elements. Whether you opt for an evergreen or a summer green hedge depends on your personal preference as well as the purpose the hedge is to fulfill. For a boundary with the outside or structuring inside the garden, you should, for example, use evergreen or wintergreen plants. Broad-leaved and needle-leaved evergreens thrive particularly well in humid situations. Yew, cherry laurel (*Prunus laurocerasus*), and common privet (*Ligustrum vulgare* "Atrovirens") are shade tolerant in addition.

For low enclosures, boxwood (*Buxus sempervirens*) or barberry (*Berberis* species) are suitable.

For medium or high hedges, the first recommendations are conifers such as yew (*Taxus* species), false cypress (*Chamaecyparis* species), arborvitae (*Thuja* species), but also European hornbeam (*Carpinus betulus*) and European beech (*Fagus sylvatica*).

Important: Keep in mind which hedges thrive well in your area. Many ornamental shrubs are also suitable for clipped hedges.

Beech hedges as a quiet background for a perennial border.

Shaped yew hedges as room dividers.

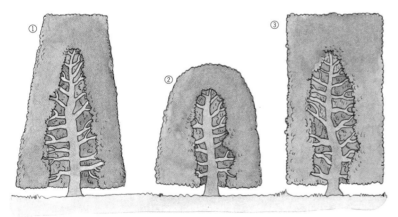

Possible Hedge Styles
① Conical hedges get good light all the way to the ground— good for evergreen shrubs.
② Rounded pruning makes a hedge look less linear and severe.
③ Vertical hedge walls are possible with hornbeam (*Carpinus betulus*). They demand less space.

Hedge Planting and Pruning
For installing a hedge, you must dig out a trench that is 16 to 20 in (40–50 cm) wide and just as deep and loosen the subsoil (see Planting and Care of Woody Plants, pages 168–169). It's best to find out about distances between plants when you buy the plants in a nursery.

Here are tips for pruning:

Pruning in the juvenile stage: With young hedge plants, you should shorten the side shoots two to three times a year (spring, summer, and late summer) in order to control branching. As soon as the hedge has reached the desired height, you can also prune the top.

Pruning large plants for shape: Hedges should if possible taper at the top so that they receive even light and don't grow bare at the bottom. You will maintain the desired height if you prune the new growth just back to the underlying branching. Stretch a string across as a pruning guide.

• Yews are ideal for the small garden, for they don't need much space and can be pruned to a clipped hedge to a width of up to only 12 in (30 cm).

• European hornbeam (*Carpinus betulus*) and many other deciduous shrubs grow fast. Therefore, prune these twice

Clipped hedges set off the growth forms and the flower display of roses to advantage. Behind, a yew hedge, in front, shaped boxwood.

Hornbeam hedge in fall color, in front, boxwood topiary.

Clipped hedge of hornbeam (behind), yew and boxwood (front).

a year: but not before the end of June the first time so as to provide protection for birds; the second time at the end of August.
• With evergreens, prune before the new growth in spring or in late summer.

Rejuvenation pruning of old plants: You can only undertake radical pruning down into the thick, heavily wooded parts with foliage shrubs and yews (*Taxus* species), and in certain circumstances with arborvitae (*Thuja* species); other conifers do not put out growth from old wood.

Natural Hedges

Free-growing hedges are the most natural way to fence, divide, or separate something. They can consist of small, medium, or large shrubs or trees, of wild plants, but also of flowering and ornamental shrubs. Size, form, and transparency of the hedge are dependent on which plants you choose for it. For a natural hedge, you must figure on a height and width of 7 to 15 ft (5 m) or more if it is to unfold in its characteristic beauty.

Importance of Hedges

Hedges are important design elements but they also serve very practical purposes.

Fencing and protective functions. Hedges surround and divide a garden and provide feelings of space and security. They conceal things, such as cars, garbage cans, or clotheslines. For sitting areas, flowers, and vegetable gardens they serve as protection from the wind and cold. They work as providers of privacy and as dust filters; and mainly the large-leaved woody species also keep out noise.

Ecological importance. Thick, wild hedges present a regular biotope. They offer food, nesting places, and cover to birds, insects, and small animals. The more native the plants you use, the more your hedge is filled with life.

Year-round ornament. Hedges that consist of different shrubs can be attractive the whole year-round with their various structures, heights, colors, and forms. Small trees and large and small shrubs as well as the perennials and wild plants set in front of them thus form a harmonious community. In spring and summer, the flowers are in the foreground, then the berries and fruits, which often retain their dots of color into the winter. In fall, the colored foliage of the shrubs shows up; and in winter, the hedge gains its charm through the structure or color of the branches or through the evergreen shrubs.

Hedges and Their Variations

The multiplicity of plants permits the formation of extremely different hedges.

Natural hedges. The usually carefree wild hedge fits well into rural areas, where gardens are tied to the landscape. They should be 10 to 15 ft (3–5 m) wide, for only then are they of particular ecological value. The height depends on what trees or large shrubs you choose. The more space at your disposal, the more rows of plants you can put next to each other, and the more various and dense your hedge will be. Large plants suitable here are field maple

Beautifully flowering shrubs in loose groups often replace dense,

(*Acer campestre*), red-stemmed dogwood (*Cornus sanguinea*), cornelian cherry (*Cornus mas*), European hazel (*Corylus avellana*), European hornbeam (*Carpinus betulus*), English hawthorn (*Crataegus monogyna*), European elderberry (*Sambucus nigra*), blackthorn (*Prunus spinosa*), and European mountain ash (*Sorbus aucuparia*). If these bushes get too high, the central shoots can be taken out (for example, with hornbeam and hazel) and thus the shrubby character is emphasized. But wild hedges can also be used for smaller gardens if the larger bushes are placed in just one row and the spaces in between are filled in with smaller shrubs like wild roses (*Rosa rubiginosa, R. rugosa*), European fly honeysuckle (*Lonicera xylosteum*), and European euonymus (*Euonymus europaea*). Such a hedge becomes about 6 to 10 ft (1.8–3 m) wide. Its protective function is then less, of course, but the variety of species of birds and insects can be just as large as with a broader hedge—especially if at the same time a plant screen of native perennials is created in front of it.

Bellflowers (*Campanula patula, C. persicifolia*), germander speedwell (*Veronica chamaedrys*), and Saint John's wort

severe hedges—but therefore, offer less privacy.

with its loose, flowery magnificence. If there is enough space, it's a good idea to plant filler shrubs in between, evergreens, for example.

Vine and fruit hedges are also an alternative in narrow space conditions. You can train many climbing plants to arbitrary heights and widths on fences, house walls, and walls. Slow-growing apple and pear varieties can be trained on horizontal trellises so that they serve the same functions as a single row flowering hedge.

Enclosures. Free growing hedges of a single plant species also serve well as low enclosures—perhaps for the front yard. Choose plants that don't go bare at the bottom, such as shrubby contoneaster (*Potentilla fruticosa*), spirea (*Spiraea bumalda* "Anthony Waterer"), barberry (*Berberis* species), wild roses (*Rosa rugosa* varieties), or box (*Buxus sempervirens*). A wonderful sight is also a uniform hedge of bridle-wreath (*Spiraea vanhouttei*), which blooms white in May–June. The bushes grow 6.5 to 10 ft (2–3 m) high, grow quickly, and have a slightly trailing, elegant growth habit.

Hedges of evergreen shrubs. Among the broad-leaved and needle-leaved evergreen shrubs are some that are as suitable for freestanding hedges as they are for clipped hedges. Yew (*Taxus* species) and box are shade-tolerant, like common privet (*Ligustrum vulgare* "Atrovirens"), cherry laurel (*Prunus laurocerasus*), and rhododendron. False cypress (*Chamaecyparis* species) and arborvitae (*Thuja* species) but also yew (for example, *Taxus media* "Hicksii") grow in pillar form by nature and can remain unpruned.

Free-growing and clipped hedges can also be combined well. At the side here and there, where the growth needs to be contained, you can prune severely linearly or irregularly; the other parts, for example the upper shoots, should retain their natural growth habit. Some very interesting structures can result this way. Foliage and flowering shrubs are best suited for such free-formed hedges.

Tips for Planting and Care

The same rules apply for hedge planting as for all herbaceous plants (see pages 168–169). The soil must be deeply loosened (20 to 32 in [51–81 cm]) and provided with compost. The planting distance between the bushes depends on their size: With shrubs, this amounts to about 5 to 6.5 ft (1.5–2 m). In hedges with several rows, the shrubs are set in gaps. A wild hedge takes care of itself. Mixed hedges are thinned every now and again in February and overaged wood is removed. Hedges composed entirely of ornamental plants must have this treatment more intensively in order to ensure regular flowering (see pages 170–171).

(*Hypericum perforatum*) often seed themselves. But you can also of course plant or sow effective perennials such as columbine (*Aquilegia vulgaris*) and foxglove (*Digitalis purpurea*), which in addition underline the natural character of the hedge.

Mixed hedges. In large gardens, mixtures of wild and ornamental shrubs also work very well. Here you should plant the wild forms as the boundary on the outside, and plant the ornamental forms on the garden side, so that you can enjoy their color and the full flowering. A border planting of perennials also does well here.

After 3 to 5 years, however, the shadow of the shrubbery and the root competition becomes so large that they must be exchanged for shade-loving plants (see pages 104–105).

Flowering hedges. In a small garden you can install a single row, mixed planting of ornamental shrubbery, at least on the sunny side, perhaps of forsythia (*Forsythia x intermedia*), crab apple (*Malus* species/varieties), and lesser flowering quince (*Chaenomeles japonica*).

Such a hedge becomes about 8 ft (2.5 m) wide and 10 to 15 ft (3–5 m) high and provides great aesthetic interest

DESIGNING WITH PLANTS
Beds As Garden Ornaments

These beds punctuate and subdivide the garden. They are especially striking because of the symmetrically planted trees and shrubs.

Beds are definite interruptions in the green of the lawn. What design possibilities they offer should become clear in the following pages.

Bed Forms
Beds can be laid out in different forms according to the size and style of your garden.

<u>Beds with austere shapes</u> have straight lines and a definite, geometric shape. You can emphasize their clear outline even more by enclosing them with box, low perennials, or curbing of wood or stone. You find the prototype of the austere bed in formal gardens (see pages 132–133) and classic kitchen gardens, or potagers (see pages 136–137).

<u>Beds with undulating, free-form</u> are well suited to natural gardens or large ornamental gardens, which they often frame, many times to end in lawn or a plaza area. It's very practical to have the beds bounded by a line of paving stones or curbstones. Unbordered beds require regular slanting and trimming of the lawn edge to keep grass and weeds from growing into it.

Which Bed for What?
Beds may be elements in a garden or may make up the entire garden itself. For example, the latter is the case in formal gardens and potagers, in which the principal elements are paths and beds.

<u>Beds as accompaniments to paths.</u> Usually it is beds with austere lines that run along beside a path as a band of flowers. In architecturally designed gardens, however, there may also be large square or rectangular bed shapes, which are almost always laid out in symmetry with the axes of paths. You can plant these beds with useful or decorative plants entirely according to your preference. Thus the contrast between the severe, composed frame and the lush planting is especially attractive.

<u>Beds along walls, fences, and hedges</u> should be laid out in the form of the classic border, which means increasing the height from the front to the back (see pages 76–77).

<u>Beds as islands in the garden.</u> Beds as rounds or ovals in the lawn or in the front yard to the left and right of an entrance have been popular for a long time. Whatever

This large perennial bed runs like a decorative ribbon throughout the garden.

form you choose for this flower island, you can plant it as a low flower carpet or in a range of heights (see page 76). Plants should be set with heights increasing from the outside toward the center, for island beds are usually seen from several sides.

Beds at the corner of a property or house can be laid out very prettily as rounded sections of circles. Because these beds are usually well protected, you can keep delicate plants here.

Beds as space dividers. Whether in free-form, in drop shape, or as a bar that extends into the yard, beds have countless possibilities for separating areas of the garden, creating corridors, or constructing niches. However, not only the bed surface plays an important role here but also the vertical accent, that is to say, the planting of the bed through smaller trees, shrubs, and climbing plants as privacy or decorative elements

Raised beds have a special charm. Their elevation makes them ideal locations for plant rarities, which can then be examined up close or whose scent can be better perceived in this way. Such raised beds can often be well placed in the vicinity of the house at the edge of a sitting area or terrace.

Beds for rock gardens and heath gardens must be designed according to the character of the planting (see pages 106–107 and 108–109). This means fashioning the bed with sand, gravel, and stones and building in boulders or natural found objects (see page 140).

Vegetable beds are usually laid out according to practical considerations. Reliable measurements are bed rows 5 ft (1.5 m) wide in as sunny and protected a location as possible.

High beds receive firm framework of timbers and planks; their inner construction corresponds to that of hill beds (see page 183). They are expensive to build, but then are easier to cultivate for older and handicapped people because all bending is unnecessary. After 6 years, however, they must be partly refilled again.

Important: In large beds, lay some stepping-stones of artificial or natural stone so that it will be easier to maintain the beds.

Plant Ideas for April/May

Every year, the first glorious color of spring bulbs is await- ed with longing and presents itself especially joyously after the dark winter. Bulbs (see pages 112–113 and 252–255) are the ones to have their chance now. Until other plants awaken to new life, bulbs add color to the picture.

Naturalized Plantings

A large number of spring flowers do not need a bed but can be naturalized under shrubs or in fields. Narcissi are particularly well suited for this. Among the early flowering rarities that love to naturalize in natural garden areas are the dog tooth violet (*Erythronium dens-canis*, see page 251) with the outstanding yellow hybrid form "Pagoda." In early spring the checkered lily (*Fritillaria meleagris*, see page 251) also blooms. Both plants are quite undemand- ing: they love moist, rich soil; the dog-tooth violet also likes a somewhat shady location and, the checkered lily flavors damp meadows.

Woody plants and bulbs. Spring flowering bulbs and corms find the ideal location near trees and shrubs. Spring bulbs love the winter soil moisture, and the light before the large plants leaf out promotes their growth. They feel especially happy within the drip line and root region of trees and shrubs. Here there are no competing plants; in addition the soil is not regularly worked. So they can easily naturalize by self seeding.

Among the late-blooming bulbs for the edge of the woods are the bluebells (*Hyacinthoides* species, see page 251), which also come in pink and white. They need fresh, nutri- ent-rich soil, just like the narcissi (*Narcissus* species/vari- eties, see pages 254–255).

Plant tips.
• Narcissi look the most beautiful when they grow togeth- er in large quantities in stands.
• The delicate white poet's narcissus (*Narcissus poeticus*) develops a special charm under a flowering fruit tree in late spring.
• The intensely brilliant yellow of forsythia (*Forsythia* species/varieties) harmonizes well with orange and the clear red of tulips (*Tulipa* varieties) as well as the blue of grape hyacinths (*Muscari armeniacum*), white-flowering narcissi (*Narcissus* species/varieties) and flowering shrubs.

Masterfully combined—crown-imperials, narcissi (variety "Professor Einstein"), and white grape hyacinths.

• The pink clouds of flowers of ornamental cherries (*Prunus* species) and crab apples (*Malus* species) on the other hand look very pretty together with pastel colors.
• You should plant the joyous yellow, white, and blue garden crocuses in small clumps in the lawn in front of white- and yellow-flowering shrubs.

Bulbs and perennials. A planting in spring is only complete with early flowering perennials. Ground covers look very pretty and cover over the withering foliage of the bulbs after they've flowered. Also thriving in chalky and humus soil in the areas around trees and shrubs are Christmas and Lenten roses (*Helleborus* species/varieties, see page 244), pink hardy cyclamen (*Cyclamen coum*, page 251), and blue hepatica (*Hepatica nobilis*), together with small bulbs (see pages 250–251) like snowdrops (*Galanthus* species), spring snowflake (*Leucojum vernum*), and winter aconite (*Eranthis hyemalis*). Christmas roses have a beautiful wintergreen foliage; there are numerous varieties in many color shades, from greenish to red.

Bed Plantings

Whereas you can let the wild forms of bulbs naturalize under trees or in the field, the highly bred bulb varieties prefer a well-prepared bed. Bulbs and corms can, however, also be set in the perennial beds. Before the perennials begin to put out new growth, the bulbs are then already blooming. Their show of flowers will be replaced by early perennials, followed by annuals and late-blooming perennials.

Plant tips.
• The dwarf narcissi—like the charming petticoat narcissus (*Narcissus bulbocodium*)—and species tulips are best suited for natural areas in sunny, dry locations, like perhaps a rock garden.
• Also, bulbs can add color to rose beds in spring. Tulips, above all, look very good with the reddish green new growth of the roses. Planted in loose groups between the rose bushes, they are hardly disturbed by the cultivation of the roses.
• The countless early- and late-blooming tulip varieties (pages 252–253) can be so combined that their flowering period stretches from April to May. Tulips look beautiful with other bulbs like hyacinths (*Hyacinthus* varieties), narcissi, and crown-imperials (*Fritillaria imperialis*).
• Garden crocus and hyacinths work to best effect as low edge plantings in colorful beds. Otherwise, hyacinths look somewhat stiff. But after a few years, they take on a natural, loose form because then the stem isn't so thick with little flowers. The spring-flowering biennials (see pages 266–267) also offer themselves as some of the best companions for the bulbs; choices include primroses (*Primula* hybrids), pansies (*Viola* x *wittrockiana* hybrids), English daisies (*Bellis* varieties), forget-me-nots (*Myosotis*

Red, white, and blue, with narcissi, tulips, and grape hyacinths.

Yellow-orange with "Fortissimo" narcissi and "Orange Emperor" tulips.

Pure primary colors with narcissi, tulips, and grape hyacinths.

hybrids), English wallflower (*Cheiranthus cheiri*), and erysimum (*Erysimum* x *allionii*), which can be planted in the fall of the previous year along with the bulbs.

Plant Ideas for May/June

Spring is in full course when the apple blossoms begin. Now the foliage comes out, the conifers put out their May growth, and chestnuts and lilacs bloom. From the middle to the end of May, in many regions there may still be frost at night. Therefore, you should only plant or sow tender annuals, tub plants, and many kinds of vegetables after this. The most intense sunshine prevails in June; the days are at their longest. The rising temperatures and the usually present spring moisture promote growth and development.

Combinations of Late-Spring and Early-Summer Flowers

Many biennial plants and early perennials, among them also some short-lived ones, now have their chief blooming period and thus create the transition from spring to summer. They go to seed rather easily and under suitable conditions can soon be found in many places in the garden.

<u>Natural locations along the woods' edge.</u> Short-lived plants like foxglove (*Digitalis purpurea*, see pages 244–245) in pink, red, or white, and columbine (*Aquilegia vulgaris*, see pages 244–245), as well as biennials like honesty (*Lunaria annua*, see pages 266–267) and dame's rocket (*Hesperis matronalis*, see pages 266–267), both with violet flowers, show to good advantage in a natural environment. They grow happily in a light woodsy border together with flowering shrubs and perennials, like the numerous cranesbill species (*Geranium* species/varieties), with whose mostly cool colors they harmonize very well. Appropriate ornamental shrubs (see page 210) are the white- or pink-flowering deutzia (*Deutzia* varieties), mock orange (*Philadelphus* varieties), or beauty bush (*Kolkwitzia amabilis*).

<u>Field flowers.</u> In May/June the meadow flora reaches its zenith. Sage (*Salvia pratensis*) and field daisies (*Leucanthemum vulgare*) spring up in delicate but also strong colors, and in damp spots there are buttercups (*Ranunculus acris*), globeflowers (*Trollius europaeus*), Siberian iris (*Iris siberica*), and Jacob's ladder (*Polemonium caeruleum*). There are also garden forms of these wildflower species that can be used in perennial borders.

<u>Bed planting.</u> Many annuals and biennials, like the perennials, like nutrient-rich, well-cultivated garden beds, like the Canterbury bells (*Campanula medium*, see pages 264–265) in white, pink, and blue, and the velvety shimmering sweet William (*Dianthus barbatus*, see pages 264–265) in every shade of red.

• The yellow-brown, strongly scented English wallflower (*Cheiranthus cheirii*) can be combined well with late tulips.

• Particularly suitable as partners in brilliantly colored borders are such country garden perennials (see pages

Blue and violet delphiniums provide the background for white and red peo

White and violet—iris in front of candytuft.

234–235) as lupins (*Lupinus polyphyllus* hybrids), pink, white, and red peonies (*Paeonia lactiflora*), delphinium (*Delphinium* hybrids) in all shades of blue, white spring and summer daisies (*Leucanthemum vulgare* and *L. maximum* hybrids), oriental poppies (*Papaver orientale*), yellow yarrow (*Achillea* species/varieties), and blue sage (*Salvia* species/varieties).

Primroses and cranesbill.

Wallflowers and honesty.

Meadowlike—poppies, cornflowers, and yellow-white auricula.

• The field flowers are also sponsors for glorious early summer pictures: cornflowers (*Centaurea cyanus*) with Flanders poppies (*Papaver rhoeas*) and wild chamomile (*Chamomilla suaveolens*) make an interesting color combination in blue, red, and white.

• However, the classic color triad blue-white-red can also be achieved with long-lived perennials, as with the mountain bluet (*Centaurea montana*), oriental poppy, and field daisies. The radiant blue of the delphinium (*Delphinium* species), the brilliant red of the campion (*Lychnis* species) or the blue and white of the campanula (*Campanula persicifolia*) add to the picture.

Iris with Suitable Companions

At this time of year, the blooming of iris presents a special high point.

Iris varieties and their location. The color range of the medium-tall and tall varieties of the fleur-de-lis (*Iris germanica*), also called bearded iris (*Iris barbata* hybrids) (see pages 234–235), runs from white to dark blue, from pink to violet, and from light yellow to brown. Many are multicolored. They are especially effective set in a gravelly dry bed, with a few large boulders or decorated with terra-cottas.

You are best placing the large-flowered and multicolored varieties singly in special spots near the house, perhaps in a carpet of low plants. Single-colored blue, yellow, or brown varieties go very well in a colorful bed of country flowers.

In their original native habitat, iris grow on walls and between rocks. The variously gray-green or bluish frosty foliage and their sensitivity to wetness makes them thrive very well in stony, porous soil in full sun. There gray-leaved and small-leaved low plants and grasses also do well. Some very interesting combinations result with all of them together.

Companions before, during, and after iris bloom. Sun-loving low perennials and semishrubs like lavender (*Lavandula angustifolia*), lavender cotton (*Santolina chamaecyparissus*), sun rose (*Helianthemum* hybrids), everlasting (*Anaphalis triplinervis*), blue flax (*Linum narbonense*), and low bellflowers (*Campanula* species), primarily blooming in white, pink, and blue-violet, underline the iris flowers and soften their stiff and somewhat unsightly foliage after they have finished flowering.

Also suitable as taller companions of iris in large gardens are desert-candle (*Eremurus* species/varieties, see pages 256–257) and giant allium (*Allium giganteum*, see pages 256–257.) Delicate-flowered roses are also a good additions to iris.

Earlier bulbs and cushion perennials (see pages 106–107 and 242–243) provide for variety, later use annuals and grasses, as well as the late-flowering redroot (*Ceanothus* hybrids) and bluebeard (*Caryopteris* x *clandonensis*)—both low shrubs.

Plant Ideas for June

June is not only the proverbial rose month but also the month in which the fields flower especially beautifully. Typical of the field flora are the loosely growing wild perennials and herbs. The wildflowers with their often single and relatively small flowers usually look more natural than the highly hybridized plants. The colors in a meadow are gaily mixed, but they never appear garish. The manifold greens of the grasses and leaves soften and mute the individual strong color areas.

Sage and lady's-mantle—a tried-and-true combination.

Bed Plantings of Field Flowers

You can carry nature's model over into your own garden. The characteristic wild floras of the various plant communities also fit very well into beds and lend more naturalness to ornamental plantings. There are suitable types for the most diverse locations and soil conditions. Among these are wild forms of perennials or those only slightly changed by hybridization, such as daisies (*Leucanthemum vulgare*); campion (*Lychnis* species); buttercup (*Ranunculus acris*); meadow rue (*Thalictrum* species); iris (*Iris* species); various annual, biennial, and triennial sage species (*Salvia* species); and the numerous forms of cranesbill (*Geranium* species/varieties), which come in many colors.

Besides these, there is a long list of perennials, annuals, and bulbs that are strongly influenced by hybridization but still look natural, like most larkspurs (*Delphinium elatum* and *D. belladonna* hybrids), Siberian iris (*I. siberica*), sun rose (*Helianthemum* varieties), yarrows (*Achillea* varieties), and summer sage (*Salvia nemorosa* varieties).

Phlomis—a rarity for dry locations.

You can achieve a very natural looking planting if you combine tall plants with low, for example, and sturdy with delicate ones. Be careful that the plants are able to develop variously in the loose combination of a community; too dense vegetation hinders their development.

You should always begin with low plants at the edge of a planting, perhaps with cranesbill or cushiony pinks (*Dianthus* species). Flat, compact plants like summer sage, for example, are loosened with the somewhat taller and looser yarrow and Maltese cross (*Lychnis chalcedonica*). Tall, sturdy mulleins, on the other hand, create accents and contrasts in carpets of low plants and grasses with a prairielike character.

Plant Combinations for Humus Soil

Bedding perennials can be considered for beds with loose and not too dry soil. Flowering in June, besides larkspur, daisies (*Leucanthemum vulgare* and *L. maximum* hybrids), and sage, are various tall bellflowers (*Campanula persicifolia* and *C. lactifolia*), veronica (*Veronica* species), and the once blooming fleabane (*Erigeron* varieties) in many delicate colors. Beside them, short-lived plants like

Lysimachia (yellow) and cranesbill (violet) for damp spots.

tall lobelias (*Lobelia splendens* and *L. gerardii*) and beard tongues (*Penstemon* varieties) also look nice.

When you combine these plants with each other, the blue-red-violet tones dominate. They can be very beautifully enhanced with white and light pink flower colors, which occur in almost all of the genera named. In addition, you

Neutral green brings peonies to brilliance.

Meadowy-feeling combinations with grasses.

Red valerian, sage, and yarrow—important summer bloomers.

can underline the loose, meadowlike character of the planting with delicate annuals like red-violet and white cosmos (*Cosmos bipinnatus*), delicate violet verbenas (*Verbena bonariensis*), white, pink, and violet spider plants (*Cleome spinosa*), and, above all, tall and low grasses. Grasses have a further advantage: They carry the summer

garden over into the fall when the flowers of the other plants are gone.

Plants for Dry Situations

In dry, somewhat stony locations in the garden, a special group of plants originating on the prairies all over the world have the advantage. Here the peach-bells (*Campanula persicifolia*, see page 237) are to be found again. It might be combined with blue and white scabiosa (*Scabiosa caucasica*), but also with mullein (*Verbascum* species, see pages 234–235) and evening primroses (*Oenothera* species, see page 237), with various species of pinks (for example, *Dianthus carthusianorum*), or the German catchfly (*Lychnis viscaria* "Plena"), with the delicate St. Bernard's lily (*Anthericum liliago*) and distinctive grasses (for example, *Stipa barbata* or *Achnatherum* x *calamagrostis*, see pages 270–271). This prairie garden has a slightly Mediterranean character and looks very lively and gauzy. The plants are delicate in growth habit, less colorful, and not so succulently green. Rather, a silvery tone dominates here.

The short-lived plants include many that because of their limited life expectancy set many seeds and, thus, ensure offspring. Among these are mulleins, evening primroses, and the rose campion (*Lychnis coronaria*). Because the seeds germinate every year in another part of the garden, as in nature, the garden scenes are constantly changing. But you can also collect the young plants in spring and then place them where you have decided they should go.

Plants for Fresh, Damp Situations

An entirely different field flora thrives in damp soil. In June, the main flowering of the many varieties of Siberian iris (*I. siberica*) occurs. The daylilies (*Hemerocallis* species) fit in wonderfully with this character. They form grasslike clumps of foliage similar to the iris and also enhance the colors very well. Blue hues predominate in the flowers of the iris, and yellows in the daylilies. However, the hemerocallis flowers first begin timorously in June. It is primarily the wild forms, with their delicate foliage, that harmonize with the also delicate iris flowers and narrow leaves. Large-leaved yellow-flowered ligularias (*Ligularia* species/varieties) create contrasts in growth form, as does the light violet meadow rue (*Thalictrum aquilegifolium*, see page 244), with delicate columbine-like foliage.

Plant Ideas for June/July

After spring and early summer have scattered their fire in sturdy colors and demonstrated their exuberance, and before high summer unfolds all its color-intensive glory with annuals and summer perennials, the vegetation in one or another section of the garden undergoes a pause. This period between the two flowering high points can be properly spanned in different ways. Rose gardens can set the tone in June/July, but you can also integrate roses into the borders. Also there are now blooming a number of plants in delicate pastel colors that harmonize especially well with roses and many other plants. In an otherwise rather colorful garden, it is comfortably restful if delicate pastel tones are seen for awhile at particular spots. But you can also bridge the time to the full flowering of the annuals and high summer perennials by choosing early and late varieties of a plant species.

Pastel Flowering Plants As Go-betweens

White and pastel shades of pink and violet have a slightly nostalgic flavor and can mediate wonderfully between other colors. These muted colors are also especially well suited for large areas. Central plants here are roses for sun and astilbes (*Astilbe* species/hybrids) for shady situations. Besides, there are many other plants in these pastel shades, like fleabane (*Erigeron* varieties) or bee balm (*Monarda* hybrids). Additional contrasts can be achieved with the beaming white of the shasta daisies (*Leucanthemum maximum* varieties), the brilliant blue of the delphiniums (*Delphinium* hybrids), and the sturdy pink, red, and purple shades of the purple coneflower (*Echinacea purpurea*) and intense color of the bee balm.

<u>Bulbs.</u> Among the plants that take on a timely, colorful, and, with their stiffly upright growth habit, a transitional role are the summer-flowering bulbs (see pages 256–257) like lilies (*Lilium* species/varieties), desert-candles (*Eremurus* species/varieties), and the giant alliums (*Allium giganteum*). They add highlights to the garden in the weeks of June before the annuals really start flowering. Alliums and mulleins, with their pastel colors, go wonderfully together, and the bright colors of the eremurus varieties are enhanced by the violets of the giant allium. Also the character of their growths is similar; both can be well integrated into perennial borders, especially on dry, well-drained soil. They show to best advantage with bearded iris (*Iris barbata* hybrids) and early lilies, combined with gray-leaved aromatic plants.

Pastel combinations with the lily hybrids "La Reve" and the small white

Gentle gray tones with blue and crimson.

<u>Gray-leaved plants.</u> The beauty of gray-leaved as well as delicate pink- and delicate blue-flowering plants develops best if one regards them close by. The low plants among them are especially suited for the formation of edging around beds, like lamb's-ears (*Stachys byzantina*), the low veronica (*Veronica incana*), the blue-gray, frosty cushions

flowers of the perennial chamomile (Chamaemelum nobile).

Tone-on-tone—only dainty white.   *Silver-gray—Stachys byzantina.*

of pinks (for instance, *Dianthus caesius*) or the wormwood (*Artemesia schmidtiana* 'Nana'), also the white-, gray-, and pink-shimmering creeping forms of baby's breath (*Gypsophila repens*), thyme (*Thymus serpyllum*), or low blue-green cushions of grasses (*Festuca* species). Gray-green lavender (*Lavandula angustifolia*), catmint (*Nepeta* x

faassenii), white and bright-red red valerian (*Centranthus ruber*) as well as sage, such as the aromatic clary sage (*Salvia sclarea*), all offer themselves as ideal partners for all pink- and lilac-colored perennials, annuals, and roses (see Roses and Companions, pages 110–111).

Such plantings can be used in many small areas around the house, on the terrace, or along the path from the entrance to the house, as well as a planting in front of an arbor or pergola. It is important that it be a sunny location. Gray-leaved and pastel-flowered plants are particularly effective in conjunction with rocks, terraces, and pathway paving.

Early- and Late-Blooming Plants as Go-betweens

If you have a small break in flowering in June/July, you can bridge it when choosing plants by selecting the particular variety as to whether it blooms early or late.

Genera that contain large numbers of species, like delphiniums (*Delphinium*), phlox, daylilies (*Hemerocallis*), and astilbes, have such a blooming spectrum. With the large number of species, you can move the particular blooming period forward or back, and new possibilities for combinations thus occur. Later delphiniums and earlier phlox, for instance, complement each other's colors very well; their blooming seasons overlap. Early delphinium varieties and late phlox varieties, on the other hand, do not flower at the same time.

A Garden Diary Helps with Planning

Seasonal and climatic imponderabilities always present surprises—for instance, by shifting the blooming period. Thus color clashes can occur sometimes, but on the other hand, sometimes very successful combinations occur this way. You should therefore proceed with extreme caution when it comes to plant combinations. Always plan in detail, especially if you want fine color matches. With a garden diary, you can keep close track of the course of the seasons, plant development, and blooming periods. This allows you to keep a good overview of your garden treasures throughout the year, to be able to reorder precisely to fill in holes in the flowering calendar, and especially, to gain much practical information as time goes by.

DESIGNING WITH PLANTS
Plant Ideas for July/August

July/August are high-summer months, and the garden presents itself in vivid color. The annuals (see pages 260–265) have now reached their zenith, and the high-summer bloomers among the perennials are showing their colors. It's best if you organize the abundance of color somewhat and put the colorful focal points in different places.

Organize Colors—But How?
You achieve a large-scale picture if you combine different plant species and thus utilize the entire palette of one or neighboring color hues, as is possible with phlox (*Phlox* species/varieties, see pages 238–239, bee balm (*Monarda* hybrids, see pages 238–239), or the sun plants (see pages 96–97 and 238–239). In small gardens, however, you should always limit yourself to a few species and thus complement with annuals in neutral white, perhaps with tall and low tobacco plants (*Nicotiana sylvestris* and *N. x sanderae*). On the other hand, you can design a garden that is entirely one color, perhaps in red or white. However, this requires superb knowledge of plants, for it isn't enough by itself to combine the white-blooming varieties of different plant genera with each other. Flowers and foliage colors as well as growth habits must harmonize so that no monotony results.

Tone-on-tone combination with purple loosestrife and wild sweet William.

Plants for Borders and/or at the Woods' Edge
At the very height of summer, with long-lasting heat and dryness, it can even be helpful for sun-loving plants if thin clumps of trees or single large shrubs cast some shadow for a few hours. Bedding plants generally need deep, fresh, nutrient-rich soil; mostly they love a spot in full sun. Some woods' edge or field plants, on the other hand, prefer light shade and a somewhat more humid location. Plants that manage in both situations are phlox (*Phlox paniculata* hybrids) and bee balm. They come from North America's damp meadows and lightly wooded areas. But both tolerate a sunny location with sufficient moisture. The astilbes (*Astilbe* hybrids, see pages 244–245) are intrinsically shade loving. In natural arrangements in conjunction with woodsy areas, they are primary providers of stunning high points at this time of year with color combinations from white to red. In fresh soils, they can also be well integrated into perennial borders.

High-Summer Perennials in Many Varieties
A portion of the garden can be designed as a gay meadow with phlox and bee balm. Many different varieties bloom in the period from June to September in shades of white, pink, red, and violet. You can create focal points of color with them, and they are outstanding for use as lead plants. Both plants grow about 39 in (1 m) tall and and display themselves through an intense, spicy fragrance of the flowers or foliage. In both, the broad spectrum of varieties is fascinating and with it the possible color variations. Within the assortment, there are early (from the end of June), mid-season (second half of July), and late (from the middle of August) varieties. Thus, the blooming time stretches over several months.

The colors of the monarda embrace the entire spectrum of shades of red, a color run from pink to purple. This rather bold tone-on-tone painting of the lead plants looks most beautiful when it is enhanced with the neutral colors of white and green. The color palette is the same with phlox, but the color effect is completely different because the hues, in contrast to the brilliant, lustrous phlox flowers are

Pastel group with monarda (left), phlox (right), tall white veronica (middle), and cream-colored achillea (front).

The fireworks of astilbes—providers of robust color for semishady places. There are many species and varity groups of astilbe, which grow to various heights and flower at different times so that with skillful combination you can provide spots of color with astilbes in lightly shaded areas from June to September. In the photo above are the Astilbe arendsii hybrids "Cattleya" (pink), "Diamant" (white), and "Glut" (red). In the background is an Astilbe thunbergii hybrid with looser panicled ears.

matte and dull. In contrast to phlox, they do not have an effect at a distance.

Appropriate companion plants, depending on shades, are coreopsis (*Coreopsis* species/varieties, see page 239) and yarrow (*Achillea* varieties, see pages 236–237) in bright yellows. The warm yellow shades of rudbeckias (*Rudbeckia* varieties, see pages 238–239) and sneezeweed (*Helenium* hybrids, see pages 238–239) harmonize better with the dark colors of the monarda. Low and tall asters (*Aster* hybrids), tall veronicas (*Veronica* species/varieties, see pages 238–239) and grasses are good partners for the late-blooming monarda hybrids.

In June/July, the vanguard of the phloxes is created by the delicate wild sweet William (*Dianthus barbatus* hybrids). Their white and pink flowers can be combined very effectively with the blue shades of fleabane (*Erigeron* varieties, see pages 236–237) and sage (*Salvia nemorosa*, see pages 234–235), but also the pretty, contrasting yellow evening primrose (*Oenothera tetragona*, see page 237).

Plant Ideas for August/September

When the summer has reached its zenith, it's time for the sun plants (see pages 238–239). With their warm tones of yellow, orange, red-brown, copper, and bronze, they announce that fall is slowly coming. The sun plants are robust and mostly long flowering. They combine well with each other, with annuals, and with grasses. Above all, sneezeweed (*Helenium* hybrids), tall and low rudbeckias (*Rudbeckia fulgida* "Goldsturm" and *R. nitida*), and oxeyes (*Heliopsis helianthoides var. scabra*) are important long bloomers in the late-summer garden.

Sunny Perennials and Other Perennials

The warm gold of the sunny perennials harmonizes very beautifully with the red-blue and violet shades of the bee balm (*Monarda* hybrids), phlox (*Phlox* species/varieties), and Michaelmas daisies (*Aster* species/varieties). Such a garden scene is also enhanced from September on by the brightly colored foliage of plants and trees. Together with colorfully matching perennials (see pages 238–239) in darker orange-yellow shades like montebretia (*Crocosmia* species), red-hot poker (*Kniphofia* species/varieties), and daylilies (*Hemerocallis* varieties), a "yellow garden" is created.

The sun perennials also look beautiful when they are against a dark or light green background, like a hedge. Because these plants are very different in growth habit, they can also be beautifully combined with one another: perhaps rudbeckia in the medium-high foreground, goldenrod (*Solidago* hybrids) and heleniums in the middle ground, and tall thin-leaf sunflowers (*Helianthus decapetalus*) in the background.

Heleniums (Helenium varieties)—*rewarding sun perennials.*

A summer picture like a painting. Yellow on yellow—with a combination dominated by annuals. Bunches of sunflowers (Helianthus annuus) *tower over a low flower carpet of marigolds* (Tagetes tenuifolia).

Sun Perennials and Annuals

The warm, full yellow shades of the sun perennials glow from afar and are very dominant. Within a plant group there are often varieties in the most different tones and shadings of yellow to copper and from bronze to ruby red, such as with the sunflowers and the annual marigolds (*Tagetes* species/varieties). Combination with the orange tones of other annuals (see pages 262–265), like the tall tithonia (*Tithonia rotundifolia*) and the delicate orange cosmos (*Cosmos sulphureus*) produces glowing tone-on-tone plantings. The darker, matte violet hues of the verbenas (*Verbena bonariensis* and *V. rigida*), on the other hand, soften the intense sun yellows. You should scatter in pure white flowers sparingly and only in small clumps in plantings of sun-colored perennials. Cream-colored and greenish yellow flowers of tobacco plants (*Nicotiana* x *sanderae* and

N. sylvestris) are much better suited. You will find more examples of annuals on pages 114–115 and 260–267.

You achieve an entirely different play of color with combinations of sun perennials with dark red and crimson flowers or with the red foliage of the massive, ornamental red castor bean (*Ricinus communis*), the tall red orache (*Atriplex hortensis*), the love-lies-bleeding (*Amaranthus caudatus*), and the perilla (*Perilla frutescens*). The warm hues with the deep ones radiate a great feeling of harmony. Also dark red gladiolas (*Gladiolus* hybrids, see page 258) and dahlias (*Dahlia*

Gorgeous—rudbeckia (Rudbeckia fulgida) *and goldenrod* (Solidago *hybrid*).

varieties, see page 258), especially the red-leaved dahlia "Bishop of Llandaff," are successful additions.

Sun Perennials and Grasses

With long-lasting grasses (see pages 268–269) like eulalia (*Miscanthus sinensis*), switchgrass (*Panicum virgatum*), and Chinese pennisetum (*Pennisetum alopecuroides*), you can hide the plant weakness of these usually tall-growing bedding perennials, whose lower foliage is often unsightly around this time because of dryness or mildew.

Plant Ideas for September/October

Fountain grass in front of eulalia and relatives.

Silvery pampas grass in front of crimson sedum in the autumn light.

Fall border with crimson boneset (Eupatorium fistulosum)*, mountain-fleece* (Polygonum amplexicaule)*, and grasses.*

By the time fall reaches its high point in October, the perennials have lost more and more of their effectiveness. Now the grasses take over a certain leadership role in the garden, whereas in the summer and early fall they can be regarded as companions to the perennials. Grasses retain their form until well into the winter and are particularly decorative when covered with hoarfrost. Above all, the tall grasses, like the molinia (*Molinia arundinacea*, see pages 268–269), stand out when their stalks, leaves, and flower panicles are colored gold. Other inflorescences, like the Amur silver grass (*Miscanthus saccariflorus*), remain silver and look particularly attractive in a cross light.

How Can Grasses Be Combined?

The neutral colors of the grasses cool down blooming beds, and their form gives plantings stability and structure. Low grasses are planted in clumps of several; taller ones can be placed in little groups or individually.
Bed plantings. You can use many of the medium-tall grasses, such as purple moor grass (*Molinia caerulea*), for between planting in the front of the bed. The flower-bearing stalks of course grow high over the clumps of grass, but they remain transparent. With the more loosely flowering grass stalks, a charming veil effect can be created in the garden, similar to that produced with the delicate baby's breath (*Gypsophila paniculata* hybrids, see pages 238), colewort (*Crambe cordifolia*, see page 237), the wild asters (*Aster sedifolius* and *A. ericoides*, see pages 240–241), which also bloom in fall, or annuals like verbena (*Verbena bonariensis*, see pages 264–265). Tall grasses between perennials and annuals can also provide a feeling of spaciousness. Single clumps are enough; but a hedgelike, loose row of tall, narrow grasses, like feather reed grass (*Calamagrostis* x *acutiflora*, see pages 268–269 and photo, page 72) lets the bedding perennials like blue delphinium (*Delphinium* hybrids, see pages 236–237), which flowers a second time in September, the late varieties of red phlox (*Phlox paniculata* hybrids, see pages 238–239) or violet fall asters show to full effect.
In September/October, grasses enter into one more pretty union with the last flowering perennials and annuals.

Reed grass as a background for fall perennials.

The warm gold tones of the mature grasses harmonize magnificently with the intense yellows of the late sun plants (see pages 96–97 and 238–239) and with the red, violet, and blue tones of the different fall asters (*Aster dumosus, A. novi-belgii,* and *A. novae-angliae,* see pages 240–241) and the different colors of winter asters (*Dendranthema* hybrids, see page 240), but also with tall late dahlias (*Dahlia* varieties, see pages 258–259). Also the choice of white or yellow grasses is large, such as zebra grass (*Miscanthus sinensis* "Zebrinus"). They look good in colorful perennial beds.

Naturalized plantings. Further interesting effects are achieved by harmony of grasses with fall foliage and ornamental fruits of trees, shrubs, and perennials. The grasses find ideal partners in late bloomers (see pages 240–241) such as sedum (*Sedum telephium* and *S. spectabile*), monkshood (*Aconitum carmichaelii*), Japanese anemone (*Anemone japonica* hybrids), white October daisies (*Chrysanthemum uliginosum*), as well as mountain fleece (*Polygonum amplexicaule*) or Chinese lantern plant (*Physalis alkekengi* var. *franchettii*). Here also, from September on, the brilliant red burning bush (*Euonymus alata*), with its corky bark, is especially attractive.

Grasses As Specimen Plants

Grasses lend good graphic structure and accents to a garden. The linear forms of the grasses contrast wonderfully with rounds and flats. As specimens, they can increase the effectiveness of particular garden situations and be placed like a sculpture or a tree or shrub. However, you should never leave them standing entirely alone. Magnificent pampas grasses (*Cortaderia selloana,* see pages 268–269) look lost and lonely by themselves in the front yard. They show to better advantage combined with small shrubs, conifers, or heathers. After the grasses are cut back in the spring, the structure of the shrubs in the combination still remains.

Crimson sedum with violet cushion asters.

The flowers of the red-hot-poker (Kniphofia hybrids) mix with those of gaura (Gaura lindheimer) and cushion asters.

DESIGNING WITH PLANTS
Plant Ideas for Winter

The garden in winter need not be monotonous and bare. It only changes its character when all the color and brilliant greens have faded. Now the structures of the trees and shrubs and grasses take prominence; now it shows whether you have planned carefully. When you are choosing trees and shrubs, consider that for almost half a year—usually in a leafless condition—they will stamp the character of the garden.

Structure Through Habit and Leaf Form
Many leaves are still present during the first half of the winter, before they decay. On the other hand, the manifold growth forms have an effect the whole winter through: linear, elegant and compact, stiffly upright, and arching, overhanging growth forms, as well as low and high growth. Above all, where large structure-forming shrubs are missing, it is important to combine plants with contrasting and long-lasting growth forms in order to maintain continuing contour, line, and structure in the garden.

Plants that also show to advantage in winter are primarily woody plants like trees and shrubs. In addition, there are the grasses and the decorative dried flowers and seed pods of perennials, like the Japanese anemone (*Anemone japonica* hybrids) or the astilbe (*Astilbe* species/hybrids), and wild herbs such as common teasel (*Dipsacus sylvestris*) or Saint John's wort (*Hypericum perforatum*). In heavy frost or snow, they take on a partially new form, in which their graceful contours are emphasized.

Structuring with Evergreen Plants
While most vegetation is resting, there are some evergreen plants that bring lively green to the garden. Evergreen and wintergreen trees and shrubs (see pages 102–103 and 212–213), low ground covers, evergreen ornamental-leaved plants, like bergenias (*Bergenia* hybrids), climbing plants (see pages 216–221), ivy (*Hedera helix* varieties, see pages 216–221), and honeysuckle (*Lonicera henryi*) as well as wintergreen ferns—they all lend color and changing forms to the winter garden. Most importantly, the structures of evergreen

Winter graphic on the water with hoarfrost on the water lily leaves.

trees and shrubs become effective in winter in a formally designed garden. Clipped evergreen hedges, perhaps of boxwood (*Buxus sempervirens*) or English yew (*Taxus baccata*), and the different tree and shrub forms not only organize a garden in summer but also in the winter season when the environment of colored flowers and leaves is missing.

Fruits, Bark, and Branches

Not only the green parts of the evergreen plants ornament the winter garden; fruit-bearing trees like the crab apple (*Malus* species), firethorn (*Pyracantha coccinea* varieties) with light and dark orange berries, the beautyberry with its lilac beads (*Callicarpa bodinieri*), or various red cotoneasters (*Cotoneaster* species/varieties) also supply individual dabs of color to the winter garden scene. However, the fruits disappear in time, for they are a favorite bird food. Or they eventually become unsightly or fall off.

Some plants draw attention in winter with a particular bark color, like birches (*Betula* species) and the Siberian dogwood (*Cornus alba* "Siberica") with its red stems or the golden twig dogwood (*Cornus sericea* "Flaviramea") with yellow-green branches. The youngest shoots are always the most intensely colored.

With others, the placement or form of the branches turns it into a eye-catcher, like the bizarre Japanese angelica (*Aralia elata*), the giant dogwood (*Cornus controversa*), the European hazel (*Corylus avallana* "Contorta"), or the dragon claw willow (*Salix matsudana* "Tortuosa").

Water plants do not lose their interest, even in winter.

Fine linear forms alternate with more compact ones—heavy frost strengthens the impact of both.

DESIGNING WITH PLANTS
Evergreen Plantings

For garden lovers who like to enjoy their gardens above all as an oasis of relaxation without exhausting themselves in the work of caring for it, the garden with evergreen shrubbery (see pages 212–215) without many time-consuming plantings of flowers is an interesting alternative. Of course, there is no garden that is absolutely carefree. Even a garden with evergreen shrubbery must be maintained and trimmed. On the other hand, a geometrically designed evergreen garden that consists of trimmed broad-leaved and needle-leaved evergreens can become a fascinating green architecture. However, in such gardens, the change of seasons with their color variations of leaves and flowers is scarcely perceptible.

Evergreen Shrubbery As a Backdrop

When a garden exclusively of evergreens at length becomes too monotonous, evergreen shrubbery can always be used as a framework or as a permanent backdrop for flowering plants as the seasons change.

- The evergreen shrubs give permanent structure to the garden in winter and add color.
- Whether free-growing or clipped, evergreens can be used outstandingly as organizing, structuring, and room-building elements.
- Because evergreens hardly change over the course of the year, they bring calm to the garden and serve as dark backdrops in front of which the lighter and more colorful leaf hues or bright and colorful flowers can then rightly be displayed to advantage. At the same time, they offer a balancing background for unruly growth forms (see photo, page 81).

Which Shrub for Which Garden?

For the average large garden of about 3,000 sq ft (300 m³) or more, the choice of evergreen shrubs isn't too large. For many treelike evergreens grow relatively slowly, to be sure, but they become very tall and—aside from the pillar-shaped ones—also very wide. They only reach the desired height after decades, but often long before that they have burst the garden space. You can quickly recognize the difficulty with a critical look at neighboring gardens. The great trick is to find the species that even after years will still fit the size of the garden. The growth potential of interesting nursery plants may not be apparent. On the contrary, at first these shrubs grow too slowly for the wishes of the garden owner, who wants to create a backdrop as quickly as possible, or a room, or a point of

Heath planting with evergreens.

interest in his garden. Therefore, get plenty of advice when you are buying, and be informed ahead of time. Otherwise, it could happen that the garden will be completely overshadowed or that some day a beautiful old shrub will have to be chopped down, which involves certain difficulties (see page 22) .

On the other hand, this danger hardly exists with broad-leaved evergreens. They don't grow so large and can be kept in check with pruning as can the conifers yew (*Taxus* species), arborvitae (*Thuja* species), or false cypress (*Chamaecyparis* species).

Needle-leaved evergreen shrubs (see pages 214–215). There are very interesting and many different forms in these. Their colors vary from light yellow, light green, silvery, golden, bluish, and dark green. Different junipers (*Juniperus* species), false cypresses (*Chamaecyparis* species), or pines (*Pinus* species) can be collected into interesting groups. On the other hand, you should avoid a combination with large deciduous trees, because these crowd the conifers in the short- or the long-term, depending on the space between the plants.

Conifers that grow in pillar forms are particularly suited

GARDEN
TIPS AND TRICKS

Warning
Some evergreens like yew, viburnum, and daphne, ivy, euonymus, cherry laurel, honeysuckle, and pachysandra are poisonous in all parts or have poisonous fruits. Anyone who has small children or house pets should avoid these plants.

Modern formal garden with low clipped boxwood.

Evergreens as backdrop (yew) and enclosure (boxwood).

for formal gardens, as companions for heathers, for gardens with a southern flair, and for parklike layouts. In other cases—especially in a natural garden—pillar- and pyramid-shaped conifers look somewhat strange. Here, aside from pillar junipers, you should if possible plant only English yew (*Taxus baccata*), pines (*Pinus sylvestris* and *P. mugo*), as well as native juniper (*Juniperus communis*). Dwarf conifers occupy a special position. They grow extremely slowly and work best in the rock garden together with small evergreen flowering woody plants such as sun roses (*Helianthemum* varieties), perennial candytuft (*Iberis sempervirens*), daphne (*Daphne cneorum*), and Saint John's wort (*Hypericum calycinum*) as well as low rock garden plants. They are also well suited to heath gardens (see pages 108–109).

Broad-leaved evergreens (see pages 212–213). In northern latitudes there are only a few wintergreen and evergreen broad-leaved evergreens. Only hollies (*Ilex* species/varieties), juniper, and ivy (*Hedera helix* species/varieties) are native. They are climatically less adaptable than conifers and should be in a protected location, for instance under a tall tree, near a building, or in front of hedges or walls.

Broad-leaved evergreens are—in contrast to the conifers, with the exception of yew—usually shade tolerant. In winter, there is the danger of dehydration for them, as there is for the conifers; when the soil is frozen for a long time, sun and wind produce evaporation. Yet their advantage over the conifers is that they look more lively and more natural in the garden. Especially recommended for the natural garden are boxwood in free-growing form, hollies, euonymus (*Euonymus fortunei* varieties), barberry (*Berberis* species), cherry laurel (*Prunus laurocerasus*), cotoneaster (*Cotoneaster* species), viburnum (*Viburnum rhytidophyllum*) and honeysuckle (*Lonicera* species/varieties) as well as firethorn (*Pyracantha coccinea*) and ivy. Rhododendron and its relatives thrive only in slightly acid, that is, lime-poor soil. Also very good as ground covers are some wintergreens like pachysandra (*Pachysandra terminalis*), Saint John's wort, myrtle (*Vinca minor*), and germander (*Teucrium chamaedrys*).

Plant Ideas for Shady Gardens

A shady garden need not be a disadvantage. There are hosts of attractive plant communities that thrive in the shade, and a wealth of design variations. Plants in shady situations have their own charm, epecially in combination with plays of light and shadow.

Almost every old garden is more or less heavily shaded. Especially shady are locations under shrubs or in front of a hedge, which has begun to run wild over the years, as well as places near buildings and walls. Also, a single widespread fruit tree often lets scarcely any light penetrate in the summer. The north side of a house or a courtyard also receives little sunlight. It is the task of all gardeners to deal with the different light conditions on their property with corresponding plantings.

Deeper and Lighter Shade

The determinants for the choice of suitable plants are soil, climate, and moisture, as well as the special light conditions. Here a differentiation is made between deep and light shade. The most delightful garden pictures appear in semishade, in places that receive some sun for several hours a day, or in the shadow cast by a roof of leaves that only filter the light and do not keep it out entirely. The choice of plants for these conditions is the largest. Here also, plants that prefer an open, sunny location will still thrive, such as bee balm (*Monarda* hybrids, see pages 238–239 or tall *(veronica)* species (see page 239). Flowers usually last longer in light shade than in full sun. Northeast and east locations are favorable: Many plants like morning light better than afternoon sun, which dries them out more with its beams.

Dryness is the greatest danger for plants anyway. As long as the ground is covered with a layer of humus, and dampness and humidity are present, shade-loving plants, such as Indian strawberry (*Duchesnea indica*) or myrtle (*Vinca* species), are happy, and also when the foliage over them becomes thicker in summer.

Real problem areas, which can only be designed with difficulty, occur where deep shade and dryness occur together: within the drip line of trees and shrubs or buildings, when the root competition of large trees and incompatible leaf- and needle-drop make it difficult for plants to grow. In such places, the only things that thrive are some grasses and moss as well as the yellow archangel (*Lamiastrum galeobdolon*) or the robust comfrey (*Symphytum grandiflorum*).

Important: With constant mulching and additional watering, as well as adding compost, you can build up a humus layer in such places in which shade-loving plants will be happy.

Ideal shade planting—hosta, ferns, and ivy.

Designing with Plants in Shady Locations

Plants that can manage with little sun often have smaller flowers by nature, but they therefore receive another endowment: ornamental foliage or an impressive structure, such as the rodgersia (*Rodgersia* species, see pages 244–245) or the ligularia (*Ligularia* species)—both tall, imposing plants. In shady locations, especially, these large-leaved plants make a good show, as do the popular hostas (*Hosta* species/varieties) with their interestingly shaped and colored foliage. But there are also some pretty flowering plants for semishady and shady spots, such as bellflowers (*Campanula latifolia*, see pages 244–245) or goatsbeard (*Aruncus dioicus*, see page 244).

The usually unpretentious color play of these shade-plant flowers stretches from new growth in the spring to the coloration of the foliage in late fall. The modest flowers in white, cream, yellow, and pink, especially, bring light into the dark parts of the garden. Exceptions are the astilbes (*Astilbe arendsii* hybrids, see pages 244–245), foxgloves (*Digitalis* species, see pages 244–245), and primroses (*Primula* species, see pages 278–279), which have stronger colors.

Garden in the light shade of high trees. Such locations, with acid soil, are exactly right for rhododendrons.

Monkshood, large-flowered betony, lady's-mantle, and others.

Birdbath between hydrangeas and hostas.

Besides the plants with ornamental leaves, the feathery ferns (see pages 272–273) are suitable for shady parts of the garden, but so are many forest grasses (see pages 270–271) and ground covers (see pages 246–247). Together they form a thick, green carpet when the soil has enough moisture and humus. Semishady areas

under the new growth of deciduous trees and shrubs develop an entirely special magic when the small spring-flowering bulbs, narcissi (see pages 112–113, 250–251, and 254–255), and early perennials form a delicately tinted carpet of flowers in the period from February to May.

Plant Ideas for Rock Gardens

A rock garden is a small world in itself. Its flora can embrace the entire plant spectrum: deciduous and coniferous woody plants, semishrubs, perennials, grasses, ferns, bulbs, and corms. The plants come from alpine regions all over the earth, from the rock/mountain plains/prairies—from meadows and woods. All members of this multicultural society are characterized by low, slow growth; cushion and rosette forms are often represented (see pages 242–243). Also typical of the sun-loving rock garden flora is the silvery gray, bluish frosted, or succulent foliage. The flowering climax of a rock garden is primarily in the spring. But with some skill in the choice of plants, you can also enjoy flowers in late fall.

In their natural environment, these plants are imprinted by the rock lying around them; it influences their growth habit and is essential for the microclimate. In lowlands, the plants don't need this protection as a rule; here the rock serves more as a natural backdrop. However, the makeup of the soil must be appropriate for the particular plants. The best conditions for a rock garden are offered by a plot facing south, with a natural or artificial slope. Often a difference in height of 1.5 to 3 ft (0.5–1 m) is enough. You can also achieve a rock garden effect by putting in a small dry wall (see pages 50–51) or a stone wall.

In large gardens or in a country setting, natural stone looks the best, also in combination with a brook. In urban settings, on the other hand, a carefully laid-out rock garden that goes with the style of the house and whose materials form a harmonious complement to terrace, paths, or steps is recommended. There are beds actually within stone enclosures, which have an entirely different decorative character from natural rock gardens. If there is only a small space at your disposal, you can fall back on small container gardens. Containers of natural stone are particularly well suited for miniature rock gardens—especially for exotics.

Rocks—Function and Effect

Rocks form the framework of the rock garden; they divide the surfaces and keep the soil from slipping away. The great art consists of laying the stones on the embankment in such a way that they give the impression that they were put there by natural means. Thus, there are some practical

Rock garden-like planting with light blue /white flax (rear), with sun roses, asphodel, and euphorbia.

as well as design criteria that you should observe (pages 140–141).

• Before you place the stones, you should rid the surface of root weeds like goutweed (*Aegopodium podagraria*), quack grass (*Agropyron repens*), horsetail (*Equisetum arvense*), and field bindweed (*Convolvulus arvensis*); they can quickly become a plague.

• The size ratio between rocks and area must be maintained. Do not use oversized rock fragments for small areas. However, use a few large rocks rather than too many small ones and keep the materials as uniform as possible.

• The most beautiful and the largest fragments should be set by themselves; smaller ones work better if they are laid in groups.

• Avoid uniformity by distributing the rock fragments irregularly. Though blocklike materials look better in even layers and grade, projections as well as irregular highs and steps can make the construction look more natural.

• Especially large and interesting individual pieces can also be set upright. But they should then stand free at the foot of the slope. They work best surrounded with low

Wall with mouse-ear chickweed, red valerian, and yellow corydalis.

Star moss, sweet Williams, and oat grass.

plants or combined with a specimen, perhaps a small mountain pine (*Pinus mugo*) or a wild rose (*Rosa glauca* or *R. rubiginosa*).

• Leave areas as flat as possible between the rocks for planting, and smooth the entire surface around the rocks with the rake.

• Put down additional stepping-stones and steps (out of the same rock material, if possible), which will make care of the garden easier.

• The soil between the plants can be covered with smaller stones and gravel. This looks nice and is good for moisture-sensitive plants.

Soil Preparation and Planting

The best preparation for a rock garden is a location in full sun and a loose, well-drained, gritty, porous, humus subsoil, which may not, however, be too rich. Almost all alpine plants need moisture, but they tolerate no standing water. According to the soil conditions and planting, an 8 to 12 in (20–30 cm) deep drainage layer of sand and gravel is recommended.

When the rocks are placed (see page 140), you should loosen the soil thoroughly and prepare for planting. Many rock garden plants remain neutral to the lime in the soil or are even lime loving. The ones that don't like lime must be planted in separate locations. Among rock garden plants, there are also some shade-tolerant ones that love it to be cool and damp in the root region. They do better in the shadow of a rock.

The front sides of the rocks should not be blocked by tall plants; here is where the low-growing, carpeting plants like pinks (*Dianthus* species) and moss pinks (*Phlox subulata*, see pages 242–243) as well as bulbs, for example botanical tulips and wild narcissi or lily leeks (*Allium moly*) belong.

On the other hand, smaller shrubs and somewhat taller plants may be placed at the top over a block of rock; they give the garden a feeling of spaciousness. Besides the rocks, conifers and evergreens provide a structure for the rock garden that remains constant and endures throughout the winter.

GARDEN
TIPS AND TRICKS

Placing Stones Properly
Each stone needs a firm foundation of gravel. The soil must be firmly compressed beforehand so the stones can't wobble or rotate. Always set the stone with the broad side down; it should only stick in the ground up to a half or a third so that the front always remains visible (see page 140). The stones must lean slightly toward the slope to allow the water to run off.

DESIGNING WITH PLANTS
Plant Ideas for Heath Gardens

Heath gardens need space in order to create an effect. This is amply demonstrated in nature by the broad flower carpet of, for example, the moors of Scotland.
If you decide to have a planting of heath plants, you should match all the rest or at least a part of your garden to it. Requirements for a heath garden are a place in full sun, as well as a soil that is nutrient-poor, as lime-free as possible, porous, and of sandy-humus content and high moisture, either in a mild coastal climate or where winter snow cover offers protection. Heath plants must be cut back regularly so that they don't calcify and fail to flower. Cut back winter and spring bloomers after flowering, and summer and fall bloomers in spring.

Heath Plants in the Garden

Heaths and heathers captivate not only with the color play of their flowers in white, pink, lilac, and red shades but also by the various colorings of their foliage. Besides the Scotch heather (*Calluna vulgaris* varieties), mainly the snow heather (*Erica carnea*), Irish heath (*Daboecia cantabrica*), and Cornish heath (*Erica vagans*) are used in heath gardens. The dwarf shrubs bloom at different times—thus, with skillful planning, you can enjoy your heath bed all year long. In winter, spring, and late summer it possesses great color interest; at other times the companion plants can provide accents. Other ericas, conifers, and ornamental shrubs are good for this purpose. Companions for dry locations. You should lay out a naturalized heath garden slightly sculptured and liven it up with plantings of differing heights so that the surface doesn't look too monotonous. Suitable neighbors are birches (*Betula* species, see pages 206–207), mountain ash (*Sorbus* species, see pages 214–215), larger and smaller pine species (*Pinus sylvestris, P. mugo, P. parviflora*, see pages 214–215) as well as various junipers (*Juniperus* species, see pages 214–215), but also flowering

Snow heather (Erica carnea) *blooms from December to April.*

Successful heath garden planting with structuring shrubs like yew, juniper, and false cypress.

shrubs, such as wild roses and other shrub roses (see pages 228–229), broom (*Cytisus* species, see page 210), golden chain (*Laburnum* hybrids, see pages 206–207), and firethorn (*Pyracantha coccinea*, see pages 212–213). In front of this backdrop, the low-lying heaths and heathers look the best when they are planted together in large groups of at least 20 to 25 plants. The proportions of the area, the flowering times of the plants, and their color and growth habit must all be in tune with one another. Small groups of cushiony plants, but also of higher-growing green and gray-blue grasses enliven these plant areas. Low ornamental shrubs, like bluebeard (*Caryopteris* hybrids, see page 210) or Russian sage (*Perovskia* species), are pretty partners. Some dry-loving, fast-growing plants also fit the character of a heath garden. Pinks (*Dianthus* species, see page 243), thymes (*Thymus* species, see page 243), and lamb's-ears (*Stachys byzantina*, see page 237) as well as low-growing species of asters (*Aster dumosus*, see pages 240–241) and evening primroses (*Oenothera missouriensis*) are good for shaping the edge. Between areas of heathers, the higher specimen plants like mulleins (*Verbascum* species,

The Scotch heather (Calluna vulgaris) *blooms from June to October.*

see pages 234–235), thistle species (*Eryngium* species), and some bulbs, such as lilies (*Lilium* species/varieties, see pages 256–257) and alliums (*Allium* species, see pages 256–257), show to advantage.

<u>Companions for damper regions.</u> Heath gardens in humid regions can have a character entirely their own. Here the conifers assume the chief role as companions (see pages 214–215). They broaden the palette of shades of green. This type of heath garden is especially attractive in winter. Here the lime-tolerant snow heather is most suitable. In acid soils and lightly shaded situations, the heath theme can be broadened with other companions in the heath family (Ericaceae).

Roses and Companions

Roses are something special—the beauty of their flowers, their rather long flowering period, and the number of varieties make them very popular. In the past decades, they've lost their special standing somewhat, but this has led them more and more to enter into association with the other garden plants. New free-flowering and everblooming varieties and the countless small ornamental shrub roses allow them to be used in many ways never possible before. They fit into any kind of garden—small, large, formal, and open-designed ones. They can be well integrated everywhere and do not require a special bed, as was the practice earlier. It has been demonstrated that roses in rose beds, that is, in monoculture, are more susceptible to diseases and pests than in combination plantings. In general, roses want good care; they need open soil as well as a free, airy, sunny location. Skillful combination of roses and other plants create beautiful garden scenes. Appropriate companions can increase the effectiveness of the roses.

Tips for Planting

Roses tolerate root competition from other plants poorly but can develop communities without any problems if you follow certain rules:
• Don't underplant roses entirely but always plant them in bunches; however, shrub roses should be by themselves.
• You should leave large spaces between the groups and fill them with suitable partners or companions, especially ones that bloom in spring and fall, like early cushion plants, bulbs, and late sedums and asters.
• Always set the companion plants at a distance from the roses. This arrangement not only looks nice, but mainly it is healthy for the roses and practical in terms of care: If the beds are organized in this fashion, the work of loosening, fertilizing, mulching, and the adding and removing of hilling can be accomplished comfortably.
Bedding roses are best suited for combinations—the simple, semidouble, and sometimes hybrid-tealike, cluster-flowered polyantha and floribunda roses; but also the modern everblooming shrub roses can be combined well with perennials, annuals, grasses, and shrubs.

Color Recipes

The smaller the area of a bed, the more important it is to limit yourself to a few colors and a definite arrangement. Roses in warm shades of red, pink, yellow, and white can be combined with restrained blue, yellow, and white flowers as well as with gray-green and blue-green foliage. Be careful with combinations of salmon-pink with cool pink. These colors must be very sensitively

The best rose companions come together—baby's breath, lady's-mantle,

Moschata (musk) hybrid "Cornelia" and Jacob's ladder.

English rose "The Miller" with catmint.

combined with one another with accompanying plants in blue, gray, and white shades. You won't make a mistake if you combine roses in exclusively warm shades (sun yellow, orange, scarlet) or entirely in cool shades (white, pink, crimson).

Roses and cranesbill.

delphinium, and grasses.   *Rose with clematis "The President."*

The robust yellow shrub rose "Lichtkönigin Lucia" underplanted with mouse-ear chickweed.

A Backdrop for Roses

Needle-leaved evergreens are outstanding as frames for bright, intensely colored roses. Yew (*Taxus* species) or hedges of blue-green or gray cypresses (*Chamaecyparis* species) and arborvitae (*Thuja* species) provide good relief. Juniper (*Juniperus* species) and pines (*Pinus* species) are particularly suitable for naturalized plantings. Shrub roses are very effective against clipped hedges of deciduous shrubs or in front of a neutral shrubbery backdrop. White-flowering ornamental shrubs like mock-orange (*Philadelphus* varieties) or summer-flowering viburnums (*Viburnum* species) underscore the color of the roses.

Roses in Dominance

Here are some plant ideas that keep the roses dominant in the bed. Roses produce the most beautiful effects when they project above a low carpet of plants. Good for enclosure or linkage between individual roses and groups of roses are
• low perennials, grasses, and cushion plants (see pages 106–107) such as baby's breath (*Gypsophila repens*) or perennial candytuft (*Iberis sempervirens*)
• low-growing conifers (see pages 214–215)
• dwarf shrubs, like lavender (*Lavandula* species) or bluebeard (*Caryopteris* varieties)
• annual flowers like sweet alyssum (*Lobularia maritima*) and annual sages (*Salvia* species/varieties).
However, make sure that you don't choose any invasive plants. Also, in large areas and long borders, low and medium-tall companion plants can be so placed that they look like a ribbon winding through islands of roses.

Roses in Partnership

Perennials and shrubs can also be equal, balancing partners of the roses. The roses are, of course, especially prominent during their main period of bloom, but their neighbors provide for stability for the rest of the year—this is the great advantage of plantings in mixed borders. When the rose bushes become unattractive in the fall, the companion plants take over the leadership once more. To frame the blooming season of roses, you should plant early-flowering relatives of the rose family like ornamental cherry (*Prunus* species/varieties, see pages 206–207), flowering quince (*Chaenomeles* hybrids), see pages 208–209), and crab apple (*Malus* species, see pages 218–219), spireas (*Spirea* hybrids, see pages 210–211), mountain ash (*Sorbus* species, see pages 204–205) as well as hawthorns (*Crataegus* species), in order to broaden the seasonal spectrum. Beautiful garden scenes are created by the combination of roses with *Clematis* (see pages 218–219). Light, freestanding trellises of wood or metal in the rose bed or arbors as an entrance over which roses and clematis climb together are very attractive. However, don't choose any vigorously growing clematis species for this purpose but only the large-flowered, summer-flowering clematis hybrids whose blooming period corresponds to that of the roses.

DESIGNING WITH PLANTS
Bulbs and Companions

When other plants are just awakening to new life in the spring, the bulbs and corms (see pages 248–259) are just providing for color on the garden scene. You can use bulbs and corms in your garden in many ways. It's important to place them suitably for their character. This is the only way to achieve good effects.

The wild forms, like the early-flowering dwarf bulbs, but also the early botanical tulips (*Tulipa* species/varieties) and wild narcissi (*Narcissus* species/varieties) belong in the natural areas of the garden, or depending on the species, along the edges of shrubbery or in the rock garden.

The hybridized forms of tulips (*Tulipa* species), lilies (*Lilium* species/varieties), and dahlias (*Dahlia* hybrids) look most beautiful in beds and borders.

Bulbs work to best effect when they are planted in large flights. The smaller the plant, the more important the total effect. Bulbs die back above ground after flowering, and their leaves wither. Thus they need neighbors in the bed that will overgrow them.

Tulips with the yellows of wallflowers, leopard's-bane, and pansies.

Bluebells with bright yellow poppies and yellow spurge.

Spring Bloomers and Their Partners

Bulbs can provide color accents almost the whole year-round. Small late-winter and spring bloomers (see pages 250–251) open the dance as early as February. The first flowers should be admired from the house. They can perhaps peep out of the leaf cover under still bare shrubbery or out of the edge of the woods or shrubbery growing in the lawn. Snowdrops (*Galanthus* species), winter aconite (*Eranthis hyemalis*), squill (*Scilla* species), glory-of-the-snow (*Chionodoxa luciliae*), and wild crocus (like, for example, *Crocus tomasinianus*) seed themselves easily and in time form carpets if they feel comfortable in a location.

Shrubs as partners. Spring-flowering ornamental shrubs are good partners for bulbs; together they create beautiful garden scenes: witch hazel (*Hamamelis* species) and buttercup witch hazel (*Corylopsis pauciflora*) with their yellow flowers and their picturesque growth habits spread over masses of blue squill (*Scilla siberica*). Between evergreen dwarf conifers and brilliant azaleas (*Rhododendron* species/varieties), the colorful flower stars of *Anemone blanda* sparkle. Also, the snow heather (*Erica carnea*) is an ideal partner for bulbs. It blooms for a very long time and can later serve as a companion for grape hyacinths (*Muscari* species), botanical tulips, and narcissi.

Wild perennials as partners. Narcissi and small spring bulbs are good for places that are shady in summer but in spring still get enough light through the light green of the new growth of foliage. There they receive a living complement from low-growing wild perennials like the yellow waldsteinia (*Waldsteinia ternata*, see pages 246–247), the brilliant blue creeping forget-me-not (*Omphalodes verna*, see pages 246–247), or the blue-violet lungwort (*Pulmonaria* species, see pages 246–247), and spring vetchling (*Lathyrus vernus*).

Spring bloomers in the rock garden. In dry areas, in rock, cliff, and terrace gardens, the early iris bulbs (*Iris reticulata* and *I. danfordiae*), the small wild narcissi, and numerous early wild tulips thrive well. They can be magnificently combined with early-flowering colorful rock garden plants (see pages 242–243) like perennial candytuft (*Iberis sempervirens*), carpeting phloxes (*Phlox douglasii* and *P. subulata*), and aubrieta (*Aubrieta* varieties). However, the colors should not be too intense so that the plants don't cancel each other out. The bulbs work best with white- and blue-flowered or gray-leaved low plants.

Spring bloomers in the country garden. Bulbs are also outstanding as partners for country garden flowers. When you combine bleeding heart (*Dicentra*

Tulip "Sweet Harmony" with deep-red "Queen of Night."

Pink tulips above violet pansies.

spectabilis), English wallflowers (*Cheiranthus cheirii*), and forget-me-nots (*Myosotis sylvatica*, see pages 266–267) with crown imperial (*Fritillaria imperialis*, see page 254) or tulips, a mixture of naturalized planting and decorative bed is created. You can plant them in a bed or along the edge of a group of shrubs, which creates a very lively effect. Yellow leopard's-bane (*Doronicum plantagineum)* and violet honesty (*Lunaria annua*, see pages 266–267) go well with them, too.

<u>Decorative beds.</u> The large-flowered hybrids of tulips, hyacinths, and narcissi go well in beds. Here suitable partners are biennial spring flowers (see pages 266–267) like pansies (*Viola x wittrockiana* hybrids), English daisies (*Bellis perennis*), and forget-me-nots. Such beds allow arrangements of intense displays of color. Tulips can unfold their full glory over a carpet of these biennials. Tulips, narcissi, hyacinths, and crown imperials can also be tied in very well in bunches among existing plantings of perennials. After flowering, however, they should be covered by the other plants.

Summer Bloomers and Their Partners

As the foliage of the spring flowers slowly fades, other bulbs take over their role. In May/June, the various alliums (*Allium* species, see pages 256–257) produce their often stately violet flower globes. The attractive flowers, which occur on stalks as tall as 39 in (1 m), loosen up the perennial bed; but above all they work together with gray-leaved plants like pink and yellow cushion plants such as cheddar pinks (*Dianthus gratia-nopolitanus*) and sedum species on gravelly subsoils. They can also be used as companions to, for instance, color-coordinated bearded iris (*Iris barbata* hybrids, see pages 234–235).

Also, camas (*Camassia* species) take on a transitional role between spring and summer bloomers. They need partners similar to those of the alliums. Desert-candle (*Eremurus* species), with their white, yellow, and pink flower candles, are imposing forms. Together with delphinium (*Delphinium* hybrids, see pages 236–237), they can produce a perennial border that will cause a sensation. However, drier rocky desert vegetation is more congenial to them.

Lilies, often pronounced fussy, count as some of the greatest beauties that a garden has to offer. However, a requirement for thriving is a well-drained soil. Most hybrids with brilliant bowl-shaped flowers and compact growth fit well into perennial borders and, depending on the variety, round out the play of color in bed plantings from early in the year until late summer.

In June, for instance, the white madonnia lily (*Lilium candidum*, see pages 258–259) and delphinium (*Delphinium* hybrids, see pages 236–237) complement one another ideally; but the yellow and orange descendents of the orange lily (*L. bulbiferum*, see pages 258–259) also achieve wonderful effects in colorful borders.

Lilies also do very well near trees and shrubbery. There they find a foothold with their feet in the shade and sun in the flower region. In this environment, the striking flowers appear to full advantage. Like the azaleas and rhododendrons, the gold-banded and showy lilies (*L. auratum* and *L. speciosum*) as well as the oriental hybrids have a preference for acid, damp locations, and they thrive well next to each other.

Fall Bloomers

Autumn crocus (*Colchicum autumnale*) and *Crocus speciosus* end the run of the bulbs and corms. The *Crocus speciocus* create their effects best in warm rock gardens, whereas the colchicums are happier in damp meadowy areas. The fall bulbs are planted in July/August.

Perennials and Annuals

Anyone who loves lushly flowering, gay summer flower beds should combine perennials and annuals.

Possibilities for Combination

In making choices, pay attention to the growth habit, color, and requirements of the plants.

• Perennials can be the focal points of a planting in which the annuals are only scattered.

• Plantings in which annuals are in the majority should be given support with biennials and with individual groups of perennials. This especially pays off in early summer or late fall, when the annuals are finished or are no longer at their peak.

• Some perennials, such as candytuft (*Iberis sempervirens*) or cushion asters (*Aster dumosus*) can serve as bed enclosures for summer flowers.

• But, turning it around, you can also use annuals for enclosures and front planting in perennial beds. Popular choices for this are low-growing annuals like sweet alyssum (*Lobularia maritima*), sanvitalia (*Sanvitalia procumbens*), lobelias (*Lobelia erinus*), moss rose (*Portulaca grandiflorum*), and annual phlox (*Phlox drummondii*).

• Some annuals are of tall or imposing growth habit so that you had better plant subordinate perennials next to them. Such annuals include castor bean (*Ricinus communis*), spider plant (*Cleome spinosa*), cosmos (*Cosmos bipinnatus*), common sunflowers (*Helianthus annuus*), Mexican sunflower (*Tithonia rotundiflora*), and tall tobacco plant (*Nicotiana sylvestris*). They can take over the function of specimens or lead perennials, serve as accents, or function in the middle or background as frames.

Practical Advantages

Combinations of perennials and annuals not only look pretty but they also have practical advantages.

• You can plant the perennial groups farther apart and fill in the holes with annuals. The perennials will thus grow more vigorously and need not be so quickly divided and replanted.

• The annual display can be done differently every year and should take account of the growth and space requirements of the perennials.

The idealized pictures of a long-flowering bed are best realized with annual flowers. They add to the border from July to frost with their long-lasting bloom.

GARDEN
TIPS AND TRICKS

Maintain Distance!

Make sure that the annuals don't crowd the perennials. The annuals and biennials must be kept at a certain distance from the perennials so that they don't deprive them of light and nutrients. If necessary, pull out annuals that are growing too thickly or spreading too much and enjoy them in a vase.

• You can use biennials to bridge the period in June in which the early-flowering perennials are already unsightly, the bulbs have finished, and the annuals aren't far enough along.

• Annuals, on the other hand, can create high points in the less lushly flowering months from July to September.

Different Locations

Annuals—even though they are only short-lived—have differing requirements. Some have similar needs to those of bedding perennials; others are rather more like the wild plants and need dry or damp locations.

In sunny borders of showy perennials with rich, fresh soil, most of the striking, colorful annuals are in the right place. Some, like annual larkspur (*Consolida ajacis*, *C. orientalis*, and *C. regalis*), Iceland poppies (*Papaver nudicaule*), or Canterbury bells (*Campanula medium*) have relatives among the bedding perennials (*Delphinium* and *Papaver*, see pages 238–239, as well as *Campanula*, see pages 238–239 and 244–245), with which they go well.

In light-poor beds in front of shrubs, which are also to some extent somewhat more damp, such biennals as honesty (*Lunaria annua*, see pages 266–267) thrive. Their wildflower-like character goes well with short-lived perennials like foxglove (*Digitalis purpurea*, see pages 244–245), columbine (*Aquilegia* hybrids, see pages 244–245), and dame's rocket (*Hesperis matronalis*). All these plants seed prolifically and thus contribute to the natural expression of the garden. Equally good for semishady beds are fuchsias (*Fuchsia* hybrids), busy Lizzy (*Impatiens walleriana*), and tuber-ous-rooted begonias (*Begonia* x *tuberhybrida*). But they should be planted rather solidly, for then they bring shining color into shady garden areas.

Near water, you can add to the bank perennials (see pages 278–279) monkey flower (*Mimulus* hybrids), prince's-feather (*Polygonum orientale*), and the tall *Impatiens glandulifera*.

In dry, stony soil, biennials like mullein (*Verbascum* species), evening primrose (*Oenothera biennis*), and Scotch thistle (*Onopordum acanthium*) thrive along with warmth-loving plants like needle palm (*Yucca fila-mentosa*), true thistles (*Eryngium* and *Echinops* species), sages (*Salvia* species), yarrow (*Achillea* species), and perennial grasses (see pages 270–271). Among the genuine annuals for these locations are included the Livingstone daisy (*Dorotheanthis bellidiformis*), flax (*Linum grandiflorum* and *L. usitatissimum*), cornflowers (*Centaurea cyanus*), and basket flower (*C. americana*).

DESIGNING WITH PLANTS
Planting Ideas for Vegetables and Herbs

Produce gardens are often regarded by gardeners as utterly different from ornamental gardens. Yet beauty and practicality need not be mutually exclusive. Colorful vegetable varieties and differing growth and leaf forms allow planting of very beautiful mixed cultures, whose effects you can enhance still more by planting herbs and flowers in between.

Planning Ahead
Consider ahead of time whether you want a purely practical garden, for example, according to the classic vegetable garden pattern (see Potager Gardens, pages 136–137) or a combination decorative and vegetable garden, or potager, in which only some rows of the bed are reserved for fruits, vegetables, and herbs. Vegetable beds should be in a fully sunny, protected place, and so laid out that they are comfortable to work (see pages 84–85 and 182–185).
When you are planning, take into consideration the visual impression you can create through successful enclosures of the bed. Charming effects are created by enclosures of boxwood (*Buxus sempervirens*) or everbearing strawberries (*Fragaria* var. *sempervirens*). Suitable here also are culinary herbs such as parsley and, above all, chives, which flower very attractively. The entire kitchen garden area can be surrounded by an edge planting of fruit trees, berry bushes, cutting flowers, and herbs.

Beautiful Vegetable Beds
In planning the vegetable garden, there is a whole list of factors, such as succession of culture, nutritional needs of the plants, and annual crop rotation (see pages 182–185), that must be taken into account. But parallel to this, design considerations should also have an influence (see pages 28–39 and 76–77), for the total picture is determined by growth habits and leaf forms as well as color combinations.
These planning criteria are put into operation in mixed-culture and hilled beds. Here are some examples of mixed plantings:
• Onions/leeks with their slender, blue-green leaves planted with wide-spreading, lush green head lettuce.
• Tall tomatoes over low lettuce or parsley.
• Feathery carrot foliage beside yellow-leaved mangel-wurzel.
An ever larger choice of different-colored varieties broadens the spectrum. So if there is green and blue kohlrabi, there is also white- and red-stemmed mangel-wurzel, green- and red-leaved lettuce, yellow and blue-violet beans, pink-violet and green cauliflower, or yellow tomatoes and zucchini. In addition, there are the differing green shades of vegetable and herb leaves. White to silver-gray, golden and purple shades of foliage are to be found in many herbs, for example the silver-leaved mugwort (*Artemisia vulgaris*) or red-leaved basil (*Ocimum basilicum*

Red-leaved head lettuce between Italian romaine lettuce.

Lanceolate black salsify leaves among filigreed dill.

Coarse cauliflower leaves beside delicate caraway greens.

"Dark Opal"). The garden scene gets still more colorful if you plant more strong dabs of color with annual flowers, like pot marigolds (*Calendula officinalis*), marigolds (*Tagetes* varieties), nasturtium (*Tropaeolum majus*), or the incomparable blue-flowering borage (*Borago officinalis*, see pages 302–303).

In the foreground, celery and red oak-leaf lettuce; behind, the decorative pyramids of bolted leaf lettuce.

Low, small-flowered marigolds between carrots.

Large red cabbage leaves between curly leaf lettuces.

Besides the colors, the various leaf shapes and structures also play a role in the vegetable garden—the delicate leaves of dill and fennel; curly, crenated, wavy, oaklike leaves of lettuce; robust and rough cabbage leaves. There are also imposing forms among the useful plants, like lovage (*Levisticum officinale*), common wormwood (*Artemisia absinthium*), common valerian (*Valeriana officinalis*), cardoon (*Cynara cardunculus*), or artichokes (*C. scolymus*). Pole beans or peas grown on pretty vine trellises or standards of currants or gooseberries are also focal points in the bed that are just as beautiful as they are practical.

Flower Meadows and Lawns

Whether you opt for a fragrant meadow of flowers or a hard-wearing lawn in your garden depends primarily on how you want to use the area. Meadows are not suitable for play areas; their sensitive flora must be protected. A lawn requires regular care, however, and unlike the meadow, looks attractive all year-round.

Flower Meadows

Flower meadows consist of wildflowers and grasses, with the composition of the plant stand depending on soil, climate, and moisture content. The drier and poorer a soil is, the more wildflower species are represented and, thus, the more flower variety and ecological value the meadow has. On the other hand, the grasses quickly lose their lush green with increasing temperatures. A meadow consists in large part of grasses. If their growth is too strong, the wildflowers will be crowded out or can't get a foothold at all. Whereas grass can form an even, thick carpet in a lawn, in the meadow, the plant stand should be as loose as possible, so that the flowers have a chance to germinate. Most wildflowers prefer poor situations; fertilizer and watering promote the growth of the grasses. You can't basically change the soil of your garden, but you can let the grasses "go hungry" to some degree.

Turning a lawn into a meadow. First, you reduce the mowing schedule to five times per season. Then discontinue watering and fertilizing. In the following years only mow once in summer (the first time not until the beginning of July because of ripening of the seeds) and once in the fall. If you let the mowings dry on the stubble, the seeds can fall out easily. It's best to scratch up the soil and the sod in some places so that the seeds falling there can germinate more easily. But you can also gather the seeds or buy them. Wildflower mixes that are suitable for the particular soil conditions are available from stores and catalogs. Make sure that they are species that will keep reseeding themselves, such as daisies (*Leucanthemum vulgare*), bellflowers (*Campanula patula* and *C. rotundiflora*), sages (*Salvia pratensis*), brown knapweed (*Centaurea jacea*), and cluster-headed and maiden pinks (*Dianthus carthusianorum* and *D. deltoides*). This is the only way a proper meadow can develop over time.

You reach the goal faster if you sow seeds of field flowers in flats or pots and then plant them in small groups—also, specialty nurseries raise wildflowers.

Flower meadow in a natural country garden.

Setout field flowers develop better. Conservation groups or a garden expert will know which species are best suited for your area.

Seeding a meadow from scratch. First, mix the soil with coarse sand in order to thin it. The seeding is done as for a lawn (see pages 166–167), only with much less seed (about 0.2 oz [5 g] per 10 sq ft [m²] instead of 0.7 to 1 oz [20 to 30 g]). Make sure when you get the seed from the store that it contains mostly weakly growing grasses like red fescue and sheep fescue (*Festuca rubra* and *F. ovina*) and less perennial ryegrass (*Lolium perenne*). In country areas, if you can get the cuttings from meadows, it can be thinly distributed over the area and the seeds allowed to fall out. It is important that there be gaps in the plant stand so that the flowers can hold out against the grasses and multiply. Wildflowers seed less uniformly than grasses, so a meadow develops much more slowly than a lawn.

Lawns under trees tend to become mossy and require special care.

Lawns

In contrast to the meadow, the lawn is kept short. Its grasses are not allowed to flower, so they grow bushier and form a thick carpet, which leaves no room for weeds. This ideal type of lawn is firm to the step, extraordinarily durable, and at the same time looks wonderfully fresh.

A beautiful lawn belongs in a cultivated garden with borders and ornamental beds. Roses, perennials, specimen plantings, and exotic plants of all kinds are most effective against the calming green. Also, a formal garden doesn't work without a lawn. Even in naturalized layouts, which are predestined for meadows, durable green areas are unavoidable, especially in near the house, where play and living take place. In more remote parts of the garden, you can turn areas of lawn into meadows. Around shrubs, in front of large trees, or in the area of a pond, it creates a special natural look.

The ideal type of lawn, the short-mowed, fine English decorative lawn, is certainly a feast for the eyes, but it is extremely time consuming to care for and very dependent on climate. In most gardens in our latitude, therefore, there is found the so-so utility lawn or the even coarser play and sports lawn, which is mowed weekly, fertilized at least twice a year, the thatch removed now and then (see pages 166–167), and watered as necessary. If it is mowed regularly, the airborne wild weed seeds hardly have a chance to get established, but the rosette-forming and creeping weeds, as well as those that form taproots, can spread excessively and completely overwhelm the grass in places where they grow into colonies. You must always hand pull white clover (*Trifolium repens*), milfoil (*Achillea millefolium*), plantain (*Plantago media*), and dandelion (*Taraxacum officinale*). Other weeds, on the other hand, loosen up a uniform lawn with their pretty flowers: English daisies (*Bellis perennis*), germander speedwell (*Veronica chamaedrys*), carpet bugleweed (*Ajuga reptans*), and self-heal (*Prunella vulgaris*). In addition, such a colorful weed garden is easy care, firm to the step, and very hard wearing.

Quiet spot amid a wild profusion of flowers.
In a natural garden, the plants are allowed to seed freely.

TYPES OF GARDENS

Garden types are garden dreams transformed into designs. Therefore, before you get into the details of planning, you need to establish for yourself which criteria are most important to you. You can rigorously adopt a particular garden type entirely or only make use of some elements of it. Gardens in which various garden styles are used in different areas can also be very interesting. Here are the most important considerations:

Use. This can be broken down into among ornamental, produce, and hobby gardens. Most gardeners want something of each.

Type of design. Here the formal (see pages 132–133) and the natural (see pages 134–135) gardens are at opposite poles from one another. A variant of the formal garden is the potager garden, which focuses on produce (see pages 136–137).

Environmentally conscious gardening is gaining more and more adherents. Anyone who wants to cultivate a garden in harmony with nature will put value on a multiplicity of species and natural methods, as found in the naturalized garden (see pages 134–135), the organic garden (see pages 138–139), and the potager garden (pages 136–137).

The location of a garden often recommends very specific design measures. Front yards (see pages 123–124) usually have a different task to perform from a garden behind the house. Anyone who has a garden on a slope (pages 140–141) must resort to other design strategies than for one on a flat piece of land.

The size. Have you the good fortune and the time to be able to manage a big garden? If so, you can realize almost all garden dreams. Many owners of small gardens have usually a wealth of dreams for their gardens, too. You will find tips for these on pages 124–129.

Formal garden—typical are the axial, symmetrical arrangements of the paths and beds. Clipped hedges and enclosures and arbors strengthen the impression of a concept of order that is maintained throughout.

Front Gardens

The front garden is the visiting card of the house: It should feel friendly and inviting and be an eye-catcher for passersby. Front gardens also determine the whole character of a street.

Basic Considerations

Here is a small checklist for you to follow in designing the front garden and choosing plants for it:

• Is the environment around the property urban or rural?

• What is the architecture of the house? The elements of the front garden should fit with it.

• How is the front garden going to be used—as a place to stop, an area to make a statement, or only as a driveway for cars and entry to the front door?

• Do you want protection from noise, dust, and view? If so, you can close off the front yard with walls or high hedges.

• Is the front yard small or large? Narrow front yards are better not enclosed with high fences, walls, or hedges. The area then appears even smaller and is very shaded.

• How are the soil, light, and climate conditions? Is the area predominantly in the sun or the shade? These are important criteria for the choice of plants.

• Can high levels of pollutants and salt (in winter) from the street be expected? If so, you must choose so-called "city" trees and plants.

Modern front garden with pebble beds and evergreen shrubs.

Design Tips

The fewer different kinds of materials you use, the more spacious and harmonious the garden will be (see Entrances and Entry Areas, pages 44–45).

The openly designed garden without fencing, walls, or enclosure with a high hedge looks spacious and inviting. If there is enough space at your disposal, you can put in a lawn area that is subdivided by a tree and groups of shrubbery. Also, pebble or gravel areas go well with modern buildings, with drought-tolerant grasses, gray-leaved plants, as well as irises and bulbs. With sandy, slightly acid soil you can establish a heath garden (see pages 108–109). Large found objects at corner points look very attractive and protect the plants

from straying cars. For privacy, provide a thicker planting directly by the house.

• An open front yard is especially nice when the grounds are large in area and have been graded.

• Open front yards are also highly recommended in settlements of row houses, where they allow more open space. Clear this with your neighbors in the planning stages.

With an enclosed front garden, walls, fences, or hedges protect against noise, dust, dogs, and curious looks. The smaller and narrower the surface, the lower and more transparent the enclosing element should be. Especially pretty here are grillwork fences of wood or metal that can be made green with climbing plants.

More tips.

• You can conjure more green into the garden with climbing plants that grow high up the front of the house.

• Plants in containers are always a friendly, welcoming greeting, and they can be as little space consuming as small trees for doormen. Suitable are evergreen shrubs formally pruned or standards of summer-flowering plants like roses or many Mediterranean tub plants.

• A larger tree lends a special accent to any front garden. With smaller areas, choose a tree with a small crown or a large shrub (see pages 204–207). Don't plant needle-leaved evergreens too close to the house, because they won't let light into the living areas in the winter.

Country front garden with central path that is lined with dahlia borders. Pear trees are espaliered against the house on both sides.

Very elegant, formally designed front garden with topiary evergreens and ivy growing around the front door.

Designing a Small Garden

Even the smallest garden can be made into a green oasis with a little imagination. The design of a small garden demands good planning, however, for it is a matter of using the tightly measured space skillfully and enlarging the design visually. Don't try to realize all the possible garden ideas. Limit yourself, and establish focuses. Only, thus, can the design appear spacious.

Tips for Planning
The usual design guidelines (see pages 28–39) are basically good for small gardens as well. However, although mistakes in planning and the wrong choice of plants don't always have massive consequences in large gardens, they strike the eye immediately in the small garden. Therefore, here are some special tips for small and/or narrow gardens:

Structure with deliberation. Divide into areas. Before you establish areas for sitting, playing, and planting, observe the light conditions. Flower and vegetable gardens need lots of sun; however, sitting and play areas can be placed in semishade.

Subdivide horizontally. With very narrow plots, avoid anything that emphasizes the length. Use room dividers (see drawings at right as well as on pages 32–33) to divide the garden into the different areas desired.

Soil grading. Even small differences in height make small gardens seem larger. For example, there can be sunken sitting areas or the piling up of a low hill. Also, land that slopes slightly toward the edge of the property increases the plot visually.

Centrally laid-out small garden with a circular path.

Path of natural stone slabs.   *Path with clinker bricks.*

Pathways. Paths are particularly important space dividing elements and, furthermore, they make it possible to experience the garden. Paths that wander around through taller plantings create a certain suspense in the beholder as to how it might go around the bend. For the garden lover, they also create an opportunty to accent these small, secluded niches and, thus, to provide for ever new impressions. However, you should avoid having a path that is too winding. It tempts people to shorten it by crossing the lawn or cutting across the planting. Also, don't make the path too broad and dominant. In small gardens, narrow walks or simple paths of stepping-stones fit in better.

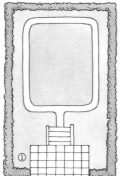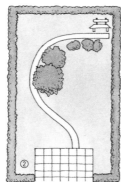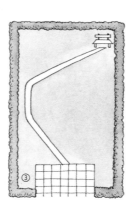

Pathways for Small Gardens
① Formal design with circular path that can be lined with perennial plantings. Central, spacious layout (see photo above).
② Natural design with pathway curving around groups of shrubs, which only opens up later with the view from the bench.
③ Modern design with a slightly diagonal pathway. The eye is, thus, directed to different areas and sides of the garden.

Designing to Make the Garden Larger and More Livable
A small garden can radiate very great intimacy and possess the atmosphere of a living room in green.
Choose uniform materials. Provide for a harmonious transition from inside to outside by keeping materials and furniture as homogeneous and matching as possible.

Small garden laid out in a circle, with formal elements like shaped boxwood, bay trees, and a roundel in the middle.

Illuminate the surroundings. The garden can also be experienced as a living space at night by skillful staging with light, perhaps through spotlighting trees, small plant groups, or light effects on a garden pond.

Design the surroundings as a backdrop. Whether it is the wall of the house itself or a wall around the garden— you can clothe both in green with climbing plants and, thus, produce the impression that the green reaches much farther.

Provide some surprises. The garden seems bigger if it can't all be taken in at one glance. A narrowing with a gatelike situation or even a low planting leaves the eye uncertain about the actual size proportions of the garden. Above all the paths (see pages 46–47) have an important function here. The garden should only gradually reveal all its details as one wanders through it.

Create focal points and illusions. An arbor or sculpture at the end of a long, narrow garden gives the eye the illusion of closeness. An arch shortly before the property line allows conjecture that it goes on farther yet behind it. A curved mirror on a wall creates the illusion of a passageway.

Pergola As Space Divider

It creates height and depth in the garden, clearly separates different parts of the garden from one another, yet possesses a large measure of transparency (see photo, page 33).

Interrupted Clipped Hedge As Space Divider

This forms a denser boundary than a pergola but still guarantees some views. It lends the garden special intimacy but can easily look too massive.

Espaliered Fruit Trees As a Space Divider

Transparent and productive dividing walls. Especially beautiful combined with plantings of roses and clematis.

Plant Ideas for Small Gardens

There are certain special things about planting the small garden. Above all, make sure that the plants don't entirely overshadow the small space that you have. A tree from a neighbor's garden can also serve as a pretty backdrop.

Shrubs for Small Gardens

In general, light deciduous shrubs are better in small gardens than dark conifers. Find out before you buy shrubs at the nursery about the ultimate height and spread. In very small gardens, you should avoid an ornamental tree by the house or large groups of woody plants altogether and instead only plant a few large shrubs. Smaller shrubs are also good screens when they are planted close to the house.

<u>Deciduous and needle-leaved shrubs</u> (see pages 102–103 as well as 202–215). Basically, you should plant more deciduous shrubs than needle-leaved shrubs in small gardens. However, if dwarf forms or hedges are used, conifers give permanent structure even in winter. A good compromise is offered by the loose-growing broad-leaved evergreens, like hollies (*Ilex* species/varieties), boxwood (*Buxus sempervirens*), common privet (*Ligustrum ovalifolium*), and cherry laurel (*Prunus laurocerasus*). But they can also be hard pruned (and thus kept small), without losing their attractiveness and then form beautiful contrasts with the free-growing plants.

<u>Climbing plants</u> (see pages 216–221). You achieve space effects best in small gardens with clipped hedges and climbing plants. These also find places to live in narrow bedding strips or planted as points in narrow spaces. Climbing on trellises or vine frames, they emphasize height the way trees do but without reaching their size. On gateways, arches, pergolas, and arbors and on (unattractive) walls, fences or wires, they form charming motifs, offer protection, and separate garden parts from one another. They provide accents as solitary plantings on trellises, pillars, or pyramids in low beds. Climbing plants can also ramble through old trees and lend them new aesthetic charm. Suitable for this are climbing roses (see pages 224–225), which rest on the branches, but also climbing hydrangea (*Hydrangea petiolaris*), fallopia (*Fallopia aubertii*), ivy (*Hedera helix*), and certain *Clematis* species.

<u>Hedges</u> (see pages 80–81 and 82–83). You should avoid free-growing hedges in the small garden; they take up too much space. For privacy, a narrow pruned hedge serves best or a fence clothed with green. Individual ornamental shrubs (see pages 208–211) are very charming for this purpose. If you want a loose divider, you can fall back on small shrubs like barberry (*Berberis* species), hydrangeas (*Hydrangea macrophylla*,

Space is left for sitting when the flowers climb up. Here yellow roses,

Small atrium garden with frothy wisteria bloom.

Small sitting area under roses climbing on a pergola.

see pages 210–211), and flowering quince (*Chaenomeles* hybrids, see pages 208–209), or choose roses, for example, *Rosa rugosa* varieties. Narrow clipped hedges of evergreen and summer green as well as flowering shrubs are good as a shield from the street and characteristically more space saving than natural-

Fruit trees (see pages 280–289) are particularly well suited to the small garden. For example, there are apples and pears in numerous miniature forms, from plants specially suitable for tubs on stems that don't grow any taller than 8 ft (2.5 m) to bush forms that also can be used as small ornamental trees by the house or as specimen plantings in the lawn. Sour cherries (*Prunus cerasus*), plum trees (*Prunus domestica*) and common quince (*Cydonia oblonga*) also remain relatively small. Berries, like currants (*Ribes rubrum* and *R. nigrum* hybrids) and gooseberries (*R. uva-crispa* var. *sativum*), can also be maintained as shrubs, hedges, and standards in ornamental and vegetable gardens.

Flowers for Small Gardens

Perennials, too, as well as annuals and biennials can be variously planted in small gardens.

Perennials (see pages 232–247). Placed singly or in groups in open space or in front of hedges and walls, perennials and grasses can to some extent take over the structuring function of shrubs in small gardens. Some perennials are also good for boundaries within the garden, perhaps tall *Phlox paniculata* hybrids, rudbeckias (*Rudbeckia* species/varieties), red-hot pokers (*Kniphofia* hybrids), and iris (*Iris germanica* and *I. siberica*). Low shrubs are also good as lawn substitutes.

Spring and summer flowers (see pages 249–267). For small ornamental beds, a place is usually found right by the house. There you can best watch the spring flowers.

Small strip beds with climbing plants and dwarf shrubs can be ideally complemented with perennial, annual, or biennial summer flowers as well as with bulbs and corms, and changed to fit the season. Annual summer flowers and climbers are also good as room dividers.

Lawns

A well-groomed green ornamental lawn or flower-and-herb lawn that is kept short provides the impression of broad area in small gardens and also here offers numerous possibilities for use. It looks particularly spacious when the lawn almost fills the garden and is only framed by a thin border planting. On the other hand, a small piece of lawn surrounded by natural stones or bricks also serves as a resting point or decorative element or as an eye-catcher.

Planted pots, tubs, troughs, and dishes often offer the

pipe vine, and honeysuckle on a large pergola.

Pretty and useful—gooseberry is standard among the red cabbages.

Flowers above and below—rose tree and campanulas.

shaped plantings. Dark conifer hedges, for example, of yew (*Taxus* species) should only reach to about eye level in order not to narrow the garden area too much visually and produce unnecessary shade. Hedges as room dividers can also be provided with gates and windows (see drawing, page 125).

(see drawing, page 125).

> ### GARDEN
> #### TIPS AND TRICKS
>
> ##### Plantings for Small Ponds and Pools
> *Even in small gardens, you needn't do without water. But the pool should be in a size proportional to the garden. Because water plants quickly grow rampant, a sparse planting is recommended: a single water lily, perhaps the pygmy water lily (Nymphaea tetragona), or small cattails (Typha minima and T. stenophylla) are already enough. (See Water Plants, pages 276–277.)*

Container Gardens

Colorfully mixed plants in pots as a terrace edging.

A round plant stand for plants in small to medium-size containers.

Plant stands are the tip-off for small-scale plant collections. Quarter sections offer the ideal solution for corners of small terraces and balconies; semicircular sections are beautiful for shelves to nestle against walls. The round plant stand pictured above is an enchanting focal point at a crossing of paths or in the middle of a bed or a lawn. Most plant stands have three levels and can also be very charming with hanging or climbing plants in containers.

Flower arrangement—tone-on-tone creates a still life.

only chance to design with plants in very crowded locations or places with impermeable soil. They can be focal points, space dividers, and screens, or lively color accents in green. Also plant collections can be put into individual pots, which, placed closely together, fill out a place in the garden or on the terrace.

What Plants Are Suitable?

You can put almost all plants into containers. But with shrubs, choose the forms that remain small.
• Spring and summer flowers provide for seasonal changes of plantings.
• Tub plants decorate the garden from May to October; after that, you must provide them with frost-free winter quarters in the house.
• Produce plants—above all herbs and vegetables, strawberries, or small fruit trees.
• Water plants and other long-lasting perennials, most of which, however, cannot survive the winter outside.
• Specimen shrubs that remain small—roses, ornamentals, broad-leaved evergreens, and conifers.
• Topiary—clipped boxwood (*Buxus* species), yew (*Taxus* species), and privet (*Ligustrum* species).

What Containers Are Suitable?

It's important that you consider ahead of time whether the materials of your choice are winter-proof. The containers should also go with the surroundings and harmonize with the plants in material, form, and scale.
Clay containers (terra-cotta) look very natural and can be well integrated into plantings. Caution: Not all are fired hard enough to be winter-proof!
Stoneware and ceramics. Among these are also the classic glazed Chinese pots. Watch out for frost hardiness here, too.

Mediterranean flair with tub plants on the terrace.

Flowers in a container as a welcoming greeting at the entrance.

Natural and artificial stone troughs, perhaps old feeding troughs of granite or sandstone, should receive a permanent location, because they are very heavy.

Wood is a natural material that can be used in numerous ways. Besides simple boxes, there are more expensive expressions in oak that are considerably more durable. Old wooden barrels are also good for water plants; white-lacquered square containers (Versailles tubs) fit especially well into formal gardens.

Wicker baskets are a charming variant for the natural garden. However, they only last for a few years and must be overwintered in the house.

Plastic and cement containers can be colorfully painted. They are an inexpensive alternative.

Found objects, such as an old washtub, can also serve as plant containers. They must only be provided with drainage or a water overflow into the ground.

Set Out Plant Tubs—But Where?

Plant containers can be used in many places.

• In entryways—the way into the house can be lined with a row of matching containers. A front door is framed when containers are placed at the left and right.

• The proper location for planted tubs is the terrace. But a sunny sitting area in the garden or a set of steps are also suitable for pot gardens.

• You can lend color to shady spots with pot plants like fuchsias (*Fuchsia* species/varieties), hydrangeas (*Hydrangea* species/varieties), or tuberous-rooted begonias (*Begonia x tuberhybrida*).

• Until a garden is grown up, movable vine and moss walls can serve as screens for privacy. Or you can hide bare spots with a planted container.

• It is practical to place containers with cooking herbs next to the house or terrace.

• The planted tub becomes a focal point in a small spot, at a path crossing or a pond.

Eye-catcher and rich harvest—strawberry jar with strawberries.

Strawberry jars are available at garden centers in different sizes. They are filled with good potting soil, and you can plant strawberries or herbs in their pockets or hanging balcony plants or annuals that stay small. Colorfully planted jars can be placed as gay color accents in green vegetable or herb beds, in front of semishady ivied walls, or on terraces and balconies.

Gardens for Children

Even if the garden is small, insofar as possible, it should be arranged for the needs of the children. In addition, the children can become comfortable with nature by dealing with plants and animals at play.

Planning a "Children's Garden"
The various developmental phases of the children and youths must be taken into consideration when planning a garden that is appropriate for children.
• At first, a sandbox close to the house is enough, because children must always remain under supervision.
• Somewhat later, you should consider your children's need to run about. A hard-wearing grass surface that remains observable from the house is important now.
• The older ones need chances to withdraw: secret wild corners, niches, hideaways, or underbrush for hiding and watching.
Divide the garden in such a way that there is enough room left for children's play. Movable materials of any kind (stones, pebbles, sand, pieces of wood and boards) are interesting play materials from which new objects can be produced over and over. Free space for children can also be created by shaping the surfaces and with trees, shrubs, and hedges.
At primary school age, many children develop the desire for a garden of their own, which they then cultivate with devotion and harvest with excitement. Others want a pet; space must be created for that, too.

Tree house with a rope ladder and sturdy seating.

Child's world in the garden with a little house and sandbox.

What's on the Wish List
Play equipment should be many sided, which permits group play and promotes creativity.
• Sandboxes, wading pools, and crawling meadows for small children belong in the immediate proximity to the house and shouldn't be in the blazing sun.

• Lawns or mowed fields invite ball playing or romping.
• A courtyard with a smooth, hard surface is good for roller skating and ball playing.
• Water and sand offer wonderful opportunities for mud pies and building. The sand should be cohesive (unwashed).
• Water in the garden is fascinating at any age: The palette ranges from wading pools and hose to streamlets and homemade water lines to the fishpond. Wastage of expensive utility water can be limited by such devices as closable supply lines or ones that stop automatically.
• Children particularly enjoy climbing. However, trees must be at least 10 years old and possess corresponding sturdiness before they are good for that. But jungle gyms can also be built and covered with growing things. Or, for example, the branches of willows can be so woven together that after a few years, stable walls of branches develop.
• Swings, seesaws, and slides are also popular play equipment. Swings can be fastened to trees, planks are good for seesaws, and tree trunks are good for balancing.

A stable swing in front of a magical area of the garden. Important for safety—a soft lawn under the swing area.

• Children also passionately desire tree houses, arbors, and huts. Huts and tents, especially, can be easily made by children themselves of wood, for example, but also of dirt (best under supervision). Huts of shrubs can be made by anyone. Wild shrubs (without stickers and thorns) are planted at intervals of 20 in (50 cm) in a circle, rectangle, or oval. The diameter should be about 8 to 10 ft (2.5–3 m). At one point, an opening is left as an entrance. The next year, the walls are already beginning to close.

A weeping elm, after some time, also creates dense foliage right down to the ground. Willow works faster as a living building material. When the flexible whips have reached the necessary height, they can be fastened together at the top and at the sides.

Also, bamboo is a living and robust material that tolerates much. A bamboo mini-forest—a few plants of the noninvasive *Sinarundinaria nitida* are enough— seems like a jungle to children.

Densely leaf-covered simple wooden frames are equally attractive for grown-ups and children alike; these can be covered with Dutchman's pipe (*Aristolochia macro-*

phylla) or woodbine (*Parthenocissus quinquefolia*).
• At a fireplace—the grilling place for the family, laid out in the form of a camp fireplace—children learn how to handle fire. Make sure that the place is not located under trees nor in the vicinity of inflammable objects.

Security for Children
Ban all poisonous plants from the garden for as long as it takes until you are certain your children recognize these dangers. Harmless plants also are often not suitable for consumption. They can form the connecting link from which children learn which plants to avoid. Even shallow water should be closed off by a fence that allows entry only under supervision and can later be removed again. As much as possible, round off corners and edges on play equipment, stairs, and landings. Don't fail to lock away all garden equipment, fertilizers, and pesticides out of reach of children (see page 187).

TYPES OF GARDENS
Formal Gardens

More or less severely formally designed gardens and classical elements are experiencing a renaissance today. With their unambiguous, architectectural structures, they are particularly suitable for small plots. Basically, the recognized design principles (see pages 29–39) apply here also. Creation of spaces ("rooms") is important, as are the framing of the garden and its subdivisions and the proper proportions of the individual elements to one another. You should take special notice of these principles of order in formal gardens as in small ones, for they preserve the garden from excess and fussiness.

Elements of Style in Formal Gardens

Geometry and symmetry characterize the formally designed garden. These include the classical style elements, which can be used singly in open design layouts as well. It is through a combination of the elements and their graphic arrangement that a formal garden gains its typical character, its architectural ground plan. This can be timelessly classic, elaborate, or contemporary.

• The framework of the garden is usually created by green walls, such as walls, fences, or clipped hedges.
• The garden space itself is again divided by clipped hedges or room dividers like trellises or arbors. High elements separate individual garden parts; low structures divide the surface areas.
• Strictly defined paths contribute to the division. They form geometric patterns or axes of symmetry.
• Essential are graphic elements, like trees clipped to geometric shapes, gates, pyramids, tree-form plants, and sculptures. They all contribute to the further vertical structuring of the garden.
• Lawns are only used in the form of closely mowed, well-groomed ornamental greens.
• Paths and beds receive distinct outlines of boxwood (*Buxus sempervirens*), flower borders, or strips of lawn.
• Focal points—perhaps round or rectangular ornamental ponds, plant containers, sculptures, or a pavilion—are placed centrally at the end of axes and vistas but are also arranged symmetrically or according to geometric basic patterns.
• Shrubs, primarily yew (*Taxus* species) and box, are arranged in rows and/or pruned into shapes.
• Characteristic of formal gardens are distant frameworks of vines as latticework walls (treillage).
• Benches and bowers are essential and are treated like the above-mentioned focal points.
• Ornamental decorative beds with difficult geometric patterns perfect the graphic austerity. However, they require a tremendous amount of effort.

Symmetrically laid-out Renaissance garden with boxwood enclosures.

Modern, formal garden with clipped shrubs.

Opportunities for Variation

The severe basic plan of a formal garden can, however, leave enough play for personal preferences and seasonal accents. You can complement the classic, ageless, and harmonious lines of the formal garden throughout with nostalgic furnishings like sculptures or with topiary

Formal order always proves its value in the herb garden with its small-leaved, often untidily growing plants.

Small formal garden with ornamental bed.

Open bed design with structuring globes of boxwood.

shrubs (primarily box or yew) clipped into shapes such as animals, spheres, or cones. Severe, geometric, enclosed beds can be planted with lush, colorful flowers. It is especially pretty when the plants are allowed to develop freely and quickly spill over the severe form.

Free plantings often gain in structure if they are combined with formal elements (like boxwood spheres or cones, see photo above).

Advantage: In winter, when the largest part of the plant structure is missing, the graphic structures become prominent and give shape to the garden scene.

Natural or Wild Gardens

For a long time, a natural garden was considered nothing more than neglected, but more and more it is regarded as a garden that is in harmony with nature. Meanwhile, many garden owners have discovered the aesthetic charm of a natural garden. Earlier, it was often only plants that were attractive and carefree that were planted. The greatly increased awareness in recent years of ecological interdependency has led to sensible handling of plants and animals in the garden areas as well. Anyone who gardens according to nature makes his or her own small contribution to the great balance of nature, but it takes much patience. The gardener must permit spontaneous developments and intervene to control only now and then. Therefore, it is extremely important to lay out a natural garden according to the landscape and to choose plants appropriate for their locations.

Designing a Natural Garden

Natural gardens should also be consciously designed (see pages 28–39). However, the individual elements and the choice of plants is more strongly oriented toward the natural. Much time passes between the new installation and the mature natural garden. An older garden also only changes into a naturalized garden very slowly. Here, however, it's imperative to use the plants on hand and not thin out the growth unnecessarily.

It goes without saying that in a natural garden, no chemical pesticides are used, if possible. But anyone who uses mostly native plants will scarcely need such radical cures.

<u>Create living areas and niches.</u> The natural garden lives through an equilibrium between plants and animals. This only succeeds when the variety of species is increased. Create living spaces and niches for animals. Examples of small biotopes are dry walls (see pages 50–51), flower meadows (see page 118), or natural ponds (see pages 62–63). Transitional areas like marshy zones or edges of woods with their margin communities are particularly valuable ecologically.

<u>Make the garden accessible.</u> So that animals can wander in and wander out of your garden, the boundaries with the neighborhood should be "porous." Therefore, plant natural hedges (see pages 82–83) or choose fencing of wire or wood that is suitable as a framework for climbing plants.

<u>Use native plants.</u> In a natural garden, it is primarily native plants that are used, which serve as sources of food and living areas for the small animals, birds, and insects. Many insects of course also like to feed on exotic flowers, but for their developmental processes, they need very particular wild plants.

The already existing plants in a garden rarely correspond to the ideal picture of a natural garden. But for a beginning, it's enough if you merely set out some wild plants at particular spots in the garden and let them spread. On the other hand, in beds and borders, you can replace the highly hybridized, often sterile species with wild forms that produce nectar, fruits, and seeds, and integrate as many wild perennials as possible into all areas of the garden. There is an appropriate plant

Spring meadow with narcissi and lady's-smock.

Natural pond with adjacent meadow and yellow flags.

Meadow Environments and Flower Lawns

Meadows and flower lawns are sumptuous areas for bees and insects because they contain great diversity of wild plants. Ideal for this purpose are old (fruit) trees or tall native shrubs. These offer optimal conditions for birds and insects.

Water Environments

Water is one of the most important elements of life for animals and plants. Plant and animal diversity is greatest in and around water. A natural garden should definitely contain water—in a pond or at least in a watering spot for birds, insects, and small animals (see pages 64–65).

species for every possible living space in the natural garden: shade-tolerant plants (see pages 244–245), also many bulbs and corms (see pages 112–113 and 242–243) for the wooded areas, sunny and dry-loving vegetation for rock gardens (see pages 106–107), as well as plants for moist zones by the water (see pages 276–277). Each of these plant communities attracts particular animal inhabitants.

Use natural materials. Above all, when creating a new natural garden, only use natural materials like wood, brick, and natural stone. Solid surfaces for sitting areas or paths must be porous to maintain the soil life underneath.

Care of the Natural Garden

A natural and unrestrictedly laid-out garden requires particularly empathetic—but not, therefore, more time consuming—care. You need to pay attention to certain things so that the garden can develop its natural character. Don't cut out every dead branch right away; leave stems that have gone to seed and dry stalks standing. Also, let the leaves stay on the ground to serve as food and shelter for insects. Included in the special care of natural gardens are gentle loosening of the soil (see pages 150–151), mulching (see pages 160–161), and organic fertilizing (see pages 156–159). Don't use any chemical pesticides, but promote useful helpers like birds and insects with provisions for nesting, birdbaths, and abundant places for feeding and sheltering (see pages 188–189).

Enchanting wild niche with flowering dog rose.

Natural garden and clothesline in one.

Spring at the woods' edge with mountain ash and wild hyacinths.

Dry Walls and Brush Piles

Lizards enjoy the heat-storing stones, and the spaces in between offer habitats for wild bees and other insects. Dead wood and stacked up brush also offer hiding places and sources of food for many creatures in the garden.

Hedge Environments

If possible, the lot should be partly or entirely enclosed by an unpruned hedge (pages 82–83). Flowers, wild fruit, brambles, and dense growth offer a habitat to birds and small mammals. A dense hedge also has a favorable effect on the climate in the garden.

Potager Gardens

The potager, a garden type that developed from the medieval cloister garden, is the original form of garden. It is very popular again today, for in it, the traditional garden culture can be joined with modern ecological philosophical ideas. Colorful potager gardens are once again not just found in the country. The basic principles of this garden form—combining the beautiful with the useful and not too strictly separating ornamental and produce plants—can ideally be translated even to small city plots. The classic defined bed shape is particularly suitable here. Even front yards or a part of the garden can be arranged in this fashion.

Elements of the Potager

A potager is characterized above all by clear divisions made by paths and simple materials. The paths usually consist of pebbles, bricks, or paving. The center of the garden is often emphasized with a focal point (see drawing, bottom left). Also typical are low enclosures of the beds (see drawing, top left). They provide calm and order among all the colorful, constantly changing plant communities within the beds. In potagers, every corner is utilized meaningfully.

• Simple wire fencing can be covered with peas and beans or sweet peas. The enclosure of a potager always consists of simple materials; usually it is a fence of vertical wooden slats (picket fence). Also, hedges fit well in the potager. They serve as protection from sight and wind; however, they need more space than fences.

Colorful riot of flowers, vegetables, and herbs—mark of a country garden

Cross Shape

The clear axial division of the produce garden is particularly emphasized by low hedging, for instance, of boxwood (which is regularly pruned and also gives structure to the garden in winter) or of annuals.

Cross Shape with Roundel

The traditional potager is laid out in cross shape. The crossing of the paths at the center is often emphasized by a fountain or a practical dipping well. But a roundel, perhaps planted with roses, can supply this central point.

Long-flowering catmint.

Orderly slab pathway.

• Roses, blackberries, or other climbing plants can be trained on pergolas, for instance, at the entrance, or can frame a bench or a corner sitting area. A densely covered arbor supplies welcome shade.
• Berry bushes or standards and small espaliered fruit trees can border a path or a fence and be underplanted with

Dovecote among the roses.

Peonies within a boxwood edging.

Typical Potager Flowers

Particular plants underlne the special lush character of the potager.

Enclosures. Boxwood (*Buxus sempervirens*), lavender (*Lavandula angustifolia*), golden carpet (*Sedum acre*), lavender cotton (*Santolina chamaecyparissus*), and ever-bearing strawberries (*Fragaria vesca* var. *semperiflorens*).

Typical shrubs. Boxwood, European elderberry (*Sambucus nigra*), French hydrangea (*Hydrangea macrophylla*), lilac (*Syringa vulgaris*), honeysuckle (*Lonicera* species), and roses (primarily Centifolia, *Rosa gallica*, and Damask roses).

Perennials. Peonies (*Paeonia officinalis* and *P. lactiflora*), foxgloves (*Digitalis* varieties), delphiniums (*Delphinium* species/hybrids), phlox (*Phlox paniculata* hybrids), bleeding hearts (*Dicentra spectabilis*), poppies (*Papaver orientale*), *Aster* species/varieties, yarrow (*Achillea* varieties), iris (*Iris barbata* groups), catmint (*Nepeta faassenii*), and rudbeckias (*Rudbeckia fulgida*).

Annuals and biennials. Tree mallow (*Lavatera trimestris*), snapdragons (*Antirrhinum majus*), marigolds (*Tagetes* hybrids), pot marigold (*Calendula officinalis*), sunflowers (*Helianthus annuus*), hollyhocks (*Alcea rosea*), sweet William (*Dianthus barbatus*), English wallflowers (*Chieranthus cheiri*), pansies (*Viola* x *wittrockiana*), forget-me-nots (*Myosotis sylvatica*), sweet peas (*Lathyrus odoratus*), zinnias (*Zinnia elegans*), and nasturtiums (*Tropaeolum* hybrids).

Bulbs and corms. Dahlias (*Dahlia* varieties), gladiolas (*Gladiolus* hybrids), lilies (*Lilium* species/varieties), crown imperials (*Fritillaria* species/varieties), and narcissi (*Narcissus* species/varieties).

A must in the vegetable garden—a shady spot with a basket.

herbs and annuals. They are also good as space dividers.
• Typical of the potager is the close association of lush, showy perennials and simple plants with a wild character. Herbs and aromatic plants, or fragrant and medicinal plants, have always been a part of this type of garden.

Entry Variation with 2 Beds

The enclosed ornamental beds can lead to a lawn or to areas planted with ground covers. The ornamental plantings look particularly effective with closely mowed lawns.

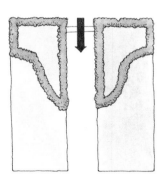

Entry Variation with 4 Beds

Beds are laid out symmetrically to the main path axis. A subdivision and enclosure with small side paths loosens up the design and emphasizes the borders.

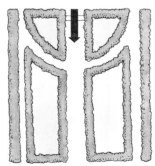

Organic Gardens

In recent years, biological and ecological considerations have gained importance in many areas and so also in garden management. Anyone who wants to cultivate a garden organically must have some exact information about natural processes and regulatory cycles. For in the organic garden, it is imperative to imitate nature and its regulatory measures, with the larger goal of reaching an ecological balance. The organic gardener does not seek to get the last drop out of the soil with "the art of artificial fertilizing." He or she gives soil and plants their appropriate requirements and receives in return soil that is fruitful over the long term, healthy plants, and a good harvest. However, until this harmony among soil, plants, and creatures has been reinstated, you need patience, for nature cannot regenerate itself from one day to the next. Keep at it consistently with natural methods, even if you have small setbacks.

Design of an Organic Garden

Any garden can be cultivated organically. Whether it is a natural garden or a formal one, ornamental or produce garden—the design is up to you. However, usually an organic garden is a produce garden in which the object is growing healthy and pesticide-free fruit and vegetables.

An organic garden need by no means appear untidy. It can be just as beautifully arranged as any other garden—perhaps with a (protective) enclosure of clipped box and with lushly colored flower borders, between which herbs, berries, and vegetables feel quite comfortable. Admittedly—the beds that have been mulched for the protection of the soil are perhaps an uncommon sight at first, but they correspond to the model of nature, where more fruitful soil is always covered with a protective layer of living and dead plants. An unavoidable element of any organic garden is the compost pile (see page 163), where the remains of plants are collected and recycled.

Cribbed from nature, too, is the large variety of plants in a narrow space. Not only is it pretty to look at, but it also promotes the health of the plants. Thus, hill and raised beds (see page 183) or herb spirals also fit into the organic garden.

Free-growing hedges of native wild shrubs, dry walls, and ponds offer additional living areas for plants and beneficial insects and animals. Thus, the ecological variety is guaranteed—the first prerequisite for reaching a biological equilibrium and a balanced relationship between damaging and beneficial insects.

Pathways to the Organic Garden

To convert an established garden into an organic garden requires time: Soil that has leached out through mono-

Beautiful and ecological. Multiplicity of fruit and colorful vegetables plante

culture and synthetic fertilizers needs years to regenerate itself. Don't be discouraged by bad harvests and invasions of pests! For the conversion to organic gardening, there are certain criteria to observe.

Soil care (see pages 150–151. The soil is the basis for the fruitfulness of the plants. Its careful maintenance and improvement with natural means forms the basis for all the gardening activities.

First, have the soil tested (see pages 148–149) to determine the type of soil, nutrient content, pH value, as well as the amount of humus, biological activity, and possible heavy metal content. With heavy, compacted soil, you should provide for a deep-reaching loosening of the compacted subsoil but without mixing in the topsoil. With light, sandy soils, it's usually enough to loosen it with a spading fork or cultivator. Then, enrich the topsoil somewhat with organic substances (compost, well-rotted manure, organic fertilizer, bone meal, and seaweed with lime).

Green manures and mulches (see pages 160–161). It is advisable to sow a green manure at the beginning or the end of the new gardening season. There are various

a small space in mixed culture.

possible plants (see page 161) appropriate to the season, depending on the type of soil . With green manure, you can loosen heavy soils or enrich thin soils with organic material so that gradually the soil organisms become activated and guarantee regular water and air control as well as a natural provision of nutrients for the plants. Thus, in the organic garden, the bare soil is never left lying exposed. Planted beds also receive an additional mulch layer of leaves, straw, or dried grass cuttings, which keeps the soil from drying out or becoming muddy and protects it from frost. In this way, too, the soil organisms are protected.

Composting (see pages 162–163). The return of all the appropriate organic materials used in the house and garden and their recycling into compost is a must in organic gardening. The microorganisms in the soil, which supply a constant source of nutrients for the plants through their excretions, are nurtured by the compost. So, the organic gardener gives back to the soil what was harvested from it somewhere else. You can also compost the waste products from agriculture, gardening, and the forest. But then, be careful that they contain no pollutants.

Fertilizing. Compost, green manures, and other organic fertilizers (see pages 156–157) are not, like synthetic fertilizers, taken up directly by the plants. They support the plant growth by feeding the soil organisms. These make the nutrients available to the plants as they need them. Where necessary, the organic gardener helps with additional preparations—besides the organic fertilizers, these are primarily all plant extracts (liquid manures and teas) and natural minerals (bone meal, blood meal, and seaweed preparations).

Mixed culture and crop rotation (see pages 182–183). These agricultural practices are important elements of organic gardening. The gardener uses them to allow plants to withdraw different strong nutrients from the soil.

• In crop rotation, plants that are weak and heavy feeders are cultivated in turn in order not to deplete the soil of one element.

• In mixed culture, as in nature's mode, various plants are cultivated next to each other and mutually protect and promote one another through their metabolic products (secretions from leaves, flowers, roots) or shield one another from pests. For example, carrots and onions planted next to each other keep onion and carrot flies away from each other. The examples on pages 116–117 show how beautifully you can design, even with vegetable plants.

Both methods can also be combined. In any case, precise planning is required. The tables on pages 183 and 185 will help you with vegetable growing.

Poison-free plant protection. Healthy soil, good locations, and careful cultivation make plants more resistant and promote their defensive power against pests. Make sure when you buy them that the plants are healthy! And there is quite a lot that can be done for prevention. There are liquid manures and teas for pests and fungus diseases (see page 189) and for the general strengthening of the plants (see page 158). A green manure with marigold or cure mixtures (specialty store) can help against tired soil and nematodes. Plant variety in the garden, that is, both flowers and wild shrubs, good nurture, and care of the plants have proven to be preventive measures to keep pests and disease in check. Above all, it is imperative to promote the beneficial insects and animals and to constantly observe the plantings. In emergencies, you can resort to natural and mechanical defenses (see pages 186–187). Some plants (see page 189), such as pot marigolds (*Calendula officinalis*) and marigolds (*Tagetes erecta*) help against tired soil, drive out nematodes— and, beyond this, look very beautiful.

Gardens on a Slope

Methods of Grading and Planting Slopes

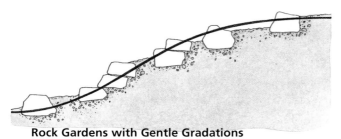

Rock Gardens with Gentle Gradations
To do this, establish the grade with stone blocks of different sizes and heights. They serve for planting and maintenance and also as stepping-stones. These variations work particularly well with rocks that are already deeply embedded. It is the ideal setting for a rock garden. Also very charming in such a garden is a small stream with a waterfall that ends in a small pond below.
Important: Always lay the stones so they rest on the the broadest side.

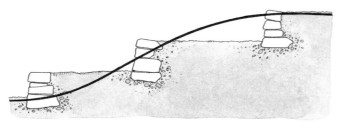

Beds with Slight Terracing
A slope can also be terraced with several small walls. In this way, beds are created for a multitude of plants: shrubs, roses, perennials, or vegetables. You can also errect several low steps of this sort yourself without the help of skilled labor.

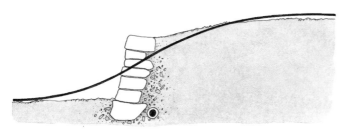

Two Levels with a Supporting Wall
A third variant is to have a single high supporting wall, which creates two almost-level surfaces. For a true dry wall (see pages 50–51), it should not be higher than 39 in (1 m). With a height of more than 32 in (81 cm), it is advisable to provide the wall with a concrete foundation and drainage pipe for safety's sake. For higher levels of landscape grading, you should always hire a professional.

Designing a sloping plot is usually relatively cost intensive and difficult, but it also offers additional charm and many opportunities to employ design imagination. Gardens on a slope can offer a specially beautiful sight if the view from living areas and the terrace look onto a slope rising opposite. On the other hand, if the arc falls under the level of the house, the view sweeps out over a part of the garden—depending on the steepness of the grade.

Prerequisites
The kind of design depends first of all on the angle of the slope and the size of the total piece of property. An extensive layout offers more possibilities for natural shaping and tie-in to the surroundings. A smaller property leaves less room to play with. In any case, it is necessary to install stairs, landings, and possibly ramps in order to be able to overcome the height.
Planning must also allow for as large a level area as possible around the house. Thus, a piece of the garden, perhaps in the area of the terrace, is lifted to the dwelling level. Furthermore, areas of the garden can be established on different levels for different uses, with bed areas for trees, shrubs, flowers, and produce plants as well as for playing and relaxing.
Beyond this, soil conditions and available sun as well as the angle of the slope are important. These points substantially determine use and accessibility of the sloping garden as well as the choice of plants.
The design of a sloping plot has its price, for construction of alterations such as earth moving, terracing, or bracing, and steps, landings, walls, and palisades are usually quite expensive. In all these contstruction measures, it is important to provide for good drainage.

Planting Tips
A slope can be "bound" in various ways (see drawings at left). After the earth-moving work, the embankment should be planted as soon as possible with a carpet of plants so that the topsoil doesn't erode.
Most gardens on a slope are facing south, that is, toward the sun; the earth here dries out faster, the water flows away easily, and the soil is often very meager because of a rocky subsoil or because it has been piled up. In this case, the most suitable plants are those that love warmth and dryness, which quickly send their roots through the soil and hold it. If, on the other hand, the garden faces the north side and receives little or no sun, you must put in shade-tolerant plants (see pages 104–105 and 244–245). Basically the plants recommended for slopes are those that like to run wild and creep; preferably medium-tall perennials as specimen plantings in a ground cover of dwarf shrubs, low-

Supported with palisades, a thickly planted flower bed on a steep slope.

Spacious terracing for sitting areas and beds.

Beautiful, lushly planted supporting wall.

growing roses, heathers, grasses, but above all rock garden plants (see pages 106–107 and 242–243). Climbing plants and plants with an overhanging habit look especially beautiful on walls and slopes. Here they can develop without supports, according to their natural character.

Water Gardens

Water can be used in many forms as a design element in the garden. Often a natural or ornamental pond (see pages 62–63 and 64–65) is installed. But you can also turn the entire garden into a water paradise: with calm water for water lilies, another part for fish—possibly tying the whole thing together with a brook (see pages 66–67).

Important: In all water layouts, there should be areas where one can walk. Large river gravel, natural stone stepping-stones, as well as wood are suitable pathways.

Planting Tips

A broad rule says that only about a third of the pond should be covered with plants. Biological grounds for this are that the water surface should be partially shaded with floating plant leaves; for aesthetic reasons, the reflective surface of the water should remain visible. You will find a beautiful choice of plants for water and marshy areas on pages 274–279.

• Depending on the species/variety, water lilies need different water depths and are very different in growth habits. A vigorously growing water lily can cover 20 to 30 sq ft (2 to 3 m²) or more of water surface.

• You should allow 2 to 3 underwater plants per 11 sq ft (m²) of water surface.

• For shallow-water zones, figure on 3 to 4 plants; for marshy areas, 4 to 6 plants per 11 sq ft (m²).

• Ponds with naturally shaped edges are particularly charming. Also, plant all perennials in groups here.

• Severely geometric pools look most beautiful with sparse planting, for instance, only a few floating-leaved plants and some contrasting tall rushes (*Juncus* species) and the native yellow flag (*Iris pseudacorus*, see pages 278–279).

Regular Care Routines

• Thin out vigorously growing plants.
• Inspect water (pH 6–7.5; dealer); too high an alkali content promotes algae growth.
• Replenish water, if possible, with rainwater or with soft tap water and regularly renew, especially the fish supply (see page 65).
• Free natural ponds gently and only partially of plant remains and mud every 2 to 3 years.

Algae—Prevention and Treatment

Algae problems often occur with the new installation of a pond; the water turns green and becomes cloudy. But, after about 2 years, as a rule, the biological balance has begun. More unpleasant is the green conferva algae, which spread out in the water like cotton and also strangle plants. They must be fished out with the rake. Avoid using chemicals. They don't provide any long-

Happy child's play by a natural pond.

Protective grill for children, overgrown with pickerelweed and horsetail.

Duckboards as a pathway through the water garden.

lasting remedies for algae.

High water temperatures (over 72° to 74° F [22°–23° C]) can also trigger an increase in algae. Therefore, avoid locations in full sun and plant water plants in the shade. It is important that no nutrients get into the pond, for example, fertilizers, dying plants, or falling leaves. This

Small garden—laid out as a water garden with yellow loosestrife, bamboo, and a quantity of water lilies.

Water garden with wooden deck and floating lamps.

A spring stone in the garden enriches the water with oxygen.

starts the rotting process, which uses oxygen, and favors the growth of algae.

Enemies of algae are snails, water fleas, and other small organisms. Underwater plants are important for oxygen production, for one thing, and for another they compete with the algae for nutrients. Also, a brook or a circula-tion pump promotes oxygen enrichment and so helps against algae.

The biological balance important for a healthy, algae-free pond depends on the size and depth of the pond. The larger and deeper the pond or pool, the less the danger of an algae plague.

GARDENING
PRACTICE

The best possible care of
the soil and the plants is
the secret of producing
splendid flowers as well as
healthy fruits and vegetables.
Whatever you might want to
learn about gardening know-
how can be found on the
following pages—all the
basic information about
gardening practice.

Garden Tools

A garden cannot be managed without the additional help of some equipment. If you have the right tools, even the hardest garden work won't be beyond you.

Basic Equipment

As a garden owner, you need a basic assortment of garden tools (see drawing, right). These include:

• Spade, spading fork, and rake for preparing the beds. Ones made of high-grade steel are more durable; these have the blade and the shaft forged in one piece and the shaft completely surrounds the handle.

• Hoe, grubber, or hook cultivator for regular soil care (loosening and weeding).

• Hand tools such as trowel and hand cultivator for planting and clearing up.

• Garden shears and saws (loppers, pruners, and rose shears as needed).

• Watering can with a sprinkling nozzle, bucket, and hose.

• Tools for lawn care (see pages 166–167).

Tips on Buying

Before you get garden tools, you should consider carefully what you need which tool for, for each item requires space and maintenance—and costs money.

The right choice depends on the type, size, and soil condition of the garden.

• There are garden tools in light and heavy models, for instance, special spades for women. Also there are various types of grips and handles.

• Multipurpose tools, such as Scott's Snap-On system, save space and are, thus, suitable for smaller gardens. There are several tool attachments for one handle.

• With larger gardens, tools are more necessary. Therefore, it is better if you choose single tools of better quality.

• For large gardens, buying motor-driven equipment pays, whereas hand tools are usually enough for the small garden.

• The garden's soil type is also a factor: With heavy soils, you need sturdier tools.

Shredders

With a shredder, woody or bulky garden waste can be ground up easily. Before buying, consider:

• Electric or gasoline power. Electric motors are quieter, but without three-phase current they are not as efficient as gasoline motors, which are used in large gardens when there is no outlet available.

• Make sure you have good noise insulation.

• The shredder should move on wheels and have a catch bag.

• If possible, it should be able to grind branches larger than 1.25 in (3 cm) and material that is damp and consisting of leaves and stems. For this purpose, hammer mechanisms are superior to pure knife mechanisms.

Caution: Best to use eye goggles when operating a chipper-shredder machine.

Important: Establish an equipment cooperative with neighbors in order to be able to buy a more efficient model.

A chipper-shredder makes it possible to compost the cuttings from trees, shrubs, and plants.

Garden Accessories

① Fruit picker
② Garden gloves
③ Watering can for watering individual plants
④ Bucket for transporting small quantities of compost
⑤ Basket for gathering garden waste and harvesting vegetables

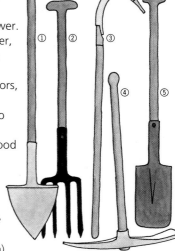

Tools for Working the Soil

① Shovel
② Spading fork for loosening the soil, for taking up plants, shrubs, tuber and root vegetables
③ Cultivator for loosening the soil
④ Pick for breaking up compacted, heavy, and stony soils
⑤ Spade for transplanting and planting

Care of Tools

To keep garden tools intact for a long time, they must be cleaned regularly and stored in a dry place.

• Helpful are wall tool holders with clips or hooks; usually single hooks are also available. These provide storage for all tools with handles. Hang the tools so that the prongs and edges are against the wall and the handle points toward the floor.

• Regularly examine the handles to be sure they don't wobble or have snags or uneven places that can injure the hand.

• With alcohol or over a flame, disinfect the blades of cutting tools that have come into contact with sick plants.

• Before winter, all tools should be carefully cleaned, metal parts oiled, and cutters sharpened.

• Have defective parts repaired so that everything is ready for the next spring.

Tools for Sowing and Planting

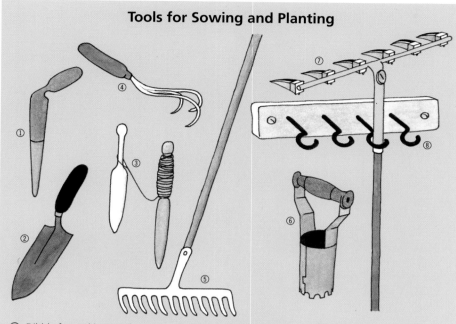

① Dibble for making seed rows and boring planting holes
② Trowel for planting and potting
③ Plant string for marking of beds, laying out seed rows, row planting of vegetables
④ Hand grubber for loosening and weeding between vegetable rows and ornamental plants
⑤ Rake for crumbling and smoothing the soil and for raking together
⑥ Bulb planter
⑦ Row maker for seed bed preparation
⑧ Wall hooks for garden tools

Pruning Tools

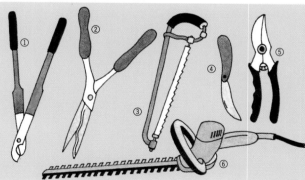

① Pruning shears with long handle grips
② Hedge clippers
③ Tree saw with replaceable blade
④ Pruning knife for smoothing the edges of cuts on trees and shrubs
⑤ Garden pruners
⑥ Electric hedge clipper

Handling Tools

The correct handling of gardening tools can protect you from injury and health stresses.

• Always dig, hoe, and rake with your back straight. To do this, the tool must fit your body height (tops of spade handles should be at waist height).

• With motorized equipment, study the operating and safety instructions carefully.

• When doing work such as shredding and hedge clipping, wear sturdy clothing, gloves, and goggles.

A stable wheelbarrow—indispensable aid for all transporting work.

Soil Tests

The soil is the most important basic element in gardening. Therefore, it is vital that it be in good condition and adequate for the particular needs of the plants. This involves the physical structure as well as the chemical composition of the soil.

Getting Acquainted with the Soil

Initially, through close examination and touch, purely external conclusions can be drawn about the kind of soil.

Color. If you dig a hole 2 spade-lengths deep, you can see differences by the colors of the cross section. Usually the topsoil layer (6 to 12 in [15–30 cm]) is darker in color than the subsoil. The dark color indicates a high content of organic material (humus). For example, marshy soils are almost black.

Structure. The individual particles of a soil can be very different. In purely sandy soils, they are large and can easily be felt between the fingers. The stickier the soil, the finer the particles and, thus, the higher the clay content. Most soils show a mixed structure.

Ideal condition. Good garden soil possesses fine and coarse particles, crumbles into loose particles in the hand, contains earthworms and other small organisms, and smells fragrantly of earth.

Soil tests. The best way to get an overview of the soil conditions is the hand-and-finger test (see right-hand page).

Soil reaction and nutrient content can be at least grossly shown on the basis of simple, commercially available tests. Only more labor-intensive soil analysis provides precise results.

The pH Value of Soil

Most plants are happiest in a slightly acid milieu (pH value 6 to7). The pH value is the measure of the degree of acid content of the soil (by measurement of the hydrogen ion concentration). On a scale of 1 to 14, 7 is the neutral point. The values below this indicate an acid reaction of the soil; those over it indicate an alkaline one. The pH value plays an important role, for it determines the amount of nutrients the plants are able to take up. If the pH is extremely high (very alkaline soil) or very low (acid soil), certain nutrients cannot be

A number of soil tests can be carried out at home with the help of a soil-testing kit or with testing sticks and a color card.

absorbed. However, some plants are specialized for just such soils and thrive in them. An example of this is the rhododendron, which, with a few exceptions, only grows well in acid soil (pH value: 4.5 to 6).

Bear in Mind When Taking a Soil Sample

Important factors are the time of year in which you take the sample and the depth of the probe.

Time of year. Soil samples are best taken in the spring or in the fall, that is, before or after the growing season. In any case, always do it before fertilizer or compost are added.

Taking Soil Samples

① Take about 10 to 15 soil samples per soil area. Distribute samplings evenly over the entire surface.

② Dig a hole (for depth, see below). With the trowel, scrape a layer along the side wall from bottom to top.

③ Collect the samples from each sample hole in a bucket and mix them all together well.

④ Put about 18 oz (500 g) of this sample in a plastic bag and label it (name, address, description of the area, and type of use).

Depth of the probe depends on the prospective planting. Usually a depth of one spade length is enough. For lawn areas, it only needs to be 4 in (10 cm) deep. If deep-rooted plants (roses, shrubs) are to be planted, you must take up to 2 spade lengths and in doing so collect the upper and under layers separately. **Important:** Garden areas that are to be differently planted and used (lawns, produce gardens, fruit, perennials) also require taking separate soil samples. Borrow a boring auger from the laboratory you are having test the soil. Soil samples are much easier to take with this special tool.

Hand and Finger Test

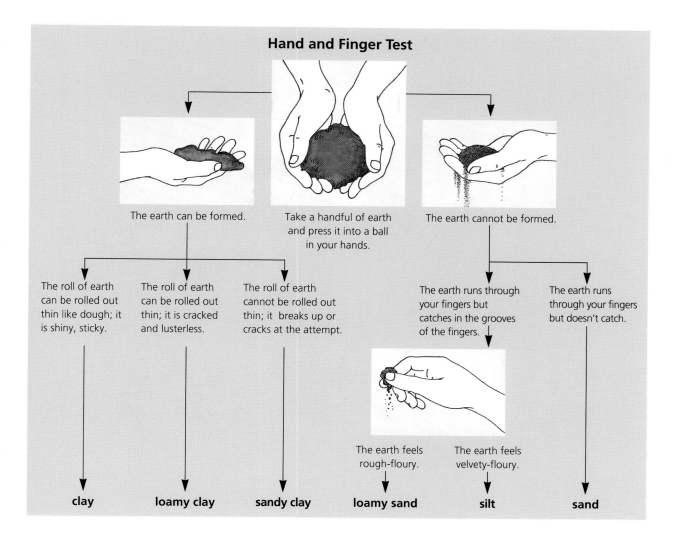

The earth can be formed.

Take a handful of earth and press it into a ball in your hands.

The earth cannot be formed.

The roll of earth can be rolled out thin like dough; it is shiny, sticky.

The roll of earth can be rolled out thin; it is cracked and lusterless.

The roll of earth cannot be rolled out thin; it breaks up or cracks at the attempt.

The earth runs through your fingers but catches in the grooves of the fingers.

The earth runs through your fingers but doesn't catch.

The earth feels rough-floury.

The earth feels velvety-floury.

clay   **loamy clay**   **sandy clay**   **loamy sand**   **silt**   **sand**

In the letter you send along with the soil sample, you should also give details about the kind of cultivation used on your garden soil (organic or conventional cultivation methods, intensive, extensive, type of fertilization, and so forth). Then, the recommendations for fertilizing can be individually tailored. For organic procedures, it is recommended to have the soil tested for heavy metals (expensive!).

Soil Analysis
Exact details about the soil contents are only produced by labor-intensive soil analysis. Such an analysis is particularly important with the installation of new gardens or of new installation of particular areas in the produce garden and by the appearance of nutrient deficiencies (see page 157). To get your soil properly tested, call your local county extension agency for complete soil testing information.

Important: In produce gardens, you should have a soil analysis performed every 2 to 3 years in order to avoid improper fertilization procedures.
A standard soil analysis as a rule includes the following values:
• Type of soil
• pH value
• Potassium and phosphorus content
Additional values to be tested for on request:
• Trace elements
• Magnesium content
• Lime content

• Humus content
• Total nitrogen
• Soil structure
• Biological activity
• Heavy metals
Fertilizing recommendations are usually enclosed with the test report or are given on request.
Soil analyses are available through your local county extension agency and private institutions. The costs vary widely, depending on the scope of the examination. Special tests are considerably more expensive.

Soil Care

Soil care includes soil preparation before planting and seeding, especially with areas that are going to be newly planted, and the treatment of the soil throughout the year—all that contributes to making the soil more productive.

Soil Improvement

There are different methods and materials that help to improve the soil, as the table on the page at the right shows. Among these are also green manures and mulches (see pages 160–161). How you should improve your soil depends on the type of soil.

Soils with a heavy clay and loam content tend to collect water, are badly aerated, and are poor in organic substances. Therefore, they must first of all be deeply loosened and aerated. In this case, you should turn the soil to the depth of 2 spade lengths. Be careful when deep cultivating that the upper and lower soil layers are not mixed, because the important soil organisms can only live in particular soil layers. While turning over the soil, additional compost, bone meal, sand or also peatmoss, and organic fertilizers (see table right) can be mixed in to the upper soil layer for loosening and aeration. The best time for this somewhat laborious work is the fall. Finally, the coarse clods of the turned soil are left to the frost, which breaks them

down still more (frost mellowing).

The alternative to deep digging is to loosen the soil only superficially and sow a green manure in the spring or the fall, using deep-rooted plants like lupines or clover species, or which may have to be repeated. Also, lime, which it's better to spread in the fall, can improve the soil structure.

Important: Don't walk on heavy soils when they are wet, or they compact even more. If necessary, lay down boards to walk on. Light soils are well aerated, dry out more quickly, and warm up quickly. Thus, they can be worked earlier in the spring. Their cultivation is easier in any case. However, they are poor in organic substances and store water and nutrients poorly. All care measures must therefore be aimed at increasing the humus content. This is possible through use of a green manure, by adding compost, and by mulching. Working in clay meal and lime also raises the soil's water retention ability at the same time.

Important: Have the lime content of the soil checked every 3 to 5 years.

Tools for Working the Soil

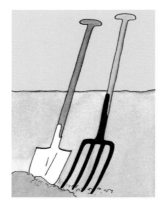

Spade
For planting, transplanting, loosening, and turning over heavy soil.

Spading Fork
For loosening medium and light soils. Sink the fork up to the top and move it backward and forward several times. This will also loosen the rooted weeds without dividing them unnecessarily.

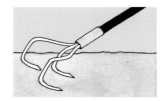

Refuse Hook
For working coarse lumps out of soil.

Cultivator
For loosening the soil and working in fertilizers.

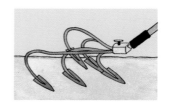

Grub Hook
For surface loosening between rows in a bed. The weeds are loosened at the same time so that you can easily pull them out.

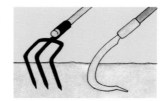

Cultivator
The "feet" of the cultivator are drawn through the topmost soil layer like little plowshares. The width of the tool head is adjustable.

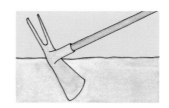

Two-pronged Hoe
This combined pulling and hacking hoe is very helpful for weeding. Because it is narrow, it is also good for loosening and weeding between rows of plants.

Rake
With this, clods of soil can be crumbled and large surfaces smoothed. Beds can be made ready for seeding and planting with the rake.

Preparation for Planting and Sowing

Before you begin sowing or planting, the beds must be prepared. Loosen the soil, which should be slightly moistened throughout, with a spading fork or a spade.

• Remove weeds.
• Work in compost, organic fertilizer, rock phosphate, and lime from the top down.
• Smooth the surface of the bed with the rake.
• Sow seeds or set out plants.

Important: Always work in the soil improvers (see table, right) from the top down only, because the active soil organisms only work in the top soil layer.

Soil Care Throughout the Year

The care of the soil depends on the season, the weather, the use, and the planting of the garden.

Spring. When the frost period is over (March/April/May), the garden year begins. Before any work can take place, the soil must dry out at least superficially.

• Remove winter debris from beds and lawns. Leaves, old mulch, or other covering material prevent the warming of the soil and, thus, the growth of plants.
• Carefully loosen planted areas, without injuring the buried spring bulbs.

• In vegetable garden beds, loosen and maybe sow a green manure.
• Throughout the garden, lightly work in compost, organic fertilizer, and rock phosphate.

Summer. During the summer months the soil dries out quickly. Therefore, it is important to loosen it regularly or to mulch.

• Scratch up the surface of open soil areas, for example between vegetables, showy perennials, or roses every 2 to 3 weeks—especially after heavy rains (air exchange, soil humidity, weed formation).
• The soil doesn't get crusted over so readily between plantings because it is shaded by branches and leaves. Here it's enough to aerate it now and then with small tools and to pull out the largest weeds.

Alternative: Cover open soil with a thin layer of mulch (see page 161); then it is not so strongly affected by weather conditions. Renew fast-rotting mulch (grass cuttings) more often.

In fall and late fall, distribute mature compost and rock phosphate thinly over the beds. Possibly add lime, potassium, and phosphate if a soil analysis has recommended this. Finally, protect the open soil with a mulch covering of straw or leaves. Thus, the beds are made secure for the winter.

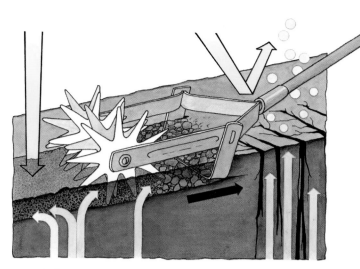

What Loosening and Crumbling Do

Sun, wind, and rain make the open soil dry out, become crusted, or turn to mud. Air can no longer penetrate into the root spaces; rainwater runs off over the surface and evaporates. On the other hand, the groundwater is sucked up to the top and evaporates (capillary effect). Loosening and crumbling (here with a hand tiller) break up the upper layer. The fine hair roots lose their connection to the outside, and the moisture remains in the soil. Also, air and water can once again enter unimpeded. Loosening and crumbling, thus, regulates the water content in the soil, makes air exchange possible, and prevents the growth of weeds.

Important Substances for Soil Improvement

Organic Material Horse/other animal manure, compost, organic fertilizer, green manure and mulching material, prepared substrate (bark or wood as peat substitute)	For all soils. Promotes formation of humus and the capacity for water, nutrient, and warmth storage. Loosens, ventilates, and fertilizes the soil.
Mineral Material Rock phosphate	Improves binding of nutrients in all soils.
Clay meal	Improves binding of water and nutrients in light soils.
Lime	Improves acid soils.
Sand/pebbles	Drainage with heavy soils.
Loam/clay	Improves binding of water and nutrients in light soils.
Synthetic Material Various flake mixtures or vermiculite	Improves the structure of heavy soils; increases binding of water in light soils.

Sowing

Sowing and watching the germination and growth of plants surely belongs to the most wonderful of gardening activities. It is always a small miracle when a sturdy flowering and fruiting plant appears out of a tiny seed grain, often in the course of one season. But before you are seduced by the colorful seed packets in the store, you should carefully consider what purpose you have for how many plants.

Sowing Indoors

You must raise frost-tender plants in the house ahead of time, before they can be set outside. You need a place for growing that is light but not in dazzling full sun (greenhouse, windowsill). The seedlings like "warm feet," that is, a temperature between 61° and 68° F (16° and 20° C) in the root zone.
Seeds can be sown from January on. But the young plants must be kept indoors until all danger of frost is past, which may be as late as the end of May in some areas. In the last weeks before being placed outside, however, they need a light, cooler, and airy location about 59° F (15° C) (attic, guest room), so that they will be somewhat hardened off before being planted out.
Alternative: If you don't have enough space for starting plants indoors, you can buy young plants in May.

Sowing in Individual Pots

Large or pelleted seed can be sown singly or in groups of three directly in a pot.
Advantage: It isn't necessary to prick them out.
Soil medium: Only use a soilless potting or seed-starting mixture available from garden centers. It is sterile and contains no fertilizer.
Containers. The pots must not be too large so that the ball can become well rooted. Ideal growing containers are peat pots ①, which make further transplanting unnecessary. But also suitable are individual pots, plastic seed-starting flats, or peat pellets ②, which swell with the addition of water. All pots can stand quite close to each other, but as the plants grow they must be pushed apart or separated. The leaves of the young plans should not touch. In the spring, the thoroughly rooted pots ③ are then planted directly in the bed.
Important: Seedlings want conditions as steady as possible and a draft-free, light place with high humidity. Ideal: a small greenhouse with ventilation and shading.

Sowing, Step by Step

① Fill seed flats with soil; smooth; press down edges. Sow evenly, not too thickly.

② With the hands or a small board, press the seeds into the soil and sprinkle or strain some soil over them.

③ Water the soil and seeds with a fine spray, or moisten with a squirt bottle.

④ Cover the seed flat with its own cover or a plate of glass. As soon as the seeds show leaves, ventilate.

Pricking Out, Step by Step

① Prick out seedlings when they begin to form the first true leaves after the 2 seed leaves.

② Shorten the roots of the seedling by about ⅓ to ½ with your fingers so they will branch well.

③ Plant singly in the smallest possible pot (better root formation).

④ Moisten the seedlings well; place in warm, bright spot. After roots are well formed, place where airy and cool.

Seeds in Various Forms

It pays to buy quality seeds, even if they are expensive. All kinds of germination protection packages are available. With appropriate storage, you can even use opened packages the next year. Then, the seeds must be closed in an airtight container, labeled, and stored in a dark, dry, cool place.

Quality seeds are correctly labeled, contain precise species and variety information, and provide detailed culture instructions as well as an expiration date.

Coated seeds. These are small pill-sized seeds that are coated to resist disease problems. The coating dissolves in damp soil. Coated seeds are expensive, but they usually need not be pricked out any further, and they can also be used in special seeding equipment (seed rollers, sowing machines).

Seed tapes, carpets, and sticks. The seeds are already placed on or in these at the proper planting distance, so that you don't have to prick out the young seedlings later. But these sowing aids absolutely must be placed with the correct side facing the soil.

Seeds from the garden. Some garden flowers seed themselves right where they are. In this case, the young plants need only be separated or transplanted. With other flowers, the seeds can be collected and sowed

again. With greatly hybridized varieties, however, it is advisable to buy the seeds new each year so that they propagate true to the variety.

Germination Characteristics

Plants germinate very differently.

Viability. Depending on the plant, this can last for a year or for many seasons. However, most seeds remain viable for 2 to 3 years.

Seed test. Sow a counted number of seeds (soil, sand), moisten, cover with plastic wrap or a pane of glass, and set in a warm place. After some time, you can see how many seeds have germinated and whether it would pay

to sow them.

Germination time. It varies from a few days and to weeks. The process may be accelerated by pregermination or soaking (see Seed test above).

Germination conditions. The seeds of most garden plants need a temperature of between 61° and 68° F (16° and 20° C). But depending on the source of the plant, it may also need cold or frost as a stimulus for germination. Almost all plants are dark germinators. But there are also some light germinators, which should not be covered with soil (read the cultural instructions).

Direct Sowing

The seeds of many garden plants may be sown directly where they are to grow, from March to May. Before sowing, the soil must be well cultivated and improved with compost and organic fertilizer. Under no circumstances should mineral fertilizer be used, because it has a corrosive effect. Then, smooth the surface with the rake; it should be fine textured.

Sow the seeds shallowly and gently compress, possibly covering with more compost. Dampen the beds well and after germination, carefully thin out the seedlings that are too close together. Water after thinning so that the soil contact is reestablished.

Sowing Outdoors

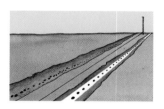

Row Sowing

In the vegetable garden, this is the best method of sowing and also makes the care easier. Using a row marker, make rows along a planting string (depth: 2 to 3 times the size of the seed). The distance between the rows depends on the mature size of the plant (8 to 16 in [20–40 cm] between plants). Lay the seeds in the row one by one, if possible, or use a seed roller.

Alternative: Lay seed tapes in the row (see drawing above, right row).

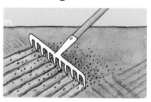

Broadcasting

Broadcasting is suitable for larger surfaces that are seeded with grass, annuals, or green manures. The seeds are simply scattered by hand over a wide area. To be sure the seed is distributed evenly, it can also be applied with a spreader.

Important: Mix grass seed with fine sand for even spreading.

Pole beans sown in clumps climb here on a teepee frame.

Clump Sowing

Sow 3 to 5 seeds of climbing plants (bush and pole beans, sweet peas, morning glories) around the edge of a support in a palm-size mound, and cover with soil.

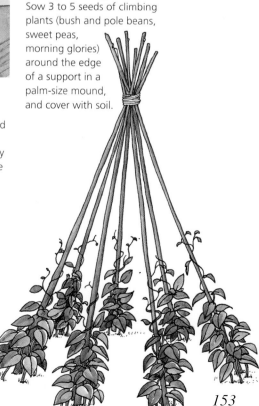

153

Vegetative Propagation

Besides sowing (generative propagation), plants are often increased by vegetative methods. To do this, new plants are produced from sprouts or roots of the mother plant, through which offspring that are true to variety are reproduced. Among the various vegetative (asexual) propagation methods, greenwood cuttings require the most intuitive feeling overall and the most demanding care (high humidity and warmth), whereas with the other vegetative methods, new roots form without any problem. But all the propagation methods are not always suitable for a particular plant species. (The table on the right-hand page shows which plants are reproduced by which method.)

Propagation by Cuttings

Various parts of the shoot are suitable for greenwood cuttings (terminal cutting = the end of a stem or branch with a terminal bud; stem cutting = a piece of a stem or branch that includes at least one node). This is how it's done:
• Take a cutting by making a cut directly under a leaf node. Callus tissue will form fastest at that spot, and the new roots will arise from this. The cutting should be about 2 to 4 in (5–10 cm) long and have 2 to 4 leaves. Remove the tips of the shoot if they are too soft.
• Summer is the best time to take cuttings. It is important that the cutting be at the right stage of maturity.

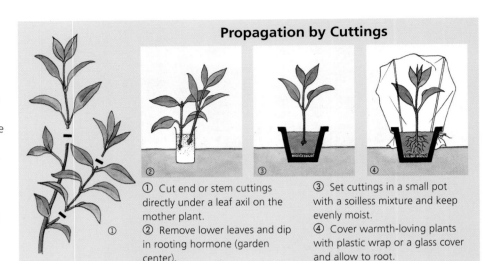

Propagation by Cuttings

① Cut end or stem cuttings directly under a leaf axil on the mother plant.
② Remove lower leaves and dip in rooting hormone (garden center).
③ Set cuttings in a small pot with a soilless mixture and keep evenly moist.
④ Cover warmth-loving plants with plastic wrap or a glass cover and allow to root.

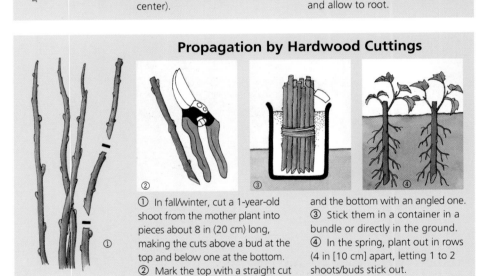

Propagation by Hardwood Cuttings

① In fall/winter, cut a 1-year-old shoot from the mother plant into pieces about 8 in (20 cm) long, making the cuts above a bud at the top and below one at the bottom.
② Mark the top with a straight cut and the bottom with an angled one.
③ Stick them in a container in a bundle or directly in the ground.
④ In the spring, plant out in rows (4 in [10 cm] apart, letting 1 to 2 shoots/buds stick out.

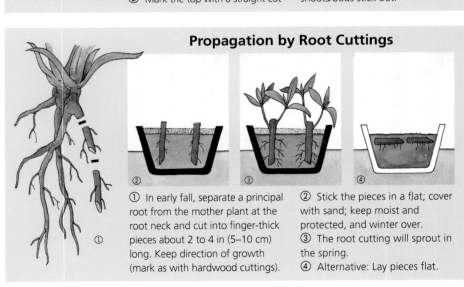

Propagation by Root Cuttings

① In early fall, separate a principal root from the mother plant at the root neck and cut into finger-thick pieces about 2 to 4 in (5–10 cm) long. Keep direction of growth (mark as with hardwood cuttings).
② Stick the pieces in a flat; cover with sand; keep moist and protected, and winter over.
③ The root cutting will sprout in the spring.
④ Alternative: Lay pieces flat.

Special Propagation Methods

Simple Layering
Suitable for woody plants with branches close to the ground and elastic, like rhododendrons. Scar the shoot where it's closest to the ground. Anchor with hooks and cover with compost.

Stolons
Strawberries and many ground covers develop long, above-ground runners, which root on contact with the earth and form new plants. They are easily separated.

Root Runners
Some plants, such as raspberries, develop runners underground, which one simply cuts off with the spade, preferably in the spring or fall, and plants anew.

Mound Layering
Hill up around gooseberries and currants. New roots form on the younger shoots in the heaped-up soil. These shoots can be cut off in the fall.

Bulb Scales
Separate the outer scales in late summer and put them in a plastic bag of damp sand. Keep dark and warm (around 68° F [20° C]). There will be bulblets in 2 to 3 months.

Dahlia Corms
They are divided right at the beginning of the root, at the spot where the corm has a bud. New plants will only form from such pieces.

Bulb Offsets
Narcissi and other bulbs form offsets, which can easily be separated and planted anew. Depending on the size, it takes 2 to 3 years for them to flower.

Hardwood cuttings may be either too soft (very new shoots) or too hard and woody. But shoots of herbaceous plants should not be too young either.
• When making softwood cuttings, hygiene is especially important. It's best to make the cut with clippers that have been disinfected (alcohol, flame). Containers, tools, and the environment should be cleaned ahead of time. Special sterile starting and potting soil, are available from garden supply stores. You should always prepare a mixture (for instance peat moss/sand in a ratio of 1:1) fresh; never use fertilized soil or compost.
• You can promote root growth with a rooting hormone (also available commercially) and support it with humidity (glass or plastic wrap cover) and warmth (tub plants also with heating up to a maximum of 68° F [20° C] or on a Styrofoam underlay).

Which Plants to Propagate How?

Propagation by Cuttings
Tub plants like oleander (*Neria*), angel's-trumpet (*Brugmansia*). Broad-leaved evergreens like holly (*Ilex*), cherry laurel (*Prunus laurocerasus*), ivy (*Hedera*), boxwood (*Buxus*). Conifers like arborvitae (*Thuja*), juniper (*Juniperus*). Also grapes (*Vitis*), roses (*Rosa*), wisteria (*Wisteria*), butterfly bush (*Buddleia*), hydrangea (*Hydrangea*), heathers (*Calluna, Erica*), lavender (*Lavandula*). Perennials like chrysanthemum (*Chrysanthemum*), delphinium (*Delphinium*), sun roses (*Helianthemum*), germander (*Teucrium*), catmint (*Nepeta*), beard-tongue (*Penstemon*), phlomis (*Phlomis*), vervain (*Verbena*), madwort (*Alyssum*), monkey flower (*Mimulus*).

Propagation by Hardwood Cuttings
Fruiting and flowering shrubs like raspberries (*Rubus*), currants (*Ribes*), hazelnut (*Corylus*), elder (*Sambucus*), grapes (*Vitis*), deutzia (*Deutzia*), mock-orange (*Philadelphus*), lilac (*Syringa*), forsythia (*Forsythia*), cornelian cherry (*Cornus*), privet (*Ligustrum*), smokebush (*Cotinus*), viburnum (*Viburnum*), witch hazel (*Hamamelis*).

Propagation by Root Cuttings
Perennials like the thistle species (*Eryngium*), Japanese anemonies (*Anemone japonica*), mullein (*Verbascum*), blanket flowers (*Gaillardia*), windflowers (*Anemone pulsatilla*), primroses (*Primula*), oriental poppies (*Papaver orientale*), baby's breath (*Gypsophila*), cranesbill (*Geranium*), bleeding heart (*Dicentra*). Shrubs like wild roses (*Rosa*), Japanese quince (*Chaenomeles*).

Propagation by Runners
Strawberries (*Fragaria*), dead nettle (*Lamium*), blue bugle (*Ajuga*), knotweed (*Polygonum*), foamflower (*Tiarella*), garden loosestrife (*Lysimachia*).

Basics of Fertilizing

Fertilizing, plant nutrition, soil condition, and soil care are in a close relationship with one another. You can learn more about this relationship in The Soil Factor (see pages 14–15). A basic prerequisite for fertilizing that is suited to soil and plant needs is a soil test (see pages 148–149). The various different fertilizers can then be considered on the basis of these results.

Type of Fertilizer

The type of fertilizer is primarily determined by the soil structure and the soil organisms. Seen over the long term, fertilizing on a pure mineral basis injures the soil. On the other hand, organic materials make the soil more productive over the long term because they nourish the microorganisms in the soil, which in turn make the nutrients available to the plants. Organic-mineral fertilizers combine the advantages of both ingredients.

Large lawn areas can be fertilized comfortably with a spreader.

Mineral fertilizers. The fertilizers are based on inorganic starting materials. They are synthetically produced or come from natural deposits. The nutrients are available in the form of easily soluble mineral salts and can be quickly taken up by the plants. This has the advantage of being able to quickly remedy recognized deficiencies. However, there is always the danger of overfertilizing the plant with too high a dosage, and injuring the life of the soil.

Important: For houseplants, you should only use chloride-free mineral (blue) fertilizers, because many plants are chlorine sensitive.

Organic fertilizers. These consist of plant and animal waste materials in fresh, dried, or rotted form. A distinction is made between natural and commercial fertilizers. Because the organic fertilizer must first be excreted by the microorganisms in the soil in order for it to become available to the plants, a lapse of several weeks occurs for the effect of fertilizing to be seen. High

temperatures, humidity, and humus-rich soil accelerate the process. Finely ground products are effective more quickly than coarse ones; also, extracts or teas work faster.

Organic fertilizing offers a steady, slow-flowing source of nutrients.

Organic-mineral fertilizers. These commercially available fertilizers offer the garden owner the nutrients in a balanced ratio. These fertilizers are of course more expensive but join long- and short-term effects with the addition of organic material.

The Most Important Fertilizers

Mineral Fertilizers

Nitrogen (N)

Ammonium sulfate potassium nitrate	fast and slow effect (lawns)
Sulfuric acid ammonia	acid effect (rhododendrons)
Sodium nitrate (Chile saltpeter)	$NaNO^3$, liming effect

Phosphorus (P)

Superphosphate	top-dressing
Thomas meal	P + Ca, reserve fertilizing (fall)

Potassium (K)

Potassium magnesium oxide	K + Mg + trace elements, reserve fertilizing (fall)

Magnesium (Mg)

Magnesium sulfate	top-dressing (conifers)

Calcium (Ca)

Calcium carbonate (carbonate of lime)	Ca + Mg, reserve fertilizing

Blue-complete fertilizer	N, P, K, Mg + trace elements, chloride-free

Organic Fertilizers

Horse, cow manure, well-rotted	N, concentrated, + trace elements
Poultry manure (dried)	N, P, K, fresh; burns
Guano, bird or bat	all important nutrients, effective quickly
Garden compost	raw: N, fast-working mature: slow-working
Horn shavings, horn meal	N, concentrated, basic fertilizing
Blood meal	N, concentrated, top-dressing
Bonemeal	P, concentrated, basic fertilizing
Horn-blood-bonemeal	N, P, K*, Ca, basic fertilizing
Castor bean pellets	N, P, K*, slow-working
Sea kelp/seaweed lime	Contains Ca + Mg + trace elements (compost additive)
Algae fertilizers	N, P, K* + trace elements
Organic complete fertilizers	N, P, K*, Ca

Organic-Mineral Fertilizers

Complete fertilizers	N, P, K, Ca, Mg + trace elements, slow- and fast-working

* contains very little potassium

Forms of Fertilizers

There are fertilizers in granular form, pulverized as meal or salts, and in liquid form.

Single- or multiple-nutrient fertilizers. These mineral fertilizers contain one or two of the principal nutrients nitrogen (N), phosphorus (P), potassium (K), calcium (Ca), and magnesium (Mg).

Complete fertilizers. Mineral and organic-mineral complete fertilizers are multinutrient fertilizers with the principal nutrients N, P, K, Ca, Mg. Complete organic fertilizers are also available; however, the potassium component is lower in these.

Slow-release fertilizers. These mineral fertilizers contain slow-flowing nutrients, are prepared by special processes, and are therefore more expensive. They provide the plants with a regular supply of nutrients for up to half a year, and these do not leach out. Therefore, one application in spring is usually enough.

Liquid fertilizers. These already contain the nutrients in soluble form, thus they work quickly at the appearance of acute deficiencies, can be accurately measured, and are easy to use (especially suitable for tub plants).

Special fertilizers. For plants with special requirements like conifers, rhododendrons, roses, and strawberries, there are fertilizers with special composition and with particular ratios of nutrients.

Horse or cow manure is a wonderful organic fertilizer. But only use it after it has been well-aged or composted; otherwise it can burn a plant.

Advantages and Disadvantages of Various Fertilizers

Mineral Fertilizers
• Immediate effect (some exceptions)
• Nutrient content can be chosen as desired

Organic Fertilizers
• No instant effect
• Long-term effect
• Nutrient content limited
• Activation by soil life
• Promotion of humus formation

Organic-Mineral Fertilizers
• Instant effect
• Also long-term effect
• Balanced supply of nutrients
• Activation by soil life
• Promotion of humus formation

Plant Nutrients and How They Work

Nutrient	Effect	Deficiency	Overfertilizing
Nitrogen (N)	Vigor of growth increased; leaf development promoted	Plants are stunted; at first, older leaves yellow; premature ripening sets in	Plants grow oversized; dark green color; tissue is bloated and susceptible to pests, frost; bad storage capability
Phosphorus (P)	Flower and fruit development promoted; maturing accelerated	Root formation and, thus, growth is limited; little development of fruit and flowers; bluish coloration of older leaves	Concentration in soil and with it the fixation of other nutrients; for example, produces iron deficiency (chlorosis)
Potassium (K)	Resistance of tissue to drought, frost, disease increased; ripening and keeping quality, stability, root and tuber development promoted	Allover growth is weakened; wilting occurs; death of leaves around the edges; frost-sensitive	As a result of concentration in the soil, calcium and magnesium deficiencies because their uptake is inhibited
Magnesium (Mg)	Synthesis of chlorophyll is promoted, thus, better growth	Lightening of the older leaves between the leaf veins	The uptake of potassium is inhibited with excess
Calcium (Ca)	New growth and tissue stability are promoted. Works in transformation of organic substances in soil, binds acids	Inhibition of growth and germination; early damage to young plant parts and fruits. Spotting in apples, acidified soil	Excess hinders the uptake of trace elements; pH of soil is increased

How to Apply Fertilizers

With applying fertilizer, the question is to determine the right combination of nutrients and dosage for the particular plant. The type of soil and its condition as well as the time of year are factors to be considered.

Tips for Fertilizing

Plants have very different nutrient requirements. However, there are some guidelines to properly establish the particular nutrient need:

Highly hybridized plants that grow and flower abundantly (roses, showy perennials) and those that grow to maturity in one season and are expected to produce a high yield like vegetables need more nutrients than plants with a wild character (ornamental shrubs, water plants, rock garden plants).

Nettles (Urtica dioica, U. urens) *are very rich in nitrogen. However, they may only be harvested before the seeds are set.*

The 10 Golden Rules of Fertilizing

① Fertilize with purpose. It is advisable when installing new gardens and afterward—especially in produce garden areas—to have the soil analyzed every 2 to 3 years (see Soil tests, pages 148–149).
② Remove old mulch material before fertilizing. Afterward, add new mulch.
③ It's best to only fertilize on dull days, if possible, just before or just after it has rained. Only spread mineral fertilizers when the ground is moist.
④ Spread solid fertilizers with the hand or with a spreader (for example, on lawns).
⑤ Only apply dusty fertilizers when there is no wind.
⑥ Be careful to keep fertilizers (particularly mineral salts and teas) from getting onto green plant parts. They cause burns. If necessary, rinse plants off after fertilizing.
⑦ Always just work solid fertilizers shallowly into the soil.
⑧ With light soils, nutrients (especially nitrogen) leach out quickly; therefore, several small applications spread out over the year and additional compost, rock phosphate, kelp, and lime for pH adjustment help improve soil.
⑨ Green manure, particularly with leguminous plants, serves to enrich the nitrogen supply.
⑩ In the fall, don't add any more nitrogen (which includes raw compost and fresh manure). The nitrates they contain are easily leached out and endanger the groundwater supply.

Fertilizing Tea of Nettles and/or Comfrey

① Chop 2 lb (1 kg) fresh plant parts or 5 to 7 oz (150–200 g) of dried plants.
② Place plants in 10 qt (9.5 L) of water that has been left standing, or rainwater.
③ Stir at least once a day so that the fermenting process is assisted by the oxygen in the air. To control odor, add a handfull of rock phosphate from time to time. After 2 to 3 weeks, the fermentation is finished. The tea no longer foams and becomes clear and dark.
④ Put the tea through a sieve and dilute with water at least 1:10 (for young plants and weak feeders 1:20). Don't moisten leaves when watering; if necessary, rinse them with water afterward.

Plants on thin soil must be fertilized more often (especially with organic fertilizers) than plants in good garden soil.

Deciduous shrubs. Trees and shrubs receive so much humus and nutrients at planting that it is sufficient for the first 2 to 3 years. In the following years, a layer of mulch of compost and leaves is enough in the fall. However, if shrubs slow down on blooming and sending up new growth (hedges), they receive 2 applications of a complete fertilizer—one in early spring and one in early summer.

Important: Shrubs should never be fertilized with nitrogen after July. Their new growth would not mature fully and would thus be susceptible to frost. Phosphorus, potassium, and calcium fertilizers are best applied in late fall. However, only use these fertilizers after a soil test

Fertilizing Correctly All Year Long

You can save yourself a great deal of trouble if you work the soil at the same time you are adding fertilizer.

In early spring (April/May) and at planting, basic and reserve fertilizing is done. Finished compost, which may also be combined with organic and mineral commercial preparations, is suitable for this.
The right amount for garden plants: 10 qt (9.5 L) compost and 1 handful each of horn-blood-bonemeal and rock phosphate. This quantity creates a compost layer of about 0.5 in per 10 sq ft (1 cm per 1 m²). Garden plants with higher requirements or that are worse situated also receive a fast-acting fertilizer like a complete fertilizer or guano.

During the growth and flowering phase, so-called top-dressing takes place. Topdressings should take effect immediately. This means that the nutrient-hungry plants receive additional fast-working fertilizers. Suitable for this purpose are the easily soluble mineral salts in solid or liquid form. Complete fertilizers or specific single nutrients can be offered as needed. If it is mainly a matter of adding nitrogen, you can also use plant or animal teas (nettle or manure tea).
Depending on the condition of the soil, fruits and vegetables, flowers for cutting, roses, and lawn areas must be provided with nutrients more often than the ordinary garden plants (see Gardening Practice text). Heavy feeders, for example, receive topdressings three to four times during the growing season.

Fertilizing in fall is not necessary in intact gardens with good soil structure. Humus and nutrient-poor soil, on the other hand, can be additionally enriched in fall with finished compost or well-rotted cow manure. If a soil analysis has indicated that calcium, potassium, or phosphorus is missing, the fall is the proper time to add these nutrients. This is only necessary every 2 to 3 years, however. The fertilizing materials used are:
• Calcium in carbonate form. In contrast to other fertilizers, calcium is always applied to dry soil.
• Thomas meal, which contains phosphate as well as calcium.

(see pages 148–149, because most soils (also compost) are abundantly provided with potassium and phosphorus (and to some degree also with calcium).
Fruit trees. Plants that are supposed to produce abundant harvests need a regular supply of nutrients.

Thus, you support the growth of shoots and flower bud formation and promote fruit setting and fruitwood development for the coming year with targeted fertilizing (see Care of Fruit Trees, page 175).
Important: Fertilize fruit trees that grow in grass a little more outside the drip line of the crown, because the grass draws away nutrients.

Conifers and broad-leafed evergreens. This plant group has no defined rest period even in winter and thus consumes water and nutrients all year-round. Therefore, either apply compost in the spring and the fall, or in the spring (if necessary also in summer), provide a complete fertilizer containing magnesium. Special fertilizers are used with lime-hating plants like rhododendron.
Roses need heavy feeding and are provided with nutrients in March/April and in June/July according to their blooming periods (see Planting and Care of Roses, pages 176–177).
Perennials. The plants in this group have widely differing nutrient requirements (see Plant Portraits, pages 232 to 247). In the spring and/or the fall, you should spread compost or organic fertilizer. In addition, showy perennials receive an application of complete fertilizer before they bloom or to stimulate a repeat flowering.
Vegetables. Produce plants receive special nutrient combinations depending on their harvested crops (leaves: nitrogen; roots/tubers: potassium; fruit/flowers: phosphorus and calcium).
With vegetables, a distinction is made among heavy, moderate, and weak feeders according to the nitrogen requirements of the plant.
Heavy feeders need addi-tional top-dressing during their growth phase, where-as weak feeders only need a basic fertilization (see Planning a Vegetable Garden, page 182).
Lawns. Lawn areas are provided with a high-nitrogen fertilizer every 4 weeks after a mowing from April to the fall. Special slow-release lawn fertilizers need only be applied once in the spring and in the summer.

Overfertilizing

If a soil analysis of your garden soil indicates too high a nitrogen content, it must be reduced. This is possible with the help of heavily feeding plants like sunflowers. However, don't plant vegetables, for these store nitrates (exception: potatoes). After they mature, all plant parts must be removed. This measure can be repeated.

Comfrey (Symphytum peregrinum) grows up to 5 ft (1.5 m) tall.

Green Manures and Mulches

Use of green manures and mulches are time-tested methods for improving the soil. Plants or plant remains cover the naked soil, rot, or are worked in right away, and so activate the soil life. Whether the soil is heavy, light, or tired, or whether the plants are fruits, vegetables, or ornamentals—they all profit from this old method of culture that today has become modern again.

Green Manure

Green manure is the term for the temporary cultivation of certain plants. For one thing, in a relatively short time, these plants form numerous roots, which loosen the soil in a natural fashion; for another, they form much green matter, which improves the soil when worked into it.
Important green manure plants are the legumes plants (Leguminosae). They are able to remove nitrogen from the air, store it in the ground, and, thus, make it available for other plants as well. The cultivation of green manure plants can be aimed at seasonal conditions and be appropriate for special soil types (see table at right). There are also ready-made green manure mixtures available commercially.

How green manure works.
• The soil is deeply loosened and improved.
• Nutrients are made available for plants.
• Weeds are suppressed.
• The soil remains moist and doesn't become muddy.

Green manure is suitable as an after crop
• before installing new gardens
• before new plantings
• for tired soil
Green manure is suitable as a pre- or in-between crop
• before and after vegetable or flower planting

Green Manure As Cover Crop

Time: Before new planting/sowing, in early spring or between first and second harvest.
① Loosen soil; rake it smooth; broadcast green manure seeds.
② Cut down or mow plants at blooming time at the latest. Use cuttings for mulch or chop up with the spade and dig in shallowly.

③ Enrich the soil with additional compost and/or organic fertilizer; rake smooth again; sow or plant.
④ The next crop grows up.
Important: If you want to bypass the cutting and chopping, work in the green manure plants when they are still small. However, the fertilization effect will be less then.

Green Manure As After-culture

Time: After the end of harvesting/clearing of a bed, in the late summer as intensive soil amendment over the winter.
① Loosen soil; broadcast green manure seeds.
② Leave the plants all winter long as a protection for the bed. In addition, cover with leaves or straw; then by the spring, it will be almost entirely rotted.

③ In early spring, when the soil has dried, rake in the remains.
④ Loosen soil; work in mature compost or organic fertilizer and stone/rock meal. Finally, rake bed smooth and plant or sow again.
Important: You can also use winter-hardy green manure plants (see table) and harvest in early spring.

Pot marigolds (Calendula officinalis) provide for good tilth and repel nematodes.

Mulching

Mulching is the term for covering the soil with organic material like leaves, grass cuttings, or other plant parts. Thus, the soil is kept from drying out and weeds are kept from growing. With mulch, you are spared the constant maintenance work like watering, hoeing, and pulling weeds. Mulch can be applied at any time, even parallel with growing the plants. Exception: Freshly seeded or planted beds. Mulching materials usually can be found in one's own garden:

• compost
• leaves
• grass cuttings
• healthy plant remains.

Also, there are straw, black plastic mulch, and wood and bark products, which are available commercially.

Important: Always mix bark mulch and woody debris you have chipped yourself with organic fertilizers, for in the breakdown process the soil and, thus, the plants will be deprived of nitrogen.

Use wood and bark chip mulch under shrubs and on paths, not for mulching of vegetables and perennials. When mulching, make sure:

• to loosen the soil, pull weeds, gently work in compost and organic fertilizer before mulching;
• to mix fine and coarse mulch material (air access hinders rotting);
• to let mulching materials dry slightly (especially grass cuttings). If this isn't possible, only spread the grass cuttings thinly;
• to have the mulch cover about 2 in (5 cm) deep;
• to remove the mulch cover in early spring so that the soil can warm (exception, black plastic mulch);
• Disdvantage: Mulched surfaces can attract voles.

Plants Used for Green Manure

Plant Species	Use	Soil Type	Sowing Time	Remarks
Yellow lupin (*Lupinus luteus*)	year-round culture, deep loosening, nitrogen enrichment	light	Apr.–Sept.	slow-growing
Blue lupin (*Lupinus angustifolius*)	pre-culture, year-round culture, deep loosening, nitrogen enrichment	light–moderately heavy	Apr.–Sept.	fast-growing
Crimson clover (*Trifolium incarnatum*)	between-, after-culture, undersowing, deep loosening, nitrogen enrichment	moderately heavy	Apr.–May July–Aug.	fast-growing, conditionally winter-hardy
Fava bean (*Vicia faba*)	pre-culture, deep loosening, nitrogen enrichment	all soils	Feb.–July	conditionally winter-hardy
Alfalfa, Lucerne (*Medicago sativa*)	deep loosening, nitrogen enrichment	moderately heavy	Mar.–Aug.	winter-hardy, attracts bees
Holy Hay (*Onobrychis viciifolia*)	nitrogen enrichment	moderately heavy	Apr.–Aug.	winter-hardy, attracts bees
(Oil) Radish (*Raphanus sativus*)	deep loosening	all soils	Apr.–Sept.	fast-growing, winter-hardy
White mustard (*Brassica hirta*)	year-round culture	light–moderately heavy	Apr.–Aug.	fast-growing, light germinator, crucifer
Rape (*Brassica napus*)	year-round culture, deep loosening	moderately heavy	Apr.–Sept.	winter-hardy, crucifer
Fiddleneck (*Phacelia tanacetifolia*)	year-round culture, pre-culture	all soils	Mar.–Sept.	fast-growing, attracts bees
Buckwheat (*Fagopyrum esculentum*)	pre-culture	light	Mar.–Apr.	fast-growing
Spinach (*Spinacia oleracea*)	pre-, between-, after-culture	all soils	Mar.–May Aug.–Oct.	fast-growing, winter-hardy
Common corn salad (*Valerianella locusta*)	after-culture	all soils	Aug.–Oct.	winter-hardy
Pot marigold (*Calendula officinalis*)	year-round culture, pre-culture, undersowing	all soils	Apr.–Aug.	against nematode
Common sunflower (*Helianthus annuus*)	year-round culture	light–moderately heavy	Apr.–July	attracts bees
Hairy vetch (*Hippocrepis* spp.)	year-round, pre-, between-, after culture	all soils	Mar.–May	Fast-growing, winter-hardy
Winter rye (*Secale cereale*)	after-culture	all soils	Aug.–Oct.	Fast-growing, winter-hardy

Phacelia tanacetifolia has beautiful, delicate blue flowers that are attractive to bees.

Composting

Compost—a magic word to the ears of gardeners and the key to long-term fertile soil. In composting, organic wastes are converted after a few months into valuable humus. It is a process wholly according to nature's model, except that it is undertaken on purpose and, thus, accelerated. It is both environmentally aware and economical to compost organic wastes instead of throwing them into the garbage can.

What Goes in the Compost Heap

Organic matter is decomposed with the aid of hydrogen, moisture, warmth, and countless microorganisms from the soil. This rotting process occurs in several phases:

Phase 1: In the first 2 weeks, it is mainly bacteria at work; in a short time, these produce high temperatures up to 158° F (70° C) through their increasing activity. This kills almost all disease germs and seeds. Then, the fungi, worms, and many other insects and microorganisms take over the breaking down of the organic matter. External sign: The compost heap falls in.

Phase 2: After 2 to 3 months, the first stage of ripening is reached: the very nitrogen-rich and still coarse-fibered raw or fresh compost. It can now be used for targeted fertilizing and for mulching (see right-hand page).

Phase 3: After another 2 to 3 months, through the activity of earthworms, dark, fragrant, mature compost, which can be used anywhere in the garden, is formed. Over the long term, the stable-structured permanent humus that makes the soil fertile develops from the mature compost.

Maturity test: You can very easily establish whether the compost is finished: Sow cress seeds on strained compost soil, press lightly, and dampen. After 3 to 4 days, a large portion of the seeds should have germinated. Sturdy, green cress leaves are a sign of mature compost.

Turning

The rotting process can be hastened if the compost is turned after 4 weeks. Then, the inside material is moved to the outside and the top to the bottom, because the main process is going on in the center of the heap. Turning is particularly effective in the summer season.

Heap or Bin?

Whether you have a heap or a bin depends on how much space there is. A heap needs more space than a bin.

Heap: For a trapezoidal heap (see drawing below), the following size has proven effective: 47 in (1.2 cm) wide, a maximum of 60 in (1.5 cm) high, length as long as you wish.

Bin: Standard measurements: 39 x 39 x 39 in (1 x 1 x 1 m). You can build your own bin of brick or wooden slats. There are commercially available ones of wood, plastic, wire netting, or metal. The material plays a subordinate role; what's important is the simplicity of movements for filling and emptying. Make sure that at least one side panel is removable.

Important: The compost container must be at least 39 inches cubed (1 m³) or no rotting process can take place. It should be open at the bottom so that microorganisms and worms can easily get in and out. The compost material must be well ventilated at the sides and be able to warm easily.

Composters

Bin of round logs.

Bin of recycled materials.

Bin of bricks.

Thermocomposter.

A compost heap does need a lot of space but it is more economical than a bin and is comfortable to work.

Layout of a Compost Area

A warm spot, protected from the wind and slightly shaded—these are the idea conditions for the compost to be able to ripen well.

When planning, consider that you need enough space to separate compost, break it up, and collect it. Furthermore, fresh green debris (remains of plants, grass, and leaves) should dry in the air before being added, or there is danger of rotting.

A three-part bin is certainly an optimal solution, if there is enough space for it in the garden. Freshly deposited, half-ripe, and ripe compost exist here side by side. When the mature compost in one bin has been used, a new supply of mature compost is available in the next.

An entry path is recommended to keep feet dry.

A wind and sight screen for neighbors and the house can be provided by undemanding plants like sunflowers, squash, or elderberry.

How Do You Compost?

Before piling compost, you must prepare the composting area.
• Loosen the soil.
• Dig up 4 in (10 cm) of soil (it will later be used to cover the heap).
• In normal to heavy soil, put in coarsely cut branches for drainage. In light, sandy soil, use loamy soil or finished compost.
• Alternative: Slightly raise the area so that superfluous standing water can run off.
• Pile up the gathered debris, after it has been cut up and mixed, in layers of 6 to 8 in (15–20 cm).
• "Inoculate" between additions (see column at right) with compost additives.
• Cover the top layer of the compost heap with garden soil or other fresh plant material.
• Add wooden boards, straw, or reed mats as protection from light, water, and rain.

Important: In hot, dry summers, water the compost once in awhile. It should feel like a squeezed-out sponge.

What Gets Composted?

Nitrogen-rich organic material:
Fresh plant parts, remains of mulch, dried grass cuttings, lawn sods, tree and hedge clippings, animal manures (horse or cow), kitchen waste (vegetable and fruit).
Nitrogen-poor organic material:
Dry leaves, straw, wooden debris, paper, and cardboard (chopped up).

What Doesn't Get Composted?

Diseased plant parts, roots and root weeds, seed-bearing plants, chemically treated substances (citrus fruits, wood), color-printed paper, severely rottable substances (bones, leather), cooked kitchen wastes, which attract vermin and smell, dairy products and meat.

Important Compost Additives

Each individual compost layer is "inoculated" with soil, compost, or compost starter and in addition is spread thinly with compost additives. This promotes the process of decay and enriches the material with nutrients. The following compost additives are spread on:

• Mature compost or loamy soil (2 to 3 shovelfuls per 10 sq ft [1 m²]) or compost starter (according to directions).
• Clay meal (bentonite) and rock phosphate (about 18 oz per 10 sq ft [500 g per m²]).
• Organic mixed fertilizer like horn-blood-bonemeal (about 7 oz per 10 sq ft [200 g per m²]) or horse manure (2 to 3 shovelfuls per 10 sq ft [per m²]).
• Algae lime/calcium (about 3.5 oz per 10 sq ft [100 g per m²]). Never use at the same time as horse or cow manure!

Using Compost Properly

Finished compost: A layer of about 0.5 to 1 in (1–2.5 cm) per year can be used in any kind of bed. Vegetables, shrubs, and trees receive—if possible—about double the quantity. Plants with high nutrient needs can receive an application in spring and fall. Work finished compost evenly into the soil.

Raw compost: For fertilizing (very rich in nitrogen) and for mulching. For fruit and vegetable culture, it's best to apply 0.5 to 1 in (1–2.5 cm) in early summer and immediately cover with a mulch layer (straw, grass).

Watering and Irrigation

Besides the type of soil and fertilizing measures, it mainly depends on proper watering as to whether your plants are healthy and strong and produce an abundant yield.

Water Requirements—a Relative Amount

Water constitutes the largest part of plants, and they can't live without it (vegetable plants, for instance, consist of almost 95% water).

Precipitation alone is usually not enough to provide garden plants with the necessary amount of water. In the spring and the early summer, during their main growing season and while the plants are fruiting and producing new buds, as well as during long dry spells, they need additional water. The water requirement is, thus, dependent on various factors.

Dependency of the plant. How thirstily and how much water a plant takes up depends on its root system and leaf mass. For

instance, shallow-rooted, herbaceous vegetable plants with large, soft leaves, over which much water is evaporated, need more frequent and more thorough watering than deep-rooted trees, shrubs, or roses. But older woody plants can also react sensitively to dry spells. Dehydration damage (retarded sprouting, poor growth, signs of deficiency in the leaves) often only becomes apparent after 1 or 2 years and then is hardly recognized as such any longer.

Dependency of the soil. The more favorable the soil conditions—subsoil, depth of water table, soil type and structure, as well as its ability to hold water—the better the conditions are for a steady supply of water.

• Medium-heavy loamy soils offer the best conditions for a steady water supply. They contain large and small soil particles (parts of sand, clay, and silt) in balanced proportions. Thus, they can hold water well, and superfluous water can easily drain off. They are also well aerated and can warm sufficiently.

• Sandy soils, of course, offer excellent drainage, but their storage capacity leaves something to be desired. They must be enriched with plenty of humus (compost, manure, or green manure, see page 160) in order to be able to store water and nutrients better.

• Heavy, clay soils, on the other hand, hold the water too well. Pooling occurs and, with it, cold is entrapped.

The 10 Golden Rules of Watering

When watering garden plants, you should follow a few important rules:

① Water in early morning or late evening—never in full sun or in midday heat.

② In general: It's better to water once thoroughly than to water a little several times.

③ On the other hand, severely dried-out areas should be watered slowly several times at short intervals. Sprinklers and spray hoses (see right-hand page) are especially suited for this.

④ Plants don't tolerate cold tap water well. The water from the sprinkler or soaker is exposed to the air and warms easily before it

reaches the plants. The ideal is water from a rain barrel.

⑤ If watering with a watering can or hose, water directly on the ground, if possible, not on the leaves. The stream should not be so hard that it washes the soil away.

⑥ Don't water newly set out plants with a hard stream; rather, sprinkle around the plants several times.

⑦ Don't keep new plants too wet (danger of rotting), because they first must form roots that can take up the water.

⑧ With freshly planted shrubs, always make a little rim of soil at least 2 in (5 cm)

high around them so that the water won't flow away so quickly.

Alternative: Lay the hose directly over the root region and let water slowly soak in over a long period.

⑨ After watering, if the soil is dried out again, loosen the soil, which saves one to two more waterings.

⑩ Water evergreen plants thoroughly once more in late fall—imperative on frost-free winter days on which the soil is not frozen—and then water well again in early spring.

The Rain Barrel with Water Collector

Rainwater is softer than tap water, warms with standing, and, therefore, is ideal for watering. It's best to catch it in a rain barrel. For this, a rain collector with an overflow stop is installed in the drainpipe. Important: After a dry spell, don't catch the first, dirty water from the roof; wait for perhaps a half hour. Close the barrel for safety (children, animals).

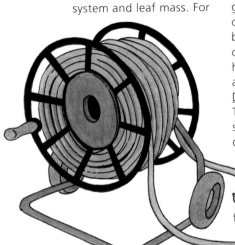

A hose cart for a mobile water supply is very helpful, primarily in large gardens.

The Most Important Sprinkler Types

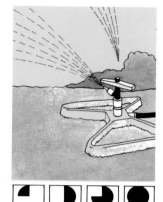

Rectangle-/Rotating Sprinkler

The apparatus swings a shower from left to right. The water is expelled through a row of spray holes on the swinging arm. A rectangular area is sprinkled.

You must cultivate deeply and work in sand or a synthetically produced vermiculite (see table, page 161) so that air spaces will be created and water can then escape.
Important: With particularly heavy, compacted, wet soil, a drainage system may have to be installed. However, this task is better left to a professional landscape construction firm.

Watering—What With?

The spectrum of watering possibilities ranges from the simple watering can to computer-controlled watering systems.

Circular Sprinkler

This sprinkler type distributes the water evenly over circular areas of different sizes. The spray is expelled from the rotating part by water pressure.

<u>Watering cans.</u>
Appropriate for small areas and delicate plants (seedlings, young plants). They should not be heavy and should have a sprinkling head (rose). Metal cans should not be used for making teas, such as suntea, because the teas will corrode them.
<u>Hoses and hose carts.</u> Very helpful for remote parts of the garden and larger gardens. There are various qualities and price ranges according to need. Double-walled, flexible hoses are expensive, but they also last longer

Pulse Sprinkler

Also called a sector sprinkler. Apparatus for evenly watering large, circular areas. Sprinkler head rotates in pulses. It can also be set to water only particular parts of an area (sectors).

and are resistant to kinking (heavy-duty rubber or PVC). There are various types of hose connectors of plastic. Hose rollers protect plantings.
<u>Spray hoses.</u> Especially suitable for rectangular beds, hedges, row culture, but also lawns, spray hoses are perforated along one side. The water sprays out in a very fine stream and gently dampens the soil.

<u>Soaker hoses.</u> The water trickles through a perforated hose directly into the soil. A soaker hose can also be buried 4 to 6 in (10–15 cm) underground as a simple irrigation system.
<u>Irrigation systems.</u> The possibilities range from simple hose connections that are joined with couplings and snap-on systems to underground networks of pipes with surface-level sprinklers and connections for every imaginable feature: from the garden shower to water-saving droplet watering for special culture—if desired, regulated by timed switches, semi- or fully automatic or computer controlled.

The slow, gentle rain of a spray hose is the most comfortable type of water for plants in bloom.

Planting and Care of Lawns

A lawn isn't just a lawn. Conceptions of garden owners often differ vastly from one to the next. The palette of requirements ranges from the manicured fine English lawn to the durable play and sports green.

Before you decide, get advice from the grass seed dealer, and be sure to give exact information about the following points:

• How is the lawn going to be used?

• What is the situation of the lawn surface (sunny or shady)?

• What is the soil consistency (sandy to dry, loamy to damp)?

Important: It always pays to choose an expensive quality grass mixture. The more durable and hard wearing a grassy surface is supposed to be, the broader and coarser the grasses it must contain.

Planting a New Lawn

The lawn is supposed to have a long life ahead of it, so it pays to prepare the soil especially carefully. For new lawns, this means removing any compaction in the subsoil and possibly also removing any construction debris. Therefore, with large areas, it is advisable to hire a gardening and landscaping firm, which can undertake thorough soil loosening and improvement at the same time or, if necessary, bring in topsoil. The upper soil layer (topsoil) should be at least 6 in (15 cm) deep— for the roots of the grass

Different Lawn-Mowing Systems

Roller, Cylinder, or Spindle Mower
This mower type offers the cleanest cut. It is particularly suited for dry, short grass on an even surface, especially for groomed ornamental lawns.

Rotating or Sickle Mower
One or several knives rotate horizontally around an axle and sickle off the blades of grass. Primarily suited to large areas and long, tough grass.

Air-cushion Mower
The machine moves on an air cushion. Suitable for slopes and moist soil. Also for corners and edges as well as useful for extremely long grass and under shrubs.

go down that far. To keep water from collecting, the upper surface of the soil must be very smooth; however, the total area should have a slight grade, if possible. The best seeding times for grass are late spring, when the soil is already somewhat dried out and warmed, and late summer or early fall (the germination temperature for grasses is around 46° F [8° C]. It's important that the seed germinate evenly; therefore, water if necessary until it comes up.

Tools for Lawn Care

① Edge clippers with long handles
② Fertilizer spreader (also good for grass seeding)
③ Aeration tool for aerating the lawn
④ String cutter with nylon string
⑤ Dethatching tool removes the thatch with the help of sharp little cutters
⑥ Electric lawn shears for edges and corners
⑦ Rake for cleaning up lawn cuttings and leaves

Seeding a Lawn

① Loosen the soil with the spade or spading fork. For large areas, it's best to use a tiller. Remove debris, stones, and roots.

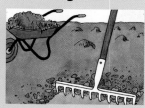

② Carefully rake the surface even. Uneven lawn surfaces make care more difficult later.

③ Finally, compact the leveled surface with boards. For large areas, it's advisable to use a roller.

④ Now scratch up the surface lightly again with the rake so that the seeds can germinate more easily and root.

⑤ Sow the seed evenly by hand or with a seed spreader (fertilizer spreader). For better distribution, mix with fine sand.

⑥ Lightly rake in the seed and use boards or a roller to make sure that the seed receives good soil contact. Finally, water it.

Year-round Lawn Care

The new grass is mowed for the first time when it has reached a height of 2 in (5 cm).

The first cut. All mower types are suitable for this; however, they should not be heavy. Important: Newly sharpened cutters. Set the cutter height to at least 1 in (2.5 cm); the first cut is only to regulate the root growth. The faster the turf fills in, the less chance the weeds have to get a toehold. Finally, carefully rake up the lawn cuttings and don't pull out any of the new plants. In the earliest phase, roll it sometimes or stamp on boards placed over it.

Watering. All the general watering rules (see pages 164–165) apply to watering a lawn.

Fertilizing. How often you have to fertilize depends on how regularly you cut and water the lawn. If you have an ornamental lawn that is mowed weekly, then at least two annual fertilizer applications are necessary:
• in late spring, after thatch has been removed.
• in summer (however, not during a very dry spell).
Slow-release fertilizers have proven to be effective. They contain mineral nitrogen in different forms: some that can be taken up by plants immediately and some that can be taken up gradually. Advantage: The lawn need not be fertilized again.

Important: Always apply fertilizer evenly, if possible using a spreader—however, the strips should not overlap as with mowing.

Mowing. The matters of how often to mow, how high the cutting blades should be set, and what happens to the clippings are settled according to the type of lawn. For utility surfaces, weekly mowing has proven valid. The cutting height should be 1 to 1.5 in (2.5–4 cm). The clippings are best collected in a grass catcher (use for compost or mulch). More frequent mowing promotes the density of the turf and thus the durability of the lawn.

Important: During heat spells, to avoid burning you shouldn't mow as short as usual.

Dethatching. Removing thatch serves to maintain the health of the lawn. Dethatching is done in the period from May to September—preferably before a cutting. The vertical cutting of the little knives on the dethatching tool cuts out the mat in the turf. Thus, air can get to the soil and the roots, which encourages water run off and avoids fungus infections.

Aeration. There are various special tools for aerating the lawn. All function according to the same principle: They work like earthworms. The resulting spaces in the soil guarantee aeration and improved water drainage.

Sod creates a usable lawn much sooner than seeding.

Planting and Care of Woody Plants

Before you plant woody plants, you should find out about their exact location requirements and ultimate height and growth form. Whether the new trees and shrubs will thrive in your garden also depends on what condition they are in when you buy them.

What to Watch for When Buying

When buying, make sure that the shrub is well branched, has sturdy roots, and exhibits no injuries or signs of disease (see pages 190–195). Also become familiar with terms in the nursery catalog:

• Sizes (height, breadth, or caliper size) at sale are usually given for all trees and shrubs.

Straw is good trunk protection for a newly planted standard with thin bark.

Planting Deciduous Woody Plants

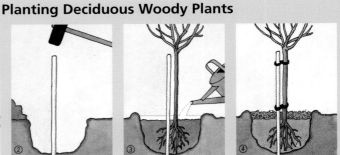

① Let bare-root trees and shrubs soak for several hours before planting; prune roots that are too long or are damaged.
② With tall plants, provide a stake before planting. It should extend 16 to 20 in (40–50 cm) below the bottom of the planting hole in order to guarantee a firm anchor.

③ Plant the tree (but no deeper in the soil than it was before). Fill in with the removed soil, which has been mixed with compost and organic fertilizer; wiggle the stem to work out any air holes. Fill the hole with water and let it seep away before filling with the remaining soil.
④ Only tie the trunk loosely to the stake at first until the soil has settled.

Planting Conifers

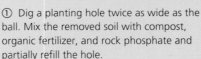

① Dig a planting hole twice as wide as the ball. Mix the removed soil with compost, organic fertilizer, and rock phosphate and partially refill the hole.
② Place the ball so that the plant's best side will be most visible. Then loosen the burlap or wires but don't remove them entirely. Any plastic should be removed.

③ Fill in with soil all around the ball; firm it lightly, but don't compact the soil.
④ Drive in the tree stake at an angle across the ball, against the direction of the wind. Only anchor firmly when the soil has settled. Build up a water lip around the hole; water well. Keep watering during the first year.

• It will say whether the shrub is balled or bare root.
• A sapling is simply a young tree (usually 1 to 2 years old). It is graded according to height.
• Shrubs are woody plants with several stems but without a trunklike center. They grow less than about 15 ft (5 m) tall.

• Zone information is provided to indicate which temperature zones the plant is hardy to and will grow in successfully.

Best Planting Times

You can plant trees and shrubs in the fall and in the spring. However, in the fall, the choice of

plants is larger. As a general rule:
• Don't plant in heat, heavy rain, or humidity.
• Plant deciduous plants after leaf drop, that is, in late fall.
• With wet and heavy soil or in regions with severe winters, it's better to plant sensitive plants in the spring.

Heeling-in Woody Plants

① If trees or shrubs are not to be planted immediately, dig a trench corresponding to the root length/size of the ball. Lay plants in at an angle.

② Shovel soil on top; tamp firm, and water. Also cover the base of the shoots. Plants can be left for several weeks this way.

Transplanting Woody Plants

① First, loosen the plant all the way around with the spading fork. The ball should be at least half as large as the diameter of the crown.

② Chop the roots all the way around and then, with angled jabs of the spade, pry the entire ball from the soil.

③ Place the rootstock on a tarpaulin; trim back any injured roots. The plant can easily be transported with the tarp.

④ Set the plant in the new, well-prepared hole and water in. If possible, prune the crown back somewhat.

• Set out conifers and evergreens in early fall or later in the spring. Water regularly and protect from the sun.

Proper Planting of Woody Plants

Prepare the soil several weeks or months before planting by deeply loosen-ing the soil and providing it with humus.
The trees or shrubs are then planted as follows:
• Dig a hole that is wider than it is deep (double the width of the ball) so that the roots can spread out sideways.
• Mix the removed soil with compost and fertilizer and partially refill the hole with it; place the plant in the hole.
• Fill the hole with earth in stages, watering in after each addition.
• Create a 2-in- (5-cm-) high rim around the planting hole to contain water.
• Remove plastic from root balls; however, burlap can remain on.
• A tree with a trunk or a shrub with a large ball must be supported. However, the stake should only be firmly anchored when the soil has settled.
• Ties of strong twine in a figure eight around the trunk and the stake or special tree ties of rubber have proven effective.

Care of the Woody Plant

The newly planted tree or shrub needs intensive care, particularly during the period of new growth. After a few years, the expenditure of care is less, but it varies from species to species (see Plant Portraits, pages 202–221).
Watering. Water young plants during long periods of drought or short-term hot spells. It's best to lay the hose there for several hours at a time at a slow rate and let water slowly seep in.
Loosen soil. This is only necessary in the first years, at best in the fall. Only loosen the soil lightly and superficially in order not to injure the fine root hairs.
Fertilizing. Good soil preparation, regular additions of compost, and mulching guarantee suffi-cient nutrients in normal soil and for newly planted shrubs or trees. Exceptions are older plants that have begun to slow in putting out new growth and/or flowering, or trees and shrubs on very thin soil.
• In the spring, provide nitrogen, just to stimulate growth—no more after the end of June, so that the wood can mature well.
• Complete fertilizers (2 oz per 10 sq ft [56 g per m^2] per year) or organic fertilizers (3.5 oz per 10 sq ft [100 g per m^2] per year) are very appro-priate.

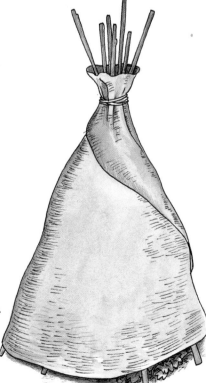

Wind and sun protector made of burlap, rush mats, or similar permeable material for freshly planted conifers and broad-leaved evergreens.

169

Pruning Woody Plants

By nature, many woody plants, if they stand alone, have a balanced, picturesque, or bizarre growth habit. Nevertheless, they still need at least some pruning for shape.

Preliminary Considerations

With newly purchased young plants, the growth habit typical for the species is not recognizable yet. Therefore, when planting, you need to allow for the height and, especially, the width the plant can attain. If they are planted too closely, shrubs and trees can never reach their full beauty and must continually undergo corrective pruning. But shrubs that are good for clipping also create a more beautiful effect when they can unfold fully and merely be thinned out now and again (see Specimens, page 78–79).

The butterfly bush (Buddleia davidii) is an ornamental shrub that can be cut back very hard every spring.

Why Prune?

The pruning of a tree or shrub should further support the special growth habit (the plant's framework has been already expertly developed in the nursery). Besides, pruning prevents the rapid aging of the plant so that it will retain its vigor over a long period.

What to Be Aware of When Pruning

Anyone who thinks to limit the vigor of a shrub by cutting it back is making a mistake. Severe pruning always promotes new growth and, therefore, is hardly appropriate for limiting the growth of a plant.

In general, the way a particular shrub is pruned varies from case to case. But there are some ground rules:

• Use only sharp shears and saws; smooth cuts heal better.
• Avoid large wounds.
• It is better to make two saw cuts for large side branches so that they don't tear out.
• Cut back to the base of a branch or to the next deeper branching.
• Cut dead branches back to healthy wood.
• Remove wild shoots and water sprouts back to their source.
• Annually remove wood that is growing too densely, turning inward, or is weak or overage.

• After the training pruning, only prune plants again when they have reached their basic form.

Flowering shrubs
With flowering shrubs, the time of pruning depends on the time of flowering (see right-hand page). With lilacs, for example, the faded flowers should always be removed, for under them develop the beginnings of next year's flowers, and the development of seeds costs the plant unnecessary strength.

Specimen plants
Only thin specimen plants (such as hazel, magnolia, golden chain, smoke bush, and Japanese maple) carefully every few years; severe pruning will have a negative effect on their beauty and the character of their growth (see Specimens, pages 78–79).

Broad-leaved evergreens
Among these are boxwood, privet, rhododendron, and cherry laurel. They really don't need pruning, but usually they tolerate a shaping or

hedge pruning very well. Exception: the evergreen *Cotoneaster* species.

Conifers (needle-leaved evergreens)
In this plant group, the regular, mostly pyramidal forms (fir, pine, cedar) are not pruned. For one thing, because the characteristic growth form would be lost, for another because these plants cannot put out new growth after a severe pruning back to old wood. Cypress, arborvitae, and yew, on the other hand, tolerate pruning well, put out new growth from the old wood, and are thus best suited for clipped hedges (see pages 80–81).

• With irregularly growing conifers, some juniper species and dwarf pines, the growth can be influenced by shortening the side shoots.
• With dwarf pines, you can shorten the May growth by about half in order to induce the plant to a branching, bushier shape.

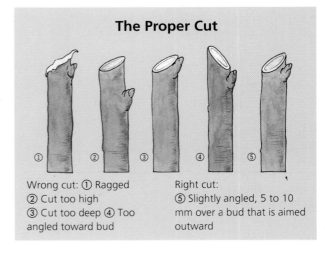

The Proper Cut

Wrong cut: ① Ragged
② Cut too high
③ Cut too deep ④ Too angled toward bud

Right cut:
⑤ Slightly angled, 5 to 10 mm over a bud that is aimed outward

Planting and Training Pruning

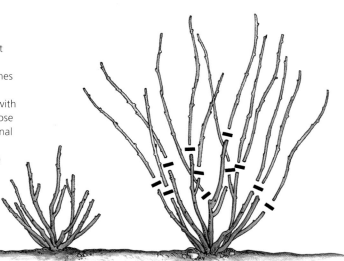

Time. Only in spring, even if planting itself is done in the fall.

Reason. Cut back bare-root woody plants after planting in order to restore the balance between the pruned roots and the aboveground parts.

How to prune. Shorten the shoots by one third or up to one half. Leave a central shoot longer and prune the side shoots evenly to form a pyramidal shape (sap level balance). In older plants, cut back the weaker shoots; in young ones, the stronger ones to encourage branching.

Important: Woody plants with few vigorous shoots and those with particularly large terminal buds (maple, magnolia, mountain ash, tree peonies) as well as balled trees and shrubs are not pruned after planting, or only very slightly.

Maintenance Pruning

Time. Every 2 or 3 years in early spring or fall. Ornamental trees and shrubs that bloom in the spring and the summer form new flower shoots for the coming year immediately after the current year's flowers fade. These should never be pruned. To keep this from happening, it is advisable to do any pruning immediately after blossoming.

Reason. Maintenance pruning serves to maintain the shrubs' vigor and/or flowering ability. First of all, they are thinned as a result.

How to prune. Remove old and weak wood, taking shoots that have finished flowering back to the base or to over the start of a younger shoot. Overaged branches are recognizable by their darker color; they may be bending mostly toward the ground or be bare down below.

Rejuvenation Pruning

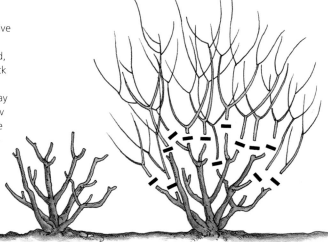

Time. Early spring or fall.

Shrubs that are pruned every year. Among these are semishrubs like Saint John's wort, fuchsia, silverberry, low ornamental shrubs like ceanothus, cotoneaster, and late-summer bloomers (butterfly bush, bluebeard, bush clover).

Reason. They only bloom lushly on this year's growth. Therefore, it's best to cut back to a few buds in March.

How to prune older shrubs. With shrubs that don't receive any regular pruning and eventually become overaged, the branches can be cut back to 12 to 20 in (30–50 cm). Remove old wood all the way down to the base. Then new shoots can develop from the remaining branches and the shrub can usually regain its natural growth form.

Planting Fruit Trees and Bushes

Fruit trees and bushes not only bring a new design element into the garden with their marvelous flowers and their varied growth forms, but they also provide the enjoyment of one's own delicious, untreated fruit. The possibilities for choice are simply inexhaustible. There are countless species and varieties of fruit, and there are also various crown and trunk forms and fruit hedges, espaliers, and bushes.

Before Buying, Consider

Fruit trees can often grow to be decades old, so you must think carefully when you plan. Before buying, consider:
• Standards and semi-dwarfs become very large, are hard to care for, and produce abundant yields that must be processed.
• With dwarf and miniature

forms or berry bushes, you can separate parts of the garden from one another, such as the produce garden from the flower garden.
• Espaliers and climbing fruit bushes are suitable for covering walls and pergolas, especially in south to southwestern exposures.
• The climate requirements of the species and varieties vary widely. Some thrive only in a mild, warmer climate (see plant portraits, pages 280–289).
• Fruit trees are grafted onto rootstocks, which influence their growth and yield and are attuned to the soil type. Dwarfs and miniatures have weakly growing rootstocks.
• It is recommended that you have a soil analysis made of the chosen location (see Soil Tests, pages 148–149).
• All fruit species need humus-rich, deeply cultivated garden soil, which should be damp but not wet and cold.

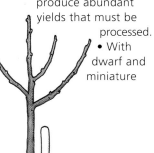

Planting fruit trees right
Prepare the soil carefully:
• *Dig the planting hole twice as wide as the rootball (see Planting and Care of Woody Plants, pages 168–169).*
• *Loosen compacted subsoil thoroughly.*
• *The graft should be about 4 in (10 cm) above the ground.*
• *Standards and semidwarfs only need a stake in the first few years; but dwarfs and miniatures need one for their entire lives, because they have a weak rootstock. The stake should be as tall as the miniature.*

Support for Berry Bushes

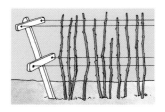

Support for Raspberries
Drive in posts at an angle. Attach crossbars with eyelets to the posts—one at the top and one in the middle—and thread wire through the eyelets.

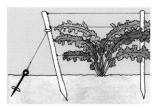

Blackberry Support
Blackberries need sturdy supports of strong wires fastened between posts. Give the outermost posts additional support with earth anchors.

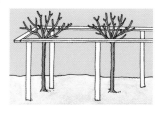

Row Frames
Standard gooseberry and currant trees can easily buckle at the base of the crown. Here use a frame on which the crowns can rest.

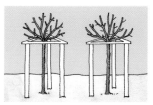

Individual Supports
Individual standards are supported with a triangular wooden support. Each corner rests on a post. Posts and the framing are nailed.

• Frost-endangered regions are always unfavorable.
• Get advice on the choice of variety from an expert. Basically, local varieties are recommended. Also important are disease resistance and, for apples and pears, keeping quality.
• There are self-fertilizing fruit species (sour cherries, peaches, apricots, quinces and Syrian plums) and non-self-fertilizing ones (apples, pears, sweet cherries, greengage plums, and some other plums). Non-self-fertilizing varieties need a pollinator in the vicinity (in your own or a neighbor's garden) if they are to bear fruit. When space is a problem, there is the possibility of having varieties that can pollinate each other grafted onto one tree.
• Fruit trees that are to pollinate each other must also flower at the same time.
• Fruit trees need intensive care. Pruning of fruit trees (page 174–175), especially, requires time and knowledge.
• Local ordinances vary with regard to the distance required from the property line for planting.

Forms of Fruit Trees

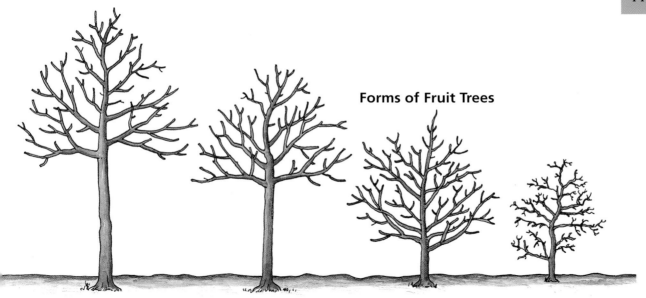

Standard
Standards can grow to be very large and many decades old. Like semidwarfs they are grafted onto vigorous seedling rootstocks. The mature height of the full tree is from 15 to 20 ft. They cast a great deal of shade and in larger gardens are splendid specimens or trees for near the house. Standards bear fruit after about 8 to 10 years (full harvest stage).

Semidwarf
A semidwarf only differs from the standard in the length of the trunk. The full mature height ranges from 10 to 15 ft (3–4.5 m), with the larger trees being apples, pears, and sweet cherries, for example. The harvest may be correspondingly large. Plums and apricots grow smaller. Semidwarfs bear fruit after 6 to 8 years.

Dwarf
Dwarfs have a small crown of 13 to 16 ft (4–5 m), but a full mature height ranging from 6 to 10 ft (2–3 m). Suitable for apples and pears, sour cherries, apricots, peaches, and quince. In small gardens, they are also charming as specimens. Harvesting and pruning are relatively easy. Dwarfs usually bear fruit after about 4 to 5 years.

Miniatures/Extra Dwarf
The miniatures and the pillar shrubs are the smallest forms of a free-growing fruit tree (only for stone fruit). Harvesting and pruning are possible without a ladder. Mature heights reach from 5 to 7 ft (1.5–2 m). Miniatures are good choices as potted plants. They are ready to bear fruit in the third year.

Espalier Forms

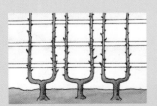
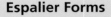
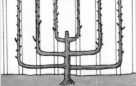

U-shaped Espalier
Apple and pear trees are well suited for pruning into shapes. The two prunings of fruitwood in the summer are the most important for this. All the side shoots are pinched out to 3 to 5 leaves in June and in August (after the new growth). The winter pruning is carried out as usual (see pages 174–175). U-shaped espaliers are good for hedges and dividers. For this purpose, they are fastened to wires or lattice extending horizontally between posts.

Six-armed Espalier
An apple or pear tree can be trained with an expensive pruning (nursery) so that it forms two or several parallel branches, which are at first trained horizontally on wire or lattice trellises and then trained vertically at regular intervals. Pruning with this 6-armed espalier is like that of the U-shaped one. This espalier form can decorate a side of a house, especially south or southwestern facing sides. The house wall serves as a heat retainer, which can produce earlier harvests.

Unformed Espalier
Fruit trees can also be grown naturally against the side of house walls—as loose or fan-shaped espaliers. Along with apples and pears, the stone-fruit species are also suitable for this purpose. The irregular growth of the unformed espalier does, however, require a larger surface, and the branches stand away from the wall somewhat more. The central leader can be removed or it can be drawn more and more to the side. The side branches are spread out against the wall.

Berries
Most berry bushes are self-fertilizing. The fruit production is often better, however, if you plant two or three varieties near each other. Different varieties offer different flavor variations and slightly staggered harvest times.
Planting times: September/October, March/April.
Planting distance: Blueberries, currants, gooseberries: 5 ft (1.5 m); raspberries: 18 in (0.5 m); blackberries: 10 to 13 ft (3–4 m).
Soil: Humus and nutrient rich, not too wet.
Important: Cultivated blueberries only thrive in acid soil (pH under 5). Make the planting hole about 10 sq ft (1 m²) in size and mix the soil with a lot of peat.

Pruning and Care of Fruit Trees

The pruning of fruit trees isn't at all simple and depends on the species of fruit, variety, and often even on the understock or the shape of the crown. It's best if you rely on the advice of the expert at the nursery or take a course in fruit tree pruning offered at a garden club or a community college.

Basics of Fruit Tree Pruning

When trees are not pruned, they grow as if "up to the sky." But you need to avoid this with fruit trees, for the fruit should remain easily within reach. Pruning makes it possible to limit the growth, promote formation of flowers, prevent disease as well as growth, and attune flowering and fruiting to one another.

In the juvenile stage, the crown is formed, usually a pyramid with a center leader and 3 or 4 lead branches. If possible, these should be in step form at a 45° angle to the trunk. Branches at too steep an angle tear out too easily, whereas more level ones let more light into the crown and produce more fruiting wood. Training pruning of the crown should be performed for at least 5 years until it has reached its final form. Important princples are: branches that are too dense, too steep, growing inward, weakly growing wood, or growing vertically on the top of the branch are removed.

With older trees, only some thinning is done every several years to let light and air into the crown and to stimulate new growth by pruning back. A radical rejuvenation is only necessary if there has not been regular pruning or thinning and the yield has rapidly dwindled. Then the tree crown is decreased by one third.

Structure of a Fruit Tree

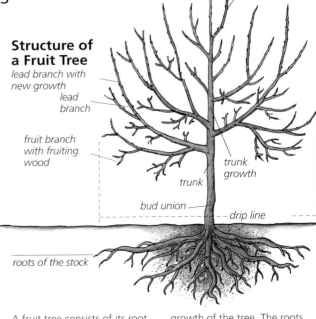

competing branch

lead branch with new growth

lead branch

fruit branch with fruiting wood

trunk growth

trunk

bud union

drip line

roots of the stock

A fruit tree consists of its root, trunk, and crown. If the tree has been grafted, the bud union should be about 4 in (10 cm) above the ground. The union must not come in contact with the soil. The rootstock influences the growth of the tree. The roots travel directly under the soil surface (careful when digging) and reach beyond the drip line of the crown (be careful when adding fertilizer and creating a bed around the tree).

Renewal of Fruiting Wood on the Slender Spindle/Pillar

1st year: Development of new wood (don't prune).

2nd year: Fruitwood formation (shorten tip).

3rd year: Harvest. Then cut back to the base of the shoot (stub with two eyes).

Pruning a Slender Miniature (Pillar)

Slender miniatures (pillars) and miniature bushes (see right-hand page) are pruned differently from other fruit trees. They have no leaders but only a continuous central shoot and loosely distributed fruiting branches around it.

With the slender miniature, the fruiting wood is continuously renewed. Prune as per drawing at the left. That way it can't develop any sturdier branches. New shoots continually develop from the central stem, which form flower buds in the second year, bear fruit in the third year, and can be cut back the following winter to the base of the shoot (stub with 2 eyes). Thus, there will be no wood more than 3 years old. Because the growing shoots on 2-year-old branches are regularly cut back, the little tree always stays small.

The starting point for the slender miniature is a 1-year-old graft.

• Leave 4 to 5 side shoots (16 to 20 in [40–50 cm] apart); these bear fruit first. Cut all the others, including the uppermost side shoots, back to stubs.

• Usually 2 new shoots will form on these, of which the most steeply angled or the weakest is again cut back to the base.

• The remaining shoot forms buds the second year, fruits in the third, after which it is cut back to a stub. Meanwhile, new fruiting wood has formed.

Pruning Measures During the Life of a Fruit Tree

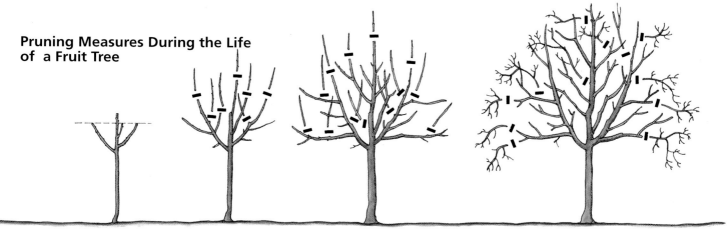

Pruning at Planting

The planting pruning has often been done at the nursery. If not, shorten the 3 lead branches by about half to two-thirds, all at the same level (sap flow balance), making sure the terminal buds face away from the center of the plant (see Pruning Woody Plants, page 170). The leader or central branch—the extension of the trunk—should be about 8 in (20 cm) longer than the lead branches.

Training Pruning

From the second year, you should again shorten the leader and the lead branches according to the diagram for planting pruning (sap level), but only by one third or at most one half. Remove all competing branches (with the lead branches) directly at the sprouting place or at the trunk (at the branch ring), as well as the new growth that points inward.

Maintenance Pruning

The crown development is also controlled in stages of yields. The goals of pruning are a balanced basic framework and thinning and aerating the crown. Steep, weak, and densely growing side branches can be tied into horizontal position from the second year to encourage early harvest. Afterward they are removed entirely.

Rejuvenation Pruning

You can interrupt the aging process of a fruit tree with a severe pruning back to old wood. External signs of age are the long, downward hanging outer branches. They must be radically pruned; the crown will be greatly lightened in addition and can be newly shaped according to the earlier training principles.

Pruning a Small Tree

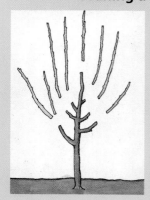

Starting point is a 2-year-old grafted small tree from the nursery:
• You need 4 or 5 branches to develop a crown. Along with the leader, these are severely pruned so that a pyramid shape is created. The branches in between are removed back to the base or may also be tied into horizontal position so that 2 years later they will bear fruit. These branches should be removed entirely after the harvest.
• After the first year, new branches have formed. Now cut back all competing branches and steeply angled branches to their bases. All the remaining fruiting branches that are pointing horizontally away from the center should remain unshortened.
• After 3 to 4 years, the branch portions that have stopped producing and are growing toward the ground should be removed.
• With older small trees (from about the 7th year) regularly shorten the new growth by about half in order to stimulate growth again.

Care of Fruit Trees

Pruning techniques alone are not enough to ensure harvesting an abundance of fruit. Targeted fertilizing, soil cultivation, and pest management complete the care.

Fertilization. In the home garden it isn't a question of massive yield, so for older, large fruit trees, 1 or 2 additions of compost per year are enough. Spread the compost around the fruit tree in the fall, up to 4 in (10 cm) deep, and cover with a layer of leaves. If there is no compost available, use organic mixed fertilizer (horn-blood and bonemeal) or organic-mineral complete fertilizer. In March or April it should be shallowly worked into the soil around the tree.

The small fruit tree forms with weak root systems receive fertilization 3 times a year:
• In the fall apply a layer of mature compost, which is covered with leaves or straw.
• In March, before the start of flowering and in summer (June/July), for bud development for the following year and the promotion of this year's fruit crop, apply organic or organic-mineral fertilizing (see Basics of Fertilizers, pages 156–157).
Important: Give liquid fertilizer to fruit trees that are situated in grass. Make about 2 holes per 10 sq ft (1 m²) with the spading fork along the drip line and add the fertilizer.

Planting and Care of Roses

Roses have high requirements for location, soil, and care; unless these are met, roses are not able to thrive well.

Optimal Location

Roses love open, airy areas, sun, and warmth. They are not tolerant of:
• heat pockets caused by being too close to the house wall or in a protected place (south terrace).
• close crowding by other plants.
• cold and drafts.
• severe temperature fluctuations (especially in early spring between day and night).
In short, roses don't like extremes but want living conditions that are as even as possible.

Soil and Soil Preparation

The best garden soil (deep, loose, airy, well-drained, and rich in nutrients) is just good enough for roses. Mostly, these are the moderately heavy, sandy-loamy or loamy-sandy soils. The soil should be slightly acid to neutral (pH 6.5–7.0). For larger rose plantings it pays to have a soil analysis with recommendations for fertilizing. Before planting, it is important to loosen the soil 2 spade-lengths deep and to improve it. Figure a bucket of mature compost per planting hole. Also add a mixture of horn-blood and bonemeal, rock phosphate and algae lime/calcium to the soil.

Tips for Fertilizing

Don't fertilize for 1 year after planting roses. Roses receive enough nutrients with the initial fertilization at planting. But after that, they need a great deal of feeding. It's best to use so-called rose fertilizer from the garden center or an organic-mineral fertilizer (see pages 156–157). Advantage: The mineral-bound nutrients are immediately available to the plants, whereas the organic nutrients are released slowly. This nutrient spurt then occurs in time for bud formation. On the other hand, acute nutrient deficiencies can be remedied with purely mineral fertilizers.

Important: Work in well-rotted horse, chicken, or cow manure or dried manure several weeks before planting.

Forms Available and Top-Quality Grades

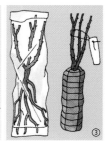

Forms available
① Bare-root roses are planted in fall or spring.
② Roses in containers can be planted anytime.
③ Packaged roses dry out easily or put out new growth early. Balled and burlapped roses can be planted immediately.
Top-quality grades:
Grafted roses of class (1½) B have at least two well-developed canes. Roses of class (1) A have at least 3 sturdy canes and a well-developed root system. Avoid No. 2 grades.

Rose Care Throughout the Year

If you create the most favorable starting conditions at planting, the amount of care required will be kept within limits.
Beginning of March/April
• First fertilization. Best to use an organic-mineral fertilizer and work lightly into the soil.
End of March/Beginning to mid-April
• Carry out spring pruning (see page 178).
• Remove hills around roses.
• Fertilize light, nutrient-poor soils once (organic fertilizer).
• Mulch as soon as the soil has warmed. Distribute a 0.5- to 1 in- (1–2.5 cm-) deep layer of compost around the plant and spread the mulching material (see page 161) over it.
May to October
• Regularly remove wilted flowers and diseased canes.

Structure of a Rose

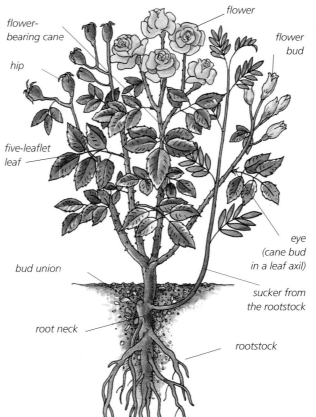

flower-bearing cane

hip

flower

flower bud

five-leaflet leaf

eye (cane bud in a leaf axil)

bud union

sucker from the rootstock

root neck

rootstock

Planting Roses

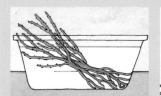

① Best planting time: October/November. Always soak bare-root roses for about 1 hour before planting.

② Prune injured roots; shorten roots that are too long to about 6 to 8 in (15–20 cm). Helpful: Just before planting, submerge in muddy water.

③ Dig a planting hole twice as large as the root system. Place the rose so that the bud union is about 2 in (5 cm) under the surface of the soil.

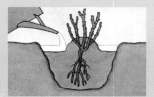

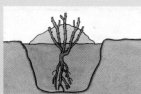

④ Fill in the planting hole with garden soil (mixed with well-aged compost, an organic fertilizer, kelp, rock phosphate, loam). Tap down gently.

⑤ Before completely filling the hole, water well several times. Make sure the roots are properly watered in so that no air pockets will be left.

⑥ Mound up the remaining soil to about 6 to 8 in (15–20 cm) around the rose. Even with spring planting, let hilling remain for about 4 weeks.

Overwintering Roses

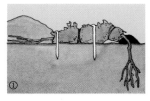

Tree and Cascade Roses

① Young tree roses are flexible. They are bent over a cone so they don't tear out. Wrap the trunk with burlap or brush to the crown. Remove leaves before anchoring the trunk to the ground with wickets. Cover crown with loose soil but don't pack it down.
② Older tree roses have their leaves removed, with excelsior or straw spread among the branches; the base of the crown should be particularly well protected. Cover with burlap or pine branches that are overlapped like roof tiles.
③ Cascade roses are protected the same way, but the trailing canes should first be tied against the trunk. This also protects the bud union at the base of the crown.

Classic and Bedding Roses

Roses can freeze back badly in severe winters. Therefore, classic, bedding, miniature, and also the repeat-flowering shrub roses should be hilled and, in addition, protected with brushwood. However, don't do it until after the first hard frost or the plants will weaken.

Climbing Roses

Protect roses on arbors, pergolas, and trellises with pine boughs or burlap. Overlap the boughs like roof tiles to protect from cold, drying winds, dangerous winter sun, and especially from temperature fluctuations in early spring.

• Gather up dropped (diseased) leaves and put them in the garbage. Don't compost them so as not to spread fungus diseases.
• Fertilize a second time at the beginning of June. Lightly scratch an organic-mineral complete fertilizer into the soil and water thoroughly.
• From the middle of July, do not add any more fertilizer so that the canes can harden off well before winter.
• Examine roses regularly for insects and disease. If necessary, institute countermeasures (see pages 190–191).
• In July/August, work the mulch layer shallowly into the soil and renew it.
• Roses need about 1 in water per week. If rainfall is low, then irrigate roses. Important: Water roses from underneath, without getting the leaves wet (fungus diseases)!
• In early fall, add a couple of inches of good finished compost to enrich soil and insulate plants. As necessary, add a handful of calcium carbonate per 10 sq ft (1 m²) every 2 to 3 years.

November/December
• Prune out any damaged, weak, or diseased canes.
• Hill up roses about 8 in (20 cm) deep with mature compost, earth, or well-rotted horse or cow manure.

Pruning Roses

Rose pruning is nowhere near so difficult as it's often made out to be. You must only observe the plants well in order to get to know the different growth habits of the various rose varieties and their blooming behavior. All the rules listed are merely guidelines.

When and How to Prune

The basic pruning of roses is done in early spring. In the summer, only the withered blossoms of the repeat-flowering roses are removed (see drawing below), in order to promote new flowers.

The right moment: The main pruning (see drawing above) takes place in early spring (March/April), when the buds begin to swell. Basic principles are: The less pruning done, the faster the cane send out shoots and flowers. The more severe the pruning, the longer you must wait for flowers, but the stronger the new growth. Less vigorous varieties can be stimulated to growth in this way.

Once-flowering roses bloom on short stems that develop on old wood. These roses do not receive a regular spring pruning, but they are thinned every few years. They are also not pruned after flowering, because these roses often produce beautiful hips.

Repeat-flowering roses first bloom on this year's shoots, later on side branches that develop out

Ground Rules for Pruning Roses

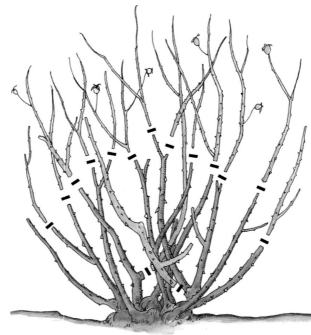

- Always prune slightly angled over an eye that is aimed toward the outside (see drawing, page 170).
- Use sharp shears to avoid crushing the wood.
- Cut dead, diseased wood

(dark center) back to healthy wood (white center).
- Remove old canes back to the ground.
- Thin out canes that are weak, too close together, crossing, or aiming inward.

Summer Pruning

① With hybrid tea roses, cut back after blossom has faded to a 5-leaflet leaf. If you want long stems, cut correspondingly deeper.

② With cluster roses, also cut the inflorescence back to a fully developed 5-leaflet leaf beneath it.

of the earlier-flowering canes—thus, a second and third flowering occurs. They must be pruned regularly in spring and also during the summer (see drawing below) in order to stimulate new flowers. If roses are only pruned a little in the spring, they branch more vigorously and bloom more abundantly. However, weak and old canes must be removed regularly.

Rejuvenation: A radical pruning of the rosebush every 3 to 5 years is recommended to rejuvenate the plant.

Tree Roses, Cascade Roses

Classic and bedding roses can be grafted onto standards and are then called tree or standard roses. Cascade roses (weeping roses), on the other hand, are climbing roses grafted onto standards.

Tree roses are pruned like bedding or classic roses (see drawing, page 179 top). However, make sure when you prune them that you create an evenly rounded crown.

With cascade roses, you need only cut back the outer branches slightly and every now and then prune out the older canes and those growing too densely from the inside.

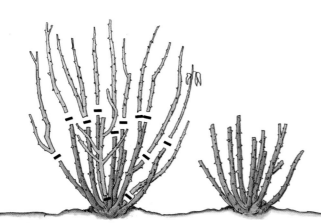

Pruning Bedding, Classic, Dwarf Roses

Bedding roses bloom in clusters, whereas the flowers of the classic roses usually occur singly at the end of a stem. Dwarf roses are small-flowered and small-growing cluster roses.

All three groups are stimulated to constant reflowering by regular summer pruning (see drawing, page 178).

Basic pruning in spring:
• Limit number of canes—depending on the age of the plant—to 3 to 8 sturdy canes.
• Shorten thinner canes more severely, up to 3 to 4 eyes, and older, sturdier canes only to 4 to 6 eyes.
• Classic roses that are supposed to flower on long stems can be cut back harder, but no more than to only 2 to 3 eyes per cane.

Pruning Climbing Roses

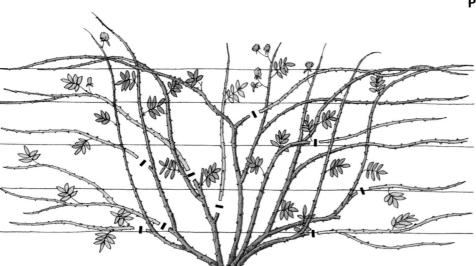

Climbing roses bloom on side branches of wood that is 1 and/or several years old. The young long canes arising from the rootstock or older side shoots are not cut back but are spread out in arches.

In spring, first of all, the old wood is shortened back to just above ground level.

For once-flowering climbers, shorten the side branches right after blooming by about half.

With repeat-flowering climbers, shorten the side branches to up to 2 to 4 eyes in spring and in summer cut off the faded flowers.

Pruning Shrub and Ground-Cover Roses

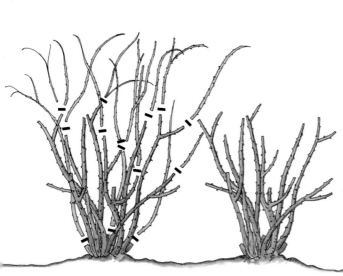

Once-flowering shrub roses (Wild, Park, and Moss Roses) are usually very strongly branched. With increasing age, they become more and more imposing and full-flowered. Usually, after the flowers, very attractive rose hips develop over the summer, so these roses are also not cut back but merely have the old wood removed from underneath now and again.

Repeat-flowering shrub roses (Ornamental shrub roses) resemble the bedding roses. After the first flush of bloom, they flower again once or several times. The spent flower clusters are removed below their branching point in order to promote development of new flowers. Like the bedding roses, these roses require intensive care (see fertilizing and watering, pages 156–159 and 164–165).

Ground-cover roses is the modern term for the shrub roses that grow closer to the ground, forming lush carpets of flowers within a very short time. This type is broken down into five different categories according to growth forms and degrees of vigor. Generally they are not pruned at all.

Planting and Care of Perennials

Perennials are winter-hardy plants with very diverse requirements. Their above ground, tender parts usually die back in the fall and winter. In the spring, they put forth new growth from their underground organs. Besides bedding and wild plants, water plants, grasses, and ferns, the perennials also include bulbs and corms.

Choice and Soil Preparation

Before you buy perennials you should have checked out your location possibilities, the soil, and the climatic conditions. The location requirements of perennials differ widely, corresponding to their different natural environments (see pages 20–21).

Planting Perennials

Perennials are usually sold in plastic containers. Advantage: The roots are protected and growing on is made easier. Therefore, you need not be so particular about the planting time.

① Water the plant once more thoroughly before planting. Then, carefully unpot without breaking any shoots. Remove the uppermost layer of soil from the root ball, for weeds and moss are likely to be growing there and will continue to develop further after planting.

② Dig out as much of the prepared, loosened soil (see below) as is needed to make space for the root ball.

③ Loosen the root ball slightly with your fingers, cut off any damaged roots, and plant at once so that the roots don't dry out unnecessarily.

It's best to plant on dull days or even in rainy weather, never in heat or drought.

④ Don't plant perennials any deeper than they were in the pot. This is especially important with plants whose buds are located directly at the soil surface (peonies, phlox). Therefore, set the plants a little high at first, then press in with the hands and water carefully several times (planting distance, see plant portraits, pages 232–247).

Tall and wide-spreading perennials like delphiniums and peonies need supports. Sprawling can be avoided with rings or stakes that link together.

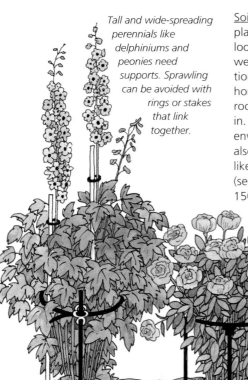

Soil preparation. Before planting, the soil must be loosened deeply and all the weeds removed. In addition, compost as well as horn-blood bonemeal and rock phosphate are worked in. Depending on the plant's environment, you should also mix in further additions like sand, gravel, or loam (see Soil Care, pages 150–151).

Planting Special Perennials

Iris

Best planting time: July/August. Plant the rhizome so that it lies horizontal to the ground and only cover with enough soil to leave the upper third exposed (sensitive to dampness). Press firmly and cover the surface with gravel or coarse crushed limestone.

Water Lilies

Best planting time: May to August. Plant the water lily in a basket furnished with special insulation (special supplier). Fill with 4 in (10 cm) of gravel, establish the rhizome on a slant in loamy soil (special pond soil from supplier), fasten with hooks, and cover with gravel or sand. Place the basket in the water.

Planting Depths for Bulbs and Corms

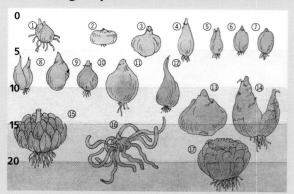

① winter aconite (*Eranthis hyemalis*), ② anemone (*Anemone blanda*), ③ crocuses (*Crocus*, wild and hybrids), ④ iris (*Iris danfordiae, I. reticulata*), ⑤ snowdrops (*Galanthus elwesii, G. nivalis*), ⑥ grape hyacinths (*Muscari* species), ⑦ squill (*Scilla siberica, S. bifolia*), ⑧ narcissi (*Narcissus*, wild forms), ⑨ species tulips (*Tulipa* species and varieties), ⑩ alliums (*Allium* species), ⑪ garden tulips (*Tulipa* varieties), ⑫ autumn crocuses (*Colchicum* hybrids),⑬ hyacinths (*Hyacinthus* varieties), ⑭ narcissi (*Narcissus* varieties), ⑮ lilies (*Lilium* species and varieties), ⑯ desert-candles (*Eremurus* species), ⑰ crown-imperial (*Fritillaria imperialis*)

When to Plant

Good planting times for perennials are the spring and the fall. Also, in general: Planting or transplanting is done after flowering. This means: the spring and early summer for early-flowering plants and early fall or even the spring for those that bloom in the second half of the year. Grasses and ferns are best planted in the spring. Some plants also have special requirements. For example, water plants are only put in when the water has warmed somewhat and danger of a frost has passed. Perennial plants develop very quickly and are usually well grown by the second year after planting.

Care of Perennials

All perennials need a certain amount of care, but the most demanding are bedding perennials.
Watering. Only necessary for freshly planted and moisture-loving plants and during long dry spells.
Loosening. Scratch up soil surface, to improve aeration, especially after heavy rain storms and dry spells.
Weeding. Important for new plantings. Root weeds (quack grass, goutweed) interfere with the development of the plants.
Fertilizing. On humus garden soil, a thin layer of compost once to twice a year is enough. Nutrient-poor soils are fertilized more (see page 150), depending, however, on the species of the plant (see plant portraits, pages 234–257 and 268–277). The most favorable time for fertilizing: either before the first flowering period or after a heavy pruning. Don't fertilize anymore after August or winter hardiness may be compromised.
Mulching. Add grass cuttings, shredded bark, or compost to decrease evaporation in summer and inhibit weeds; use leaves for winter protection.
Staking. If plants grow very tall or very wide, they must be supported (see drawing, page 180).
Cutting back. Remove spent flowers immediately, which stimulates the plant to put out new shoots, prolongs the flowering time, or induces a second flowering. Remove dead plant parts in early spring.

Rejuvenating Perennials

Dividing Roots

Even with long-lived perennials, it is advisable to rejuvenate by dividing the plants every few years. Especially when the flower production wanes or the ball gets too dense and the plant becomes bare from the inside out, it's time to thin out old plants. With daisies and asters, for example, after the plant has been dug up, separate out individual rooted shoots. The strongest of them are replanted, and after 2 to 3 years they have again developed into lushly flowering plants.

Dividing Rhizomes

Plant rejuvenation and plant propagation go hand in hand. Fleshy rootstocks (rhizomes) are cut straight through with a knife at the thinnest places. Damaged root parts are cut away. The wounds heal by themselves.

Important: Plants with taproots don't divide well because of the shape of their rootstock. It is easier to propagate the plant with root cuttings (see Vegetative Propagation, page 154) or sow again.

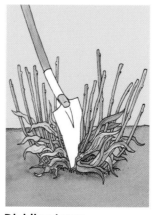

Dividing Large Rootstocks

The simple way to rejuvenate is to divide the rootstock with a spade or a spading fork. First loosen the root ball all around, pull out manageable hunks, remove intergrown and old root parts, and replant.

Planning a Vegetable Garden

Fresh-picked vegetables are rich in the nutrients necessary for life and are particularly flavorful. There is scarcely a gardener who wants to do without them entirely. However, correct planning of the succession and combination of the different vegetable species is important to achieve a rewarding and healthy yield.

Planning the Garden

It's best if you use the winter months for this, for you need to consider the following:

Division of the beds. The optimum is to have 2 or 3 areas for different crops, which can be divided into different beds so you can switch between vigorous and less vigorous growers one time around and among the individual vegetable species another time (see rotation of crops, right).

Order of cultivation within the year. This means that you plan what you grow as a brief early-season crop, as a main crop, and as a late crop so that the bed is used to the best advantage over the entire year (see Tips for Planting, page 184 and table, page 185).

Mixed cultivation. Also to be considered is what vegetables should be combined (or not combined) with one another (see right and table, page 183).

Crop Rotation

The basic idea is to keep the soil from being exhausted in any one respect by rotating crops annually.

Feeding Requirements of Vegetables

The nutrient needs of the individual vegetable species vary. Differentiation is made among heavy, moderate, and weak feeders, depending on the nitrogen need of the plant in question. Preparation and fertilization of the beds must take account of the requirements of the particular plants.

Heavy feeders
(high nutrient requirement): white, red, savoy cabbage; Chinese cabbage; kale; brussels sprouts and cauliflower; broccoli; celery; corn, leeks; Swiss chard; tomatoes; cucumbers; peppers; zucchini; pumpkins, melons

Moderate feeders
(moderate nutrient requirement): carrots; beets; animal feed radishes, salsify; kohlrabi; onions; potatoes; fennel; eggplant; spinach; corn-salad; head lettuce; chicory

Weak feeders
(low nutrient requirement): peas; beans; salad radishes; cresses; kitchen herbs

Rotation of Crops

Year 1   Year 2

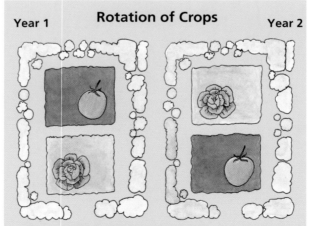

Year 1: Divide area. Prepare one part with manure and compost (also basic fertilization) in the fall or spring for the heavy and some moderate feeders. Cultivate the weak feeders in the second bed.

Year 2: Now change. After 3 years, at the earliest, the same vegetable species are back in the same bed.

This changing rhythm of cultivation hinders
• the depletion of one nutrient from the soil;
• the unilateral stressing of the soil by the root exudates of certain plants;
• the spreading of diseases and destructive insects that specialize in certain plants. So you should never plant crucifers (Cruciferae) after one another in the same area, because dread diseases (see Clubroot, page 193) and insect pests (see Cabbage fly, page 191) are specialized in this plant family. The crucifers include all the cabbage species, radishes, turnips, and some green manure plants like yellow mustard and winter rape.
Important: Separate beds for long-term crops like asparagus, rhubarb, or strawberries have proven valuable; these are not included in the annual rotation.

Mixed Cultivation

This term refers to the combination of vegetable species that promote each other (see table, page 183). In addition, head-forming species like cabbage and lettuce should be alternated with deep-rooted vegetables, and tuber-forming species with shallow-rooted ones. This way, competition for light, water, and nutrients does not develop either above or below ground.

With mixed cultivation, you can plant closer and harvest more.

Mixed Culture—Vegetable Species and Their Mutual Tolerances

Vegetable	Goes Well With	Goes Badly With
Beans (Leguminosae)	Beets, cabbage, carrots, celery, cucumbers, kohlrabi, lettuce, potatoes, radishes, savory, spinach, tomatoes	Garlic, fennel, leek, onions, peas
Beets (Chenopodiaceae)	Beans, cucumbers, garlic, kohlrabi, lettuce, onions, zucchini	Leeks, potatoes, spinach
Cabbage species (Cruciferae)	Beans, beets, celery, cucumbers, dill, lettuce, peas, radishes, spinach, tomatoes	Garlic, leek, onions
Carrots (Umbelliferae)	Garlic, leeks, lettuce, onions, peas, radishes, salsify, tomatoes	Celery
Celery (Umbelliferae)	Beans, cabbage, cucumbers, kohlrabi, leeks, spinach, tomatoes	Carrots, lettuce, potatoes
Cucumbers (Cucurbitaceae)	Beans, beets, cabbage, celery, dill, garlic, leeks, lettuce, onions, peas	Potatoes, radishes, tomatoes
Fennel (Umbelliferae)	Lettuce, peas	Beans, tomatoes
Kohlrabi (Cruciferae)	Beets, celery, leeks, lettuce, peas, potatoes, radishes, salsify, spinach	Cabbage
Leek, Garlic (Liliaceae)	Carrots, celery, cucumbers, kohlrabi, salsify, tomatoes	Beets, beans, peas
Lettuce (Compositae)	Cabbage, carrots, cucumber, fennel, kohlrabi, onions, peas, radishes, tomatoes	Celery
Onions (Liliaceae)	Beets, carrots, cucumbers, lettuce, tomatoes, zucchini	Beans, cabbage, peas, radishes
Peas (Leguminosae)	Cabbage, carrots, cucumbers, fennel, kohlrabi, lettuce, radishes, zucchini	Beans, leeks, onions, potatoes, tomatoes,
Peppers (Solanaceae)	Cucumbers, kohlrabi	Beans, tomatoes
Potatoes (Solanaceae)	Beans, cabbage, kohlrabi, spinach	Beets, celery, cucumbers, tomatoes
Radish (Cruciferae)	Beans, carrots, lettuce, peas, spinach, tomatoes	Cabbage, cucumbers, onions
Salsify (Compositae)	Carrots, kohlrabi, leeks, onions	Lettuce
Spinach (Chenopodiaceae)	Beans, cabbage, celery, kohlrabi, potatoes, radishes, tomatoes	Beets
Tomatoes (Solanaceae)	Beans, carrots, celery, garlic, leeks, onions, radishes, spinach	Cucumbers, fennel, peas, peppers, potatoes
Zucchini (Concurbitaceae)	Beans, beets, onions, peas	Cucumbers

Hill Beds

As in a compost heap, the rotting process goes on inside the hill bed, setting free nutrients for the plants. The growing season is extended by the warmth that is being created by this rotting in the substrate. A hill bed can produce up to 4 harvests a year. The curved shape makes the soil outside it warm faster, the plants receive more light, the usable surface is increased by about a third, and there is excellent water drainage. Hill beds are especially useful in areas with clay or heavy soils.

Tips for Installing

Hill beds are best oriented in a north-south direction so as to catch the sun evenly.

<u>Size:</u> 5 ft (1.5 m) wide, 39 in (1 m) high, length as desired.

<u>How to make it:</u>
• Dig out 8 in (20 cm) of soil.
• Lay down wire mesh as a protection against voles; later bend it upward.
• Pile up coarse brush in the middle, about 20 in (50 cm) deep. Now, make layers of the following:
• fresh compost or grass sods (6 in [15 cm] deep);
• leaves and garden waste (about 8 in [20 cm] deep);
• raw compost or horse manure (about 6 in [15 cm] deep).
• Finally, heap up soil mixed with finished compost over the hill bed.

• Only plant the bed with vigorous growers in the first year because of the high nutrient content.

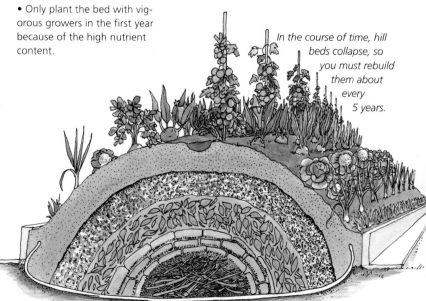

In the course of time, hill beds collapse, so you must rebuild them about every 5 years.

Planting, Care, and Harvesting of Vegetables

Reserve a sunny, warm, and wind-protected area of your garden for the vegetable beds, for most vegetables have originated in warmer climates.

Bed Preparation

Basic requirements for all produce plants to thrive are the best possible soil preparation and deep, loose earth, rich in humus and nutrients. Divide your vegetable beds into 2 or 3 areas (see Crop Rotation, page 182). In the fall, you can seed all the empty beds with a green manure (see pages 160–161).

Areas for heavy and moderate feeders are given lots of compost or well-rotted manure and some horn-blood bonemeal for basic fertilizing in the fall or early spring. Before planting or sowing, loosen the soil and rake it smooth.

Areas for weak feeders have been fertilized for heavy feeders the previous year, and except for some compost, receive no fertilizers but are well cultivated.

Areas for long-term culture receive basic fertilizing—according to the plant species.

Tips for Planting

Vegetables have growing seasons of different lengths. Anyone who uses these skillfully can harvest three or four times in succession from one bed.

Main crops are vegetables that occupy the bed for almost the entire growing season, like tomatoes, cucumbers, cabbage, peppers, pumpkins, squash, eggplants, and corn.

Interim crops can be vegetables with a short growing period, like lettuce and kohlrabi, which can be cultivated at the same time as the main crop but ripen earlier and so contribute to better use of the area.

Early crops must be fast-growing vegetables such as radishes and spinach.

Late crops are primarily the winter-hardy vegetables like endives, spinach, leeks, and corn salad, which can be planted in late summer.

Permanent crops are plants that remain in a bed for several years, like asparagus, artichokes, strawberries, and rhubarb.

Important: Plant your vegetables mixed together as much as possible (see table, page 183). This is the best prevention against disease and pests!

Fertilizing Correctly

Moderate and heavy feeders receive one or several additional top-dressings during their growing season (see page 159)—depending on their need for nutrients (see table, page 182).

The weak feeders are not fertilized.

To prevent overfertilizing or nitrate concentration, it is advisable to have a soil analysis done every 3 years for the vegetable garden (see Soil Tests, pages 148–149).

Cultivating Vegetables

Vegetables want to be hoed and repay good care with splendid yields.

• Don't let the soil dry out; water regularly during dry spells (see pages 164–165). Tomatoes, cucumbers, and zucchini especially need a lot of water,

about 1 in (2.5 cm) per week.

• Mulch surfaces between the plants.

• Weed regularly and loosen the soil.

• Pinch back tomatoes, that is, regularly shorten the new shoots that keep forming between the main stem and the leaves.

• Hill up 4 in (10 cm) around beans, peas, and tomatoes; this makes them grow stronger. The tops of hilled potatoes and carrots don't get green.

• Some vegetable species become especially delicate with bleaching: Tie endives together or cover them with bleaching caps. Cover celery and fennel bulbs up to the beginnings of the leaves with soil. With cardoon, wrap the long stalk with black plastic wrap.

Special Harvesting Tips

• Harvest pumpkins when stems can be easily twisted and pulled apart.

• Harvest kohlrabi and zucchini as soon as possible; they are tenderer then.

• Potatoes are ripe when their foliage is yellow.

• Pull out onions when their foliage becomes yellow and bends over. Let them dry in the bed for 2 to 3 days in the sun.

• Prop melons on a support 1 to 2 weeks before harvest to prevent rot where the melon touches the ground in wet weather.

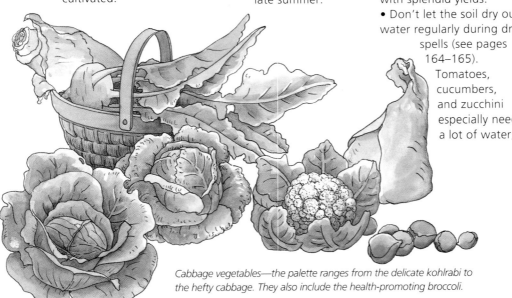

Cabbage vegetables—the palette ranges from the delicate kohlrabi to the hefty cabbage. They also include the health-promoting broccoli.

Culture Times for Vegetables

Note: These times are quite accurate for most parts of the country, especially zones 4–7. In zones higher or lower, one should mentally add or subtract a few weeks to 1 month to 6 weeks onto either beginning or planting and harvest dates.

Vegetable	Pre-culture Indoors	Sowing Outdoors	Planting	Harvest Date	Plant Portrait and Care Instructions
Beans	—	from mid-May–June/July	—	July–beginning October	see pages 294–295
Beets	—	mid-May–mid-June	—	August–mid-November	see pages 300–301
Broccoli	February-April	mid-April–mid-July	from May; from April (hot caps)	from June-October	see pages 298–299
Brussels sprouts	—	mid-April–mid-May	mid-May–end June	beginning October–end February	see pages 298–299
Cabbage, red and white	February-March	mid-April–mid-May	from April	July–November	see pages 298–299
Carrots	—	March–May	—	mid-June–September	see pages 300–301
Cauliflower	February-March	mid-April–May	beginnng May–mid-July	beginning August–October	see pages 298–299
Celery	middle/end March	—	mid-/end May early June	September/October	see pages 300–301
Corn salad	—	mid-August–mid-September	—	October–March	see pages 296–297
Cucumbers	April	mid-May–mid-June	from mid-May	from end July	see pages 292–293
Fennel	from March	mid-April–mid-July	from May; from April (hot caps)	from August	see pages 300–301
Garlic	—	—	April	from August	see pages 294–295
Kale	—	from May	from mid-June	end October–beginning March	see pages 298–299
Kohlrabi	February–March	April–June	from mid-April	from June–end October	see pages 298–299
Leeks	mid-February	April/May	beginning May	mid-September–February	see pages 294–295
Lettuce	from February	from April–end July	March-April (protected)	from June–October	see pages 296–297
Onions	February–March	mid-March	—	July–September	see pages 294–295
Peas	—	mid-April–beginning July	—	July–mid-September	see pages 294–295
Peppers	March	—	mid-May–mid-June	from end July	see pages 292–293
Potatoes	—	—	from mid-April–end May	from mid-June	see pages 300–301
Radishes	—	beginning March–August	—	mid-April–September	see pages 300–301
Salsify	—	March–April	—	October–March	see pages 300–301
Savoy cabbage	January–end March	end April–end May	from April	mid-July–mid-October	see pages 298–299
Spinach	—	March or August/September	—	from April or from September	see pages 296–297
Tomatoes	early March early April	—	from middle–end May	from July–end October	see pages 292–293
Zucchini	April	from mid-May	mid-May	July–October	see pages 292–293

Basics of Pest Control

Conventional chemical pest control is regarded very critically today. The methods of natural control are the wave of the future, and they are being used in the home garden with ever greater success. In this milieu, there is no need for record yields. And there is no wide-scale monoculture on which insect pests can multiply. Using natural growing methods (see vegetables, pages 182–185), taking care of all garden plants, and having a large variety of plant species are the requirements for establishing a balance between desirable and undesirable creatures. Nevertheless, situations will arise in which you need to protect yourself against the inroads made by pests. There are many remedies at your disposal, but you should only turn to synthetic pesticides as a very last resort.

Practical for large gardens:
A backpack sprayer for spraying pesticides or fertilizer teas and extracts. It should hold 5 to 10 qt (4.7–9.5 L) and have an extensible sprayer.

Integrated Pest Control

Integrated pest control combines prevention and direct measures to protect plants from disease and insects. The basic rule is: Prevention is better than cure. Follow these important tips:

• Only choose plants that fit the existing location, soil, and climate.

• Buy disease-resistant seed and plant varieties and, above all, only buy healthy plants.

• Cultivate and feed (fertilize) plants appropriately, for strong, healthy plants are more disease resistant. Avoid nutrient deficiencies as well as overfertilizing—both make the plant weak and more vulnerable.

• Be careful not to injure the plants, so that no small germs can gain entrance.

• Examine ornamental and produce plants regularly to catch pest or disease infestations early. Weather also plays a large role.

• Always resort first to mechanical, biotechnical, or biological measures (see page 187).

• Only turn to synthetic materials in an emergency, using only those with specific effects and biologically valid preparations that will not injure animals.

• Follow directions carefully and wear protective gloves and eye goggles if using a sprayer apparatus.

Aids to Pest Control

Snail Fences
Turned edge of white tin or plastic, insurmountable for snails. Don't put any tall plants in front of it; they can serve as snail bridges.

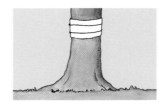

Grease or Sticky Bands
Fasten around tree trunks at the beginning of October to combat winter moths; remove again in the spring. This prevents the wingless female from laying eggs.

Netting and Row Covers
Effective means to prevent eating and egg laying of vegetable flies and white cabbage moth. They are air- and water-permeable, store the heat, and so also promote growth.

Cabbage Collars
Made of paper (easy to make oneself) or plastic, they fit tightly around the stem of newly planted cabbage. Prevent insects' laying eggs at the base of the stem.

Vole Traps
Various types that catch or kill the voles are available commercially. Wear gloves when placing the trap; the animals are extraordinarily sensitive to smells.

Sticky Traps
Sticky yellow cards that attract insects. They serve primarily as controls during infestations. In greenhouses, they are good for whiteflies and fungus gnats (Sciarid).

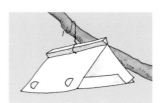

Pheromone Traps
Lure traps, that serve in large orchards to control the attacks of apple and plum codling moths, help establish the optimal time for combat measures.

Mechanical Measures

This term refers to the repelling of insects with hands and tools—not with preparations.

Collecting. Good to carry out in the early stages of insect attacks. Susceptible areas are the undersides of leaves, young shoots, bark, and the neck of the root. Look for egg deposits on the soil around the plant (especially with vegetables), for sick leaves and fruits (with fruit and woody plants). Snails and slugs collect in dark, damp hiding places, under boards, stones, and large leaves.

Cut off. Always remove affected plant parts immediately.

Shake off. Helps with insect control of trees. Before doing it, spread a cloth under the tree.

Rinsing off. Aphids can be sprayed off with a stream of water. This is only possible with sturdy plants.

Scratching, brushing off. Treatment method for fruit tree trunks in the fall. Some insects hide under the bark or lay their eggs there.

Catching with grease band or sticky tape. Insects get stuck on the sticky tape or grease. Then, they can be gathered easily and destroyed.

Disadvantage: They must be renewed often and are also a danger for other insects.

Defense with bird netting. Nets protect the fruit harvest from birds. They must also be fastened at the bottom so that birds can't get caught inside them.

Defense with wire guards. Fine wire mesh 31.5 in (80 cm) high can be fastened to 3 or 4 stakes around the trunks of fruit trees in order to protect them from rabbits.

Biotechnical Measures

These procedures use chemical materials or physical stimuli to lure or ward off pests.

Lures. These include the sexual scents (phero-mones) of particular female moths by which the male moth can be lured and trapped (see Pheromone Traps, page 186), and also beer, whose aroma snails and slugs find irresistible. Therefore, you can also use shallow containers of beer sunken into the ground as snail traps. However, they must be refilled daily.

Light traps. These attract moths active at night (bell moth species) but are not recommended because they also trap beneficial insects.

Color traps. These are special baits targeted for particular insects. White, yellow, red, and blue have differing powers of attraction for the particular species (see sticky traps, page 186).

Acoustic lures: To repel birds and voles, garden stores offer some equipment whose sound drives off these animals with more or less success.

Important: If you have a question about pest control or are not certain what insect or what disease is involved, you can turn to the appropriate pest control or agricultural office in your local county extension agency.

Synthetic Pest Controls and How to Use Them

Pest control materials are sold in garden centers by specially trained salespeople only after appropriate consultation. They are mostly very dangerous to humans. Never use any highly poisonous material that is labeled with "warning" or "poison/danger" without the proper training or certification required by law. Pesticides are categorized in 3 safety levels: caution (relatively nontoxic); warning (moderately toxic), and danger/poison (highly toxic).

Insecticides are effective against insects. The term "harmless to beneficial insects" merely says that this preparation did not harm the particular beneficial insect tested.

• In the garden only use materials that expressly certify that bees will not be harmed.

• Insecticides poisonous to fish should not be used near a pond or water.

• Pyrethrum is poisonous for humans and should not be used with open wounds or mucous membrane inflammations. Pyrethrum is also lethal to all insects and fish.

• Also effective against insects are materials with a soap foundation or paraffin oil products. The latter are particularly effective against scale insects, but should only be used on robust, hard-leaved plants and for dormant and new growth sprays on fruit and ornamental trees.

Fungicides for fungus diseases are generally nontoxic to humans and pets—also for bees—but not for fish.

Acaricides kill mites.
Nematicides kill nematodes.
Herbicides work against weeds.

Be careful to:
• Follow exactly the instructions for use and the dosages specified on the package.
• Keep to the recommended spraying intervals to destroy the next generation of pests.
• Not use any sprays containing fluorocarbons.
• Keep the material tightly closed, in the original packaging, out of reach of children and pets, and not anywhere near food.
• Not to inhale the spray fog.
• Wear gloves and eye goggles when handling these materials.
• Never apply sprays on windy days.
• Put any leftovers in the hazardous waste collection. (Call your local county extension agency or EPA for information on safely disposing of any chemicals.)

Beneficial Animals and Plants

Plant injuries can have many causes that are not always just the result of parasites. The injuries are often linked to physiological problems and, therefore, lead back to poor conditions of location and climate. Recognizing what is wrong with a particular plant is very difficult for the beginner. But through observation, inspection, comparison, and acquired experience, you can reach the correct diagnosis and then choose the correct treatment. Far better than healing and battling pests is prevention by making use of the natural resistance of the plants and the natural enemies of the pests. A certain amount of tolerance of harmful insects is also included in this, for without the harmful insects, the beneficial animals couldn't live.

The crown imperial (Fritillaria imperialis) is not only an imposing spring flower but through the garliclike smell of its bulb, it repels voles.

Beneficial Creatures

Besides the many recognized beneficial garden creatures (see drawings, right) there are quantities of small and tiny creatures in the soil, such as pill bugs, springtails, and millipedes, which demolish the pathogens on diseased plant parts along with the organic debris. But beneficials are also insects like beetles, flies, and bugs and their larvae. Many of these hunt their own kind. For example, the larva of the ladybug (depending on the species) eats about 500 aphids in the mere 4 to 8 weeks of its life. Other insects like the various hymenopterous wasps lay their eggs directly on the living leaf louse (aphid), in the larvae of the whitefly, and in the white cabbage moth larva. These then serve the beneficial larvae as food. The judgment as "beneficial" or "harmful" is always applied from the point of view of the human being and is oriented toward human interests. Often the borderlines are fluid. The use of poisons affects both the harmful and the beneficial and at the same time disturbs the biological equilibrium. As a garden owner, you can do a lot to promote the variety of species: Provide for a natural garden area with numerous different plants, which also permits some wild growth, offers fruits, seeds, and shelter, and contains water somewhere.

Beneficial Animals and Their Shelters

Birds
The traditional insect exterminators in the garden, they search out eggs and larvae even when hidden. Provide additional brooding areas with nest boxes and places to build nests.

Lacewings
("Aphis lions") act as predators, especially their larvae. Offer the pretty insects winter protection in a lacewing box filled with straw.

Syrphid Flies
Look very much like wasps but they aren't. They lay their eggs in aphid colonies, which then serve the larvae as food. Good for overwintering: pieces of wood with holes bored in them.

Earwigs
Destroy aphids, mites, egg deposits, and even fungus spores. They take shelter in such places as flowerpots stuffed with straw that are hung from branches.

Blindworm
These harmless lizards are important destroyers of nocturnal snails. For living areas, they need small, damp cavities, like a heap of stones piled out of the way in the shade.

Toads and Frogs
These insect- and nocturnal-snail-exterminators will quickly take up residence in the garden if offered a damp environment (natural pond) and hiding places under stones, leaves, or wood.

Hedgehog
Destroys insects and nocturnal snails. For living and overwintering, they need heaps of brush or a heaped up pile of fall leaves under a bush or a hedgehog-house (store).

Beneficial Plants

Plants are in a position to promote or inhibit the growth of other plants with the aid of specific materials. This allows the gardener to, for example, use promoting neighbors directly beside one another —as in mixed cultivation (see pages 184 and table, page 183). However, plants also yield their curative principles to teas, broths, extracts, or liquid manures (see table at right). Some repel insect pests and disease and, therefore, as defending plants, are welcome guests in the garden.

Crown imperials (Fritillaria imperialis) work through the powerful garlicky odor of their bulbs to repel voles.

Garlic should be interplanted all through the garden if plants are subject to powdery mildew or rust. Also for roses!

Nasturtium planted in the space around fruit trees keeps off aphids and woolly aphids.

Wormwood (Artemisia absinthium) smells very strong and a weak wormwood tea can repel aphids, black flea beetles, and cabbage moths. (Note: not a good companion plant because its roots secrete a substance that can inhibit growth of nearby plants.)

Savory has a strong smell. It protects beans from the black bean aphid and the bean fly.

Lavender protects roses from aphids, and it also looks pretty.

Wormwood— (Artemesia absinthium) Cold-Water Extract

For aphids, caterpillars, and ants in the spring, spray undiluted; also helps in the summer against white cabbage moth.
Let 10.6 oz (300 g) of fresh, or 1 oz (30 g) dried, wormwood steep in 10 qt (9.5 L) water for several hours; strain, and spray undiluted.

Soft-Soap—Alcohol Broth

For aphids.
Dissolve 7 oz (200 g) soft soap in 10 qt (9.5 L) hot water; let cool, and add 0.5 qt (0.5 L) denatured alcohol. Spray undiluted on affected plants.
Important: Don't use on plants that are to be harvested within the next 14 days.

First Aid—Homemade

Tansy (Tanacetum vulgare) Broth

For sawflies, strawberry blossom weevils, strawberry and blackberry mites, raspberry beetles. Also prevention for mildew and rust. Steep 18 oz (500 g) fresh, or 2 oz (56 g) dried, tansy for 24 hr in 10 qt (9.5 L) water. Then boil for 30 min, strain, and let cool. Spray undiluted on the ground.
Warning: Tansy is poisonous. Keep plants and broth secure.

Stinging Nettle (Urtica dioica) Extract

For aphids.
Soften 2 lb (1 kg) stinging nettles for several hours in 10 qt (9.5 L) water; strain, and then spray immediately, undiluted.

Field Horsetail (Equisetum arvense) Broth

Preventive for fungus diseases (see pages 194–195).
Steep 2 lb (1 kg) fresh or 3.5 oz (100 g) dried plants in 10 qt (9.5 L) water for 24 hr. Then boil for 30 min; strain, and let cool. From the spring to the summer, spray the broth on the plants regularly in good weather using a dilution of 1:5.

Note: The quantities given can be changed as necessary. However, you should not store the sprays for more than 1 week.

Calendulas and marigolds drive away nematodes and are, therefore, good as a soil cure.

Commercial Biological Preparations

These consist of using pathogens that are transmitted to the pests and produce lethal infections in them or waste them.

Bacillus thuringiensis. (Bt). A spray powder for combatting leaf chewing larvae of harmful butterflies and moths on fruit, vegetables, and ornamental plants.

Baccillus popilliae. Also known as milky spore disease, it is used to control Japanese beetle grubs, which cause damage to lawns.

A colorful assortment of healthful garden plants: wormwood, savory, and lavender (behind from left to right), with garlic and nasturtium in the foreground.

Animal Pests

Aphids

These insects form entire colonies in a very short time and especially reproduce during dry, hot spells. Some species are specialized for only a few plants; others use many hosts. They weaken plants by sucking on them. This can lead to malformation and growth disturbances. They can also transmit virus diseases. In addition, black sooty fungus often colonizes on the insects' sticky excretion (honeydew). Combat: Aphids have many natural enemies such as birds, ladybugs, syrphid flies, and hymenopterous wasps. It is most important to control the attack at the beginning. Remove infested leaves and shoots entirely. Keep plants well watered. Remove aphids from plants with a cold stream of water.

Mites

Their appearance en masse is typical in warmth and dryness. These are also sucking insects and can cause entire plantings to wither.
Combat. Regular watering and high humidity help to inhibit further spread. Natural enemies are predatory mites and masked hunters (assassin bugs). If necessary, use special preparations (acaricides). With fruit trees, a winter spraying with a dormant oil spray is helpful.

Nematodes

(Threadworms, eelworms) These tiny little worms can attack many different plants and plant parts (inside and outside). Often they are difficult to diagnose. Remove ailing plants with any suspicion of nematodes entirely. Eelworms are easily transmitted and can survive unfavorable conditions for long periods. Combat. In home gardens, only preventive and hygienic methods are possible. This means primarily rotation of crops, mixed cultivation, and soil cures with "hostile plants" like marigolds and pot marigolds (calendulas) sown as interplantings.

Chewing and Sucking Insects

These include many beetles, moths, flies, and sawflies, which primarily do injury through the voraciousness of the larvae (caterpillars, maggots). After pupation, the particular insect emerges. It is important to know the devlopmental stages of each insect in order to know the right defense measures to take depending on the flying phase, egg laying, and larvae hatching.
Combat. Mechanical, biotechnical, and plant defense measures. Further possibilities: Move the seeding of vegetables before or after the particular flying phase of the insect; choose early or late varieties! Dust with hydrated lime and wood ashes around plants.

Damage Done by Insect Pests

Aphids
Green or black aphids, predominantly on young plant parts. Young leaves/shoots roll in, are stunted, or crinkle. Primarily in the spring and early summer.

Woolly Agelid
White, waxy excretions make them appear woolly. Special species attack conifers like hemlock, larch, cedar, pine. Primarily on young trees in the spring.

Whitefly
They park on the undersides of leaves and fly up when touched. Common on greenhouse plants and fuchsias. The adult animals die with first frost.

Scale Insect
Unmoving animal, hidden under a firm covering. Only unprotected and moving in the juvenile stage. On hard-leaved plants and fruit trees.

Rose Cicada
About 4 mm long, pale insect on undersides of leaves. Leaves under attack lightly spotted, similar to spider mites. Animals move with a jerk when touched.

Rose Leaf-Roller Wasp
Black, 3 to 4 mm long. Lays eggs in May/June on the edges of rose leaves. Later, the leaves fed on by the larvae hang down in tubelike rolls.

Rose Leaf Wasp
Black, about 5 mm long. Eggs deposited on the underside of leaves. Larvae less than 0.5 in (1 cm) long, eat windowlike holes in the rose leaves all summer.

Damage Done by Insect Pests

Nematodes (Eelworms)

Up to 1 mm long, transparent threadworms. Cause malformations and growth disturbances in plants. Primarily at the roots, stems, leaves of roses, perennials, strawberries.

Apple Codling Moth (Fruit Maggot)

Small, gray-brown moth. Eggs laid in June/July, primarily on apples and pears. Larvae make the fruit wormy. Leads to premature ripening and fruit drop.

Spider Mites (Red Spider)

Yellow to reddish, 0.5 mm long, 8-legged mites. At first, on undersides of leaves; with severe attack, fine webs on all shoots. Especially on cucumbers, beans, and fruit trees.

Winter Moth

Females are unable to fly, climb up tree trunks in fall/winter. Eggs laid in the bark. The bright green caterpillars, typical inchworms, are voracious in spring.

Currant Gall Mite

Unnaturally swollen round buds—most visible in winter. On gooseberries and currants. Massive spreading in spring.

Strawberry Blossom Weevil

Beetles lay eggs in buds and puncture the inflorescence. Larvae pupate at the spot. New generations are harmless. Endangered: mainly large-fruited varieties.

Cherry Fruit Fly

Black-yellow insect 5 mm long. Loves sun and warmth. Egg deposits on the ripe fruit of cherries and plums. The maggots develop in the fruit flesh.

Snout Weevil

Eggs laid in soil at end of June. After 3 weeks, the larvae develop. Tremendous root damage! Catch beetles at night! Nematodes against larvae. Symptom: holes at edges of leaves.

Onion Fly

Gray-black insect with 2 to 3 generations per summer. Eggs laid in May at the base of young onion and leek plants. Dryness hinders development.

Flea Beetle

Small, black, shiny beetle, lays eggs in May in the soil. Larvae damage by eating seedlings and young leaves. Second generation is less damaging.

Cabbage Fly

When chestnut trees come into flower, eggs are deposited at the root neck or in the soil next to it. Damage from maggots eating young cabbage plants and radishes.

Carrot Fly

Small flies with yellow legs. Egg laying at the end of May and in June at the root neck and in the soil. Maggots eat outsides from the tip up in carrots and celery.

White Cabbage Moth

Small butterfly, which lays its eggs in a typical cone shape on the undersides of cabbage leaves. There is a generation each in the spring and in the summer. Caterpillars eat cabbage leaves.

Fungus Diseases

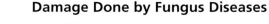

Damage Done by Fungus Diseases

Powdery Mildew
Fungus specialized to different plants. Symptoms: Upper sides of leaves, stems, flowers are covered with whitish deposit. On roses, vegetables, berries, and perennials.

Downy Mildew
Gray-white deposit on the undersides of leaves. Upper sides show yellow to red-brown spots. Fungi are specialized to grapes and various vegetables.

Black Spot
Various fungus species that readily settle on the honeydew excreted by aphids. They form a sooty, blackish deposit, which suffocates the leaves.

Spot Anthracnose
Round, jagged-edged, spreading spots on the upper sides of leaves. Leaves yellow and fall off early. Primarily on roses—especially during rainy, cool summers.

Rust
Typical are the first light, then dark pustules on the undersides of leaves. Almost all mallow species are infected with it. A similar rust fungus also appears on roses.

Monilinia
The fungus survives in the wood. Infection begins in the flower. A short time later, the ends of the shoots wither. The leaves droop. Mostly with stone fruit and ornamental shrubs.

Monilinia–Brown Rot
Rings of mold develop around wounds in the fruit. The rotten spots enlarge quickly. End stages are fruit mummies. Remove. In stone fruit and cherries.

Scab
Infection begins on the leaves and spreads to the fruit. Round, dark spots develop. They look like scars covering mainly apples and pears (depends on variety).

Fruit Tree Canker
Young branches and old trunks are infected—usually through injury. The tissue sinks in or proliferates. Especially at risk are apple and pear trees.

Pear Cluster Cup Rust
Orange spots on the upper sides of leaves, cartilaginous pustules on the undersides. Remove the intermediate host of the fungus (savin tree, *Juniperus sabina*).

Leaf Curl
Bladder-shaped, distended leaves are typical for this fungus, which is specialized to peach trees. Infection can cause branches and fruit to die off.

Raspberry Cane Disease
Begins with white spots on young canes. Later typical violet coloration of the cane and finally the bark turns silvery. Leads to dying off.

Red Pustule Disease
Bright-red pustules on the bark of withered branches of deciduous woody plants are pin-sized the second year and dark red. Infection follows injury (weakness parasites).

Botrytis
Botrytis fungi cover leaves, corms, and fruit of many fruits and vegetables, such as cucumbers, lettuce, as well as bulbs and perennials with gray fields of mold.

Damage Done by Fungus Diseases

Leaf Rot, Potato Rot
Phytophthora fungi infect and destroy first the leaves, then the fruits of tomatoes and potatoes. Spreads especially in summer with warmth and high humidity.

Aster Wilt
Different *Fusarium* and *Verticillium* fungi can attack garden plants. The stem area becomes black, the plants collapse suddenly.

Damping Off
Typical disease of seedlings. Plants die from the bottom up. The fungus spreads in the seed-bed. Affects both ornamental plants and vegetables. Main cause: inadequate hygiene.

Clubroot
Tuberlike growths on the main and side roots. External similarity to damage done by the cabbage gall weevil. At risk are cabbage species and other crucifers.

Leaf Spot
Various fungus diseases but also bacteria produce different colored spots on ornamental plants, vegetables, and fruits. Recognizable only by the reddish yellow fungus spores.

Plum Pockets
Unmistakably deformed damsons and plums point to this disease. The infection begins in the flower. In late summer, the fruits become brown and dry.

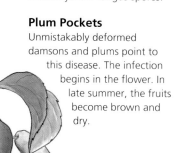

Fungus Diseases
Fungi that can be dangerous for plants are primarily parasites on weakness. They attack where damage is already present, for instance, as a result of injury or of poor maintenance such as overfertilization or dryness. In contrast to bacteria and viruses, fungi can invade plant tissues directly.

Fungi multiply through microscopic spores. Water and wind carry them over large distances. They are viable for a long time, especially on plants and in soil. In humidity accompanied by much warmth, they germinate and multiply. The spores either enter through the soil and roots of the plant or from outside through the air. The fungi that enter through the soil (soil-borne fungi) are characteristically harder to fight (athlete's foot, damping off, clubroot, raspberry cane blight) than those attacking above ground (like powdery mildew or *Monilia*).

Most fungi primarily attack leaves and young shoots; others clog the conduction pathways. This often leads to sudden death, as in aster wilt. All plant parts may be affected by fungus diseases—roots, root neck, leaves, stem, shoots/canes, flowers, and fruits. The means of defense differ accordingly.

Combat.
• For soil-borne fungi, which are usually recognized too late, only preventive measures can help, like hygiene at sowing and propagation, choice of healthy varieties, disinfection of seeds, and constantly good culture conditions.

• For aboveground fungi, the symptoms are more easily recognized. It is advisable to observe the plants carefully, particularly in dangerously warm and humid weather conditions, in order to prevent any severe outbreak of disease. Often the undersides of the leaves are affected first. The signs are frequently yellowish coloration, which later becomes brown and black.
Preventive measures:
Wider sowing and planting distance, thinning out close-standing shrubs and trees. Moving air provides for fast drying of plant parts.

Important: Regularly, gather up diseased leaves and fruits and cut off infected plant parts as well. The fungus spores usually winter over at the same spot and attack the plant anew the next spring.

Plant tonics—for example, horsetail broth (*Equisetum arvense*) (see page 189), whose silicic acid content strengthens the cell tissue—and the best possible culture methods promote the resistance of the plants. Only resort to fungicides in emergencies (see page 187).

Bacteria, Viruses, and Improper Culture

Bacterial Diseases

Bacteria are single-celled organisms that occur everywhere in nature, but only certain species play a role as causes of disease in plants. When infection occurs, there is scarcely any help for the plant. Transmission. Bacteria are carried by wind, water, sucking insects, infected tools, and infected soil. The disease organisms enter the plants through wounds and fissures. Symptoms. They are easy to confuse with those of fungus diseases: Wilt, cancerlike growths, or rotten spots may appear on all plant parts. Leaf spots are particularly difficult to classify. Typical signs of a bacteriosis here are slimy, wet, brown-black spots. One of the most dangerous bacterial disease is fire blight. It mainly attacks members of the rose family (pears, quince), many ornamental shrubs, especially ever-greens, tall *Cotoneaster* species, shadblow, mountain ash, and hawthorn. Preventive measures.
• Use healthy plants and resistant seeds.
• Provide for constantly good culture conditions.
• Burn infected plants (don't put them in compost).
• Prune out infested branches well below diseased area.
• Avoid heavy fertilization, which makes plants more susceptible to fire blight.

Virus Diseases

Viruses are the smallest and most feared disease organisms—they can also affect plants. There are harmless forms but also ones that are dangerous. If there is an infection, there is no help: the plants must be destroyed (burning, garbage). Transmittal. Chiefly through aphids and other sucking animal pests. But viruses can also be spread through the soil and through seeds. Just touching with the plant juices in the course of handling, propagation, and cultivating them can spread the virus further. Symptoms. Virus can cause very different malforma-tions, growth inhibitions, curling, or ringspots, which are often confused with other diseases and deficiency symptoms. On the other hand, other viruses produce positive changes in appearance. Thus, the colored leaves of many decorative plants as well as the colored stripes in some flowers (for example, flamed tulips) can be traced to the mosaic virus. Symptoms such as these need not be treated or combatted. The plants can live very well and for a long time with them. Preventive measures. As with bacterioses, however, plants must always be completely destroyed. Hygiene is very important.

Damage Done by Bacteria and Viruses

Fire Blight
Bacteriosis. Crooked branches, which turn from brown to black in the spring, looking as if they'd been burned. At risk: stone fruit and some ornamental shrubs.

Bacterial Blight
Round spots on the leaves, which become holes. Flowers/fruits dry out. Flow of sap and death of branches possible. Primarily on young fruit trees.

Halo Blight
Bacteriosis. First watery spots with yellow centers on leaves of bush and scarlet runner beans, then on beans round, waxy greasy spots with slimy secretion.

Bacterial Leaf Spot Diseases
A bacteriosis is present when the leaf spots have traces of bacterial slime (in contrast to the fungal leaf spots).

Mosaic Diseases
Virus. Typical are the light-dark marbled leaves. Especially on cucumbers, beans, and tomatoes, fruit trees, and berry bushes.

Stonefruitedness
Virus. Yellow-green leaf spots. Fruits have knobs and dents. The flesh of the fruit is partly stippled with hardened, granular places. Chiefly pears and quinces.

Mummification/Plum Virus
Virus. Carrier: aphids. Sometimes the fruit of plums falls from the tree before it is ripe, other times it becomes pockmarked and rubbery.

Damage Done by Improper Care

Nitrogen Deficiency
The foliage is continuously yellowing, the overall growth is weak and small. The older leaves are the first to yellow, become brown, and fall off. The plants often bloom ahead of time.

Potassium Deficiency
The foliage dies back. The edges of older leaves are first yellow, then brown; they dry out and roll up. Plants appear withered all over.

Phosphorus Deficiency
Expresses itself mainly in younger shoots and leaves going from deep dark green to blue-violet. The overall growth is somewhat slowed.

Magnesium Deficiency
Shows itself first on the older lower leaves. The leaf edges remain green at first. The area between the leaf nerves becomes brown and dry.

Iron Deficiency
Begins first on the younger shoots. The network of leaf nerves remains the typical green, whereas the space in between can appear light yellow to whitish.

Overfertilization/Dryness
High content of mineral salts in the soil works like lack of water. Plants fail and wilt. Leaves become brown around the edges and die back.

Needle Drop
Conifers respond to prolonged drought with the loss of the older, interior needles. Typical with this is the fresh new growth.

Improper Culture
Too little feeding or care of plants can cause the appearance of damage that may greatly resemble insect or fungus attack (see drawings at left). Only basic knowledge about the requirements of the different plants as well as careful observation and the consideration of culture measures can clear up the cause.

Problem: Snails
Snails are one of the most feared plagues in the garden. Particularly in years with a lot of rain, great damage occurs to almost all bright green plants—be they vegetables, perennials, or annuals. The worst offenders are mainly the large and small nocturnal snails. The animals live in damp, dark hiding places during the day and are active at night. You can make use of this and lay down planks, cardboard, or large leaves, under which you can then collect the snails during the day.
Combat: Snail fences are best suited for the seed beds. Beer traps will drown the animals.
Important: Don't use snail granules under any circumstances! They endanger children, pets, and beneficial creatures.

Snails have a preference for tender lettuce.

Problem: Voles
Voles undermine the soil with a widespread system of passageways that is usually very visible, with shallow humps. In contrast to moles, voles chew on roots.
Combat. Traps have proven to be the most effective (if possible, distribute several at once over the passageway system). But check first to be sure the passageways are used. Open the passageway at some places. If the voles are using it, the opening will be stopped with earth within a very short time.
Special vole bait should be laid very deep in the working tunnels in order not to endanger other animals.
Important: Carry out all these measures wearing gloves; voles are very sensitive to odors! Because their territory often extends beyond the borders of one garden, it is wise to carry out the extermination program at the same time as neighbors.

Garden Calendar

This calendar is a general guide for all gardening regions; gardeners living in more extreme northern, southern, or western regions should use the calendar guidelines but keep in mind their own climatic variations.

January

Winter is the best time to study the new garden catalogs and books to gather inspiration for the coming season at leisure.
Ornamental garden. Free shrubs of heavy burdens of snow. Feed birds. If there are fish in the garden pond, keep a hole open in the ice.
Produce garden. Prepare the layout for the current and the following year. Plan for mixed cultivation and rotation of crops. Thin trees; remove branches that are diseased or are growing too close together.

February

Now is the time to sharpen, oil, and repair garden equipment if necessary, or get new tools.
Ornamental garden. You can now prune summer-flowering shrubs. However, only cut back shrubs that bloom in the spring after they have flowered. Cut back old growth or branches that are too dense all the way to the ground. Rejuvenate hedges if necessary. With frost, protect delicate shrubs and evergreens from sun and wind.
Produce garden. Toward the end of the month, start indoor sowing of early vegetables and annuals. Cut back berry bushes. Whitewash fruit tree trunks as a protectection against frost.

March

The garden comes alive. Small bulbs bloom and the first green leaflets appear. Remove winter protection and mulches. Provide all plants in the garden with nutrients (basic fertilization). Add compost and manure and work in lightly.
Ornamental garden. Allow the soil to dry out and prepare for new plantings. In severe climates, maintain further protection for delicate plants.
Produce garden. Continue indoor sowing of vegetables and indoor seeding cultivation. First planting of early vegetables under plastic or cold frame. End of March begins outdoor sowing of some early cold-tolerant vegetables.

April

Now you should remove the last winter protections so as not to impede new growth.
Ornamental garden.
Remove hilling from roses, fertilize, and prune them. Favorable planting time for woody plants and perennials (especially for evergreens). Set hardy annuals out and sow delicate ones indoors.
Produce garden. Planting time for many cool weather vegetable plants and lettuce. Warmth-loving vegetables (cucumbers, zucchini, tomatoes) can still be sown indoors. You can sow peas, radishes, and other tough vegetables directly outdoors.

May

Height of flowering of bulbs and biennial spring bloomers. Flowering of apple and pear trees. The first few weeks of May can still bring occasional frosts. Only set out warmth-loving vegetables, flowers, and tub plants after this.
Ornamental garden. Still good planting times, primarily for perennials, grasses, and water plants. Good time for seeding a lawn. Remove seedpods from bulbs.
Produce garden. Tender vegetable plants can only go outdoors after all danger of frost is past. Plant the next crop of vegetables. Mulch exposed bed surfaces.

June

Many ornamental shrubs and early-summer perennials bloom. First and most abundant burst of rose bloom.
Ornamental garden. Thin ornamental shrubs immediately after flowering. Annual summer flowers can still be sown and planted. Sow biennials now. Break off rhododendron seedpods after flowering. Important growth period, still fertilize! Water in dry spells. Further maintenance tasks: staking, tying, mulching, and mowing grass.
Produce garden. Berry harvest! Maintenance jobs like soil loosening, thinning, mulching, and giving heavy feeders a top-dressing of liquid fertilizer while watering.

July

Before going on vacation, deadhead flowers, loosen soil, and weed. Examine plants for pests and disease; treat if necessary.
Ornamental garden. Top-dressing for annuals. Last fertilizing for woody shrubs and roses. Prune hedges at the beginning of the month; by then, the birds will have raised their young. Mow flower meadows for the first time now.
Produce garden. Plant harvested beds with next crop. For long-term crops like tomatoes, cucumbers, and cabbage, apply a top-dressing. Dwarf fruit trees receive their summer pruning. Loosen soil around strawberries after the harvest, and fertilize.

August

In late summer, the peaches, plums, and early pears ripen. In dry spells, water where needed, loosen soil, and mulch.
Ornamental gardens. Hedges can be pruned at the end of the month (first or second pruning). Separate biennials sown in June and plant them in their future locations. Planting time for madonna lilies.
Produce garden. Sow cool weather vegetables (corn salad, spinach). Head lettuce and kohlrabi can still be planted. Prune sour cherries, currants, and gooseberries; remove finished raspberry canes. Fasten up blackberry canes; thin strawberries.

September

Early fall is the chief harvest time for pears. Depending on weather and location, the first frosts may occur. The garden begins to change color. It is again fresher and damper—good planting time (root formation), because the soil is still warm.
Ornamental garden. Favorable time for planting of perennials and evergreens as well as for sowing a lawn. Beginning of bulb planting of spring flowers for the coming year.
Produce garden. Last date for sowing of winter vegetables and green manure plants. Fruit and vegetable harvest. Fertilize strawberries again.

October

Night frosts can appear at any time during the fall. The leaf coloring reaches its high point. The apple harvest is in process.
Ornamental garden. Now is the time to put all bulbs into the ground if possible. Chief planting time for woody shrubs. Use fall leaves for mulching. Cut lawns/meadows once more and remove thatch. Get nonhardy plants (tub plants, gladiolus, dahlias) under winter cover at the end of the month.
Produce garden. Protect storage vegetables against frost by the end of the month. Clean up beds, loosen, fertilize, and mulch. Compost leaves and plant remains. Plant fruit trees and berry bushes.

November

Often the month becomes wet and cold and everyone is glad when the necessary garden work is done.
Ornamental garden. As long as the soil is workable, planting can be done. Deciduous shrubs and roses are often not available any sooner. Hill up roses, but first remove all diseased leaves—also from the ground around them. Remove leaves from the lawn. If necessary, protect water plants for the winter. Cut back woody plants and perennials. Bulbs can still be planted.
Produce garden. Harvest late vegetables and store them. Leave brussels sprouts and kale in the bed until they've had a frost. This improves their flavor. Put sticky bands around fruit trees.

December

The winter comes on slowly —time to begin feeding the birds. Also, there is still enough to do in the garden.
Ornamental garden. In severe climates, before heavy frosts set in, pine brush is laid over all roses, rhododendrons, and freshly planted evergreens in order to protect them from winter sun and drying winds. Can also apply a burlap covering to shrubs for winter protection.
Produce garden. Harvest time for corn salad begins. Dig out chives, pot them, and bring into the house. Then, they can also be harvested in winter. Mulch around fruit trees.

GARDEN
PLANTS

Whether brightly colored and full of fragrance, green and easy to care for, or rich with fruits and vegetables—your garden's pleasures depend on its plants. The following pages present you with a choice of the most beautiful of the ornamental and useful plants.

Plant Names and Symbols

Why experts don't call plants by their common names may not quite make sense to hobby gardeners. But there are various different names for the same plants, even just in English, besides there being a need for a uniform name throughout the entire world for trade and for science.

The Classification of Plants

The most famous founder of the plant classification system in effect all over the world was the Swedish naturalist Carl Linnaeus (1707–1778). He introduced binomial nomenclature for unambiguous description of organisms; this system employs a capitalized genus name and a lowercase species name. He himself described many plants. Even today his initial L. is often still found after plant names. The systematic classification of plants is made on the basis of their similarities in internal and external structure; however, the flower structure is considered first. These family relationships are not always easy for lay people to perceive at first. The classification of plants is based on different rankings:

<u>Species</u> are identical in their most essential characteristics. Within a species, there are also crosses.

Although, in general, no reproduction is possible between two different species by natural means, breeders develop methods by which such crosses become possible.

<u>Genus</u> (pl. genera) is the next higher step within the classification system. Closely related species belong to one genus.

<u>Families</u> comprise several genera.

<u>Orders, classes, and phyla</u> (sing. phylum), the upper rankings, only play a role in science.

The nomenclature of the dog rose, for example, looks as follows:

Phylum: Covered-seed plants (Angiospermae)
Class: Plants with two-chambered embryos (Dicotyledoneae)
Order: Rose-like (Rosales)
Family: Rose (Rosaceae)
Genus: *Rosa*
Species: *canina*

Knowing the family relationship is also useful for the hobby gardener, for diseases and predators are often limited to certain plant families, such as the crucifers (Cruciferae), which include not only the cabbage vegetables but also the radish (*Raphanus sativus* var. *niger*), green manure plants like mustard (*Sinapis alba*), ornamental plants like stock (*Matthiola incana*), and weeds like shepherd's purse (*Capsella bursa pastoris*). Cabbage flies, white cabbage moth, and clubroot can affect all these plants but do not damage other vegetables or flowers. Family bonds often also allow conclusions as to similar plant care.

Thus, two terms are always required for correct scientific naming of a plant. So the common pine or fir is called

Plant diversity at a glance—the poisonous fruits of the cuckoopint (Arum

Pinus sylvestris. But there are a great number of different pines besides this one: the Swiss stone pine (*Pinus cembra*), the bristle-cone pine (*Pinus aristata*), the shore pine (*Pinus contorta*), the Bosnian pine (*Pinus leucodermis*), the mountain pine (*Pinus mugo*) and many, many more. Therefore, it isn't enough to ask in the nursery for just a pine, for each individual species has an entirely different pattern of growth, and that is decisive for placing it in a particular spot the garden.

Gardeners' Terminology

The practice of gardening includes some other important terms that describe a plant in more detail. In nature, small variations often appear within a species, and these then receive a third name with an abbreviation before it, either:

• ssp. = subspecies
• var. = variety
• f. = form
• cv. = cultivar
• Varieties occur when plants with special characteristics are selected from a wild or garden form, and these charac-

...maculatum) between the silvery leaves of Artemisia ludoviciana.

Origin of Names

Even in ancient times, people gave names to plants. Therefore, most botanical descriptions are of Greek or Latin origin. Often they have very particular meanings, indicate the origin of the plant, describe a morphological characteristic, or also honor a particular person. Here are some examples.

• Boneset—*Symphytum officinale*—(*symphein* = Greek for grow together—reference to healing effect in broken bones)

• Fragrant sumac—*Rhus aromatica*—(*aromatica* = strong smell—the leaves have a pleasant fragrance when rubbed lightly)

• Fennel—*Foeniculum vulgare*—(*foenum* = Latin for hay or *feniculatus* = thread shaped—reference to fine foliage)

• False acacia, robinia—*Robinia pseudoacacia* (Robin was the one who introduced the plant to Europe in around 1600)

Many botanical names have been taken over into English, for example fuchsia, aster, iris, magnolia, rose, and many more. But because these terms cover a number of very particular different individual plants, use of the species names is unavoidable, for example, to make a planting plan. Therefore, the botanical names are always listed in italics after the common name. Scientists are always recognizing new relationships and reclassifying. For example, just most recently there has been a great deal of annoyance generated because the well-known daisy is no longer listed under *Chrysanthemum* but under *Leucanthemum*. When it comes to fruit, vegetables, and roses, the scientific names have scarcely any meaning; here only the variety names count. However, these can all change again from country to country—there is not always a correct translation for them. The rose known as "Peace" in English-speaking countries, for instance, is known as "Gloria Dei" in German-speaking countries. Clearly, it can sometimes be difficult for gardening enthusiasts to understand one another.

teristics are retained by sexual or asexual reproduction. Such changes occur through changes in genes (mutations). The gardener is glad to make use of these in order to increase the number of varieties. Especially interesting are color and shape mutations, perhaps doubled or otherwise marked flowers or leaves. But quality features like size, yield, stability, health, and frost hardiness also play a role in breeding.

• Hybrids are descendants of crossing of genetically different parents—either between different species or between closely related genera; these were also formerly called bastards. The first generation of the crossing of two parent plants are called F$_1$ hybrids. Uniform offspring with higher qualities are created here, but their seeds do not show the species-typical characteristics. The next, F$_2$, generation no longer appears uniform. The indication for a bastard is the *x* between the genus and species name, like *Lobelia x gerardii*. When there are a number of hybrids, they are divided into groups like *Delphinium belladonna* hybrids or *Phlox paniculata* hybrids.

A comfy place to sit amid flowering shrubs and trees.

WOODY PLANTS IN THE GARDEN

Woody plants perform an important function in a garden: They create a structure and a framework, defining the garden as space, establishing a boundary with the outside, and, thus, providing privacy and protection from wind and noise. Trees and shrubs are the essential green elements with which the garden is structured. In the form of hedges—either free-growing or clipped, evergreen or flowering—woody plants frame the garden. Low shrubs enclose beds, border paths, or separate sections of the garden from one another; taller shrubs offer privacy or focal points. Many trees and shrubs are particularly appropriate for specimen plantings because of their impressive growth habits; others can be beautiful in groups; and still others form a good backdrop for specimens, roses, perennials, and annuals.

Trees and shrubs play a special role in the garden in winter, when their shape, their branches, and the beauty of their bark and fruits become more prominent. This is a reason for choosing the right ones—particularly in the small garden, where there is only room for a few large trees or shrubs—which will guarantee attractiveness all year long. So, for instance, you can plant shrubs with staggered flowering times, whose fruits and fall coloring create additional garden climaxes. Evergreens are suitable for interplanting and with their constant green in the winter create additional beautiful contrasts. Dwarf trees and shrubs lend structure to some parts of the garden, and also ground-covering shrubs have important functions as underplantings.

This variety of the Japanese maple (Acer palmatum *"Dissectum") changes its color in the fall from fresh green to glowing yellow.*

Deciduous Trees and Large Shrubs

Trees and shrubs are the impressive vegetative design elements of a garden. A single tree can completely change the appearance and character of the garden. When making a choice, keep in mind:

• First of all, the conditions of the available locations in the garden are the deciding factors. Crown and roots need appropriate space for the woody plant to develop to its full glory. You will find the necessary information in good catalogs.

• Before you begin to plan, find out from the local authorities about minimum planting distances from neighboring properties that must be maintained (see pages 22–23), as well as guidelines for the use of particular trees or shrubs in the garden.

• Learn beforehand from the nursery catalogs about species and varieties. There information will be given about growth forms and average mature sizes of the plants. In some cases, the full growth appears early; however, in others it only appears after years. Trees often take decades to attain their characteristic habits. However, the particular location exercises a definite influence on the vigor of a tree or shrub. Get advice before selecting, for large trees and shrubs can hardly be transplanted again later.

• Also important is the spread of a tree or large shrub. It determines the shading of the soil and the possibilities for underplanting (see pages 104–105). Neighboring plants can be influenced or inhibited by planting too close, but the tree or shrub itself can also be restricted in its development. You should never try to solve the placement problem by constant pruning. It's better to take the woody plant out altogether.

• For a tree or shrub to develop its utterly characteristic growth form, you must either place it alone or provide it with a weaker partner. With a stepwise increase in heights of plantings through combination of tall and low plants, you create a transition to lower plantings. However, you can also decide at the beginning to have a grouping of shrubs in which the individuality of the single shrubs increases the total effect.

• The habitat of a plant and especially of a tree is a fundamental design factor in your garden (see page 18). For example, a solitary standard lets the eye roam past it, making the garden seem larger. On the other hand, a freestanding tree with a picturesque branch structure all the way to the ground can provide a stop and focus in a large garden.

• If you plant a tree close to the house, consider the effect of shade on the living quarters. There are deciduous

The Chinese magnolia is a spring beauty.

Chinese, Saucer magnolia
Magnolia x soulangiana
Very slow-growing, shrubby tree; the star magnolia (*Magnolia stellata*) blooms at the end of Mar. and remains small (Z. 3–8). <u>Flowers</u> from the age of about 10 years with upright, tulip-like bells, white to pink, Apr.–May, before the foliage comes out.

<u>Foliage</u> large, thickish leaves, elliptical, light green. <u>Growth</u> short trunk, spreading with age, H: up to 20 to 30 ft (6–9 m); S: up to 13 ft (4 m). <u>Location</u> sunny, warm, protected from late frosts; acid to neutral soil, damp, rich, no surface compaction or dryness. Z: 4–9 (*M. soulangiana*).

trees that leaf out or drop their leaves late or early. But also the drop of fruits and seeds can have an impact on the living area.

Flowering crab.

The catalpa *in full bloom.*

Flowering crab
Malus x purpurea
Many varieties, also other species. Flowers single, ruby red, later paler, Apr.–May; roundish, red ornamental apples. Foliage oval, in early spring reddish, later green. Growth spreading, H: 26 ft in (8 m); S: 33 ft (10 m). Location sunny, damp; acid to neutral soil. Z: 5–8.

Common catalpa or Southern catalpa
Catalpa bignoniodes
Large summer-flowering ornamental tree with strikingly ornamental fruit. Flowers up to 12 in (30 cm) long, white panicles, beautiful individual flowers, trumpet shaped with a yellow throat and purple flecks, sweetly fragrant, June–July;

fruits long, beanlike capsules hanging down. Foliage large, heart-shaped leaves, light green, only appears end of May to beginning of June. Growth broad-crowned, H: up to 49 ft (15 m), S: up to 40 ft (12 m). Location sunny to semishady, protected. Z: 4–9.

Katsura tree.

The shadbush is captivating with its fall color.

European mountain ash.

Katsura tree
Cercidiphyllum japonicum
Red-brown branches. Flowers crimson, Apr. Foliage fragrant, heart shaped, red when new, later bright green, in fall yellow or orange. Growth multistemmed, H: 40 to 60 ft (12–18 m); S: 20 to 30 ft (6–9 m). Location sunny to semishady, protected; likes moist, well-drained soil. Z: 4–8.

Serviceberry or shadbush
Amelanchier arborea (N.)
Undemanding large shrub with reddish bark and enchanting fall color. Flowers from the age of about 5 years with creamy white racemes; Apr.–May, small, globular, purplish to black, edible fruits, Aug–Sept. Foliage grayish when new, elliptical, at first silvery hairy

leaves, green; from Oct. yellow to orange-red, early leaf drop, quickly rotting. Growth multistemmed, picturesque, H: 16 to 26 ft (5–8 m), S: 10 to 16 ft (3–5 m). Location sunny to semishady; chalky soil. Z: 4–9.

European mountain ash, Rowan ☠
Sorbus aucuparia
Medium-high tree. Flowers white umbelliferous, May, fragrant; Sept., round, red berries (skin irritant). Foliage pinnate, green, in fall yellow to orange. Growth tree- or bush-like, H: 20 to 60 ft (6–18 m). Location sunny to semishady; moderately dry. Z: 3–6 or 7.

Deciduous Trees and Large Shrubs

Larger woody plants form the framework of the garden and create atmosphere and the proper conditions for shade-loving plants at the same time. The growth of flowering and sun-loving ornamental shrubs, perennials, and annuals is, however, affected by the shadows and root pressure of trees and shrubs. In older gardens the woody plants are often so large already that the garden must be redesigned (see pages 26–27).

Therefore, you should consider when planning, especially with a small property, whether a single large tree might not be enough for an outstanding design element, otherwise shrubs might be better used. In very small gardens, a shrub with a height of 16 to 23 ft (5–7 m) can usually also take the place of a small to medium-size tree (about 33 to 49 ft [10–5 m] tall).

The color plays an important role in the choice of a tree or shrub. Not only do the various shades of green enliven the garden, but also golden, red, or variegated foliage contributes to the design variety in the garden. Combining too many colors usually creates a busy effect, however. In a small garden, a single unusually colored specimen is enough to provide contrast. The white-variegated foliage of the ash-leaved maple (*Acer negundo* "Variegatum") or the yellow leaves of the robinia (*Robinia pseudoacacia* "Frisia") is in no way inferior in its distant effect to a flowering tree or shrub. You should also take into consideration the form and color of the flowers and fruits as well as the autumn coloring as you plan your garden design. Many woody plants, like the flowering crab, are covered with flowers in the spring, then develop fruits, which remain on the branches for a long time and enrich the garden scene with their attractive fall coloring.

At the same time, you should keep your eye on the possibilities for colorful enhancement of the shrubbery with appropriate perennials. Especially in spring, at the best flowering time, there can be wonderful combinations of bulbs flowering in front of the trees or shrubs. And once again, as the final notes to the season, the coloring of the leaves in harmony with the yellow or violet shades of late perennials enhance the fall garden scene.

The growth characteristics of the woody plants are also used as a means of design. Many small trees have several trunks; others grow in bizarre forms or are extremely picturesque.

The proper proportions are also important in the choice of trees or shrubs to create structure: It looks very well balanced if the fully grown tree or large shrub reaches over the house by one third or remains about one third the height of it.

Japanese ornamental cherry.

Japanese flowering cherry, Oriental cherry
Prunus serrulata
Many varieties. Flowers white to pink, somewhat doubled, Apr.–June. Foliage bronze when new, then green, in fall orange to yellow. Growth depending on variety, pillar shaped, treelike, weeping, or bushy. Location sunny, humid air; porous, humus soil, lime loving.
Important: Many early-flowering species are descended from *Prunus sargentii* and *P. subhirtella*, such as "Accolade" with pink flowers. The white and double-flowered bird cherry *P. avium* "Plena" can grow to 33 ft (10 m) high. Z: 5–9.

Goldenchain tree "Vossii."

Goldenchain tree ☠
Laburnum x watereni
Easy, profusely flowering. Flowers bright yellow panicles up to 8 in (20 cm), May–June; beanlike fruits, Sept., very poisonous. Foliage medium green, tripartite. Growth multistemmed, H: 16 to 23 ft (5–7 m), S: 10 to 13 ft (3–4 m). Location sunny to semishady. Important: Prune after flowering. Z: 5–7.

Weeping birch "Youngii."

Weeping birch, European white birch
Betula pendula
Umbrella-shaped crown. Flowers yellow catkins, Mar.–Apr. Foliage roundish to heart shaped, serrated, bright green when new, then darker, yellow in fall. Growth manelike pendulous branches, H: 40 to 50 ft (12–15 m), S: 20 to 30 ft (6–9 m). Location sunny to semishady; well-drained, moist soil. Z: 2–6 (7).

False acacia "Umbraculifera."

Chinese elm.

Black locust, ☠
Common locust
Robinia pseudoacacia (N.)

Small, globular tree. Flowers none. Foliage pinnate, light green, yellow fall coloring. Growth long trunk with densely branched globular crown, slow growing, H: 30 to 50 ft (9–15 m), S: 20 to 35 ft (6–10 m). Location sunny; dry to loamy or chalky soil. Z: 3–8 (9).

Chinese elm, Lacebark elm
Ulmus parvifolia

Medium tree. Flowers inconspicuous Aug–Sept. Foliage dark green; yellowish, reddish in fall. Growth graceful, rounded habit, pendulous branches, some upright, H: 40 to 50 ft (12–15 m). S: similar. Location many soils, preferably moist, well-drained; Full sun to semishady. Z: 4–9.

Cherry plum.

Staghorn sumac.

Cherry plum
Prunus cerasifera "Nigra"

Outstanding dark red leaves. Flowers abundant, pink, single, Apr.–May; plum like fruits. Foliage oval, dark red, shiny. Growth crown cone shaped, H: 15 to 30 ft (5–9 m), S: up to 15 to 25 ft (5–7.6 m). Location sunny to semishady, as warm as possible; all well-drained soils. Z: 3–8.

Staghorn sumac ☠
Rhus typhina (N.)

Easy. Flowers candlelike green panicles, June–July, Aug. reddish fruits in clusters. Foliage pinnate, orange in fall. Growth umbrella shaped with age, H: 15 to 25 ft (5–7.6 m), S: 10 to 20 ft (3–6 m). Location sunny, prefers dry, well-drained soils. Z: 3–8. Important: To prevent runners don't injure roots.

Other Woody Deciduous Plants

Hedge maple; *Acer campestre* Wild shrub; flowers insignificant; foliage 5-lobed, dark green, yellow from Oct; growth shrubby, H: 10 to 49 ft. S: 26 to 39 ft; location sunny to semishady. Z: 4–8.

Amur maple; *Acer ginnala* Undemanding; flowers green-white, May; foliage 3-lobed, from Oct., brilliant orange; growth H: 16 to 20 ft, S: 13 to 33 ft; location sunny to semishady. Z: 2–8.

Bottle-brush buckeye; Dwarf horse chestnut *Aesculus parviflora* (N.) Shrub; flowers white, candles, July–Aug; foliage pinnate, bronze when new, fall coloring; growth H: 10 to 20 ft, S: 16 to 26 ft; location sunny. Z: 4–10.

Devil's walking stick, or Hercules-club; *Aralia spinosa* Large shrub; flowers white, panicles, Aug.–Sept; fruits globular; foliage pinnate, fall coloring; growth umbrella-like, H: 10 to 16 ft, S: 10 ft; location sunny, warm. Z: 4–9.

European hornbeam *Carpinus betulus* Hedge shrub; flowers insignificant, May; foliage dark green, from Oct. yellow, drop in spring; growth H: 40 to 60 ft, S: 30 to 40 ft; location sunny to semishady. Z: 4–7.

Eastern redbud *Cercis canadensis* (N.) Striking; flowers before new growth, purplish pink, April; foliage dull green, growth H: 20 to 30 ft, S: 25 to 35 ft; location full sun to light shade; moist, well-drained soil. Z: 3–9.

Japanese dogwood, Kousa dogwood; *Cornus kousa* Decorative; flowers small, large white bracts, May; red fruits Sept.; foliage green, from Oct. brilliant yellow to red; growth H: 20 to 30 ft, S: 20 to 30 ft; location sunny to semishady; acidic, well-drained, sandy soil. Z: 5–8.

Cornelian cherry, Dogwood *Cornus mas* Wild shrub; flowers yellow, Feb.–Mar.; red fruits from Aug.; foliage yellow-orange from Oct.; growth H: up to 26 ft, S: up to 16 ft; location sunny to semishady. Z: 4–8.

European filbert, American filbert *Corylus avellana, C. americana* Wild shrub; flowers yellow catkins, Feb.–Mar.; nuts Sept.; foliage broadly ovate; growth H: 12 to 20 ft, S: 8 to 15 ft; location sunny to semishady; well-drained, loamy soil. Z: 4–7.

Green ash *Fraxinus pennsylvanica* (N.) Undemanding; flowers green to reddish purple, May; foliage deep green; growth H: 50 to 60 ft, S: 13 to 20 ft; location sunny, warm; alkaline soil. Z: 3–9.

American sweet gum *Liquidambar styraciflua* (N.) Tree; flowers insignificant; foliage oak-like, from Sept. firey red; growth H: 60 to 75 ft, S: 40 to 50 ft; location sunny; acid, rich-humus deep soil. Z: 5–9.

Nothofagus, Antarctic beech *Nothofagus antarctica* Bizarre tree; flowers insignificant; foliage glossy green, wavy edged; growth 13 to 20 ft, S: 10 to 13 ft; location sunny; no lime. Z: 8–9.

Goat willow; *Salix caprea* Honey producing; flowers silvery, later golden yellow, Mar.–Apr.; foliage dark green above, grayish beneath; growth H: 15 to 25 ft, S: 12 to 15 ft; location sunny to semishady. Z: 4–8.

Japanese pagodatree, Scholar-tree; *Sophora japonica* Decorative; flowers cream white, racemes, Aug.; foliage bluish green; growth H: 50 to 75 ft, S: 40–60 ft; location sunny. Z: 4–8.

Willow-leaf pear *Pyrus salicifolia* Pretty tree; flowers white, racemes, Apr.–May; foliage gray-green; growth H: 15 to 20 ft, S: 10 to 15 ft; location sunny, dry, no acid soil. Z: 4.

Ornamental Shrubs

As a general rule, shrubs grow differently from the trunk-forming trees. They usually branch out from a base or form several ground shoots of equal size, which then develop like trunks. But in tiny gardens, a large shrub can take over the function of a decorative tree altogether. There are varieties of a great many ornamental shrubs that only grow slowly and, therefore, are suitable for smaller gardens. You will find information about them at a nursery or in a good catalog.

Special characteristics of ornamental shrubs. Ornamental shrubs are distinguished by especially lush flowering or they are decorated with multicolored leaves. Often they also have a special growth form.

There are ornamental shrubs that are suitable even for extreme locations in the garden. Some tolerate heat and dryness—which frequently occur in city locations—and also temperature fluctuations because they have learned to adapt to them in their native habitats. Among these are the Russian olive (*Elaeagnus angustifolia*), the Siberian peashrub (*Caragana arborescens*), and many barberries (*Berberis* species). Some are also somewhat more delicate and in our climate don't have extensive frost hardiness.

Flowers of forsythia.

They often freeze back and must be cut down every year. This is the case with butterfly bushes (*Buddleia davidii* hybrids), with bluebeard (*Caryopteris x clandonensis*), and with shrub bushclover (*Lespedeza thunbergii*), a fall bloomer. Some are also so-called half-shrubs, with lower stems that become woody while the upper parts remain herbaceous and die back after the growing season ends, such as the lavender (*Lavandula* species). With decorative shrubs, many hybrid forms are grafted onto an understock—similarly to roses. Wild shoots, or suckers, can grow from this base, as for example with lilacs. These must be cut back as close as possible to their base. If you let the suckers grow, the plant will be weakened.

Native wild shrubs. Many of our native shrubs can take over the function of the ornamental shrubs, for they are hardly inferior in abundance of flowers, decorative fruits, and leaf coloration than their exotic relatives. Furthermore, they are winter hardy and offer birds and insects shelter and food. Therefore, you should choose at least some wild shrubs for your free stand or hedge, for instance the bayberry (*Myrica pensylvanica*) or the spring-flowering western sand cherry (*Prunus besseyi*). Z: 3–9.

The witch hazel, a valuable winter bloomer.

Witch hazel
Hamamelis x intermedia

Valuable winter-bloomer, specimen shrub. Flowers filamentous, spidery, yellow, orange, red, Feb.–Apr. Foliage broad oval, dark green, from Oct. yellow, orange, or red fall coloring. Growth H: 15 to 20 ft (5–6 m), S: 10 to 15 ft (3–5 m), horn-shaped, short-stemmed, branches aimed steeply upright, slow growing. Location sun to semishade; rich, weakly acid soil, fresh to moist. Z: 5–9.

Important: Do not prune if possible, except for small branches for a vase; numerous large-flowered varieties with various flower colors.

There are countless varieties of flowering quince.

Forsythia
Forsythia x intermedia

(photo left) Common spring bloomer, many varieties. Flowers golden yellow bells; April. Foliage oval to lanceolate, dull green. Growth H: 8 to 13 ft (2.5–4 m), S: 10 to 12 ft (3–3.7 m). Location full sun, loose, rich soil. Care thin older branches every 2 to 3 years; prune after flowering. Z: 4–8 (9).

Common flowering quince
Chaenomeles species

Outstanding spring bloomer. Flowers red, pink, white; March–Apr. Foliage oval, dark green. Growth H: 6 to 10 ft (1.8–3 m), S: 6 to 10 ft (1.8–3 m). Location sun to semishade; warm, well-drained, rich, semidry to moist soil, acid to neutral. Z: 4–8 (9).

Spike winterhazel—a charming early-spring bloomer.

Fothergilla.

Spike winterhazel
Corylopsis spicata

Fragrant spring bloomer.
Flowers bright yellow ears;
Apr. Foliage heart-shaped,
bluish green, outstanding yellow to orange-red fall coloring.
Growth H: 4 to 7 ft (1.2–2 m),
S: 4 to 10 ft (1.2–3 m), several
upright stems from the
ground, in age broader than

high, slow growing. Location
full sun to semishade, avoid
heat and dryness; prefers rich
moist well-drained, slightly
alkaline to acid, soil.
Important: *Corylopsis pauciflora* blooms earlier (Mar.) and at
5 ft (1.5 m) remains distinctly
smaller. Z: 5–8.

Fothergilla,
Large fothergilla
Fothergilla major (N.)

Unusually beautiful small specimen shrub. Flowers cream
white, up to 8-in- (20-cm-)
long, bottlebrush-like ears;
May. Foliage oval, bright
green, from Sept. colored
golden yellow to orange-red.
Growth 6 to 10 ft (1.8–3 m),

S: up to 5 ft (1.5 m), spreadingly bushy, cone shaped, slow
growing. Location sun to semishade, protected; humus rich
to moist acidic soil. No hot, full
sun places with dry soil.
Important: Combines well with
azaleas, rhododendrons, and
Japanese maple, which have
similar cultural requirements.

Rewarding and undemanding—the Japanese rose.

European euonymus.

Japanese rose,
Japanese kennia
Kerria japonica "Plena"

Many stems, very undemanding
bouquets of flowers for flowering hedge. Flowers densely doubled, golden yellow flower balls;
May, dish shaped in the single
wild species. Foliage oval- lanceolate, pointed, bright green.
Growth H: 3 to 7 ft (0.9–2 m),

S: 6 to 5 ft (1.82.7 m), little
branching ground shoots,
spreads through root runners,
thicketlike. Location sun to
shade; damp, moderately rich
soil, acid to weakly alkaline
Important: Every 2 to 3 years
remove older shoots at the base.
With too much fertilizing, the
shrub spreads vigorously but
forms few flowers. Z: 4–9.

European euonymus ☠
Euonymus europaea

Wild shrub ornamented with outstanding fruits. Flowers undistinguished, yellow-green; May,
from Aug. coral pink "pope's
hats" with orange seed hulls.
Foliage oval, light green, in fall
yellow to crimson. Growth wide,
upright, H: 12 to 30 ft (3.7–9 m),
S: 10 to 25 ft (3–7.6 m).

Location full sun to semishady;
ph adaptable, dry to moist,
well-drained, and rich soils.
Important: The winged
euonymus (*Euonymus alata*) only
grows 15 to 20 ft (5–6 m) high,
with similar spread; it captivates
with its brilliant red fall coloring
and attracts particular attention
with its 4 finlike corky growths
on the branches. Z: 3–8.

Ornamental Shrubs

The growth form of a shrub—its habit—is the first thing that determines whether it works better as a specimen planting or in a group of shrubs. Shrubs with outstanding forms or that develop characteristically shaped branches can be used in the garden as striking single forms. Others would scarcely attract any attention by themselves; they show to best effect in small groups or are also suitable for hedges.

Groups of shrubs. From the multitude of ornamental shrubs, you can seek out those that—planted in a group—create interesting effects. Here you can play with flower colors and forms. If you choose shrubs with uniform flowering times, once a year they will present an entire fireworks display of flowers. Of course, you can also select the species and varieties so that something is blooming almost all year long. Besides the flowering time, the various leaf colors and shapes provide interest. Differing growth forms can also provide interesting contrasts, perhaps if you plant shrubs that grow slender and tall with globular or cushion-shaped ones.

Combination with perennials. Shrubs create a pretty background for flowering perennials; species with an upright growth habit are best suited for this. Along paths or beds, you should plant the ornamentals in such a way that they have enough space for their development but don't crowd any weakly growing plants.

Magnificent display throughout the year. If you select species and varieties skillfully, you can have flowering shrubs in the garden from early spring until late fall. The winter and early-spring bloomers are rarer and less strikingly colored, but seen from close up they promise the enchantment of early spring. The scene becomes brilliant and gay in early April, when the forsythias (*Forsythia x intermedia*) appear in many front yards like yellow flames. In May come the colorful butterfly flowers of the brooms (*Cytisus scoparius*), the lilacs in all colors (*Syringa vulgaris*), the viburnums (*Viburnum* species), and the white cascades of flowers of the bridal-wreaths (*Spiraea* species). In June, a wealth of ornamental shrubs come into flower, with white and pink shades predominating. By high and and late summer, the glory of bloom is beginning to wane. Only the butterfly bushes (*Buddleia davidii* cultivars) display white to black-purple flowers, depending on the variety, and the rose-of-Sharon (*Hibiscus syriacus)* flowers in many beautiful white, pink, and blue shades, as do the hydrangeas (*Hydrangea* species) with their outstanding sterile flowers in white, blue, or red.

Recommended Ornamental Shrubs

Alternate-leaf, Butterfly bush
Buddleia alternifolia
Easy-care flowering shrub; flowers pale lavender, fragrant, June; foliage gray-green; growth H/S: 15 to 20 ft; location sunny, protected, moderately dry. Z: 5.

Butterfly bush
Buddleia davidii cultivars
Attracts butterflies; flowers long panicles purple, red, white, July; foliage lanceolate, dull green; growth H: up to 15 ft, S: up to 7 ft; location warm, full sun, well-drained, fertile soil. Z: 5–9.

Bluebeard, Blue-spirea
Caryopteris x *clandonensis*
Small late-summer bloomer; flowers blue panicles, Aug.–Sept., on new growth; foliage lanceolate, gray-green, fragrant; growth H/S: 2–3 ft; location sunny, protected. Z: 7–9.

February daphne ☠
Daphne mezereum
Fragrant spring-bloomer; flowers crimson, Mar.–Apr.; foliage elliptical, dull green; growth H/S: 3 to 5 ft, upright; location semishady; humus, alkaline soil. Z: 5–8.

Deutzia
Deutzia species and varieties
Popular summer bloomer; flowers white or pink, somewhat doubled, May–June; growth H: up to 13 ft, S: up to 7 ft; location sunny to semi-shady. Z: 4–8.

Russian olive
Elaeagnus angustifolia
Heat-tolerant large shrub; flowers yellow, fragrant, May–June; Sept. olive-like fruits; foliage lanceolate, silver-green; growth H: up to 23 ft , S: up to 15 ft; location sunny, dry, lime-loving prefers light, well-drained sandy loam soil, salt tolerant. Z: 2–7.

Rose-of-Sharon
Hibiscus syriacus
Pretty late-summer bloomer, many varieties; flowers saucer shaped, white, pink, red, violet, June–Sept.; foliage oval, dark green; growth H: up to 12 ft, S: up to 10 ft, upright; location full sun to part shade, warm, protected; best in moist, organically amended, well-drained soil. Important: First year, protect from frost with branches. Z: 5–8. (9).

Beautybush
Kolkwitzia amabilis
Weigelia-like, easy shrub; flowers many pink to light pink little bells, May–June; foliage oval, dull green; growth H/S: up to 10 ft, overhanging; location sunny to semishady with well-drained soil. Z: 4–8.

Lavender
Lavandula angustifolia
Small shrub; violet-blue flower panicles, from June, fragrant; foliage elongated, silver-gray, evergreen; growth H/S: up to 3 ft; location sunny, warm, alkaline, well-drained, dryish soils. Z: 5–9.

Tree peony
Paeonia suffruticosa
Magnificent spring bloomer; flowers very large, white, yellow, pink, red, partly doubled, Apr.–May; foliage laciniate, medium green; growth H/S: up to 7 ft; location sunny; rich, neutral soil. Z: 4–8.

Mockorange
Philadelphus hybrids (N.)
Richly flowering, fragrant shrub; flowers white to cream, partly doubled, May–June; foliage oval, dark green; growth H: up to 13 ft, S: up to 10 ft; location sunny to semi-shady, moist, well-drained soil with organic matter. Z: 4–8.

Shrubby cinquefoil
Potentilla fruticosa (N.)
Heavily blooming small shrub; flowers yellow, white, orange, red, May–Oct.; foliage pinnate; growth H: up to 4 ft, S: 2–4 ft; location sunny to semi-shady; likes fertile, well-drained, moist soil. Z: 2–7.

Hydrangea "Annabelle."

Various hydrangeas—at right, a red smokebush.

Smokebush in flower.

Wild hydrangea
Hydrangea arborescens (N.)
Large-flowered shrub, shady areas. Flowers white in broad, globular corymbose cymes; June–Aug. Foliage oval, green. Growth H: and S: 4 to 7 ft (1.2–2 m), slightly overhanging, larger in spread. Location semishade to shade; humus, rich and well-drained, moist, slightly acidic soil. Z: 3–9.

Hydrangea
Hydrangea aspera
Important late-summer bloomer. Flowers flat inflorescences up to 12 in (30 cm) in diameter, small fertile inner flowers in pink, violet, or blue, encircled by outer, sterile flowers in white or pink, July–Sept. Foliage large, oval, velvety, dull green. Growth H: up to 10 ft (3 m), S: up to 3 ft (0.9 m), upright, little branching. Location semishady; humus, rich, fresh to moist soil, acid to neutral.

Important: Also widely distributed is *Hydrangea macrophylla* with pink flowers in neutral to alkaline soil or blue in acid soil; all hydrangeas are sensitive to winter dryness. Z: 7–9.

Smokebush
Cotinus coggygria
Large shrub, wiglike arrangement of fruits. Flowers whitish, feathery panicles; June–July. Foliage oval, orange to red in fall. Growth H: 10 to 16 ft (3–5 m), S: 10 to 15 ft (3–5 m). Location sunny; dry to well-drained loamy soil. Cultivars "Royal Purple" has dark red foliage. Z: 4–8.

Popular variety "Charles Joly."

Doublefile viburnum "Mariesii."

Bell-shaped flowers.

Flowering marvel—garland spirea.

Common lilac
Syringa vulgaris hybrids
Classics among the late-spring bloomers. Flowers upright, loose panicles, doubled or single, lavender, purple, pink, white; May. Foliage heart shaped, fresh green. Growth H: 10 to 20 ft (3–6 m), S: 6 to 16 ft (1.8–5 m), multistemmed, forms runners. Location sunny to semishady, lime-loving, neutral pH. Z: 3–7.

Japanese snowball, Doublefile viburnum
Viburnum plicatum var. *tomentosum*
Extravagant flowering shrub. Flowers cymes surrounded by white flowers; May–June. Foliage broadly elliptical, dark red to orange in fall. Growth H: up to 15 ft (5 m), S: up to 10 ft (3 m), forming horizontal layers of branches. Location sunny to semishady. Z: 5–8.

Weigelia
Weigelia cultivars
Hedge shrub. Flowers bell shaped in cymes, pink, red; May–Aug. Foliage elliptical, light green. Growth H: and S: 6 to 10 ft (1.8–3 m), many stemmed, upright to arching overhanging, fast growing. Location sun to semishade, well-drained soil. Pollution tolerant. Z: 5–8. Important: Many cultivars are available.

Garland spirea
Spiraea x arguta
Robust flowering shrub with lush display of many flowers. Flowers small, white corymbs on the upper sides of the branches; from Apr. Foliage small, lanceolate, fresh green. Growth H and S: 5 to 7 ft (1.5–2 m), tending to arch over with age. Location sun to semishade; any well-drained soil.

Broad-leaved Evergreen Shrubs

Evergreens don't lose their leaves in the fall but replace the old leaves with young ones throughout the growing season. Some broad-leaved evergreens are ivy (*Hedera helix*), holly (*Ilex aquifolium*), myrtle (*Vinca minor*), and some heaths and heathers. They thrive primarily in the shady understory and their leaves are protected by a waxy layer from excessive evaporation. Native broad-leaved evergreens include: Florida privet (*Forestiera segregata*), inkberry (*Ilex glabra*), and Oregon grape holly (*Mahonia aquifolium*). The inkberry and Florida privet thrive in sunny conditions, whereas the Oregon grape holly prefers shadier sites. Many species of evergreen are found growing in North America. There is an evergreen shrub available to suit all growing climates in North America. In winter, these plants need protection: When the ground is frozen, the roots can't take up water but the leaves continue to evaporate water. The missing supply of fluid then causes the broad-leaved evergreens to dry out; inexperienced gardeners often confuse this damage from dryness with frost damage. Keep freezing off for as long as possible with leaf mulch and branches and if necessary provide protection from the sun—perhaps with burlap—so that it doesn't produce excessive evaporation. Also, you should water your evergreens regularly on frost-free days. The higher the moisture content of the soil and the air, the better unfavorable conditions are tolerated. However, if injury does occur in spite of protection, you should remove the dessicated branches. Most of these shrubs will stand pruning. In our gardens, evergreens are especially suitable for underplanting light stands of trees. They like a humus-filled, loose, and rich-moist acidic soil.

Rhododendrons. Rhododendrons and their relatives, the heath family, hold an important place among the broad-leaved evergreens. But these attractive flowering shrubs require mild winters and a humid climate as well as acid soil with a low pH (see pages 148–149). However, breeding of "lime-tolerant" rhododendrons is under way today. The new varieties not only offer many colors, but suitability for sunny locations is also a declared goal of breeders. However, in general, rhododendrons and the heath family still have special care requirements. Therefore, in many areas, it is hardly possible to make them grow under natural conditions.

Rhododendron
Rhododendron **hybrids (N.)**
Popular flowering shrubs for regions with mild winters, numerous varieties available. Flowers trumpet shaped to bell-like, in dense clusters, white, yellow, orange, pink, red, and purple; April–June. Foliage lanceolate, oval to roundish, dark green, leathery. Growth broadly bushy to spherical, H: up to 13 ft (4 m). Location light shade; soil rich in humus, porous, neutral to acid. Care don't dig in root region; leaves that roll up in winter are a sign of dryness; don't fail to water in frost-free weather; cut off dead flowers without injuring new buds. Generally hardy in Z: 4–8.

Skimmia.

Skimmia,
Japanese skimmia
Skimmia japonica
Beautiful fruits. Flowers yellowish white panicles, May, dioecious, fragrant; Oct. shining red fruits, if male and female plants present. Foliage baylike, evergreen. Growth half round, compact, H: 3 to 4 ft (0.9–1.2 m), S: 3 to 5 ft (0.9–1.5 m). Location semishady to shady; acidic, moist, rich, well-drained soil. Z: 7 (6)–8 (9).

Cherry laurel—the wide-spreading variety "Otto Luyken."

Holly.

Cherry laurel ☠
Prunus laurocerasus

Small shrub, frost-hardy. Flowers white, candle-shaped racemes, May–June, Aug.; strong smell; black cherries. Foliage thick, leathery, lanceolate, upright. Growth broad, vigorous to half round, H: 10 to 18 ft (3–5.5 m), S: 6 to 10 ft (1.8–3 m), slow-vigorous. Location sunny to shady;

semidry to moist, well-drained, organically amended soils. Z: 6. Cultivars "Otto Luyken" (photo), dense, compact, H: 3 to 4 ft (0.9– 1.2 m). S: 6 to 8 ft (1.8– 2.5 m). "Herbergii," cone-shaped, H: 7 ft (2 m); "Schipkaensis Macrophylla," large-leaved, flowering; "Zabeliana," low-growing, H: 3 ft (0.9 m). Z: 5.

English holly ☠
Ilex aquifolium

Tolerates pruning; female plants develop fruit. Flowers insignificant, white, May; Sept. red fruits. Foliage oval, dark green, also variegated, leaf edges wavy with stiff, spiny teeth. Growth H: 30 to 50 ft (9–16 m), S: up to 20 ft (6 m). Location sunny to shady, damp, acidic soil. Z: 6–9.

Cotoneaster.

"Emerald 'n Gold."

"Orange Glow" is resistant to scab.

Cotoneaster, Willowleaf cotoneaster ☠
Cotoneaster salcifolius var. floccosus

Undemanding shrub with poisonous fruits. Flowers dense, white umbels, June–July, strongly fragrant; from Sept. numerous round, bright red fruits, long-lasting. Foliage lanceolar, glossy dark green,

furrowed. Growth multi-stemmed, broadly spreading; H: 10 to 13 ft (3–4 m), S: up to 10 ft (3 m). Location sunny to shady, also hot. Varieties Dwarf cotoneasters can be planted as ground covers; varieties like "Scarlet leader," "Gnom," "Parkteppich," "Repens" grow into compact, cushion shapes. Z: 3–7.

Wintercreeper euonymus
Euonymus fortunei

Climbs by rootlets. Flowers only with age, yellow-green umbels; June. Foliage elliptical, colored; Oct. reddish. Growth H: 1 ft (0.3 m) to 2 ft (0.6 m), S: 3 ft (0.9 m), forms mats. Acts as a climber up to 40 ft (12 m) if given support. Location sunny to semishady; rich soil, pH adaptable, no dryness in hot spells. Z: 4–9.

Firethorn, Scarlet firethorn
Pyracantha coccinea

Tolerates pruning. Flowers white corymbose cymes, May–June; fruits from Aug. in yellow, orange, red, long lasting. Foliage glossy dark green, partly only winter-green. Growth twiggy, H/S: 6 to 18 ft (1.8–5.5 m). Location sunny to semishady. Important: Choose hardy cultivars, resistant to scab and fireblight problems. Z: 6–9.

Needle-leaved Plants, Conifers

Conifers have needle-shaped leaves. A very few species lose these in the fall, but most are evergreen. The needles have only a very limited life span and are replaced throughout the entire growing season. The needle drop is even increased in unfavorable conditions and drought. One advantage, however, is that the resulting layer of dropped needles is useful as mulch for certain plant groups like the acid-loving heath and pine families.

Evergreen needle-leaved shrubs are indispensable for creating structures and protective screens that stay green in the winter garden. But often positives turn into negatives when proportions are ignored and the conifers are too many or too large for the size of the garden (see pages 98–99). With evergreens, you don't see the seasonal changes, nor does light play on their "foliage." They cast shadows all year-round and underplanting is only possible in a few cases. A dearth of falling deciduous leaves in the garden also results in a lack of humus for the soil. A humusy soil allows perennials and bulbs to thrive.

Pruning. False cypress (*Chamaecyparis* species), arborvitae (*Thuja* species), and yew (*Taxus* species) can be pruned hard and are suitable for clipped hedges (see pages 80–81), but they can also be pruned into other shapes. The other species will not put out new growth if cut back to old wood. However, many conifers grow by nature into spherical, cone, or pillar shapes.

Uses. Conifers form a beautiful, quiet background for flowers and other ornamental striking plants. In large gardens, they can also form charming/interesting groups of mixed dwarf and tall conifers. Less successful, however, are combinations with tall deciduous trees, whose broad crowns impinge on the needle-leaved plants. An exception is the shade-tolerant yew, which still thrives under the canopies of large trees.

Needle-leaved plants do not fit into every landscape. Often they appear foreign, and, with age, most of them outgrow the dimensions of a home garden. However, within many species, there are usually some less vigorously growing natural and cultivated varieties. First mention here goes to the pines (*Pinus* species) and junipers (*Juniperus* species), the latter especially for sunny locations.

Dwarf forms. Woody plants with dwarf forms exist in a great variety of colors and shapes, in green, gray, blue, silver, and gold tones. They are especially good for rock gardens and slopes, for framing beds of roses or perennials, as well as for container planters on balconies, terraces, and in entry areas. But dwarf conifers shouldn't be combined indiscriminately either; even with them, too many can easily become monotonous.

Korean fir.

Arborvitae.

Korean fir
Abies koreana
Slow-growing, robust. Fruit at first violet, then brown, upright. Foliage dark green, light undersides, arranged in whorls. Growth H: maximal 26 to 33 ft (8–10 m), cone shaped with age, branches horizontal. Location sunny to semishady; rich, moist soil. Z: 6–8

American arborvitae, ☠
Thuja occidentalis (N.)
Diverse, many varieties. Fruit small brown cones. Foliage dull green, close-lying, scale-shaped. Growth H: by variety, 40 to 60 ft (12–18 m), S: 10–15 ft (3–5 m), pillar, cone, spherical shapes. Location sunny to semishady; prefers moist, loamy, well-drained soils; high atmospheric moisture. Z: 2–8.

The mountain pine fits into almost any garden.

Mountain pine
Pinus mugo
Universally useful. Fruit oval, dark brown, cones in juvenile stage. Needles double-veined, medium size, close together, stiff. Growth H: 10 to 20 ft (3–6 m), S: 20 to 30 ft (6–9 m), trunk prostrate with age, arching upward somewhat. Location sunny, easily loses needles in shade, otherwise tolerant of all climate and soil conditions. Prefers deep, moist, loamy soil. Z: 2–7. Important: Caution when buying; there are cultivars with many different growth habits and heights from 6 in (15 cm) to 10 ft (3 m), also those that will actually remain dwarfed; in the juvenile stage they all look the same. "Compacta"—this cultivar will reach a mature size of only about H: 4 ft (1.2 m), S: 5 ft (1.5 m).

Pillar juniper.

Dwarf white spruce.

Common juniper
Juniperus communis (N.)

Undemanding. Fruit insignificant. Needles blue-gray to blue-green, pointed not sharp. Growth by variety, flattened spherical to pillar shaped, H: 8 in (20 cm) to 13 ft (4 m). Location full sun; partly dry, adaptable. Variety "Hibernica" has columnar growth habit. Z: 2–6 (7).

Dwarf white spruce
Picea glauca "Conica" (N.)

Regular, tightly contained cone-shaped conifer. Fruit insignificant. Needles short and sharp, new growth light green, soft, later bluish green. Growth H: 7 to 12 ft (2–3.7 m), S: up to 5 ft (1.5 m) with age. Location sunny, cool; rich, loamy, moist soils. Tolerant of heat, cold, winds. Z: 2–6.

The blue white pine bears fruit even as a young plant.

White spruce
Picea glauca "Echiniformis" (N.)

Spreading dwarf conifer with lively needle coloration. Fruit insignificant. Needles short, blue-green, undersides light. Growth H: up to 20 in (50 cm), S: up to 3 ft (0.9 m), cushion shaped to flattened sphere. Location semi-shady, cool, humid; acid to alka-line, porous, damp soil. Cultivars "Alberta Globe" is a mutation of *P. glauca* "Conica"; it grows loosely round to cone shaped, about 20 in (50 cm) high, with thin, green needles; "Laurin" resembles the *P. glauca* "Conica" in habit but grows much less vigorously, only about 0.5 to 1 in (1.5–2.5 cm) per year, ideal for alpine garden. Z: 2–6.

Conifers That Remain Small

Balsam fir
Abies balsamea "Nana"
Compact dwarf form; needles dark green, dense; growth H: up to 3 ft (0.9 m), S: up to 7 ft (2 m), flattened sphere; location sunny to semishady; moist, acidic soil. Z: 3–6.

Hinoki cypress
Chamaecyparis obtusa "Nana Gracilis"
Compressed, lush green, shining scales; growth H: 5 to 10 ft (1.5–3 m), S: 3 to 7 ft (0.9–2 m), round to cone shaped; location semishady to shady, moist, well-drained soil. Z: 4–8.

Sawara cypress,
Japanese false cypress
Chamaecyparis pisifera "Filifera Nana"
Drooping; foliage dark green, shining, needle-like; growth H: up to 7 ft (2m), S: up to 10 ft (3 m); location sunny to semishady, with moist, loamy, acidic soil. Z: 3–8.

Common juniper
Juniperus communis "Hornibrookii"
Prostrate; dull green needles; growth H: 19 in (0.5 m), S: 5 to 7 ft (1.5–2 m), center curved; location sunny. Z: 2–6 (7).

Norway spruce
Picea abies "Nidiformis"
Hemispherical shrub; needles dark green, pointed; growth H: 3 to 6 ft (0.9–1.8 m), nest-shaped hollowing; location sunny. Z: 2–7.

Colorado blue spruce
Picea pungens "Glauca Globosa"
Shallowly spherical to cone shaped; silver-blue needles; growth H: 3 to 5 ft (0.9–1.5 m), S: up to 10 ft (3 m); location sunny with rich and moist soil. Z: 2–7.

Mountain pine
Pinus mugo var. *mugo*
Vigorously spreading; dark green needles; growth H: up to 10 ft (3 m), S: up to 16 ft (5 m); location sunny. Z: 2–7.

Japanese white pine
Pinus parviflora "Glauca"
Charming small tree; fruit medium size brown, oval cones; blue-green-silvery needles; growth H: 10 to 16 ft (3–5 m), sometimes up to 45 ft (14 m) very slow-growing; location sunny; sandy-humus well-drained soil. Z: 4–7.

Dwarf Siberian pine
Pinus pumila "Glauca"
Broadly bushy, striking red flowers; egg-shaped violet-brown cones; silvery blue needles; growth up to 3 ft (0.9 m), S: up to 10 ft (3 m); location sunny, humid. Z: 5.

Scotch pine
Pinus sylvestris "Watereri"
Half-round, cone shaped; brown cones; steel blue needles; growth H/S: 10 to 13 ft (3–4 m); location sunny, likes well-drained, acidic soil.

Eastern white pine
Pinus strobus "Radiata"
Spherical; blue-green needles; growth H: 3 to 5 ft (1–1.5 m), S: 7 to 10 ft (2–3 m); location sunny to semishady. Z: 3–8.

English yew ☠
Taxus baccata "Repandens"
Prostrate; round, red, poisonous fruits, needles dark green; growth H: 2 to 4 ft (0.6–1.4 m), S: up to 10 ft (3 m); location sunny to shady. Z: 6 (5)–7.

Japanese yew
Taxus cuspidata "Nana"
Irregularly growing; fresh green needles; growth H: up to 10 ft (3 m), S: up to 16 ft (5 m); location sunny to semishady. Z: 4–7.

Dwarf hemlock
Tsuga canadensis "Nana"
Low-growing, arching overhanging; dark green needles; growth H: up to 3 ft (0.9 m), S: up to 7 ft (2 m), center indented in nest shape; location semishady to shady. Z: 3–7.

Different varieties of ivy here create a bower for mischievous cherubs.

CLIMBING PLANTS

Climbing plants exist in great variety—annual plants (see page 265) are included among them as well as perennials and woody plants. Some love the sun, others the shade, and, thus, they grow, flower, and fruit very differently. All have in common the ability to climb and to survive on very little soil area. They either grow up on their own (self-climbers) or with the aid of some kind of support. Regarded from a design standpoint, climbing plants are the most multipurpose of the plants (see pages 126–127). They are best suited for greening of space separations. As living fences, they can provide protection from view, wind, and sun. They can twine enchantingly on trellises, columns, arches, and pergolas, where the combination of different climbers is especially pretty. Climbing plants even form green roofs, whether it is a "bean tent" of densely growing leaves or an imaginative plant house.

On the one hand, a web of climbing plants can be used to conceal some unattractive things, but on the other, special features can also be emphasized. In addition, climbing plants become attractive hanging plants when they trail down luxuriantly over walls and arbors.

Don't forget: Many animals find shelter in the protection of their dense cloaks of leaves. Beyond this, a "green pelt" on the house has an insulating effect. However, vigorously growing plants should be policed regularly and kept within bounds because they can damage roof, drainpipes, and gutters.

The honeysuckle (Lonicera periclymenum) *has produced some beautiful, fragrant varieties.*

Clematis

Clematis naturally prefer a rich, humus soil (see pages 14–15). Besides the approximately 250 wild forms, there are today more than 500 varieties and cultivars recognized. Flower form and size can be very different. Clematis climb by means of their leaf stems (petioles), by winding the stem around thin twigs or other supports. They can be divided into the following groups:

• Climbing wild species and their varieties. Almost all are robust, vigorously growing, and flower abundantly. Many wild species form pretty, feathery fruits after the flower has finished.

• Large-flowered hybrids. Their great blossoms reach diameters of up to 6 in (15 cm).

• Bush clematis. Most of these do not climb; many are suitable for ground covers. Bush clematis form shoots up to 7 ft (2 m) long and are predominantly small flowered.

Design ideas. Clematis are highlights in the garden; the most diverse supports—including shrubs and trees—interact enchantingly with them, but clematis can also be used to hang over walls or creep over arbors. Combined with roses, they create magical garden scenes.

Pruning rules. Pruning depends on the time of flowering.

• Varieties flowering in April/May don't need pruning. Remove the dead wood immediately after flowering.

• Clematis flowering in May/June should be pruned in late fall, but only about 4 to 8 in (10–20 cm), for they flower on last year's wood.

• Plants blooming in July/August or later, however, form their flowers on new wood. They are, therefore, cut back hard in the fall (maximum to 8 in [20 cm]).

• Cut back bush clematis to the ground in the fall or spring.

Planting. Dig a large planting hole (16 x 16 in [40 x 40 cm]) and set the root ball 4 to 6 in (10–15 cm) under the ground level and angled toward the climbing support. Enrich the planting soil with compost or humus and apply mulch over planting area to keep root areas cool and moist. Shade the clematis's feet or put perennials or small shrubs in front of it.

Clematis wilt. This fungus disease attacks the large-flowered hybrid forms most often. In a short time, the shoots wither and turn brown. All diseased parts must be cut out and destroyed (don't compost!). For prevention, avoid all injuries to the plant through which fungus spores can enter.

Clematis montana rubens *variety "Rubens."*

Clematis montana, Anemone clematis !
Clematis montana **(N.)**
Very vigorously growing, popular wild species with many varieties, ideal for greening old trees, fences, or garden houses. Flowers 4 petals, diameter 0.5 to 2 in (1.3–5 cm), originally white, many pink varieties, some fragrant; May–June. Foliage dark green, reddish shoots, fall coloring brown-red. Growth H: up to 33 ft (10 m), also trailing, overhanging with loose cascades of flowers. Location sun to shade, young plants need protection from late frosts. Varieties "Rubens" delicate pink flowers with yellow stamens; "Tetrarose" more intense pink than "Rubens"; "Grandiflora" white. Z: 6–10.

Clematis* Species and Varieties !

Clematis alpina "Frances Rivis"
Pale-blue hanging bells, Apr.–May, feathery fruits, H: 8 ft (2.5 m), shade-tolerant.

Large-flowered clematis
Clematis macropetala "Markham's Pink"
Rose-red, hanging bells, May–June, H: 10 ft (3 m), location sunny to semishady.

Clematis tangutica "Aureolin"
Golden yellow bell-shaped flowers, June–Oct., feathery fruit, H: 20 ft (6 m), sunny location.

"Gypsy Queen" hybrid
Purple flowers, red stamens, diameter 5 in (13 cm), Aug.–Sept., H: 11 ft (3.5 m), sunny to semishady location.

"Huldine" hybrid
White flowers with purplish cast, diameter 3 in (8 cm), Aug.–Sept., H: 16 ft (5 m), sunny location.

"Lasurstern" hybrid
Lavender-blue flowers with white stamens, diameter 7 in (18 cm), May–June, second flowering Sept., H: 8 ft (2.5 m), sunny to semishady location.

"Nelly Moser" hybrid
Delicate pink flowers with violet center stripe, red stamens, diameter 7 in (18 cm), June, second flowering Sept., H: 10 ft (3 m), semishady location.

"The President" hybrid
Blue-violet flowers, reddish brown stamens, diameter 7 in (18 cm), May, H: 10 ft (3 m), all locations.

*Most clematis are hardy from Z: 5–8.

Hybrid "Jackmanii."

"Marie Boisselot" is also known in the trade as "Mme Le Coultre."

"Ville de Lyon."

Clematis x jackmanii ! "Jackmanii"

Clematis hybrid, classic clematis hybrid, the similar variety "Jackmanii Superba" is some-what darker in color. <u>Flower</u> bluish purple, green stamens, diameter 4 in (10 cm) July–Aug. <u>Foliage</u> pinnate, medium green. <u>Growth</u> H: 10 ft (3 m). <u>Location</u> sun to shade. Z: 3–8.

Clematis patens ! "Marie Boisselot"

Large-flowered early-summer bloomer, often offered as "Mme Le Coultre"; this markedly beautiful variety thrives very well in a shady place, its flowers shining there especially intensely. <u>Flowers</u> pure white, very symmetrical, stamens yellow, light green stripes on the petals when open, diameter about 7 in (18 cm), June, second flowering Sept. <u>Foliage</u> pinnate, medium green. <u>Growth</u> H: 10 ft (3 m), also well suited for planter culture. <u>Location</u> sun to shade. Z: 4–8.

Clematis viticella ! "Ville de Lyon"

Round-flowered garden variety, abundant fertilizer and water promote lush flowering. <u>Flowers</u> crimson, stamens yellow, diameter 5 in (12 cm), July–Sept. <u>Foliage</u> pinnate, fresh green. <u>Growth</u> H: 13 ft (4 m). <u>Location</u> sun to semishade. Z: 4–8.

"Etoile Violette" and "Abundance."

"Perle d'Azur."

"Rouge Cardinal."

Double variety "Vyvyan Pennell."

Clematis viticella ! "Etoile Violette"

Healthy, lushly blooming. <u>Flowers</u> dark violet, flat; July–Sept. <u>Foliage</u> medium green. <u>Growth</u> 13 ft (4 m). <u>Location</u> sun to shade. <u>Other varieties</u> "Abundance" mauve red (see photo above); "Alba Luxurians" white; "Minuet" white flowers with red border; "Rubra" brilliant red. Z: 4–8.

Clematis x jackmanii ! "Perle d'Azur"

Superior garden variety. <u>Flowers</u> light blue, stamens creamy white to green, flower edges slightly curved back-ward, diameter 4 in (10 cm), July–Sept. <u>Foliage</u> pinnate, fresh green. <u>Growth</u> H: 15 ft (4.5 m). <u>Location</u> sun to shade. Z: 3–8.

Clematis hybrid ! "Rouge Cardinal"

Heavily flowering, healthy garden variety with compact growth and a long flowering period. <u>Flowers</u> crimson, stamens reddish brown, July–Sept. <u>Foliage</u> pinnate, fresh green. <u>Growth</u> H: 10 ft (3 m). <u>Location</u> sun to semishade, not good for strictly northern exposures. Z: 3–8.

Clematis patens ! "Vyvyan Pennell"

Best double variety. <u>Flowers</u> lavender-blue, densely doubled, stamens yellow, diameter 6 in (15 cm); June, second flowering Aug.–Sept., but undoubled. <u>Foliage</u> pinnate, fresh green. <u>Growth</u> H: 10 ft (3 m). <u>Location</u> sunny to semishady, protected from wind. Z: 4–8.

Other Climbing Woody Plants

If there is no frame for the climbing plants, they need a suitable base or an artificial support to be able to grow toward the light. The manners and modes these plants use to gain height vary:

<u>Self-climbers</u> can climb a wall by themselves without any support. Among these are climbers with aerial roots, like English ivy (*Hedera helix*) and climbers with disks at the ends of tendrils, like some species of woodbine (*Parthenocissus*).

<u>Twiners</u> raise themselves by winding their entire stem around a support. This is by far the most widely prevailing climbing technique. Twiners are usually vigorous growers; they even twine around themselves at the beginning and form a kind of stem if support is lacking. Frames of all kinds are suitable supports; often even just a sturdy, stretched wire is enough.

<u>Vines with tendrils</u> have climbing organs that are developments of stem, leaf, or leaf stem (petiole). Climbing supports can be wires, lattices, and trellises with small openings.

<u>Spreading climbers</u> have long, flexible, sometimes thorny or prickly canes, with which they can hold onto supports. Possible supports are pillars and espaliers, which have many horizontal bars over which the soft canes can be spread and fastened.

Important: Espaliers, lattice, and wires should always be at least 4 in (10 cm) away from the wall (spacers) to allow air to circulate.

Woody Climbers

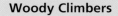

Five-leaf akebia, Chocolate vine
Akebia quinata
Red-brown, fragrant flower racemes, Apr.–May, H: up to 20 to 40 ft (6–12 m), sunny to shady. Z: 4–8.

Trumpet vine
Campsis radicans (N.)
Orange flowers in clusters, July–Sept., H: up to 30 to 40 ft (9–12 m), location sunny, protected. Z: 4–9.

Chinese bittersweet
Celastrus orbiculatus
Dioecious, flowers insignificant, June, fruits yellow-orange Oct–Feb., H: up to 39 ft (12 m), location sunny to no sun. Z: (4) 5.

Italian woodbine ☠
Lonicera caprifolium
Yellowish white, fragrant flower umbels, May, H: up to 13 ft (4 m), location semishady. Z: 5–9.

Boston ivy, Japanese creeper
Parthenocissus tricuspidata
Flowers yellow-green, June–July, fruits dark-blue, from Sept.. H: up to 39 ft (12 m), location sunny to semishady. Z: 4–8.

Blue passionflower
Passiflora caerulea
Climbs by tendrils, pale blue flowers, foliage lobed, H: 7 to 13 ft (2–4 m), location sunny, protected; in winter even the woody parts freeze back to the ground; only perennial in vineyard climate with winter protection. Z: 10—11.

Climbing bramble
Rubus henryi
Evergreen, spreading climber, flowers insignificant, foliage lobed, H: up to 20 ft (6 m), location warm, protected. Z: 6–9.

Chinese wisteria ☠
Wisteria sinensis
(see photo above)
Attractive twining plant.
<u>Flowers</u> long, light blue to blue-violet racemes before leaves appear; Apr.–May, fragrant; long, pea-pod-shaped seed capsules from Aug.
<u>Foliage</u> long pinnate, medium green. <u>Growth</u> H: up to 49 ft (15 m), S: up to 33 ft (10 m), very powerfully twisting.
<u>Location</u> sunny, warm; no lime, fresh, rich soil.
<u>Important:</u> Only plant on very strong supports, because the shoots will otherwise strangle themselves. Never plant on smaller trees or drainpipes. Pruning regularly after flowering as well as severely cutting back the new shoots in the summer increases flower production. Z: 5.

Winter jasmine.

Winter jasmine
Jasminum nudiflorum
Valuable pre-spring-bloomer, spreading climber, needs support.
<u>Flowers</u> yellow, star shaped; Dec. or Feb.–Mar. <u>Foliage</u> deep green, small. <u>Growth</u> H: 10 to 12 ft (3.7–5 m). <u>Location</u> sunny to semishady, warm, and protected.
<u>Important:</u> Water well before first frost. Z: 6–10.

Ivy variety "Cathedral."

Kiwi flowers are about 1 in across and have a delicate fragrance.

Climbing hydrangea.

English ivy ☠
Hedera helix

Evergreen self-climber. <u>Flowers</u> only on old plants, green-yellow umbels, Sept.; later black fruits (poisonous). <u>Foliage</u> 3 to 5 lobed, leathery, glossy, old form oval. <u>Growth</u> up to 66 ft (20 m), S: up to 49 ft (15 m). <u>Location</u> sun to shade. Z: 4–9.

Kiwi, Chinese gooseberry
Actinidia chinensis

Fruits only in protected situations in a warm southern climate. <u>Flowers</u> white pseudo-umbels, male and female flowers on separate plants, May–June; edible fruit brown, hairy, male and female plants necessary for fruit development, 1 male pollinates 4 to 5 females, harvest in November. <u>Foliage</u> heart shaped, hairy, up to 6 in (15 cm) long. <u>Growth</u> fast growing, H: up to 33 ft (10 m). <u>Location</u> sunny, warm, protected; well drained, rich soil, constant moisture. <u>Care</u> constant pruning of young shoots. Z: 7–9.

Climbing hydrangea
Hydrangea anomala ssp
petiolaris

Attractive self-climber. <u>Flowers</u> flat, white umbels, large, sterile flowers around edge, up to 8 in (20 cm), June–July. <u>Foliage</u> heart shaped. <u>Growth</u> H: up to 50 ft or more (15 m), S: up to 20 ft (6 m). <u>Location</u> sun to shade; cool-moist, no lime. Z: 4–7.

Virginia creeper, fall coloring.

Flowers of the Russian vine.

Pipevine.

Woodbine, honeysuckle.

Virginia creeper, Woodbine
*Parthenocissus
quinquefolia* (N.)

Self-climber with striking fall color. <u>Flowers</u> insignificant, June–July; black, blue-frosted fruits from Sept. <u>Foliage</u> hand-shaped, 5 to a cluster, dark green, glossy, from Sept. red. <u>Growth</u> 30 to 50 ft (9–12 m). <u>Location</u> sun to shade; tolerates any soil condition. Z: 3–9.

Mile-a-minute plant,
Russian vine
Polygonum aubertii

Fast- and dense-growing vine with special requirements. <u>Flowers</u> white, loose panicles, July–Sept. <u>Foliage</u> oval, green. <u>Growth</u> up to 49 ft (15 m), annual growth several yards, shoots trailing and overhanging. <u>Location</u> sun to shade. Z: 5–9.

Dutchman's pipe,
Pipevine
Aristolochia durior (N.)

Large-leaved twining vine. <u>Flowers</u> green-brown, pipelike, insignificant; June–July. <u>Foliage</u> large, heart shaped, dark green, overlapping like scales, remain long on the branch. <u>Growth</u> H: 26 to 33 ft (8–10 m), S: 3 to 26 ft (0.9–8 m). <u>Location</u> sun to shade, no dryness. Z: 4–8.

Common woodbine, ☠
Common honeysuckle
Lonicera periclymenum

Twining climber with intensely fragrant flowers. <u>Flowers</u> long barreled, depending on variety yellow-white or dark crimson, pink inside; May–July. <u>Foliage</u> oval to long, gray-green. <u>Growth</u> H: up to 23 ft (7 m). <u>Location</u> sun to semishade; porous, rich soil. Z: 5–9.

221

Rambler rose "Paul's Himalayan Musk" climbs up to 20 ft (6 m) into a tree.

ROSES

The rose continues to be the incarnation of the beautiful flower, a symbol for abundance of forms, splendid color, and fragrance. There are enchanting rose gardens and old varieties that are intensely fragrant. But many new hybrids once again possess this quality as well. Wild roses and almost all old roses flower lushly, but only once. Most modern hybrids, on the other hand, marry beauty with the characteristic of flowering several times a year.

The ancestors of all modern hybrids and varieties are the wild roses. They grow on their own roots and in the fall develop very beautiful hips. Native wild roses are extremely robust and winter hardy. Hybrid roses, however, are usually grafted and are therefore more delicate.

Roses grow in the most diverse forms; some can even climb and creep. As a result they are also suited for a variety of design purposes. The following categorization of the roses is arranged according to these various uses:

• Climbing roses, see pages 224–225
• Old and English roses, see pages 226–227
• Shrub roses, see pages 228–229
• Bedding roses, see pages 230–231

Before you decide on a variety, find out how healthy it is, for ailing roses are a burden for any gardener and demand the regular application of sprays. Especially in regions with a cold climate, you should always choose frost-hardy varieties. But proper planting and care are also crucial for your roses to thrive splendidly. You will learn all about this in the Gardening Practice section (pages 176–179). Most cultivated varieties listed are in zones 4–9. It is always best to check with a garden center before purchasing an unfamiliar variety.

The climbing rose "Raubritter" is bedecked with its old-fashioned round flowers only once a year—but then lavishly. The rose is vigorous and frost-hardy, but unfortunately it is somewhat susceptible to mildew.

Climbing Roses

Climbing roses have a remarkable long growth. There are once- and ever-blooming varieties, fragrant and scentless ones, vigorous and weakly growing ones, cluster-flowered ones and those with large, mostly singly occurring flowers. Ideal locations for climbing roses are southeast and southwest walls, somewhat protected from sharp winds. On hot south walls, the leaves burn easily and the flowers bleach out. Lack of air circulation promotes infestation of spider mites and fungus diseases. Climbing roses will bloom more lushly when plants form more branches.

You will find all you need to know about planting and care of roses on pages 176–177. Pruning often depends on whether the rose is one that blooms once or blooms several times (see each growing season on page 179). In contrast to bedding roses, which are cut back hard annually, climbing roses are only thinnned out. However, it is important to keep providing for sufficient offspring on young canes.

Rambler roses have soft, hanging or creeping canes. Almost all bloom only once and usually have small flowers, but these occur in lush thich clusters. Rambler roses look particularly beautiful if they are trained to grow several yards upward—for instance up poles, pillars, and walls, but also up into tree crowns—where they can hang down in cascades. They are also grafted onto standards about 4.5 ft (1.4 m) high. These "cascade roses" make charming and elegant specimen plantings.

Climbers. These stout-caned climbing roses are spreading climbers that grow straight up and can reach 7 to 13 ft (2–4 m) without support. They are decidedly useful in many different ways and excellent for rose arbors and pergolas. Climbing roses need a support or a trellis, because they do not have any climbing attachments. They cover house walls, walls, and trellises of all kinds beautifully, especially the attractive, old-fashioned, wooden latticework ones. Steel mesh mats or simple wires offer a cheaper solution. Suitable for a simple support or space divider are wooden posts with diagonal latticing above and in the middle or even connected to each other by wires stretched horizontally between them. Somewhat less vigorous growing climbers form a pretty focal point if they are merely allowed to grow free.

Note: Most all of the roses listed are hardy in zones 4–9. Mulch for overwinter protection.

"New Dawn" possesses bewitching charm.

Climbing rose "New Dawn"

One of the best known and most rewarding climbing roses with an old-fashioned flair, useful in many different ways, robust and frost-hardy. Flowers delicate pale whitish pink, medium size, in clusters, self-cleaning, weather-fast, second flowering until frost. Foliage glossy, dark green, long lasting, resistant to mildew and spot anthracnose. Growth H: up to 15 ft (5 m), at first stiffly upright, then archingly outspread and overhanging, rambler. Z: 4–9.

Important: Beautiful for walls, fences, trellises, and arbors because of long, trailing canes.

Recommended Rambler Roses*

"Bobbie James"
Vigorous, lushly flowering; flowers creamy white, saucer shaped in clusters; oval, dark red hips; foliage light to medium green, glossy; growth H: to 23 ft (7 m), grows rampantly; location sunny to semi-shady, protected.

"Madeleine Seltzer"
Frost-hardy; doubled flowers, lemon-yellow to white, medium size, fragrant, dense clusters, early; foliage bronze-green; growth H: up to 10 ft (3 m), moderately vigorous; location sunny.

"Paul's Himalayan Musk"
Old-fashioned, delicate variety with very vigorous growth habit; flowers pale pink, double, slightly fragrant, rosette shaped, repeat flowering, large, dense clusters; foliage medium green; growth H: up to 33 ft (10 m), trailing; location sunny.

"Paul Noel"
Healthy, lushly flowering variety; flowers apricot pink, large-flowered, doubled, repeat flowering, slightly fragrant; foliage lush green, glossy; growth H: up to 10 ft (3 m), bushy; location sunny.

"Super Excelsa"
Pompom-flowered variety; flowers crimson- pink with white center stripe, second flowering; foliage medium green, glossy; growth H: 5 to 8 ft (1.5–2.5 m); location sunny; also as ground cover.

"Veilchenblau"
Vigorous grower, also known as "Blue Rambler"; flowers crimson-violet with white stripes, single or semidouble, in large corymbose cymes, fruity scent, early; foliage light green, healthy; growth H: up to 16 ft (5 m); location sunny.

* Z: 4–9.

"Santana."

"Compassion" with a beguiling scent.

"Golden Showers."

Climbing rose "Santana"

Robust, frost-hardy climbing rose. <u>Flowers</u> brilliant, dark blue-red, large, double, long lasting, weather-fast, slightly fragrant. <u>Foliage</u> glossy green, leathery, large. <u>Growth</u> H: up to 7 ft (2 m), densely bushy, upright, forms sturdy new canes.

Climbing rose "Compassion"

Marvelously fragrant climbing rose, robust and frost hardy. <u>Flowers</u> salmon-pink, slightly silvery, changing to pink, beautifully shaped, classic rose buds—yellow with red border—large flowered, loosely double, weather-fast, good second flowering, intensely fragrant. <u>Foliage</u> glossy dark green, leathery tough. <u>Growth</u> H: up to 10 ft (3 m), dense and broadly bushy, sturdy and stiffly upright.
<u>Important:</u> For covering trellises and pillars, but also as specimen shrub and hedge plant.

Climbing rose "Golden Showers"

Rewarding early-flowering variety. <u>Flowers</u> lemon yellow, lightening as they open, large flowered, saucer shaped, loosely double, occurring singly or in bunches, flowering until late in fall, soft scent. <u>Foliage</u> glossy green, firm. <u>Growth</u> 7 to 10 ft (2–3 m). Z: 4–9.

"Lawinia."

"Ilse Krohn Superior"

"Rosarium Uetersen," one of the most rewarding varieties.

Climbing rose "Lawinia"

Very abundantly flowering climbing rose. <u>Flowers</u> intense rose, later light rose, large, loosely double, saucer-shaped, last well, strongly fragrant. <u>Foliage</u> dark green, dully glossy, large. <u>Growth</u> H: 7 to 10 ft (2–3 m) broadly bushy, moderately vigorous, slightly trailing.

Climbing rose "Ilse Krohn Superior"

Wonderfully fragrant and robust. <u>Flowers</u> white, classic bud shape, medium size, saucer shaped, very double, good second flowering, weather-fast. <u>Foliage</u> brilliant green, but matte. <u>Growth</u> H: up to 10 ft (3 m), long canes, sturdily bushy, upright to slightly arching.

Climbing rose "Rosarium Uetersen"

Lushly blooming rewarding and robust rose. <u>Flowers</u> brilliant rose, buds light red, medium size, densely doubled, somewhat rosettelike, occurring in clusters, continuously flowering abundantly and well, light fragrance. <u>Foliage</u> glossy green, medium size, dense.

<u>Growth</u> H: 7 to 10 ft (2–3 m), moderately vigorous, twiggy, bushy, upright.
<u>Important:</u> Useful for pillars, pyramids, and covering walls, but also freestanding and as a tree form with the crown pruned into a sphere.

Old Roses and English Roses

Working with old and English roses can become a real passion if you trace the family trees of the individual varieties back to their beginnings, even if the origins of some remain uncertain. The various different flower forms also evoke the pleasure of collecting. Harmonious blending of colors, forms, and growth habits also allow old and modern roses to be successfully combined with one another.

Old roses. Today this term is used for the varieties of the *Gallica*, *Damascena*, *Alba*, and *Centifolia* roses. What make these fascinating are the densely doubled and typical "old-fashioned" shaped flowers, the delicate colors, and lastly their incomparable fragrance. All these things together constitute the charm of the old roses. That many of them flower only once or only a little again in late summer is not perceived as a disadvantage by their admirers. With skillful choice of varieties, early, late, and reblooming varieties can be planted in combination so that there will be roses in bloom from May through the fall. The once-flowering roses impress with their seductive abundance of flowers, many also remaining in bloom for a long time. Often they form pretty hips and have beautiful, healthy foliage. The once-flowering varieties, are especially robust. Many old roses, in contrast to modern hybrids, also tolerate a partly shaded location, perhaps under trees. Depending on the variety, they grow upright or slightly trailing. Usually they develop into sturdy and widespreading shrubs.

Among the old roses are also the remontant roses (remontant = repeat-flowering). They were developed through crossing with Portland, Bourbon, Noisette, and Tearoses, have a robust growth habit, and have strong colors. They bloom somewhat again in late summer. However, they are a little less resistant to disease than their once-flowering relatives.

English roses. The boundaries between old and new rose varieties are fluid. In 1961, David Austin succeeded in breeding the first English roses with "Constance Spry." This stems from old *Gallica*, *Damascus*, and *Centifolia* roses and unites the flair of old roses with good characteristics of the modern rose: Most flower more often, are disease resistant, have densely doubled flowers, and an alluring fragrance. Many English roses have the classic pastel shades of the old roses, but their palette has been extended with enchanting yellow, orange, and red shades.

Important: Climate and location generally exercise great influence on roses' resistance to disease and pests. Roses need an airy, open location and loose, deeply cultivated fertile soil. You will find out all you need to know about planting, care, and pruning on pages 176–178.

The cabbage rose, Rosa centifolia "Minor."

Cabbage rose
Rosa centifolia
The hundred-petaled rose is one of the hybrids resulting from several wild species. Reputedly it was already in cultivation in Holland in the 16th century. Since then, a great number of varieties have developed. The moss roses (Rosa centifolia muscosa) are descended from the centifolias. *The stems, ovaries, and sepals of the moss roses are covered with a mosslike tissue.* Flowers *white, pink, or red, densely doubled, often quartered, round, once-flowering, strong centifolia fragrance, only rarely hips.* Foliage *fresh green.* Growth *moderately vigorous, loose, arching overhanging, H: up to 7 ft (2 m).*

Delicate pink—"Maiden's Blush."

Rosa alba
"Maiden's Blush"
Long-lived shrub rose, classic among old roses, known since the Middle Ages. Flowers light pink, large, plumply double, in clusters, fragrant, once-flowering, weather-fast. Foliage blue-green, large, loose. Growth H: up to 7 ft (2 m), overhanging, vigorous.

Fuchsia red—"Rose de Rescht."

Damask rose
"Rose de Rescht"
Old rose, cultivated in Persia before 1880. Flowers fuchsia red, lavender as they fade, small flowers, densely double in rosette form, in clusters, strong fragrance, repeat-flowering. Foliage dark green, large, dense. Growth H: up to 3 ft (0.9 m), upright, well branched, compact, sturdy.

Rosa gallica "Versicolor."

"La Reine Victoria."

Rosa gallica, Rosa mundi "Versicolor"

Old rose with interesting play of colors. <u>Flowers</u> light pink with crimson stripes, golden yellow stamens, medium size, loosely double, abundantly flowering, strongly fragrant. <u>Foliage</u> medium green, matte, dense, large. <u>Growth</u> H: up to 5 ft (1.5 m), upright, bushy.

Bourbon rose "La Reine Victoria"

Particularly impressive variety with much charm. <u>Flowers</u> silky, irridescent rose, large, roundish, densely doubled, repeat-flowering. <u>Foliage</u> light green, large, loose. <u>Growth</u> H: up to 5 ft (1.5 m), upright, slender canes <u>Important:</u> Needs a support; beautiful on pillars or fences.

"Constance Spry."

"Charles Austin."

English rose "Constance Spry"

Robust shrub and climbing rose. <u>Flowers</u> strong pink, up to 5 in (13 cm) in diameter, well doubled, round at first, then saucer shaped when wide open, myrrh fragrance, blooms once but for a long time. <u>Foliage</u> large, light green. <u>Growth</u> sturdy, H: up to 7 ft (2 m).

English rose "Charles Austin"

Nostalgic effect. <u>Flowers</u> apricot with pinkish cast, large flowered, very double, cup shaped, abundantly flowering, strongly fragrant, second flowering rarely. <u>Foliage</u> light green, glossy, large. <u>Growth</u> H: up to 5 ft (1.5 m), bushy, upright, vigorously growing.

Old Roses

<u>Hybrid perpetual</u>
"Ferdinand Pichard"
Flowers red-and-pink-striped on white ground, large-flowered, doubled, strongly fragrant; foliage dark green; growth H: up to 4 ft (1.2 m).

<u>Noisette, Tea rose</u>
"Gloire de Dijon"
Winter-hardy, early-flowering climbing rose, flowers light orange-yellow, large, doubled, strong fragrance; foliage dark green; growth H: up to 16 ft (5 m).

<u>Portland rose</u>
"Jacques Cartier"
Easy-care; flowers intense pink, large-flowered, doubled, with a "Damask button" in the center, fragrant, twice blooming; foliage dark green; growth H: up to 3 ft (1 m).

<u>Bourbon rose</u>
"Mme Pierre Oger"
Romantic variety, flowers mother-of-pearl pink, round, medium size, loosely doubled, in clusters, twice blooming, fragrant; foliage dark green; growth H: up to 5 ft (1.5 m), also thrives in semishade.

<u>Hybrid perpetual</u>
"Mrs. John Lang"
Long-flowering, flowers pure pink, large, doubled, in clusters, fragrant; foliage light green; growth up to 5 ft (1.5 m), suitable for elevations.

<u>Bourbon rose</u>
"Souvenir de la Malmaison"
Famous variety; flowers delicate pink to white, very double, large, fragrant, repeat-flowering; foliage light green; growth H: up to 2 ft (0.6 m).

<u>*Pimpinellifolia* x
Damask rose</u>
"Stanwell Perpetual"
Easy care; flowers light pink to white, medium size, densely double, shallow with "Damask button," long-lasting, fragrant; foliage gray-green; growth up to 2 ft (0.6 m).

English Roses

"Abraham Darby"
Very healthy; flowers apricot-yellow with pink, large, doubled, fragrant; foliage medium green, glossy; growth H: 5 to 7 ft (1.5–2 m).

"Heritage"
Abundantly blooming shrub rose; flowers pure pink, medium size, densely doubled, quartered, fragrant, rain-fast; foliage dark green; growth sturdy, H: 4 ft (1.2 m).

"Lilian Austin"
Arching, overhanging variety; flowers salmon-pink, orange in the center, large flowered, doubled in rosette shape, fragrant, in clusters; foliage dark green; growth H: up to 4 ft (1.2 m).

"Mary Rose"
Bushy, abundantly flowering variety; flowers pink, cup shaped, densely doubled, slightly fragrant; foliage medium green; growth broadly bushy, H: up to 4 ft (1.2 m).

"The Squire"
Unfading, carmine red flowers, chalice shaped, very large, very double, fragrant; foliage rust-brown when new, then dark green; growth vigorous, H: up to 4 ft (1.2 m).

"The Yeoman"
Shrub rose; flowers large, salmon-pink with orange and yellow, rosette shaped, strong myrrh fragrance; foliage dark green; growth H: up to 35 in (90 cm).

"William Shakespeare"
Shrub rose, rarity; flowers dark crimson-red to purple, quartered petals, fragrant; foliage light green; growth H: up to 4 ft (1.2 m).

"Graham Thomas"
Upright growth; flowers amber yellow, roundish, doubled, weakly fragrant; foliage brilliant green, glossy; growth H: up to 5 ft (1.5 m).

Shrub Roses

The term shrub roses includes all roses that grow tall and bushy, which can then be subdivided into the once-flowering and repeat-flowering ones. Shrub roses include most old roses and English roses (see pages 226–227) and the wild roses. The so-called park roses also fit in under shrub roses. Some of the old, once-flowering cultivated varieties are also so termed. The growth habits of the shrub roses are really quite different. Many—especially the wild and park roses—are unsuitable for small gardens because of the amount of space they require: They grow as wide as they do high. Old roses and modern hybrids, on the other hand, fit into any garden.

Modern shrub roses or ornamental roses developed in the last 100 years through crossing of hybrid teas. Ornamental roses are thus smaller and more delicate in their growth habit, with their sizes ranging between 3 and 7 ft (0.9 and 2 m). They bloom all summer long, which makes them ideal and attractive ornamental shrubs even for small gardens.

Small shrub roses or ground-cover roses protect the soil from erosion with their dense growth and prevent weeds from coming up. Ground-cover roses can grow up to 32 in (81 cm) high and 7 ft (2 m) wide. The distances between plants varies according to the choice of plants. They can obviously also be planted singly and in small groups.

The shrub rose "Red Yesterday" makes a good ground cover.

Shrub rose "Red Yesterday"

Small, broadly bushy shrub rose, which can also be used as a ground cover. Flowers brilliantly dark red with white center, flower diameter 0.5 to 1 in (1.3–2.5 cm), single, in large clusters, buds small and cherry red. Foliage light green, coppery when new, glossy, small, loose. Growth H: up to 2.5 in (6.3 cm), moderately vigorous, partly upright, partly loosely trailing.

Important: When using as a ground cover, figure 3 to 4 plants per 10.75 sq ft (1 m²) with a distance between plants of 2 ft (60 cm).

Wild Roses

Rosa hugonis
Very early flowers, golden yellow, small, single, May, dark red hips; foliage light green, pinnate; growth H: up to 7 ft, broadly shrubby, trailing.

Rosa moyesii
Different wild rose from China; flowers blood red, abundantly blooming, June, bottle-shaped hips; foliage pinnate; growth H: up to 7 ft, wide-spreading.

Rosa rugosa
Robust wild species; flowers lavender to pink, large, single, fragrant, May–June, orange hips; foliage dark green; growth H: up to 6 ft, erectly upright, forms runners, no lime.

Rosa sweginzowii
"Macrocarpa"
Old Chinese garden rose; flowers crimson, medium size, single, abundantly flowering, June, orange hips; foliage fern green, pinnate; growth H: up to 8 ft, arching overhanging.

Repeat-flowering Shrub Roses

"Bischofstadt Paderborn"
Classic shrub rose; flowers scarlet with light center, semidouble; foliage dark green; growth H: up to 5 ft, upright, heavily branched.

"Centenaire de Lourdes"
Robust and frost-hardy; flowers brilliant rose with light centers, double, fragrant, blooms once again in fall very lushly; foliage medium green; growth H: up to 5 ft, archingly overhanging.

"Iga 83 München"
Frost-hardy, suitable both for bedding or ground-cover rose; flowers crimson, large, semidouble; foliage fern green; growth H: up to 4 ft, broadly shrubby.

"Vogelpark Walsrode"
Healthy long-bloomer; flowers pink, later white, large, loosely doubled, fragrant; foliage fresh green; growth H: up to 5 ft, broadly bushy, loose.

"Marguerite Hilling"
Specimen shrub with wild-rose character; flowers dark pink, lightening toward center, single, lushly flowering; foliage brilliant green; growth H: up to 7 ft, sturdy.

"Elmshorn"
Broadly spreading shrub for specimen planting; flowers sturdy pink, doubled, blooming in dense clusters until frost; growth H/S: up to 7 ft.

"Mozart"
Small bush; flowers dark pink with white eye, single and very small, but in many-flowered clusters; growth H: up to 32 to 39 in.

"Mountbatten"
Slightly fragrant variety also for group plantings; flowers yellow with pinkish shimmer, classic rose shape, double, abundant flowering; foliage dense; growth H: up to 4 ft, sturdily upright.

Ground-cover Roses

"Ballerina"
Bushy; flowers delicate pink with white eye, small, single, large clusters, abundant second flowering; foliage light green; growth 2 to 3 ft, spreading, archingly overhanging.

"Heidetraum"
Healthy and frost-hardy; flowers rose red, medium size, semidouble, everblooming; foliage medium green; growth H: 3 ft, broadly shrubby.

"White Immensee"
Vigorously growing; flowers pure white, yellow stamens, small, single, once-flowering; foliage dark and winter green; growth H: up to 1 ft, canes dense and close lying, up to 7 ft.

"Mainaufeuer"
Wide-spreading; flowers blood red, medium size, doubled, everblooming; foliage lush-green; growth H: up to 19 in, overhanging with fullness of flowers.

"Lichtkönigen Lucia" is very robust and frost-hardy.

"Westerland" blooms until frost with a fascinating play of colors.

Shrub rose "Lichtkönigen Lucia"

Retains flowers for a long time. Flowers brilliant lemon yellow with red stamens in the center, fades with aging, large flowered, flower diameter up to 4 in (10 cm), doubled, fragrant, abundantly flowering, starts early. Foliage fern green, somewhat lighter when new, large, leathery, glossy. Growth H: up to 5 ft (1.5 m), vigorous, stiffly upright, bushy.
Important: Suitable also for small garden areas. Good combined with perennials. Ideal backgrounds are dark green shrubs.

Shrub rose "Westerland"

Robust shrub rose with interesting flower color, blooms from summer to fall. Flowers brilliant copper-orange with yellow, large flowered, diameter 4 to 5 in (10–13 cm), loosely double, open center, fragrant, in large clusters, often trailing, early and abundantly flowering; orange, flattish round hips. Foliage deep green, reddish when new, leathery, glossy, dense. Growth H: up to 7 ft (2 m), well branched, upright at first, later broadly shrubby and spreading. Important: Regularly remove spent flowers to promote formation of new ones.

"Schneewittchen" blooms for quite a long time.

"Grandhotel."

"Sommerwind."

Shrub rose "Schneewittchen"

Tirelessly blooming shrub rose, one of the best white varieties. Flowers white, slightly pink cast, pink after lower temperatures, yellow stamens in center very visible, fragrant, medium size with flower diameter 2.75 to 3 in (7–8 cm), loosely doubled, saucer shaped, in loose bunches, abundantly flowering, rain-fast, self-cleaning. Foliage fern green, dully glossy, medium size, slender. Growth H: up to 5 ft (1.5 m), bushy, upright, loose, flower canes archingly overhanging.
Important: Use both as hedge or specimen. With planting in beds, prune the rose severely every year.

Shrub rose "Grandhotel"

Robust, lushly blooming. Flowers scarlet, large, double, classic rose shape, in bunches, ever-blooming, weather-resistant. Foliage dark green, young leaves reddish at first, very glossy. Growth H: over 7 ft (2 m), S: up to 5 ft (1.5 m), vigorously growing, broadly bushy.

Ground-cover rose "Sommerwind"

Lush- and long-flowering variety. Flowers brilliant rose, medium size, flower diameter 2 in (5 cm), loosely doubled, edges of petals wavy, in loose clusters. Foliage medium green, slightly glossy, small. Growth H: up to 2 ft (0.6 m), well-branched, broadly bushy.

Bedding Roses

The term bedding roses includes the most various bush roses that can be planted in groups or over wide areas. Large-flowered classic roses, hybrid teas. These roses usually bear their large, doubled, and often fragrant blossoms singly on long stems. They look most beautiful in small groups but are suitable for combinations with delicate, loose plants like perennials, grasses, and annuals. Hybrid teas usually possess especially beautifully formed buds and elegant flowers. They are more for viewing up close and are less effective at a distance.

Cluster-flowered roses. Their breeding—like that of the hybrid teas—started about 100 years ago. Their multiflowered clusters are typical. Several individual flowers, whether large, small, single, semidouble, or double, are situated together in densely or loosely arranged clusters. Differentiations are made among:

• Polyanthas, which bloom all summer long and form small flowers on large corymbose cymes.

• Floribundas or polyantha hybrids, which developed through crossing with large-flowered varieties. They offer a wide range of colors including yellow.

• Grandifloras, which were created by crossing cluster-flowered varieties with hybrid teas.

The lush flowering of these rose groups over months makes them ideal for continuous color in the garden. In a sunny location, they can—depending on size, color, and growth habit—be used either as uniform bedding plants or combined with perennials. If desired, these roses can be kept at the same height with regular pruning.

Miniature or dwarf roses. These ornamental roses are also considered bedding roses. They have small, doubled flowers, fine foliage, and become about 12 in (30 cm) high. They are especially appropriate for trough beds and rock and heath gardens.

Many of the bedding roses are hardly different from small shrub roses, particularly if they are only pruned very little. Hybrid teas and floribundas can then reach heights of 7 ft (2 m). It is important to remove old wood at the base from time to time and to rejuvenate the bushes (see page 178) in order to retain their capacity to continue to flower.

Standards or tree roses. Classic roses can also be grafted onto standards; a stem with a height of up to 16 in (40 cm) is known as a semistandard, with 35 in (90 cm) being a high standard. Tree roses are ideal for the small garden; they can be underplanted wonderfully. In architectural gardens they define beds and paths and establish pretty accents.

Bedding Roses

"Bella Rosa"
Floribunda; flowers pink, yellow stamens, densely doubled, in thick clusters, weather-fast, everblooming; foliage medium green; growth H: 2 ft (0.6 m).

"Bernstein Rose"
Old-fashioned floribunda; flowers amber yellow, double, weather-fast; foliage dark green; growth H: 2 ft (0.6 m).

"Duftwolke" (Fragrant Cloud)
Hybrid tea, good cut flower; flowers coral red, well doubled, fragrant, lasting; foliage dark green; growth H: 2 to 2.5 ft (0.6–0.8 m), sturdy.

"Escapade"
Reliable floribunda; flowers lavender-pink, semidouble, fragrant, everblooming; foliage light green; growth H: up to 2.5 ft (0.8 m), upright.

"Peace"
Most popular hybrid tea; flowers light yellow with pink edge, later pink, loosely double, weather-fast, fragrant, long- flowering; foliage dark green; growth H: up to 3 ft (0.9 m), bushy.

"Gruss an Bayern"
Floribunda; flowers blood red with velvety shimmer, semidouble, slightly fragrant; foliage dark green; growth up to 2 ft (0.6 m), very branching.

"La Sevillana"
Floribunda; flowers brilliant red, yellow stamens, semidouble, everblooming; foliage dark green; growth H: up to 2.5 ft (0.8 m).

"Märchenland"
Floribunda; flowers salmon-pink, semidouble, fragrant, second flowering; foliage green, reddish at first; growth H: 2.5 to 4 ft (0.8–1.2 m), canes trailing.

"Margret Merill"
Floribunda; flowers pearl white-pink, large, semidouble, fragrant, weather-fast; foliage green, reddish when new; growth H: up to 2.5 ft (0.8 m).

"Mildred Scheel"
Fragrant hybrid tea; flowers crimson, velvety, lighter when opening, double; foliage dark green, reddish when new; growth H: up to 2.5 ft (0.8 m).

"Pascali"
Hybrid tea; flowers pure white, medium size, classic, abundant flowers, loosely doubled; foliage deep green, lighter when new; growth H: up to 2 ft (0.6 m).

"Sarabande"
Floribunda; flowers geranium red, golden yellow stamens, slightly doubled, rain-fast; foliage light green; growth H: 19 in (0.5 m).

"Sutter's Gold"
Hybrid tea with classic buds; flowers light orange-yellow with reddish shimmer along the edge, loosely doubled, very fragrant; foliage dark green, glossy, new growth light green; growth H: up to 3 ft (0.9 m).

"The McCartney Rose"
Strongly fragrant hybrid tea; flowers pink, loosely double; foliage sturdy green; growth H: up to 2 ft (0.6 m).

"Vatertag"
Dwarf polyantha; flowers orange, round balls, loosely doubled, abundantly flowering, second flowering; foliage light green; growth H: up to 1 ft (0.3 m).

"Whisky"
Hybrid tea flowering until fall; flowers amber yellow, double, strongly fragrant; foliage dark green; growth H: up to 35 in (90 cm), bushy, makes new growth fast.

"Bonica '82."

"Blue River."

"Gruss an Aachen."

"Friesia."

Floribunda rose "Bonica '82"

Charming, lushly blooming. <u>Flowers</u> dark pink, lightening, medium, well doubled, dense clusters, long lasting. <u>Foliage</u> dark green, reddish when new, small, leathery, glossy. <u>Growth</u> H: 2 to 3 ft (0.6–0.9 m), bushy, loosely branching. Z: 4–9. <u>Important:</u> Also for semishade.

Hybrid tea rose "Blue River"

Robust, wonderfully fragrant. <u>Flowers</u> magenta lilac with darker edge on petals, lightly powdered with white at the center, medium size, very double, in loose clusters. <u>Foliage</u> dark green, glossy, dense. <u>Growth</u> H: up to 2 ft (0.6 m), bushy, branching.

Floribunda rose "Gruss an Aachen"

First floribunda rose, nostalgic-looking variety for a not too sunny location. <u>Flowers</u> cream-white, yellowish pink inside, large, densly doubled, eager to flower, slightly fragrant. <u>Foliage</u> dark green, tough. <u>Growth</u> moderately strong, compact, bushy, H; up to 19 in (0.5 m).

Floribunda rose "Friesia"

Long, lushly flowering. <u>Flowers</u> brilliant golden yellow, medium size, densely doubled, clusters, fragrant, second flowering, self-cleaning, weather-resistant. <u>Foliage</u> medium green, glossy, leathery. <u>Growth</u> H: up to 2.5 ft (0.8 m), S: 2 ft (0.6 m), upright, well branched. Z: 4–9.

"Queen Elizabeth"

"Edelweiss."

"Erotika."

"Montana."

Floribunda rose "Queen Elizabeth"

Very healthy. <u>Flowers</u> salmon-pink when opening, then lightening, large flowered, loosely doubled, in clusters on long stems, long-lasting flowers. <u>Foliage</u> reddish to dark green, glossy, tough, large, loose. <u>Growth</u> H: 3 to 6 ft (0.9 to 1.8 m), upright, sturdy. Z: 4–9.

Floribunda rose "Edelweiss"

Robust, lushly flowering. <u>Flowers</u> cream-white, medium size, doubled, outer petals standing out horizontally, inner ones curving roundly toward center, in large clusters. <u>Foliage</u> dark green, reddish when new, glossy. <u>Growth</u> H: up to 1 ft (0.3 m), broadly bushy, compact.

Hybrid tea rose "Erotika"

Long stems, healthy and frost hardy. <u>Flowers</u> velvety, dark red, very large, well doubled, abundant flowers, very fragrant, rain- and sun-fast. <u>Foliage</u> deep green, reddish when new, glossy. <u>Growth</u> H: up to 2.5 ft (0.8 m), strong, upright. <u>Important:</u> Good cut flower.

Floribunda rose "Montana"

Robust and frost hardy. <u>Flowers</u> glowing red, medium size, saucer shaped with open centers, in thick clusters, weather-fast, consistent color. <u>Foliage</u> dark green, glossy, reddish when new, large, leathery. <u>Growth</u> H: up to 35 in (0.9 m), erectly upright, compact, sturdy.

Small perennials also thrive in containers, like the baskets shown here.

PERENNIALS

The perennials include all the long-lived herbaceous plants, whose upper parts die back in the winter. The underground organs—rootstock, rhizomes, bulbs, and corms—possess buds for overwintering from which they produce new growth in the spring.

Besides the familiar border plants, the perennials include the rock garden, marsh, and water plants, grasses, ferns, and bulbs and corms. The plants have very varied life spans. Only a few, like the peonies (*Paeonia* species), thrive for years undisturbed in the same spot. Most need to be divided every 2–3 years. In contrast to the annuals, many perennials can be propagated by other means as well as seeds; they form runners (stolons) or can be divided (see pages 154–155 and 180–181). The kingdom of the perennials is gigantic; distinctions are made between:

Border plants, also known as showy or ornamental perennials. These are plants that have been highly cultivated through breeding. They exhibit lush growth and splendid flowers, and their requirements for soil, climate, and nutrients are correspondingly high. They are planted in beds or borders that must be well maintained.

Native perennials are less demanding and more robust by nature, often specializing in a particular type of natural habitat. The mountain flora and water and marsh plants are among these, as are grasses and ferns and the shade-loving woodland plants. When a natural garden is being created, the native perennial component of the garden design becomes important. But even there, it is not only the purely native species that are used but also cultivars and varieties that can maintain the charm of the native forms. As there are throughout nature, there are also fluid transitions among the perennials.

The Siberian iris (here the variety "Blue Burgee") is a species with an abundance of forms with fragrant flowers in violet-blue and striking patterns.

Perennial Plants for Early Summer

The transition from spring to summer is a very exciting period: the late tulips are still blooming, the biennials and the ornamental shrubs are at their peak. Now the first ornamental perennials join the dance.

Bearded iris and other iris species are the outstanding perennials of this season. The genus is extremely varied in its origins and lifestyles, but nevertheless its members have very similar flower forms. There are iris from colder regions and for dry locations, for normal soil conditions, but there are also some for damp and marsh zones. Their growing patterns, their requirements, and their uses in the garden are correspondingly different. With the proper selection, an iris lover can take pleasure in these striking flowers from spring through mid-summer and even early fall.

The flowers consists of 3 inner and 3 outer petals. In the bearded iris, the inner petals are raised and closed together—they form the so-called standards. The 3 outer petals—the falls, hang down and have on top the small brushlike growth—the beard, from which they take their name. In other species, such as the Japanese iris (*Iris kaempferi*, see pages 278–279), Z: 5–9, the standards are less typical in shape, often even being curved or bent down toward the outside. In modern hybrids, especially, the falls are often spread out horizontally and, thus, are important attractions and landing surfaces for insects.

With the bearded iris (*I. germanica* var. *germanica*), Z: 3–9, the number of hybrids has come to be innumerable. However, very rough categories can be established according to size and time of flowering:

• *I. barbata nana* hybrids are already flowering from early spring to mid-spring and grow 8 to 12 in (20–30 cm) tall. They are particularly good as front plantings in borders.

• *I. barbata media* hybrids are medium-tall 1.5 to 2 ft (0.5–0.6 m) and flower in May (late spring).

• *I. barbata elatior* hybrids, the tall bearded irises, grow to be 2 to 4 ft (0.6–1.2 m) in height and bloom from the end of May into July (late spring to mid-summer).

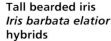

Bearded iris with orange beard.

Medium-tall and tall hybrids in the perennial border always work best planted in groups of 3 to 5 in 2 to 3 color shades. They look most attractive when their vertical forms rise from a low carpet of plants. Other important species are:

Butterfly iris (*I. spuria*) can be combined well with bearded iris. This less well-known but showy iris grows up to 4.5 ft (1.4 cm) tall and loves full sun as well as rich soil. Unfortunately, it is not entirely frost hardy.

The tall Dutch bulb iris (*I. hollandica* hybrids), Z: 5–8, are very slender in habit and are good cut flowers. They bloom

Tall bearded iris
***Iris barbata elatior*
hybrids**

(see photo above and left)
Classic with a rich spectrum of colors. Flowers all flower colors except pure red, falls and standards often different colors, a brushlike "beard" on the falls, fragrant, several flowers on sturdy stems, May–June. Foliage blue-gray, sword shaped, stiff, arranged in fan shape beside each other,

partially wintergreen. Growth H: 2 to 4 ft (0.6–1.2 m), clumps, spreading, thick rhizomes. Location full sun; soil warm, dry to rich, well-drained, containing lime, alkaline, even sandy-stony. Important: Plant bearded iris shallowly so that the rhizomes can dry out quickly, won't rot, and can mature (see page 180). If you want to plant a large group, lay out the rhizomes in a large circle.

in May and must be replanted each year.

Among the low bulb iris are *I. reticulata*, a blue-violet species, (Z: 5–9) up to 6 in (15 cm) tall for the spring garden. It flowers in February/March (early spring) as does the tiny, brilliantly yellow *I. danfordiae* (Z: 5–9).

The water flag, Japanese iris, and Siberian iris (*I. pseudacorus, I. kaempferi,* and *I. siberica*) (Z: 5–9, Z: 5–9, Z: 4–9) can be found on pages 278–279.

Mullein.

Catmint "Six Hills Giant."

Mullein
Verbascum hybrids
Short-lived, decorative. Flowers yellow, saucer shaped, tall candles of flowers, June–Aug. Foliage grayish, furry, broad oval. Growth 4 to 6 ft (1.2–1.8 m), basal rosette of leaves. Location sunny, warm to hot; dry, porous, rich soil. Z: 5–9 (depending upon species).

Catmint
Nepeta x faassenii
Aromatic perennial. Cut back after first flowering in July, which will produce a second—though weaker—flowering. Flowers lilac-blue labiate flowers in loose whorls, May–Sept. Foliage gray, broadly oval, toothed, aromatically fragrant.

Growth H: 12 to 20 in (30–50 cm), loose clumps. Location sunny, warm; dry to fresh but no heavy soils. Z: 4–8. Important: As the name suggests, cats are magically attracted to the scent. They can dig up the cushions or roll around on them.

Asphodel.

Violet sage "Blauhügel."

Pearly everlasting.

Speedwell.

Asphodel, King's spear
Asphodeline lutea
Decorative plant of the lily family. Flowers golden yellow, star shaped in dense racemes, May–June. Foliage gray-green grasslike in dense clumps. Growth H: 2 to 4 ft (0.9–1.2 m) nestlike, short runners. Location sunny, warm; well-drained, rich soil. Z: 6–9.

Violet sage
Salvia nemorosa
Long-flowering. Flowers blue to violet, labiate flowers in dense, candlelike ears, May–Aug. Foliage dull green, furrowed, elongated oval. Growth H: 16 to 32 in (40–81 cm), clumping. Location sunny, warm; moderately dry to moist, well-drained, rich soil. Z: 5–9.

Pearly everlasting
Anaphalis margeritacea
Undemanding cushion plant. Flowers silvery white, small round blooms in dense umbel-like racemes, July–Sept. Foliage gray tomentose, lanceolate. Growth H: 8 to 36 in (20–91 cm), carpet-like, spreading by means of creeping shoots. Location warm, sunny; porous soil. Z: (3) 4–8.

Silver-gray speedwell
Veronica spicata ssp. *incana*
Thick, gray carpet. Flowers dark blue, star shaped, small in dense ears at the ends of shoots, June–Aug. Foliage lanceolate, silver-gray. Growth H: 2 to 4 ft (0.6–1.2 m), runners. Location sunny, warm; moderately dry to moist, well-drained soil. Z: 4–8.

Perennial Plants for Early Summer

In early summer, the peonies (*Paeonia* species and hybrids) and the delphiniums (*Delphinium* hybrids) make their entrance. Both can function as lead plants in the perennial border. Ideal companion perennials are presented on these pages.

Peonies. They only develop their full beauty after years and should remain undisturbed in their location. The following peonies are worthy of note:

• Piney peonies (*P. officinalis*) (Z: 2–9), with single to double flowers appears at the end of May in white, pink, and red. The extremely double flowers are often bent way over with rain.

• The Chinese or common garden peonies (*P. lactiflora* hybrids) (Z: 4–8), with many single to double varieties in the same palette of colors, appear 2 weeks later.

• Show peonies (*Paeonia* hybrids), with very large flowers in uncommon shades such as yellow.

• The magnificent tree peonies (*P. suffruticosa* hybrids) (Z: 4–8), which need a protected location.

• Wild species like the delicate *P. tenuifolia* (Z: 5–8), for warm spots and the single yellow *P. mlokosewitschii* (Z: 5–8), with bluish-green foliage.

Important: Peonies contain poisonous parts.

Delphinium. With its majestic form and the rich palette of shades of blue, this is one of the most popular garden flowers for locations that are sunny but not too hot. It will bloom for 3 weeks at a time and once again in September if it is cut back. For best effect, you should plant several varieties with differing flowering times, heights, and colors. The following groupings can be made:

• *Delphinium belladonna* hybrids (2.5 to 4 ft [0.8–1.2 m]) (Z: 4–9), come in white and blue. Flowers and growth habit are somewhat looser and more delicate than in the other hybrids.

• *Delphinium elatum* hybrids (Z: 3–9), with different shades of blue (also two-tone); they grow 4 to 7 ft (1.2–2 m) tall.

• *Delphinium* Pacific hybrids in white, pink, and blue (also two-tone) are the largest flowered but least stable and reach heights of 5 to 6 ft (1.5–1.8 m).

Important: The entire plant is poisonous.

Delphiniums go well with roses (see pages 110–111), but they also are good in the potager (see pages 136–137) or with wild perennials (see pages 90–91). Also interesting is a community of perennials in blue and white with the very similar-looking monkshood (*Aconitum napellus*—caution, very poisonous!). Other ideal companions are poppies (*Papaver orientale*) and Maltese-cross (*Lychnis chalcedonica*), which is an exciting scarlet that makes a wonderful contrast with the blue. Like delphiniums, lupines (*Lupinus polyphyllus*), fleabane (*Erigeron* hybrids), and fern- leaf yarrow (*Achillea filipendulina*) can be induced to flower a second time if they are cut back.

Delphiniums have flowers with intense colors.

Delphinium ☠
Delphinium elatum hybrids

Showy perennial in unique blues. Flowers blue to lilac, white, white or black eye, candlelike, dense racemes, rarely branched, June–July, a second flowering can be induced from Aug.–Oct with cutting back of flowers. Foliage fresh green, palmate, divided to lobed. Growth sunny to semishady, cool; moist, fertile, deeply cultivated, loamy soil. Z: 3–9.

Important: There are numerous varieties, which vary primarily in the color of the flowers; check before buying.

Pink variety "Holbein."

Common garden peony ☠
Paeonia lactiflora

Long lived. Flowers red, pink, white, single to double, sometimes fragrant, May–June. Foliage dark green, sturdy, single leaves. Growth H: 20 to 43 in (50–110 cm), broadly bushy. Location sunny; moderately dry to moist, rich, deeply cultivated soil. Z: 4–8.

Lupine "My Castle."

Lupine
Lupinus polyphyllus

Popular perennial. Flowers blue, white, yellow, pink, crimson, sometimes two-tone in long, upright, cylindrical panicles, June–July. Foliage blue-green, divided palmate. Growth H: 32 to 39 in (81–100 cm), clumps. Location sunny, warm; moderately dry. Z: 4–9.

Golden achillea "Parker."

Oriental poppy "Frührot."

Fern-leaf yarrow
Achillea filipendulina

Popular long-bloomer. Flowers golden yellow, umbrella-like, compact umbels, July–Sept. Foliage gray-green, pinnate, strong aromatic fragrance. Growth H: 28 to 51 in (71–130 cm), nestlike, forms runners. Location sunny, warm; moderately dry, well-drained soil. Z: 3–10.

Oriental poppy ☠ !
Papaver orientale

Striking. Flowers red, pink, salmon, thick, brushy black stamens, thick stigma, saucer shaped, May–June. Foliage dull green, densely hairy, large, dies back early. Growth H: 16 to 39 in (41–100 cm), nestlike. Location sunny, warm; moderately dry, well-drained, soils. Z: 3–9.

Maltese-cross.

White variety of fleabane.

Maltese-cross
Lychnis chalcedonica

Campion or catchfly. Flowers fire red, star shaped, in umbrella-like umbels at the ends of shoots, June–July. Foliage dark green, oval. Growth H: 32 to 39 in (81–100 cm), nestlike. Location sunny; moist, humus, rich soil. Important: The brilliant red is often hard to combine; looks lovely with silvery gray foliage plants like Artemesia species.

Fleabane
Erigeron hybrids (N.)

Aster-like. Flowers pink, purple, lilac, blue-violet, white with golden yellow centers, marguerite-like on multibranching stems, June–July. Foliage dull green, lanceolate. Growth H: 20 to 32 in (50–81 cm), nestlike. Location sunny, warm; rich well-drained soil. Z: 2–9—depending upon species.

Ornamental Perennials for Early Summer

Bugloss, Alkanet
Anchusa azurea
Short-lived; flowers gentian blue, May–June; foliage lanceolate, dull green; growth H: up to 59 in, nestlike; location sunny, warm; no winter wetness. Z: 4–8.

Peach-bells
Campanula persicifolia
Native; flowers blue or white, June–Aug.; foliage oblong-lanceolate; growth H: 20 to 39 in; location sunny to semi-shady; fresh soil. Z: 4–8.

Knapweed
Centaurea dealbata
Flowers pink to purple, insides white, June–July, second flowering in Sept.; foliage oblong-lanceolate, pinnatilobate, green; growth 20 to 32 in, nestlike; location sunny; fresh soil. Z: 4–8.

Colewort
Crambe cordifolia
Specimen perennial; flowers white, June, strong fragrance; foliage green, roundish; growth H: up to 7 ft, dense nests; location sunny; limey soil. Z: 6–9.

Spurge ☠
Euphorbia griffithii
Bracts brilliant orange red, May–June; foliage dull green, lanceolate; growth H: 20 to 32 in, nestlike, runners; location sunny to semishady. Z: 4–9.

Geum
Geum hybrids
Long-flowering; flowers orange red, salmon, yellow, May–Aug.; foliage roundish, wintergreen; growth H: 8 to 16 in, creeps along ground; location sunny to semishady. Z: 5–9.

Daylily
Hemerocallis species
Easy-care; flowers yellow, orange, and red, May–June; foliage wintergreen to some extent; growth H: 16 to 43 in, clumps; location sunny to semishady. Z: 4–9.

Shasta daisies !
Chrysanthemum x superbum hybrids
Classic; flowers white with yellow centers, sometimes doubled, June–July; foliage dark green, lanceolate; growth H: 20 to 35 in; location sunny. Z: 4–8.

Evening primrose
Oenothera tetragona (N.)
Flowers golden yellow, saucer shaped, fragrant, June–Aug.; foliage blue green, oval; growth H: 16 to 28 in, clumps; location sunny, warm. Z: 3–9.

Phlomis
Phlomis russeliana
Ground cover; flowers bright yellow, June–Aug.; foliage dull green, lanceolate; growth H: 24 to 32 in, slowly spreading; location sunny, warm. Z: 5–9.

Common buttercup ☠
Ranunculus acris
Flowers golden yellow, May–July; foliage fresh green, divided; growth H: up to 39 in; location sunny; fresh to moist, humus soil. Z: 5–9.

Scabious, Pincushion flower
Scabiosa caucasica
Cutting plant, several varieties; flowers light blue to lilac, also white, July–Sept.; foliage oblong-lanceolate basal leaves, feathery stem leaves; growth 20 to 32 in, nestlike; location sunny; moderately dry. Z: 4–9.

Betony
Stachys grandiflora
Striking; purple-pink flower candles, June–July; foliage dull green, heart shaped; growth H: 16 to 24 in, clumps; location sunny to semishady. Z: 4–9.

Pyrethrum, Painted daisy !
Chrysanthemum coccineum
Flowers pink, wine red, purple, or white, sometimes doubled, May–July; foliage dull green, finely laciniated; growth H: 20 to 32 in, clumps; location sunny, warm. Z: 4–9.

Perennial Plants for Mid-Summer

July and August are the high season for the composite or daisy-like flowers and the daylilies.

Composite flowers. They all are quite undemanding, flower at about the same time, and usually are in warm yellow tones. Therefore, they combine best with perennials that provide other colors. There are countless genera and species among the composites, and with some, the family resemblance is not apparent at the very first look.

• Goldenrods (*Solidago* hybrids) are very rewarding summer perennials. There are very valuable and also very ornamental hybrids with long periods of bloom.

• Not to be overlooked for the summer garden are the typical composites like the rudbeckias (*Rudbeckia* species), heliopsis (*Heliopsis helianthoides* var. *scabra*), and sneezeweed (*Helenium* hybrids). The heliopsis, in particular, blooms very well after being cut back.

• The less well-known species include the golden marguerite (*Anthemis tinctoria*), the oxeye (*Buphthalmum salcifolium*), and the undemanding, tirelessly blooming inula (*Inula ensifolia*). They grow low and are suitable for carpet-like foreground planting in the perennial bed.

• The counterweight can be created by such imposing large plants as the giant *Inula magnifica* (see table), sunflower (*Helianthus salcifolius*), tickseed (*Coreopsis tripteris*), and tall rudbeckias (*Rudbeckia* species, see table). All are suitable for naturalizing and look interesting in the background of borders or in front of dark shrubs.

• The globe thistle (*Echinops bannaticus*) and alpine eryngo (*Eryngium alpinum*) are also members of the Compositae. With their steel-blue-gray color they look extravagant and create a beautiful contrast. An additional complement to the yellow hues of the composites are bedding perennials in all the shades of red such as phlox (*Phlox paniculata*) and wild bergamot (*Monarda* hybrids) as well as blue and white tall bellflowers (*Campanula lactiflora*) and the daylilies (*Hemerocallis* hybrids).

Daylilies. Their star-shaped, lily-like flowers occur in many shades of yellow and red, also often bicolored or banded. In time, the easy-care plants form decorative grasslike clumps. Many highly crossed hybrids are not long lived, however, so you should get good advice before buying. Daylilies prefer sunny to semishady places. They look beautiful with other wild perennials like the Siberian iris (*Iris siberica*), also by a pond or along the sunny edge of a clump of shrubbery and, of course, in the border. They are best planted in small groups. The large range of choices allows you to plan for flowering from May to October.

Heliopsis "Venus" and sneezeweed "Moerheim Beauty" (front).

Heliopsis
Heliopsis helianthoides var. *scabra* (N.)
Continuous bloomer. Flowers golden yellow, sometimes greenish or orange, daisy-like, single, semidouble, or double, July–Sept. Foliage dark green, rough, pointed oval. Growth H: 32 to 59 in (81–150 cm), clumps, vigorous. Location like *Helenium*. Z: 4–9.

Sneezeweed
Helenium hybrids (N.)
Many varieties. Flowers yellow, orange, brown-red with black or brown center, June–Sept. Foliage fresh green, lanceolate. Growth H: 2 to 5 ft (0.6–1.5 m), clumps, spreads slowly. Location sunny, warm; moist, rich, loamy soil. Z: 3–9 (depending upon species).

Daylily "Turned On."

Popular variety "Goldsturm."

Daylily
Hemerocallis hybrids
Many varieties. Flowers yellow and red shades, trumpet to star shaped, June–Sept. Foliage fresh green, also wintergreen, narrow, straplike, arching. Growth H: 16 to 43 in (41–110 cm), clumps, spreading slowly. Location sunny to semishady; moist, rich soil. Z: 3–9 (depends on species).

Rudbeckia
Rudbeckia fulgida var. *sullivantii* (N.)
Flowers until fall. Flowers golden yellow with dark brown, buttonlike, high-curved center, daisy-like, July–Sept. Foliage dark green, oval. Growth H: 20 to 32 in (50–81 cm), clumps, broad. Location sunny, warm; rich, loamy soil. Z: 3–9.

Perennials for Mid-Summer

Acanthus
Acanthus hungaricus
Decorative, pink-white ears, June–Aug.; foliage blue-green, oval; growth H: up to 39 in; location sunny to semishady, winter protection. Z: 7–9.

Turtlehead
Chelone obliqua (N.)
Wild-plant character, dark pink ears, July–Sept.; foliage lance-olate; growth H: 15 to 36 in; location sunny to semishady; fresh to moist soil. Z: 5–9.

Tickseed
Coreopsis species (N.)
Continuous bloomer, extraordinarily easy-care, golden yellow composite flowers, June–Sept.; foliage fresh green, pinnate or lanceolate; growth H: 12 to 35 in, clumping; location sunny; fresh soil. Z: 3–10.

Purple coneflower !
Echinacea purpurea (N.)
Butterfly plant; flowers violet-red with brownish red centers, July–Sept.; foliage dark green, pointed oval; growth 28 to 39 in, clumping; location sunny, warm. Z: 4–8.

Globe thistle; *Echinops ritro*
Cutting plant; flowers lavender-blue, round, July–Sept.; foliage dull green, deeply lobed, prickly edge; growth H: 32 to 39 in, clumping; location sunny, warm; alkaline soil. Z: 4–10.

Blanket flower
Gaillardia hybrids (N.)
Short-lived; flowers yellow, red-brown, July–Sept.; foliage dark green, lanceolate; growth H: up to 24 in, clumping; location sunny. Z: 4–11.

Baby's-breath
Gypsophila paniculata
Good companion plant; flowers white, pink, sometimes double, June–Aug.; foliage gray-green; growth H: 32 to 47 in, bushy; location sunny; dry, alkaline soil. Z: 4–8.

Inula; *Inula magnifica*
Specimen; flowers golden yellow, July–Aug.; foliage oval, large; growth 55 to 71 in, broadly bushy; location sunny. Z: 5–8.

Red-hot poker
Kniphofia hybrids
Decorative yellow-orange spikes, July–Sept.; foliage gray-green, wintergreen; growth H: 24 to 55 in, clumping; location sunny, warm. Z: 5–9.

Beard-tongue; *Penstemon barbatus* hybrids (N.)
Attractive; flowers white, pink, violet, red, July–Sept.; foliage fresh green; growth H: to 39 in, clumping; location sunny, mulch for winter protection. Z: 3–9.

Cape fuchsia
Phygelius capensis
Flowers orange-red, tube shaped, July–Oct.; foliage dark green; growth H: up to 47 in; location sunny, winter protection. Z: 5–9.

Balloon flower
Platycodon grandiflorus
Flowers violet, blue, pink, white, bell shaped, July–Aug.; foliage blue-green, leathery; growth H: 8 to 28 in, clumping; location sunny. Z: 3–9.

Rudbeckia
Rudbeckia laciniata (N.)
Imposing; flowers golden yellow, sometimes double, July–Oct.; foliage green, divided; growth H: 63 to 79 in; location sunny. Z: 3–9.

Goldenrod
Solidago hybrids (N.)
Robust; flowers yellow panicles, July–Sept.; foliage willow-like; growth H: up to 32 in; location sunny to semishady; all soils. Z: 3–9.

Speedwell; *Veronica longifolia*
Elegant flower spikes, lavender-blue, July–Aug.; foliage dark green, lanceolate; growth H: 20 to 39 in, clumping; location sunny, warm. Z: 4–11.

Phlox—the varieties "Flamingo" and "Rosa Pastell."

Perennial phlox
Phlox paniculata hybrids (N.)
Popular, fragrant ornamental perennial with numerous varieties. Flowers white, pink, salmon, crimson, violet, sometimes with an eye of another color, roundish with a long tube, densely gathered into dome-shaped corymbs, June–Sept., second flowering from side axils. Foliage green, firm, lanceolate. Growth H: 28 to 59 in (70–150 cm), clumps. Location sunny, cool; moist, rich, humus, well-drained soil. Z: 3–9. Important: The first few years plant *Tagetes* with them in order to prevent infestation with nematodes, which often occurs.

"Loddon Anne" grows to 35 in.

Bellflower
Campanula lactiflora
Magnificent bellflowers. Flowers light blue, white, violet, or lavender-pink, bells opening out into star shapes, occurring in heavy panicles, June–July. Foliage fresh green, lanceolate to oval. Growth H: 32 to 59 in (81–150 cm), clumps. Location sunny to semishady, humid, may need staking. Z: 4–8.

Wild bergamot "Mohawk."

Wild bergamot, Bee balm
Monarda hybrids (N.)
Bee and butterfly plants. Flowers crimson, purple, scarlet, violet, pink, white, labiate, July–Sept. Foliage lush to dark green, broadly lanceolate, coarsely toothed, fragrant. Growth H: 28 to 51 in (71–130 cm), clumping. Location sunny to semishady, warm, adaptable to most soil conditions. Z: 4–9.

Perennial Plants for Fall

The fall colors glow in the gentle light of the sun as it stands lower in the sky. The pink, blue, and crimson of the flowers stand out, accompanied by the warm ocher of the grasses and the yellows and reds of the slowly changing leaves.

Perennials like the tall and low fall asters (*Aster* species and varieties) and the obedient plant (*Physostegia virginiana*) dominate in this season. If you have cut back your delphiniums (*Delphinium* hybrids, see pages 236–237) to a hand's breadth after they flowered in June/July, they will now produce a second flowering.

Naturalized design. Many plants contributing to the fall atmosphere have a pronounced wild character like the very poisonous monkshood (*Aconitum carmichaelii*), the fall anemones (*Anemone hupehensis,* include: *A. japonica* and other *Anemone* species and hybrids) as well as the numerous, far too-little-known wild asters such as *Aster cordifolius* and *A. sedifolius*. With their delicate flowers and loose growth habit—especially when they are planted with grasses—they cast a slight veil over the garden. Spiderwebs glittering in the air, the dew, and the first morning mists strengthen this fall atmosphere. A pretty combination is created with *Aster linosyris* in yellow, *A. laevis* in lavender, goldenrod (*Solidago* hybrids), and the stiffly upright gay-feather (*Liatris spicata*) in violet and white, whose flowers last a long time and—very uncommon—bloom from top to bottom.

Diversity of species and variety. Besides the *Anemone hupehensis* presented here, there are also *A. japonica* hybrids of importance with many recognized good varieties like the white, single-flowered "Honorine Jobert" and the lilac-pink "Königen Charlotte" and the red "Prinz Heinrich," both semidouble. A single pink-flowered variety is *A. tomentosa* "Robustissima." The red-hot poker (*Kniphofia* hybrids), with its many beautiful varieties, flowers until fall, but it must be tied together and covered with leaves for winter protection. At the end of the growing season, the garden without the rewarding stonecrops (*Sedum* species, see table) is unimaginable. They have small, fleshy leaves in which they can store water. Therefore, they do well in very dry locations. When other perennials are already exhibiting signs of passing, the sedums lend a planting a still-succulent, fresh appearance. Many species, such as the showy *S. spectabile* "Autumn Joy," develop very beautiful umbels of flowers in purple-red, which last until the first frost like a dried bouquet.

Obedient plant—here the variety "Vivid."

Obedient plant
Physostegia virginiana (N.)
Flowers for cutting with spiked inflorescences; the individual flowers are movable, which may contribute to the common name; stake weak stalks. Flowers pink, violet-red, white, tube-shaped labiate flowers, regular spikes at ends of stems, July–Sept. Foliage grass-green, glossy, narrow lanceolate, saw-toothed. Growth H: 24 to 47 in (60–120 cm), forms large clumps by means of stolons. Location sunny to semishady; moist, rich, slightly acidic soil. Z: 3–9.

Important: Ideal for planting edges of ponds, sunny brook courses, and wild flower gardens. Stake taller plants.

Japanese anemone "Ouverture."

Monkshood "Arendsii."

Japanese anemone
Anemone japonica
Picturesque. Flowers pink to white, yellow stamens, saucer shaped, Aug–Oct. Foliage dull green, trifid. Growth H: 2 to 4 ft (0.6–1.2 m), clumping, with age broadly bushy. Location semishady, cool; moist, fertile and humus soil: apply mulch for winter protection. Z: 5.

Monkshood ☠
Aconitum carmichaelii
Brilliant blue edge-of-the-wood perennial. Flowers medium blue to purple, hoodlike, large in dense, long panicles, Sept.–Oct. Foliage lush green, glossy, 3 to 5 clefts. Growth H: 39 to 55 in (99–140 cm), clumping. Location semishady; cool, humusy, acidic, rich soil. Z: 4–8.

"Mönch."

"Veilchenkönigen."

"Herbstgruss vom Bresserhof."

"Rubinkuppel."

Michaelmas daisy
Aster x frikartii
Valuable hybrid. <u>Flowers</u> blue, lavender, yellow center, up to 2.75 in (7 cm) wide, Aug.–Sept. <u>Foliage</u> dark green, lanceolate. <u>Growth</u> H: 24 to 32 in (60–81 cm), clumping. <u>Location</u> sunny, warm; dry to moist, chalky, well–drained soil. Z: (4), 5–8. <u>Important:</u> Plant spring only.

Italian aster
Aster amellus
<u>Flowers</u> pink, lavender, violet, yellow center, daisy-like, July–Sept. <u>Foliage</u> dull green, broadly lanceolate. <u>Growth</u> H: 16 to 24 in (40–61 cm), clumping. <u>Location</u> sunny, warm; dry to fresh, porous, alkaline soil, not too rich. Z: 4–9.

Michaelmas daisy
Aster dumosus
Many varieties. <u>Flowers</u> lavender, white, pink, crimson, centers yellow, sometimes densely double, Aug.–Oct. <u>Foliage</u> dark green, lanceolate. <u>Growth</u> H: 2 to 20 in (15 to 50 cm), clumping with more or less vigorous stolon formation. <u>Location</u> sunny, cool; fresh, rich, humus soil. Z: 4–8.

Michaelmas daisy
Aster novi-belgii (N.)
Popular. <u>Flowers</u> white, pink, lavender, violet, crimson, purple, blue, with yellow centers, sometimes double, loose panicles, dense, Sept.–Oct. <u>Foliage</u> dark green, smooth, lanceolate. <u>Growth</u> H: 32 to 55 in (81–140 cm), clumping, short runners. <u>Location</u> like *Aster dumosus.* Z: 4–9.

Perennials for Fall

White wood aster
Aster divaricatus
Rarity; flowers white with brownish yellow centers, Sept.–Oct.; foliage dark green; growth H: up to 30 in, clumping; location sunny to semishady. Z: 3–9.

New England aster
Aster novae-angliae (N.)
Robust, many varieties; flowers white, pink, violet, blue, crimson, may be double, Sept.–Oct.; foliage dull green; growth H: 39–63 in, clumping; location sunny, warm. Z: 4–9.

Boltonia; *Boltonia asteroides*
Undemanding; flowers white with yellow centers, Aug–Oct.; foliage dull green; growth H: up to 71 in; location sunny. Z: 3–8.

Florists' chrysanthemum
Dendranthemum x grandiflorum hybrids
Flowers white, pink, yellow, orange, red, single to double, Aug.–Nov.; foliage dull green; growth H: 16 to 39 in, clumping; location sunny, warm. Z: 4–9.

Perennial sunflower
Helianthus species (N.)
Large perennials; flowers golden yellow, July–Oct.; foliage dark green; growth H: 47 to 79 in; location sunny, warm. Z: 3–11 (depending on species).

Field daisy, Oxeye daisy !
Leucanthemella serotina
Flowers white, yellow centers; foliage fresh green, lanceolate, toothed; growth H: 51 to 63 in, clumping; location sunny to semishady. Z: 4–9.

Orpine, Live-forever, Stone crop
Sedum telephium
Striking; flowers pink, purplish red, star shaped; foliage blue-green, fleshy, oval; growth H: 16 to 24 in, clumping; location sunny. Z: 3–9.

The variety "Erlkönig" forms with delicate violet flowers.

Heath aster
Aster ericoides
Forms veil-like clouds of flowers. <u>Flowers</u> white to delicate pink or pale lavender, yellow to brown centers, daisy-like, in heavily branched panicles, Sept.–Oct. <u>Foliage</u> narrow, lanceolate, sometimes almost needle-like, dark green. <u>Growth</u> H: 32 to 47 in (81–120 cm), clumping.

<u>Location</u> sunny, warm; moderately dry to rich, well-drained soil, no standing water. Z: 5–8.

<u>Important:</u> Also blooming wonderfully and until November is the white *Aster pringlei* "Monte Cassino" (H: 47 in [120 cm]). It is used as a cut flower and is the "September weed" of the florists.

Perennials for the Rock Garden

The major portion of the plants in the rock garden is composed of those perennials that prefer warm, dry, and neutral to alkaline soil.

Cushion and rosette plants. These hug the ground to better be able to resist wind and rain; they are typical rock garden plants. Often they have long taproots, with which they can find a hold and food among the existing stones. Among the numerous rock garden perennials, there are some that are particularly robust and undemanding and that transform the rock garden or dry wall in the spring. First and foremost come the brilliant flower cushions of the *Aubrieta* hybrids, moss pinks (*Phlox subulata* hybrids), perennial candytuft (*Iberis sempervirens*), and tussock bellflower (*Campanula carpatica*). Also recommended are the pretty, carefree stonecrops (*Sedum* species). The carpeting primroses (*Primula juliae* hybrids), rockfoils (*Saxifraga* species), and yellow corydalis (*Corydalis lutea*) are good for shady areas. Rock garden beginners are better off starting with undemanding plants. Gentian and edelweiss can of course be bought from specialty nurseries, but usually they don't thrive long because as alpine rarities they have special requirements.

Other rock garden plants. Besides the perennials, which nestle so picturesquely against the rocks or trail down them, dwarf shrubs also belong in a rock garden. Best of all are pines (*Pinus mugo* dwarf forms) or creeping junipers (*Juniperus* species), but also garland flower (*Daphne cneorum*), cushion-forming broom species (*Genista lydia* and *Cytisus* x *kewensis*) and tiny dwarf shrubs like the sun rose (*Helianthemum* hybrids).

In addition, some taller-growing shrubs are suitable for focal points, such as the white spruce (*Picea glauca* "Conica" and the small shrubby cotoneaster (*Potentilla fruticosa*). Low grasses (see pages 270–271) and small ferns (see pages 272–273) can broaden and round out the planting.

The rock garden location. The term rock garden is all-inclusive. Except for the truly alpine, it includes rock gardens on slopes, man-made small hills, but also even flat areas that have been enhanced with added rocks (see pages 106–107 and 140–141). Hot, dry locations are required, for most rock garden plants come from higher altitude locations and regions with high ultraviolet irradiation and wide temperature ranges. But typical rock garden plants also grow in shady, damp places and forest regions. With some skill, you can design a diverse rock garden for yourself.

Thrift.

Tussock bellflower.

Thrift
Armeria maritima (N.)
Cushion perennial, loves dryness. Flowers red, pink, white, small, globular, May–June. Foliage dark green, elongated, grasslike bunches. Growth 8 to 12 in (20–30 cm), mounded, dense. Location sunny; well-drained, dryish, sandy soil. Z: 3–8.

Tussock bellflower
Campanula carpatica
Everbloomer, seeds itself easily. Flowers violet, blue, also white, large bells or saucers, June–Aug. Foliage heart shaped, fresh green, dense. Growth H: 8 to 12 in (20–30 cm), button shaped, nestlike cushion. Location sunny to semishady; well-drained, moist soil. (Not dry or wet.) Z: 4–8.

Perennial candytuft.

Moss pink.

Perennial candytuft
Iberis sempervirens
Lushly flowering semishrub. Flowers white, terminal cymes. Foliage dark green, evergreen, lanceolate. Growth H: 6 to 12 in (15–30 cm), broadly bushy to cushioned, long-lived. Location sunny, warm; dry well-drained soil, poor in humus. Z: 3–9.

Moss pink
Phlox subulata (N.)
Lushly flowering. Flowers lavender, violet, white, pink, crimson, some with eyes, star shaped, Apr.–May. Foliage dull green, narrow, needle shaped. Growth H: 2 to 8 in (5–20 cm), cushion shaped, vigorously growing. Location sunny, warm; dry to well drained, rich gritty soil. Z: 4–9.

Variety "Huntercombe Purple."

Houseleek varieties.

Horned viola
Viola cornuta

Long-flowering small perennial.
<u>Flowers</u> yellow, violet, blue,
white, sometimes bicolored,
pansy-like, May–Oct. <u>Foliage</u>
dark green, ovate. <u>Growth</u>
H: 4 to 10 in (10–25 cm), nestlike, creeping rootstock. <u>Location</u>
sunny to semishady, cool; moist,
well-drained soil. Z: 6–9.

Houseleek, Hen-and-chickens
Sempervivum hybrids

Easy care. <u>Flowers</u> pink to red,
star shaped, dense umbels,
June–July. <u>Foliage</u> gray-green,
fleshy, in rosettes. <u>Growth</u> slow,
H: 4 to 10 in (10–25 cm), forming daughter rosettes. <u>Location</u>
sunny, hot; dry-nutrient-poor,
well-drained, gritty soil. Z: 5–9.

Aubrieta "Moerheimii."

Rockfoil.

Aubrieta, False rockcress
Aubrieta deltoidea

Cushion plant. <u>Flowers</u> lavender-
blue, violet, velvety red, pink,
roundish, Apr.–May. <u>Foliage</u>
gray-green, evergreen, oval lanceolate. <u>Growth</u> H: 2 to 6 in (5–15
cm), rooting stems. <u>Location</u>
sunny, warm; moderately dry to
fresh, rich, porous, alkaline soil.
Z: 4–9.

Rockfoil, Mossy saxifrage
Saxifraga x arendsii hybrids

Spring bloomers. <u>Flowers</u> pink,
red, yellow, white, in clusters,
Mar.–June. <u>Foliage</u> narrow, lanceolate, fresh green, evergreen.
<u>Growth</u> H: 2 to 6 in (5–15 cm),
rosette like, dense cushions.
<u>Location</u> sunny to semishady,
cool, humid air; well-drained soil.
Doesn't like hot, dry areas. Z: 4–6.

Perennials for the Rock Garden

<u>Basket-of-gold</u>
Aurinia saxatilis
Cushion plant; flowers brilliant
yellow, Apr.–May; foliage gray-
green, spatulate; growth H: 10
to 16 in; location sunny,
warm, dry. Z: 4–7.

<u>Rock cress</u>
Arabis caucasica
Cushion plant; flowers white
or pink, Apr.–May; foliage
gray, tomentose; growth
H: 6 to 8 in, creeping; location
sunny. Z: 5–9.

<u>Alpine aster; *Aster alpinus*</u>
Lushly flowering, short-lived;
flowers white, violet, pink,
May–June; foliage dull green,
oval; growth H: 8 to 12 in,
small cushions; location sunny,
porous soil. Z: 4–9.

<u>Adriatic campanula</u>
Campanula garganica
Cushion-forming; flowers
small, lavender, June–Aug.;
foliage lush green, small;
growth H: 6 in; location sunny
to semishady; alkaline. Z: 4–8.

<u>Yellow corydalis</u>
Corydalis lutea
Self-sowing; flowers yellow,
Apr.–Sept.; foliage blue-green;
growth H: 12 in; location
sunny to semishady. Z: 5–9.

<u>Cottage pink</u>
Dianthus plumarius
Fragrant; flowers pink, red,
white, may be double, May–
June; foliage gray-green;
growth H: 8 to 12 in, cushion
shaped; location sunny. Z: 4–9.

<u>Dryas</u>
Dryas x suendermannii
Flowers cream-colored,
May–June, from July feather
seed pods; foliage dark green,
evergreen; growth vigorous,
H: 6 in; location sunny. Z: 3–6.

<u>Cranesbill</u>
Geranium dalmaticum
Abundant flowering; flowers
brilliant pink, July–Aug.;
foliage fresh green, wintergreen to some extent; growth
H: 4 to 6 in, cushion; location
sunny. Z: 5–8.

<u>Creeping baby's-breath</u>
Gypsophila repens
Flowers white to pink,
May–Sept.; foliage gray-green,
lanceolate; growth H: 4 to 8 in,
cushion; location sunny;
alkaline.

<u>Sun rose</u>
Helianthemum hybrids
Semishrub; flowers pink, red,
yellow, orange, white, sometimes double, May–Sept.;
foliage gray-green, linear to
ovate, wintergreen; growth
H: 6 to 12 in, cushion shaped
to shrubby; location sunny;
chalky soil. Z: 5–8.

<u>Coralbells</u>
Heuchera x brizoides
Wintergreen; flowers pink,
red, white, bell shaped,
May–July; foliage heart-
shaped, dark green; growth
H: 12 to 20 in; location sunny
to semishady, humid air.
Z: 4–8.

<u>Iceland poppies</u>
Papaver nudicaule (N.)
Delicate; flowers red, pink,
orange, yellow, white,
May–Aug.; foliage blue-gray;
growth H: 8 to 16 in; location
sunny. Z: 4–8.

<u>Soapwort</u>
Saponaria ocymoides
Undemanding; flowers rose-
red, fragrant, May–July; foliage dull green; growth H: 4 to
8 in, cushion; location sunny;
chalky soil. Z: 4–8.

<u>Stonecrop</u>
Sedum floriferum
"Weihenstephaner Gold"
Ground cover, easy-care;
flowers little golden yellow
stars, July–Oct.; foliage dark
green; growth H: 4 to 6 in;
location sunny, warm. Z: 5–9.

<u>Creeping thyme,
Mother-of-thyme;</u>
Thymus serpyllum
Flowers small, crimson,
May–Oct.; foliage dark geen,
fragrant; growth H: 2 to 6 in,
flat carpet; location sunny;
lime-poor, sandy soil. Z: 5–9.

Perennials for the Edge of the Wood

When the edge of the wood is referred to, it does not mean the forest edge, as in free nature, for that exists in a very few gardens. It refers to an area where there are enough groups of trees or shrubs or single woody plants, in whose shadow those perennials that prefer cooler and fresher locations thrive, in contrast to those that want a sunny spot all day long if possible. Often they resign themselves to the narrowest areas—in the circle around a single shrub, for example, and to considerable differences in light conditions, caused by the daily and seasonal changes in the sun's position and possibly also by the leafless conditions during the winter. Designs for plantings in the areas around these woody plants are equally diverse.

Sunny locations. The soil and the air are particularly warm on the sunny side of a hedge or shrub grouping, because the planting acts as a wind break and, thus, offers protection from the cold. Because it is warmer, soils are usually drier. Many flowering perennials that in nature prefer to locate in warm, open area sites between forest and field or meadow, thrive in loose, well-drained-humus soil. Among these are foxglove (*Digitalis purpurea*), bellflower (*Campanula latifolia*), and black cohosh (*Cimicifuga racemosa*). Or there can be plants that like it sunny but also want somewhat moist soil conditions, like the very poisonous garden monkshood (*Aconitum napellus*, see table) and meadow rue (*Thalictrum aquilegifolium*).

Shady locations. Where the sun hardly shines at all or only for a few hours a day—between evergreens or in the light shade of larger trees—the ornamental-leaved plants like the hostas (*Hosta* species and varieties) do extremely well. The wonderfully colored astilbes (*Astilbe* species and hybrids) provide color accents in such places. These are flower and foliage plants in one, and enrich the summer months with their extraordinary wealth of color to brighten shady sections. With the right choices of variety, flowering can be made to extend from June to October (early summer to fall).

Fluffy flowers of the meadow rue.

Astilbe—here the varieties "Hyazinth" and "Augustfeuer."

Meadow rue
Thalictrum aquilegifolium
(photo left)
Flowers pink, light violet, finely radiate, in loose cymes, May–July. Foliage blue-green, columbine-like, delicate. Growth H: 32 to 47 in (81–120 cm), clumping, self-seeding. Location semishady; moist to damp, humus soil. Z: 5–8.

Astilbe, False spirea
***Astilbe x arendsii* hybrids**
Many species, hybrids, and varieties. Flowers white, pink, red, purple, spike like panicles, early to mid-summer, June–July. Foliage dark green. Growth H: 2 to 3 ft (0.6–0.9m), clumping. Location semishady, cool, humid; moist to damp, rich, humus soil. Z: 4–8.

Perennials for the Edge of the Woods

Garden monkshood ☠
Aconitum napellus
For semishade; flowers dark blue, helmet like, June–July; foliage dark green; growth H: 35 to 59 in, nestlike; location cool; fresh soil. Z: 4–8.

Windflower
Anemone sylvestris
Creeping; flowers white, saucer shaped, slightly fragrant, May–June; foliage fresh green; growth H: 12 to 20 in; location semishady. Z: 3–9.

Goat's beard
Aruncus dioicus (N.)
Specimen; cream-colored panicles, June–July; foliage fresh green; growth H: 59 to 79 in, clumps; location semishady. Z: 4–8.

Clematis; *Clematis recta*
Wild shrub; flowers cream white, fragrant, July–Aug., feathery seeds; foliage lush green; growth H: up to 5 ft;

location sunny to semishady. Z: 3–9.

Christmas rose
Helleborus niger
Winter bloomer; flowers white, Dec.–Mar.; foliage evergreen; growth H: 12 in, clumps; location semishady. Z: 4–9.

Kirengeshoma
Kirengeshoma palmata
Ornamental perennial; flowers yellow, Aug.–Sept.; foliage fresh green; growth 24 to 35 in, clumping; location semishady. Z: 5–8.

Solomon's-seal ☠
Polygonatum hybrids (N.)
Flowers milk white bells, May–June; foliage oval; growth H: 24 to 39 in; location semishady. Z: 3–9.

Toad lily; *Tricyrtis hirta*
Extravagant; flowers white, spotted with purple-violet, Aug.–Oct.; foliage blue green; growth H: 20 to 35 in; location semishady. Z: 4–9.

Rodgersia with gigantic leaves.

Hosta sieboldiana, H. crispula, H. fortunei *(from left to right).*

Black cohosh.

Rodgersia
Rodgersia podophylla

Specimen. <u>Flowers</u> cream colored, large, loose panicles over leaves, June–Aug. <u>Foliage</u> dark green, divided, coarse, deeply grooved. <u>Growth</u> H: 32 to 71 in (81–180 cm), clumping. <u>Location</u> sunny to semishady to shady, cool, humid; moist, humus soil. Z: 5–8.

Hosta, Plantain lily
Hosta species and hybrids

Popular, diverse, and easy care ornamental-leaved perennial with a rich range of species and varieties. <u>Flowers</u> white, lavender, tube or bell-shaped, fragrant, in racemes over the foliage, June–Aug. <u>Foliage</u> blue-green to fresh green, sometimes marked with white or yellow, heart-shaped to narrow lanceolate, leathery, with deep, parallel veins. <u>Growth</u> H: 4 to 47 in (10–120 cm), clumping, new growth late. <u>Location</u> semishady to shady (variegated varieties green in shade); cool, moist, humus rich soil.
<u>Important:</u> Hostas are much beloved by snails and slugs.

Black cohosh
Cimicifuga racemosa

Picturesque large perennial. <u>Flowers</u> cream colored, small, in cylindrical spikes, standing erect over leaves, July–Aug. <u>Foliage</u> dark green, pinnate. <u>Growth</u> H: 59 to 79 in (150–201 cm), clumping. <u>Location</u> semishady, cool, humid; fresh, loose, humus soil.

Masterwort.

Columbine.

Foxglove.

Bellflowers.

Masterwort
Astrantia major

<u>Flowers</u> silvery white to pink, star-shaped involucral leaves around the panicles, June–Aug. <u>Foliage</u> dark green, glossy, palmate, divided. <u>Growth</u> H: 20 to 28 in (51–71 cm), clumping. <u>Location</u> semishady, cool; moist, humus soil. Z: 5–8.

Columbine ☠
Aquilegia vulgaris

Short-lived wild perennial, seeds easily. <u>Flowers</u> blue, pink, white, spurred, May–June. <u>Foliage</u> blue-green, delicate. <u>Growth</u> H: 16 to 24 in (40–60 cm), loosely clumped, dies back after flowering. <u>Location</u> semishady; humus soil. Z: 5–9. <u>Important:</u> Magnificent hybrids for sunny locations are commercially available.

Foxglove ☠
Digitalis purpurea

Usually biennial. <u>Flowers</u> pink, purple, white, spotted, June–July. <u>Foliage</u> dull green, ovate. <u>Growth</u> H: 39 to 55 in (99–140 cm), only a low rosette of flowers in first year. <u>Location</u> semishady to shady; acid, humus soil. <u>Important:</u> Remove spent flowers.

Bellflower
Campanula latifolia

Native wild plant. <u>Flowers</u> blue, white, in loose racemes, June–July. <u>Foliage</u> dark green, lanceolate pointed stem leaves. <u>Growth</u> H: 32 to 39 in (81–99 cm), clumping. <u>Location</u> full sun to semishady, cool; moist to damp, humus, rich soil.

Perennial Ground Covers

There is no bare ground in nature, as a rule. A plant cover offers protection, and the decay of its dead portions contributes to the buildup of the soil. There are species in every genus that will cover the soil entirely within a few years. The plants achieve this in different ways:
- creeping flat over the ground
- through aboveground runners
- through underground runners
- through long, arching canes
- by growing bushy and spreading

The height of growth generally varies between 2 and 20 in (5 and 50 cm). Ground covers include woody plants and low shrub roses as well as annuals. Among the perennials, however, there are an especially large number with appropriate growth characteristics. It is important for them to form an enduring, dense cover. Many plants are unsuitable for this purpose because they become bare from the inside out and must be repeatedly divided. There are ground-covering perennials for almost every location. Among the sun- and warmth-loving plants, the lawn-and cushion-forming rock garden plants are especially good (see pages 242–243).

Ground covers for shade. They are presented here. They can be used particularly well under trees and shrubs, in their natural setting. A thick cover of plants also inhibits weeds. However, it is all the more important to thoroughly clear out weed roots before any planting. The soil should also be prepared to its best possible condition, and the type of soil and the layout measured. How many plants per square foot (square meter) will be needed depends on the species and growth habit of the plant. To get the planting established more quickly, plants may also be set somewhat more closely together. However, there is also the risk that the plants can grow unattractively crowding on top of each other instead of spreading out flat. Normally it takes 3 to 4 years until a planting is completely filled in and needs scarcely any care. Let the fall foliage lie there and contribute to the protection and nutrition of the planting.

Designing with ground covers. Ground covers are the ideal substitute for a grass lawn:
- in shady areas, for grass lawns need light
- on steep slopes, where mowing is difficult
- as a quiet underlay to bring specimens and decorative elements to full effect

Depending on the species, this carpet of plants can even be walked on, or some stepping-stones help to define and structure the area.

Spotted dead nettle "Chequers."

Spotted dead nettle
Lamium maculatum (N.)
Easy-care wild perennial with decorative foliage. Flowers dark rose, pink, white, labiate, in dense, leafed whorls, May–July. Foliage dark green with more or less regular silvery white spots, pointed ovate, toothed, furrowed.

Growth H: 6 to 16 in (15–40 cm), runner shoots, but not invasive. Location semishady, cool; moist, loose, rich, soil. Z: 3–8.
Important: There are different varieties that come in other colors and leaf markings; most can also be mowed.

Pachysandra with evergreen leaves.   *Lungwort "Reginald Key."*

Pachysandra ☠
Pachysandra terminalis
Robust, evergreen semishrub. Flowers insignificant, green, Apr.–May. Foliage dark green, hard, leathery, coarsely toothed, oval. Growth H: 8 to 12 in (20–30 cm), bushy, runners. Location semishady to shady; moderately dry to moist acidic soil. Z: 5.

Lungwort
Pulmonaria saccharata
Decorative leaf plant. Flowers dark rose fading to lavender-blue, Mar.–May. Foliage dull green with silvery spots. Growth H: 6 to 12 in (15–30 cm), creeping, forms a closed plant cover. Location semishady to shady; moist, loose, humus, fertile soil. Z: 3–9.

Myrtle.

False miterwort.

Carpet bugleweed.

Waldsteinia.

Common myrtle ☠
Vinca minor

Evergreen ground cover. <u>Flowers</u> violet to light blue, star shaped, Apr.–May. <u>Foliage</u> dark green, shiny, leathery, dense. <u>Growth</u> H: 4 to 8 in (10–20 cm), large carpet by means of long runners. <u>Location</u> semishady to shady, cool; dry to moist, loose soil. Z: 3–9.

False miterwort
Tiarella wherryi (N.)

Ground cover. <u>Flowers</u> white, in upright spikes, May–June. <u>Foliage</u> heart shaped, lobed, linden green. <u>Growth</u> H: 6 to 12 in (15–30 cm), carpets through runners, not invasive. <u>Location</u> semishady to shady, cool; moist, porous, humus soil. Z: 3–8.

Carpet bugleweed
Ajuga reptans

Native wild perennial. <u>Flowers</u> brilliant blue, small, densely flowered spikes, Apr.–May. <u>Foliage</u> fresh green to reddish, wintergreen. <u>Growth</u> H: 6 to 8 in (15–20 cm), carpetlike. <u>Location</u> semishady, cool; dry to moist, nutrient-rich, loamy soil. Z: 4–8

Waldsteinia
Waldsteinia geoides

Dense clumps. <u>Flowers</u> golden yellow, saucer shaped, Apr.–May. <u>Foliage</u> fresh green, lobed. <u>Growth</u> H: 8 to 12 in (20–30 cm), broad clumps. <u>Location</u> sunny to shady; dry to moist soil. Z: 5. <u>Important</u>: *Waldsteinia ternata* grows like a carpet.

Perennial Ground Covers

Lady's-mantle
Alchemilla mollis
Flowers greenish yellow; foliage gray-green; growth H: 12 to 20 in, clumping; location sunny to semishady. Z: 4–8.

European wild ginger
Asarum europaeum
Evergreen; foliage dark green; growth H: 4 in, creeping; location semishady to shady. Z: 5–7.

Siberian bugloss
Brunnera macrophylla
Flowers gentian blue, May–June; foliage gray-green; growth H: 12 to 18 in, prostrate; location sunny to semishady. Z: 4–8.

Plumbago
Ceratostigma plumbaginoides
Flowers gentian blue, Sept.–Oct.; foliage lush green, from Sept. orange; growth H: 8 to 18 in, runners; location sunny to semishady. Z: 6–8.

Mock strawberry
Duchesnea indica
Vigorous; flowers yellow, May–Sept.; fruits strawberry-like; foliage fresh green; growth H: 4 in, runners; location sunny to semishady. Z: 4–9.

Cranesbill, *Geranium endressii*
Flowers pink, June–Aug.; foliage dark green; growth H: 12 to 20 in; location semishady. Z: 4–8.

Ground ivy
Glechoma hederacea
Flowers blue-violet, Mar.–June, then Sept.–Oct.; foliage kidney shaped, winter green; growth H: 4 to 8 in; location semishady. Z: 5–9.

Comfrey
Symphytum grandiflorum
Flowers yellow, also blue, Mar.–May; foliage wintergreen; growth H: 12 to 16 in, developing runners; location sunny to shady. Z: 5–9.

Epimedium "Sulphureum."

Creeping forget-me-not.

Epimedium
Epimedium x versicolor

Vigorously growing. <u>Flowers</u> sulphur yellow, bell shaped, Apr.–May. <u>Foliage</u> fresh green, bronze when new, greening later, somewhat wintergreen. <u>Growth</u> H: 12 to 14 in (30 to 35 cm), forms runners. <u>Location</u> semishady to shady; moderately dry to moist, humus soil. Z: 5.

Creeping forget-me-not
Omphalodes verna

Delicate spring bloomer. <u>Flowers</u> brilliant blue with white center, similar to the forget-me-not, Apr.–May. <u>Foliage</u> fresh green, ovate, pointed. <u>Growth</u> H: 6 to 10 in (15–25 cm), forming a dense carpet with runners. <u>Location</u> semishady, warm, fresh to moist soil. Z: 5–8.

Narcissi exude slime when cut. Therefore it's better
not to combine them with other cut flowers.

FLOWERS FROM BULBS AND CORMS

Bulbs and corms make up a special group within the perennials. They survive their resting phase by means of underground storage organs. The shape, size, and development of these organs are as different as the plants themselves. Every genus has special flowering and resting times. The requirements of these plants as to location and care vary according to their native origins. Fundamentally, the hybrid forms produced from the wild species want a well-prepared garden soil, but then they are usually robust and will flower abundantly.

Bulbs and corms can be combined well with perennials and trees and shrubs (see pages 112–113). They can be planted in loose arrangements or between the plants. The time of planting depends on the flowering time: Spring bloomers go into the ground from September until November; fall bloomers in summer; summer bloomers in fall or spring. As a rule of thumb for planting depth: Place them about three times as deep as the diameter of the bulb or corm (see page 181). Every few years, the clumps of bulbs should be transplanted to a new location. Fertilizing with compost and organic fertilizer is generally done at the time of planting as well as at the beginning of growth. You should regularly cut off flowers when they have finished blooming so that seeds are not produced. The foliage is only removed after it has completely yellowed so that the storage organs can build up new reserves.

These Darwin hybrid tulips (variety "Gudoshnik") look like a painting with their alluring play of colors.

Small Spring Bloomers

The small spring bulbs occupy a very special place in the garden as the harbingers of a new growing season. They are the first spots of color, beginning delicately in shades of white and yellow, then adding blues and purples. Some varieties also possess stronger colors, but everything still looks small and restrained in contrast to the colorful glory of the tulips later.

The many wild species play the leading role with the spring bulbs, but the hybrids have also largely retained their wild character. An exception is the hybrid crocuses, which look like colored Easter eggs and also are much more bulbous than their delicate, slender ancestors. In country gardens, small and large bulbs usually are grown mixed up colorfully together, the small ones sometimes used as low bed enclosures, together with early-flowering perennials. By their nature, however, these small spring bulbs fit better in the naturalized areas of the garden: The warmth-loving ones among them feel better on sunny and dry slopes in the rock garden. All those that prefer a damp location from fall to spring thrive under or in front of groupings of trees or shrubs, in the transition area between woods and fields. Scatter the small bulbs or corms over a wide area in the fall, perhaps 20 to 25 to about 1 sq ft (30 x 30 cm).

When the fall leaves are left lying over the winter, a natural mulch layer is created. This situation is agreeable to the small bulbs. The plantings increase and spread like a carpet if they are just left entirely to themselves and not disturbed by the soil's being worked.

With poor soils, compost or a light application of complete fertilizer can be provided in the fall or at the appearance of new growth in the spring.

Spring-flowering bulbs also die back, in time. The yellowed foliage can be removed easily or better still, covered by succeeding perennials or grass. But wait to mow until the leaves have died. Where the spring bulbs are not desired or when the garden is being rearranged, they are best transplanted immediately after flowering as long as the location is still recognizable. It is wise to dig out whole clumps and replant them; however, there is also a chance to divide the bulbs at this point. In lawns, the garden crocuses usually only last for a few years; they must continually be replaced.

Snowdrops.

Winter aconite ☠
Eranthis hyemalis
(see photo above)
Earliest spring bloomers for naturalizing under trees and shrubs, self-seed vigorously, form dense carpets. <u>Flowers</u> brilliant yellow, fragrant; Feb.–Mar. <u>Foliage</u> finely divided, light green. <u>Growth:</u> 2 to 4 in (6–10 cm). <u>Location:</u> semishade to shade; fresh, humus soil. Z: 5–9.
<u>Important:</u> Soften the small corms overnight in warm water before planting; they will then root better.

Snowdrops ☠
Galanthus nivalis
(see photo left)
For naturalizing along the edges of trees and shrubs or under specimens. <u>Flowers</u> white, trifid, inner circle with greenish border, nodding; Feb.–Mar. <u>Foliage</u> blue-green, narrow linear. <u>Growth</u> H: 4 in (10 cm). <u>Location</u> sun to shade. Z: 3–9.

Spring snowflake.

Snowflake ☠
Leucojum vernum
Spring-flowering tuber, self-seeding. <u>Flowers</u> white with green dots on the points, wide bells; Feb.–Mar. <u>Foliage</u> dark green, shining, strap shaped, short. <u>Growth</u> H: 8 in (20 cm). <u>Location</u> semishade to shade; moist soil. Z: 4–8.

Scilla "Spring Beauty."

Glory-of-the-snow.

Grape hyacinths.

Squill, Bluebell ☠ !
Scilla siberica
Masses of flowers, naturalizes easily. <u>Flowers</u> light lavender-blue, also white and blue, star shaped, nodding, in loose racemes; Mar.–Apr. <u>Foliage</u> sturdy green, strap shaped. <u>Growth</u> H: 4 to 6 in (10–15 cm), dense carpets. <u>Location</u> semishade; fresh and humus soil. Z: 4–8.

Glory-of-the-snow !
Chionodoxa luciliae
Delicate early spring flower. <u>Flowers</u> light blue, white, or light pink, star shaped, yellow stamens, loose racemes; Mar.–Apr. <u>Foliage</u> linear, grass green. <u>Growth</u> H: 4 to 10 in (10–25 cm), carpeting. <u>Location</u> sun to semishade. Z: 3–9.

Grape hyacinths ☠
Muscari armeniacum
Robust and long flowering, many species and varieties. <u>Flowers</u> blue with white edge, variety "Alba" with white flowers; Apr. <u>Foliage</u> narrow linear, gray-green. <u>Growth</u> H: 6 to 8 in (15–20 cm), clumping, spreading. <u>Location</u> sun to semishade; porous and also dry soil. Z: 2–9.

Crocus.

Windflower.

Crocus
Crocus tomasinianus
Abundantly flowering crocus for naturalizing; forms dense carpet of flowers. <u>Flowers</u> light lavender, funnel shaped, also white; Feb.–Mar. <u>Foliage</u> narrow, light center stripe. <u>Growth</u> H: 2 to 4 in (5–10 cm). <u>Location</u> sunny; porous soil. Z: 3–8.

Windflower ☠
Anemone blanda
Charming very early spring bloomer for the edge of wooded areas and rock gardens, also for naturalizing. <u>Flowers</u> blue, white, pink, lavender, also with white eye, daisy-like; Mar.–Apr. <u>Foliage</u> trifid, laciniated, bright green. <u>Growth</u> H: 4 in (10 cm). <u>Location</u> sun to semishade. Z: 5–10.

Small Spring Bloomers

<u>Crocus</u>
<u>*Crocus* hybrids</u>
Flowers white, yellow, lavender, blue, bicolored, funnel shaped, Mar.–Apr.; H: 4 to 6 in (10–15 cm); location sunny to semishady, warm. 3–8.

<u>Alpine violet</u>
<u>*Cyclamen coum*</u>
Flowers pink, purple, white, fragrant, Feb.–Apr.; H: 4 in (10 cm); location sunny to semishady; humus soil. 5–9.

<u>Dog-tooth violet</u>
<u>*Erythronium dens-canis*</u>
Flowers lavender-pink, white, nodding, Mar–Apr.; H: 3 to 4 in (8–10 cm); location semishady; cool, humus soil. Z: 3–9.

<u>Checkered lily</u> ☠
<u>*Fritillaria meleagris*</u>
Flowers purple-lavender with checkered pattern, Apr.–May; H: 8 to 12 in (20–30 cm); location semishady to shady;

humus, loamy, alkaline soil. Z: 3–8.

<u>Spanish bluebell</u>
<u>*Hyacinthoides hispanica*</u>
Ideal for naturalizing; flowers blue, bell shaped, May; H: 8 to 12 in (20–30 cm); location semishady to shady; moist, humus soil. Z: 4–9.

<u>Purple gem</u>
<u>*Iris reticulata*</u> !
Flowers violet-blue, Mar.–Apr.; H: 4 to 8 in (10–20 cm); location sunny, warm; dry, porous soil. Z: 5–9.

<u>Puschkinia, Striped squill</u>
<u>*Puschkinia scilloides*</u>
Flowers light blue, also white, bell shaped, Apr.–May; H: 4 to 6 in (10–15 cm); location sunny to semishady, warm. Z: 4–10.

Tulips

Tulips embody the spring with a wealth of colors and forms that are almost immeasurable. All colors are represented except for a true blue. Tulips are divided into different groups:

Species tulips. These are suitable above all for naturalized plantings, grow 6 to 16 in (15–40 cm) high, and flower from March to May. Recommended are the yellow *Tulipa sylvestris*, as well as *T. batalinii, T. clusiana, T. pulchella, T. tarda, T. turkestanica, T. praestans,* and *T. urumiensis.* Among the *T. kaufmanniana, T. fosteriana,* and *T. greigii,* it is mainly the large-flowered hybrids that are important; some of these have marbled foliage. They are particularly effective as edge plantings in front of shrubs and along paths as well as in beds with narcissi and grape hyacinths.

Cultivated tulips. They grow 16 to 28 in (40–70 cm) high and are divided into three groups according to when they flower. Each group also contains several different classifications:

• Early tulips (beginning to middle Apr.). In this group there are single and double varieties.

• Mid-season tulips (middle Apr. to beginning May). Among these are the Mendel tulips, the robust Triumph tulips, and the large-flowered, splendidly colored Darwin hybrid tulips.

• Late tulips (beginning to end of May). Tulips of this group grow to 20 to 28 in (50–70 cm) tall. The first to appear are the sturdy, single Darwin tulips, then the cottage or single late tulips, as well as the elegant lily-flowered tulips, the parrot tulips with their baroque shapes, the not very vigorous, flamed Rembrandt tulips, the double late peony-flowered tulips, the multiflowered tulips, the viridiflora tulips with their striking green stripes, and the crispa tulips, whose single flowers are delicately fringed along the edges.

Tulip planting and care. Planting time runs from September until the ground freezes. The location should be predominantly sunny, the soil sandy-humus. It is important that the soil not hold water, particularly in the summer, or the bulbs will rot. The planting depth is about 6 in (15 cm), with the planting distance depending on the size of the flowers—for single tulips it is about 6 to 8 in (15–20 cm), somewhat more for the large-flowered ones. The bulbs are planted in loose groups. You should plant at least 10 of any one variety to achieve a good effect. Tulips propagate themselves through bulblets, which are developed anew each year.

Important: Tulip bulbs can also be planted up to the beginning of December where seasons are mild. Make sure that the bulbs you buy are healthy. Most tulips are hardy to Z: (3) 4.

One of the best-known Greigii hybrids "Red Riding Hood."

Botanical tulips !
Tulipa greigii hybrids

Attractive late-flowering species tulips with gray-green, brown-striped, or marbled leaves. Flowers one- to several-colored, often with contrasting stripes, longe, narrow calyxes, which open wide in sunlight; Mar.–Apr. Growth H: 8 to 18 in (20–46 cm).

Varieties "Red Riding Hood" (see photo), brilliant scarlet with black basal spot and beautifully patterned leaves; "Oriental Splendour," lemon yellow, green-red basal spot, red-yellow edge, foliage striped, long-lasting variety; "Plaisir," cream-yellow with red stripes, leaves brownish striped. Z: 3–8.

Tulipa kaufmannia *hybrids.*

The multiflowerd Tulipa tarda.

Species tulip !
Tulipa kaufmanniana

Parent form for many hybrid tulips, also called water-lily tulip. Flowers cream-white with rosy cast, narrow calyx, which opens star shaped; Mar.–Apr. Growth H: 6 to 10 in (15–25 cm).

Important: Many hybrid varieties in brilliant colors, often with striped foliage.

Species tulip !
Tulipa tarda

Very undemanding delicate species tulip, which develops large stands and self-sows. Flowers white with large yellow centers, gray-green outside, star shaped, several flowers per stem; Mar.–Apr. Growth H: 4 to 6 in (10–15 cm).

"Coleur Cardinal."

"Mrs. John T. Scheepers."

"Orange Princess."

Lily-flowered tulip.

Single early tulips ❗
Tulipa
Early-flowering tall tulips. <u>Flowers</u> many colors, oval calyx; Apr. <u>Growth</u> 10 to 16 in (25–40 cm), sturdy stems. <u>Varieties</u> "Coleur Cardinal" (see photo), dark scarlet with bluish cast, 14 in (36 cm); "Apricot Beauty," apricot colored; "Princess Irene," orange with purple flames.

Single late tulips ❗
Tulipa
Also called cottage tulips. <u>Flowers</u> almost all colors, slender, oval calyxes; May. <u>Growth</u> H: 16 to 20 in (40–50 cm), sturdy stems. <u>Varieties</u> "Mrs. John T. Scheepers" (photo), pure yellow, large flowered, spreads vigorously, 24 in (60 cm), very late flowering, best yellow variety.

Double late tulips ❗
Tulipa
Peony-flowered tulips. <u>Flowers</u> usually multicolored, also flamed, very large; Apr–May. <u>Growth</u> H: 16 to 24 in (40–60 cm). <u>Varieties</u> "Orange Princess" (photo); "Bonanza" red with yellow border, 16 in (40 cm); "Angelique" light pink 18 in (46 cm). <u>Important</u> location protected from weather.

Lily-flowered tulips ❗
Tulipa
Very elegant-looking late tulips. <u>Flowers</u> many beautiful colors, long, slender calyxes; Apr–May. <u>Growth</u> H: 20 to 24 in (50–60 in), elegant to sturdy. <u>Varieties</u> "West Point" primrose-yellow, elongated calyx, 20 in (50 cm); "White Triumphator" pure white, very elegant, 24 in (60 cm).

Baroque beauty—parrot tulip "Flaming Parrot."

Viridiflora tulip "Hummingbird."

Parrot tulips ❗
Tulipa
Extravagant late-flowering collector's variety. <u>Flowers</u> multicolored, often flamed, in strong colors, large, heavy calyxes, which open wide, bizarrely slit and wavy edged; May. <u>Growth</u> H: 16 to 24 in (40–60 cm). <u>Varieties</u> "Flaming Parrot" (see photo), yellow and red flamed, 22 in (56 cm); "Black Parrot" dark purple, 22 in (56 cm); "Fantasy" salmon pink, green flecked, 24 in (60 cm); "Rococo" crimson red, green outside, 14 in (36 cm); "Texas Flame" yellow-crimson flamed, 22 in (56 cm); "White Parrot" white, stable variety, 16 in (40 cm).

Viridiflora tulips ❗
Tulipa
Very striking single, late-flowering cultivated tulips, many new hybrids. <u>Flowers</u> predominately delicate colors with characteristic green markings especially on the outsides of the petals, slender, beautifully shaped calyxes; May. <u>Growth</u> H: 12 to 20 in (30–50 cm). <u>Varieties</u> "Hummingbird" (see photo), mimosa yellow outside and inside with green markings, 16 in (40 cm); '"Golden Artist" yellow-and-green striped, 12 in (30 cm); "Artist" inside salmon pink and green, outside purple and salmon, 12 in (30 cm), late variety; "Greenland" light-green center stripe, yellow border, pink cast, 20 in (50 cm).

Narcissi

Narcissi are the absolute messengers of spring. Their flowering period begins in March with the earliest varieties; the main portion extends throughout April, with the late varieties reaching into May. Yellow and white are the predominant color shades. For better differentiation, narcissi are classified into groups according to their flower form and origins:
- Trumpet narcissi with thus-formed perianths
- Large-cupped narcissi with saucer-shaped perianths
- Small-cupped narcissi with delicate perianths
- Double-flowered narcissi
- Angel's-tears (triandrus) narcissi with multiflowered, fragrant, long stems
- Cyclamineus narcissi with reflexly curving petals
- Jonquils, multiflowered with captivating fragrance
- Tazettas with several small flowers per stem
- Poeticus narcissi with dazzling white petals

The flower is clearly divided into the main corolla and the perianth in the center. The perianth can be trumpet, saucer, cup, or bowl shaped. With many varieties, it is a different color from the petals, often even reddish.

The bulb has a characteristically pointed shape with a so-called nose. Double noses are of special quality and flower heavily. The roots are strikingly long and unbranched. They are sloughed off and redevelop again after September (caution when planting!).

The leaf is narrow and grasslike. The foliage dies back

late—often only by the end of June/beginning of July—and may not be mowed until it is completely yellow. Therefore, you should place bulbs along the woods edge as far as possible into the background. The location should be sunny to semishady, the soil fresh to moist, rich, humus, and well-drained.

Use. Robust narcissus varieties are best planted under early-spring-flowering ornamental shrubs (see pages 202–215), as well as in the transition areas at the edges of fields or lawns. Under favorable conditions, they will naturalize and form large clumps. Varieties with unusual colors and shapes as well as the multiflowered, delicate narcissi grow better in beds and bor-

Crown imperial (Fritillaria imperialis).

ders, whereas the wild forms and low-growing varieties look beautiful in rock gardens and in plantings of wild or native perennials.

Planting takes place in September/October, about 4 to 6 in (10–15 cm) deep, depending on the size of the bulb, and at distances of 6 to 8 in (15–20 cm) apart. If the bulbs are too late getting into the ground, flowers and foliage will not appear. Always plant bulbs in groups—separated according to class, variety, and color. Highly hybridized varieties are transplanted as soon as their foliage dies down. The bulbs

Crown imperial ☠ !
Fritillaria imperialis
(photo left)
Typical country garden plant. Flowers orange, brick red, or yellow; bells in whorls at the end of the stem, with a crown of leaves over it; Apr. Foliage narrow ovate, grass-green. Growth H: 24 to 39 in (60–99 cm), one stalk, stiffly upright. Location sunny, warm; porous, fresh, nourishing soil; avoid heavy soil or improve with sand. Z: 5–9.

Poet's narcissus ☠ !
Narcissus poeticus
(photo above)
Famed for their fragrance. Flowers petals white, bowl-shaped perianth, sometimes with a red edge; Apr.–May. Foliage narrow, blue- or gray-green. Growth H: 12 to 16 in (30–40 cm). Varieties "Actaea" old, proven variety with lemon-yellow, red-bordered, shallow perianth; "Recurvus" with yellow-red perianth; "Queen of Narcissi" with red perianth. Z: 3–9.

are removed after the yellowing and removal of the foliage, divided, and planted in a new spot.

Care. While the flowers are blooming in the spring, water during dry spells. After flowering and during the summer, watering is not necessary. Fertilize them when new growth appears and during or directly after flowering with an organic-mineral complete fertilizer (about 1 oz/10.75 sq ft [30 g/m²]).

Warning: The entire plant—also the bulb—contains a poisonous alkaloid. The slippery plant juice can lead to irritations of the skin.

N. cyclamineus *"Jack Snipe."*

N. cyclamineus *"February Gold."*

Double variety *"Unique."*

Dwarf narcissi ☠ !
Especially beautiful in naturalized plantings and rock gardens. <u>Flowers</u> very lush, long-lived; Feb.–Apr. <u>Foliage</u> narrow, fresh green. <u>Growth</u> H: 6 to 12 in (15–30 cm). <u>Location</u> sunny to semishady. <u>Varieties</u> "Jack Snipe" with narrow, white main corona and primrose-yellow perianth; "February Gold" with golden yel-

low main corona and somewhat darker perianth; "Thalia" with white flowers; "Peeping Tom" yellow flowers with very slender trumpets; "Tête á Tête" yellow and multiflowered; "Minnow" cream-white with yellow perianth; "Jet Fire" with yellow flowers and orange-red trumpets; "Tittle Tattle" light yellow, strong scent, multiflowered. Z: 3–9.

Double narcissi ☠ !
From trumpet narcissi. <u>Flowers</u> main corolla and perianth or just perianth may be doubled; one flower per stem, often bicolored; Apr.–May. <u>Foliage</u> narrow, gray-green. <u>Growth</u> H: 14 to 20 in (36–50 cm). <u>Varieties</u> "Unique" very large; "Rose of May" white, fragrant; "Tahiti" dark yellow-orange. Z: 3–9.

The most famous trumpet narcissus *"Golden Harvest."*

Large cupped—*"Gabriel Kleber."*

Small-cup variety *"Birma."*

Trumpet narcissi ☠ !
Yellow Easter bells are the personification of spring. <u>Flowers</u> long, trumpet-shaped perianths, edge usually ruffled; white, yellow, or bicolored; Apr. <u>Foliage</u> narrow, gray-green. <u>Growth</u> H: 16 to 20 in (40 to 50 cm). <u>Yellow varieties</u> "Golden Harvest" proven variety; "Dutch Master" flowers somewhat

upward-tilted; "Exception" and "Modoc" both very heavily flowering; "King Alfred" huge flowers. <u>White varieties</u> "Empress of Ireland" large flowered; "Cantatrice" pure white. <u>Bicolored</u> <u>varieties</u> "Bravoure" and "Magnet" with white petals and yellow trumpets; "Glenfarclas" petals yellow, trumpet orange. Z: 3–9.

Large-cupped ☠ ! narcissi
Ancestors are trumpet and poet's narcissi. <u>Flowers</u> perianth saucer shaped, often bicolored; Mar.–May. <u>Foliage</u> gray-green. Growth H: 14 to 20 in (36–50 cm). <u>Varieties</u> "Gabriel Kleber," white; "Ice Follies," white, yellow perianth; "Carlton" yellow; "Ceylon" yellow, orange perianth. Z: 3–9.

Small-cupped ☠ ! narcissi
Are also called flat-cup narcissi. <u>Flowers</u> usually bicolored, perianth plate shaped, very short; Mar.–May. <u>Foliage</u> blue- to gray-green. <u>Growth</u> H: 12 to 20 in (30–50 cm). <u>Varieties</u> "Birma" yellow, perianth brilliant orange; "Snow Crest" white, perianth greenish center. Z: 3–9.

Summer-flowering Bulbs

Even though most of the bulbs flower in the spring, there are still some attractive species and hybrids that provide flowering climaxes in the garden over the course of the gardening year. First among them are the lilies. The number of offerings has become inconceivably large. Besides the countless wild forms and their descendants, there is a wealth of hybrids that have been produced by various crossings. Wild forms are often quite demanding and also are bound to a certain location. But even among these are species that will thrive in the garden throughout the year such as the orange lily (*Lilium bulbiferum*), the Madonna lily (*L. candidum*), the David lily (*L. davidii*), the Japanese turk's-cap lily (*L. hansonii*), the turk's-cap lily (*L. martagon*), the regal lily (*L. regale*), and the tiger lily (*L. lancifolium*). The spectrum of colors contains all shades of white, yellow, pink, and red. The height of the plants, depending on species and variety, ranges from 16 in to 7 ft (40 cm–2 m). With careful planning, you can rejoice in lilies over the entire summer. The earliest flower in May/June, like the Madonna and orange lilies, but most in June/July/August. Late lilies such as the tiger lily, gold-banded lily (*L. auratum*), and showy lily (*L. speciosum*) bloom in August/September.

Lilies love sunny places but they have a dislike for hot, dry locations. In nature, they grow in a carpet of low perennials. This loose plant cover shades the soil and keeps it cool and damp. Some distance is maintained from larger shrubs and trees in order to avoid root pressure.

Planting is done in the fall; late-flowering species can be planted in the spring as well. An exception is the Madonna lily (*L.candidum*), which is planted in August. Lilies need a very well-cultivated, deep, and well-drained soil.

Therefore, before planting, it is best—depending on the type of soil—to lay a 0.5- to 2-in (1–5 cm) layer of sand or gravel for drainage; on top of that comes soil, and then the bulbs. Lily bulbs do not possess any protective skin; so they, therefore, may not be left out in the air for long. Take care when buying that the bulbs and the roots at the base of the bulb are not injured or shriveled. Lilies are fertilized as soon as they begin to appear with 2 oz (56 g) of chlorine-free complete fertilizer per 10 sq ft (1 m²), which is gently worked into the top layer of soil. In the fall, a layer of some 4 to 6 in (10–15 cm) of leaves or compost is laid down. Injury can be caused by mice, lily beetles, molds, bacteria, and viruses (see pages 190–193). Buy varieties that are as disease resistant as possible.
Warning: Lily bulbs are poisonous!

Flowers and seeds of the giant allium are good for cutting.

Allium
Allium giganteum
Attractive tall ornamental allium for perennial beds. Flowers red-violet large globular umbels, up to 8 in (20 cm) in diameter, singly on sturdy stems; June–July. Foliage strap-shaped, basal rosettes, blue-green, early yellowing. Growth H: 32 to 59 in (81–150 cm). Location sunny; dry to fresh and porous, warm soil.
Important: There are other allium species such as A. aflatuense, A. rosenbachianum, and A. christophii. The bulbs of all allium species are left undisturbed by shrews. Z: 4–9.

Desert-candles.

Camass.

Desert-candle
Eremurus stenophyllus
Striking plant. Flowers brilliant yellow-orange, small single flowers form long spikes; June–July. Foliage gray-green, strap shaped. Growth H: 39 to 79 in (99–201 cm). Location sun; warm; well drained soil, no sogginess, fertile. Z: 6–9.

Camass, Missouri hyacinth
Camassia leichtlinii (N.)
Striking plant with delicate look. Flowers violet-blue, also white, star-shaped single flowers form the inflorescence; Apr.–June. Foliage narrow, gray-green, rosette forming. Growth H: 28 to 32 in (70–81 cm). Location sun to semi-shade; damp, rich soil. Z: 7–9.

Madonna lily.

Orange lily.

Turk's-cap lily.

Japanese turk's-cap lily.

Madonna lily ☠
Lilium candidum

Wonderful traditional country garden flower. Flowers pure white, fragrant, trumpet shaped; June–July. Foliage light-green, dense leaf rosettes. Growth H: 32 to 47 in (81–120 cm). Location sun; warm, alkaline soil. Z: 4–9.
Important: Plant in August.

Orange lily ☠
Lilium bulbiferum

Flowers orange-red, saucer-shaped flowers facing upward, clusters at the end of the stem; May–July. Foliage glossy green, small, around the stem, bulblets in leaf axils. Growth H: 24 to 47 in (60–120 cm). Location sun. Z: 4–8.

Turk's-cap lily ☠
Lilium martagon

Flowers reddish, nodding; June–July. Foliage light green, narrow, whorled around stem. Growth H: up to 59 in (150 cm). Location semishady; humus, fresh, alkaline soil. Z: 4–8. Important: *L. martagon* var. *album* has larger, white flowers.

Japanese turk's-cap lily ☠
Lilium hansonii

Floriferous species. Flowers orange, speckled with brown, nodding, fragrant; June–Aug. Foliage dark green, broad, in whorls. Growth up to 47 in (120 cm). Location semishade, protect from frost. Z: 4–8. Important: Hybrid groups from *L. martagon* and *L. hansonii*.

Hybrid "Stargazer."

Regal lily.

Lily hybrid "La Reve."

Oriental lily ☠
"Stargazer"

Vigorous, fragrant garden lily. Flowers large saucers of extraordinary intense pink with dark spots, standing upright; July–Aug. Foliage oval, pointed, opposite. Growth H: 59 in (150 cm). Location sun to semishade; acid-humus, porous soil. Z: 5–8.

Regal lily ☠
Lilium regale

Captivatingly fragrant, robust lily. Flowers white inside, pink outside, trumpet shaped, yellowish throat; July–Aug. Foliage linear, situated around the stem. Growth H: 32 to 72 in (81–183 cm). Location sun to semishade; fresh to moist, also alkaline soil.

Important: All trumpet- and funnel-shaped lilies are strongly fragrant and can have narrow tube- shaped or large, saucer-shaped flowers. Their spring growth is at risk of late frosts. They should, therefore, be protected with branches. Z: 3–8.

Asiatic hybrids ☠
Lilium hybrids

They are the easiest to cultivate. Flowers white, yellow, orange, pink, red, saucer- or turk's-cap-shaped, from June. Foliage whorled. Growth H: 20 to 72 in (50–183 cm). Location sun to semishade. Z: 4–8.

Gladiolas and Dahlias

These corm plants are not winter hardy in most areas of the country; therefore, they are planted in late May and lifted again before the first frost. But the lush splendor of the flowers compensates anew every year for this trouble. Garden gladiolas (*Gladiolus* hybrids) exist in almost every color except blue, even bi- or more colors. They bloom from June to September and are divided into the following groups:

- large-flowered gladiolas with dense racemes of flowers, height 39 to 55 in (99–140 cm)
- butterfly gladiolas with small, multicolored flowers and wavy edges, height 20 to 32 in (50–81 cm)
- *primulinus* hybrids with hood-shaped flowers, height 20 to 32 in (50–81 cm)
- baby or *nanus* gladiolas, even somewhat more delicate in growth, with loose racemes, height about 20 in (50 cm).

Gladiolas want sun and well-drained soil and tolerate no sogginess. The corms are planted at the beginning of May about 4 in (10 cm) deep; tall varieties need a support. At the end of October, or before a hard frost, they are lifted again. The stems are cut back to 2 in (5 cm) and the corms are cleaned, dried, and stored in a place protected from frost.

Dahlias (*Dahlia* hybrids) can be planted in the same bed as gladiolas, which makes care easier. There are dahlias in the same color palette, and they bloom from June to the first frost. The dahlias are classified according to their flower forms:

- single-flowered varieties like the dwarf and mignon dahlias
- semidouble forms like the anemone and peony dahlias as well as the collared dahlias
- double-flowered varieties like the water lily, decorative, globe, pompon, cactus, and semicactus dahlias.

In each group, there are varieties with different heights: dwarf forms reaching only 8 in (20 cm) and vigorously growing ones over 39 in (1 m).

Dahlias also want sunny, well-drained soil and tolerate no sogginess. Before planting they can be propagated by division (see page 155). The corms are planted at the beginning of May; they are covered by about 2 in (5 cm) of soil. Dahlias need a lot of space; the shorter varieties 12 to 16 in (30 to 40 cm), the taller ones 20 to 24 in (50–61 cm). Tall varieties also need a support, which is best placed before planting in order to avoid injuring the corm. At the end of October, cut back the stems to about 2 in (4 to 5 cm) above the ground. Then pick out the corms with the spading fork and let them dry well for several days before you store them in a cool, dark place.

Gladiolas and dahlias can be very beautifully combined with annual summer flowers (see pages 262–265) and with tall ornamental grasses (see pages 270–271).

Garden gladiolus hybrid "Charme."

Garden gladiola
Gladiolus hybrids

Popular late-summer bloomer, especially well suited for cutting. Flowers all colors except pure blue shades, often with markings, with eyes or in several colors, flowering time dependent on variety; June–Sept (early, midseason, and late varieties), the individual flower is slanting/funnel shaped, with several individual flowers occurring in pairs on a long shaft. Foliage light green, sword shaped, standing vertical. Growth H: 20 to over 39 in (50 to over 99 cm), stiffly upright. Location sunny, warm; any good garden soil, optimal sandy-loamy. Perennial, Z: 7–10. Important: The larger the corm, the sturdier the flower stalk will be later.

Butterfly gladiolus.

Butterfly gladiola
Gladiolus hybrid

Flowers somewhat butterfly-like. Flowers multicolored with wavy edges. Foliage light green, sword shaped. Growth H: 32 to 39 in (81–99 cm). Location sunny, warm.

Important: Baby and primulinus gladiolas also belong to the newer small varieties.

Gladiolus hybrid "Jester."

Garden gladiola
"Jester"

Striking, late-flowering variety. Flowers yellow with red spot, large-flowered. Foliage light-green, sword-shaped, firmly placed on stalk, standing vertical. Growth H: over 39 in (100 cm), stiffly upright. Location sunny, warm; any good garden soil, optimal sandy-loamy.

"Fellbacher Gold."

"Bishop of Llandaff."

Collarette dahlia.

"Kaiser Wilhelm."

Single dahlia
Mignon dahlia

Dahlias of various different heights. <u>Flowers</u> usually a single color, single, rayed flowers wreathed around a yellow center. <u>Foliage</u> dark green, opposite, pinnatipartite. <u>Growth</u> H: 8 to 39 in (20–99 cm). <u>Varieties</u> "Fellbacher Gold" yellow, 16 in (40 cm); "Feuerrad" red, 39 in (99 cm).

Semidouble dahlias
Peony dahlias

Shallow, open flower faces. <u>Flowers</u> wreath of 2 to 3 circles of rayed flowers surrounding the involucre, medium size. <u>Foliage</u> dark green, pinnatipartite. <u>Growth</u> H: 24 to 47 in (60–120 cm). <u>Varieties</u> "Bishop of Llandaff" brilliant red, dark red leaves, bushy.

Semidouble dahlias
Collarette dahlia

Very striking dahlia. <u>Flowers</u> different circles of petals, inner circle smaller, differently colored and shaped, small flowers. <u>Foliage</u> dark green, pinnatipartite. <u>Growth</u> narrow upright. <u>Varieties</u> "Grand Duc" (yellow-orange flamed), "Libretto" (white and purple).

Double dahlia
Pompon dahlia

Like the ball dahlia, but more petite. <u>Flowers</u> closed and spherical, dainty flowers rolled into cornets, open at the ends; June–Oct. <u>Foliage</u> dark green, situated opposite on sturdy, hollow stems, pinnatipartite. <u>Growth</u> narrow upright.

Cactus dahlia with rolled petals.

Water lily-flowered dahlia.

Ornamental dahlia "Purple Joy."

Double dahlia
Cactus dahlia

Double-flowered dahlia with cornet-shaped rolled petals. <u>Flowers</u> all colors except for pure blues; flowering time depending on variety June–Oct; individual flowers situated on stems of differing length occurring at a leaf axil, strongly recurved quill-like flowers in the center, outside colored petals transforming to tongue or ray flowers, which are all that is visible in the very double dahlias. <u>Foliage</u> dark green, opposite on sturdy hollow stems, pinnatipartite. <u>Growth</u> H: around 39 in (99 cm), broadly bushy. <u>Important:</u> With semicactus dahlias the flowers are only partially rolled.

Double dahlia
Water lily-flowered dahlia

Reminiscent of water lilies. <u>Flowers</u> regularly arranged broad, spoon-shaped ray flowers in yellow-red or rose-purple; Jun–Oct., depending on variety. <u>Foliage</u> dark green, opposite on sturdy, hollow stems, pinnatipartite. <u>Growth</u> H: around 39 in (99 cm).

Double dahlia
Ornamental dahlia

Is also reckoned among the decorative dahlias. <u>Flowers</u> somewhat curved petals, all colors except for pure blue; June–Oct. depending on variety. <u>Foliage</u> dark green, opposite, pinnatipartite. <u>Growth</u> H: around 39 in (99 cm).

Zinnias (Zinnia elegans) come in many warm colors. They are very effective, especially in groups.

ANNUALS AND BIENNIALS

You can achieve the most lush glory of bloom with the short-lived flowers. When these are combined with bulbs and corms, you can have beds enchantingly in flower from April to October (early spring to fall) of every year with ever-changing displays. In the spring, the small flowering bulbs create sensations with the biennials. Later in the year, it is mainly the dahlias that, together with the annuals, create the garden high points. You can avoid the less happy combinations the next year by simply choosing other plants. The art consists in producing a continuing display of flowers and color and avoiding the so-called "June gap" as well as possible. With skillful planning, you can bridge this period with the aid of biennials as well as the perennials, bulbs, and roses that flower in early summer.

Annual summer flowers. This is the term for plants that grow within one season, flower, fruit, and form seeds, and then die.

Biennial summer flowers. Their sowing or self-seeding takes place during the summer. The young plants winter over and come into flower in the spring of the second year. But with these plants, too, the growing season takes place within 1 year. They are usually planted anew from seed every year, although some of them can occasionally last for 2 or 3 years. Then they are considered short-lived perennials.

Exotics. Also treated as annuals are perennials, half-shrubs, and woody plants from subtropical and tropical regions like the fuchsias (*Fuchsia* hybrids), which are not winter-hardy, or only partially so, with us. They must usually be grown anew each year from seed or cuttings.

Combination of red annuals. Love-lies-bleeding (Amaranthus caudatus), nicotiana (Nicotiana x sanderae), and groundsel (Senecio hybrid) come together here in an unusual ensemble.

Annuals

When the tulips finish flowering at the end of May, (spring) a change takes place in the garden: The spring flowers yield to the summer flowers; the bulbs die down or are moved to other quarters until fall.

Using annuals. Their variety produces the best effects in decorative beds, perhaps in the front yard, at the entrance, or near the house. But these aren't the only possibilities. Annuals let you:

• close existing holes that occur during the summer months when plants die back,

• create low bed enclosures,

• bring movement and rhythm into a planting with taller annuals,

• span periods with little show of bloom and extend the flowering season until frost,

• lend color to vegetable gardens (see pages 116–117),

• create cutting gardens,

• close the holes between still-small perennials and shrubs in newly planted areas.

• You can even augment natural plantings with appropriate annual flowers: for dry rock gardens and gravel beds, the sun-loving icicle plants (*Mesembranthemum*), gazenias (*Gazania* hybrids), cape marigolds (*Dimorphotheca sinuata*), rose moss (*Portulaca grandiflora*), or California poppy (*Eschscholzia californica*) are good. For shady areas there are only a few possibilities: fuchsias (*Fuchsia* hybrids), tuberous-rooted begonias (*Begonia* tuberous hybrids) and busy Lizzy (*Impatiens* hybrids).

General design rules. When dealing with annuals, it's important to establish a plant and color concept—whether it is a matter of a particular ornamental bed or of annuals that are to be integrated into an already existing planting. The same guidelines apply as for planting perennials (see pages 74–77). Growth height, form, and color must be coordinated to create a harmonious display. Large groups of one variety achieve a stronger color effect. But even prettier than the massed look is the overlapping and interflowing of forms and colors. Make sure that there is no hard distinction between the individual groups. You can also place very tall plants or grasses above low plantings. This profusion of varieties and multiplicity of forms side-by-side and rising one above the other is what constitutes the interest in a colorful planting of annuals.

However, so-called *millefleurs* plantings are also enchanting: Low, medium, and tall plants combined singly with one another—with colors finely tuned—creating a scattered-flower effect. This is a pretty idea for small areas and ribbon-shaped borders.

African marigolds !
Tagetes erecta hybrids

(see yellow flowers, photo above)
Vigorous, undemanding annuals with numerous species, varieties, and hybrids, one of the most diverse genera in wealth of forms. Flowers lemon yellow, golden yellow, orange, red-brown involucre, sometimes semidouble or double, strong smell; June–Oct. Foliage dark green, pinnate, unusually strongly scented. Growth H: 6 to 47 in (15–120 cm), nestlike, broad. Location sunny, warm; damp to moderately dry soil. Species and hybrids *T. patula* hybrids (French marigolds) are the most widespread marigolds, H: 8 to 20 in (20–50 cm). *T. tenuifolia* (signet marigolds) are very petite, with single flowers, H: 8 to 12 in (20–30 cm). *T. erecta* hybrids have the largest flowers. **Warning:** Plants can produce skin irritations.

Groundsel, Dusty-miller ☠
Senecio bicolor

(see silver-leaved plants, photo above)
Silver-gray ornamental leaves, forms beautiful contrast to colorful bedding plants, biennial, not winter-hardy. Flowers yellow, small flower heads, do not appear with culture as annual, only in second year with frost-free wintering over; July–Sept. Foliage silver-gray, tomentose, deeply lobed or laciniate. Growth H: 8 to 12 in (20–30 cm), bushy. Location sunny, warm, protected from rain; sandy, porous, moderately moist to dry soil. Varieties "Cirrus" has roundish, silvery leaves, H: 10 in (25 cm); "Silberzwerg" with delicate cut leaves, H: 6 to 8 in (15–20 cm). Important: Watch out for mildew, rust, and aphids. **Warning:** Plant contains poisonous alkaloids.

Mexican sunflower.

Sunflower.

Mexican sunflower
Tithonia rotundifolia

Tall annual, healthy and easy to care for, also as lead plant in perennial bed, still little known. <u>Flowers</u> orange to orange-red, yellow-orange in the center, daisy-like, strong stem; Aug–Sept. <u>Foliage</u> large, heart shaped, dull green, and rough. <u>Growth</u> H: 47 to 71 in (120–180 cm), upright, bushy clumps. <u>Location</u> sunny; rich, loose, fresh soil, not too sandy. <u>Varieties</u> "Fackel" is strong orange-red, support in early stages promotes branching. <u>Important:</u> Goes well with calendulas, marigolds, rudbeckias, and verbena.

Sunflower
Helianthus annuus (N.)

Familiar and widespread. <u>Flowers</u> yellow with brown centers, strong stem; July–Oct. <u>Foliage</u> dark green, rough, large pointed oval. <u>Growth</u> H: 16 to 99 in (40–251 cm), upright, not always stable. <u>Location</u> sunny, warm; moderately dry to fresh, rich, loose soil.

Orange cosmos.

Pot marigold.

Zinnia.

Black-eyed Susan "Marmalade."

Orange cosmos
Cosmos sulphureus

Rare beauty. <u>Flowers</u> orange, golden yellow, large saucer shaped daisy-like; July–Oct. <u>Foliage</u> fresh green, simply pinnate. <u>Growth</u> H: 16 to 28 in (40 to 70 cm), broadly bushy. <u>Location</u> sunny, warm; dry to moist, loose, rich soil.

Pot marigold
Calendula officinalis

Ornamental and medicinal plant. <u>Flowers</u> light to golden yellow, orange, daisy flowered, sometimes double or semidouble; May–Sept. <u>Foliage</u> fresh green, rough, oblong. <u>Growth</u> H: 12 to 28 in (30–70 cm), upright, spreading in clumps. <u>Location</u> sunny, warm; fresh, rich, loose soil.

Zinnia
Zinnia elegans

Many different forms. <u>Flowers</u> white, yellow, orange, salmon, pink, red, double or semidouble, depending on variety diameter from 0.5 to about 3 in (1–8 cm); July–Oct. <u>Foliage</u> grass green, ovate. <u>Growth</u> H: 6 to 39 in (15–99 cm). <u>Location</u> sunny, warm; fresh to moist soil.

Black-eyed Susan
Rudbeckia hirta (N.)

Long flowering. <u>Flowers</u> sunflower-like, yellow to orange with dark brown centers; July–Sept. <u>Foliage</u> dull green, hairy, lanceolate to narrow, toothed edges. <u>Growth</u> H: 16 to 32 in (40–81 cm), upright, clumping. <u>Location</u> sunny, warm; slightly moist, rich soil. Short-lived perennial, annual.

Annuals

Annuals are usually easy to grow from seed, although you can get many of them from garden centers as young plants, starting at the end of spring. If you are intending to grow your own, you should consider ahead of time how much space you have available and what facilities you have for raising the plants.

Early starting on the windowsill or under glass has the advantage that sturdy little plants can be ready at planting time after the last danger of frost has passed so that they will come into flower sooner. You can have a great deal of pleasure and save money while doing it.

• Sowing takes place in pots, flats (see pages 152–153), or directly into the cold frame. As soon as the first leaves have formed, the seedlings are pricked out singly or in small groups into a container. The young plants must be hardened off before they are placed outdoors. Therefore, provide for sufficient fresh air and light.

• All frost-sensitive plants—and this includes most annuals—are only planted outdoors after all danger of frost has passed (See Frost Map, back inside cover).

• Annuals should be located in as sunny, warm, and protected spots as possible. This guarantees abundant bloom later. The soil preparation corresponds to that for perennials (see pages 180–181).

• The planting distance depends on the size and vigor of the plants, which again are also dependent on the conditions of the soil and cultivation.

• Before planting, you should mark the surface; then you have a chance to correct the placement when you set out the plants (see pages 180–181).

Direct sowing in the garden is recommended when you need a great many plants. The right time is usually in mid- to late spring (see instructions on the seed packet). You can broadcast the seeds or sow them in rows. When the little plants are about 1 in (2.5 cm) tall, the planting must be thinned. After plants are a few inches tall, apply a complete fertilizer (formulations vary) and work into the top soil layer along with cultivation and weeding. Depending on the weather, the plants must also be watered.

With direct sowing, you can form groups, as in a planting. It's best if you mark the areas beforehand with a stick or sand. Then sow the various kinds of seeds according to your plan and label the areas.

Care. Besides watering, cultivating, and fertilizing, the most important thing is to remove the spent flowers regularly in order to prevent setting of seed. Don't be shy about cutting flowers for the house. Cutting spurs the plants to form new flower buds.

The cosmos develops silky-shimmering saucers of flowers.

Cosmos
Cosmos bipinnatus
Classic annual flowers with fine, decorative foliage; the white varieties go with almost all annuals and perennials; good cut flower. Flowers white, pink, crimson, yellow stamens in center, saucer shaped, composite; June–Oct. Foliage bright green, double pinnate, narrow. Growth H: 32 to 55 in (81–140 cm), upright, broadly bushy. Location sunny, warm; fresh, rich soil. Varieties "Carminkönig" crimson, H: 39 in (99 cm); "Unschuld" pure white, H: 39 in (99 cm); "Gloria" pink with crimson edge, H: 35 in (90 cm). "Sensation Mix" pink, rose, and crimson, H: 48 in (123 cm).

Mealy-cup sage.

Tall nicotiana.

Mealy-cup sage
Salvia farinacea (N.)
Undemanding annual. Flowers dark blue, labiate in dense spikes; June–Oct. Foliage grass green with gray down, lanceolate. Growth H: 20 to 32 in (50–81 cm), upright, branching clumps. Location sunny; fresh, loose, rich soil. Perennial treated as an annual in northern areas.

Nicotiana ☠
Nicotiana sylvestris
Very decorative. Flowers white, yellow, or crimson, tube shaped; July–Sept. Foliage fresh green, large, ovate. Growth H: 39 to 59 in (99–150 cm), nestlike. Location sunny, warm; fresh, rich, loose soil. Important: Popular in containers *Nicotiana* x *sanderae*.

Snapdragons.

Spider plant.

Common snapdragon
Antirrhinum majus
Popular garden flower. Flowers pink, red, yellow, salmon, orange, white, dense in candle-like inflorescences, large-throated flowers, June–Oct. Foliage fresh green, narrow ovate. Growth H: 8 to 39 in (20–99 cm), upright, bushy. Location sunny; fresh, rich, loose soil.

Spider plant
Cleome spinosa
Tall, filigreed, and unique. Flowers white, pink, crimson, needle-shaped prominent stamens in terminal racemes; July–Oct. Foliage dark green, 5- to 7-lobed. Growth H: 32 to 55 in (81–140 cm), upright. Location sunny, warm; humus soil.

Vervain.

Rose mallow.

Vervain
Verbena bonariensis
Loosely vigorous. Flowers blue to delicate violet, small umbels; July–Oct. Foliage dark green. Growth H: 32 to 47 in (81–120 cm), branching with spurs. Location sunny, warm; fresh soil. Important: Best placed in groups to rise above lower flowers in beds.

Rose mallow
Hibiscus moscheutos
Lushly blooming. Flowers pink, white, crimson, dark veined, trumpet-shaped saucers; July–Sept. Foliage dark green, heart shaped, rough. Growth H: 20 to 32 in (50–81 cm), upright, broadly bushy. Location sunny, warm; fresh, loose, porous, moderately rich soil.

Annual Summer Flowers

California poppy ☠
Eschscholzia californica (N.)
Abundantly flowering; flowers yellow, orange, pink, red, June–Oct.; growth H: up to 16 in; location sunny, warm.

Edging lobelia
Lobelia erinus
Cushion; flowers blue, violet, pink, white, small, May–Sept.; growth H: 4 to 8 in; location sunny.

Sweet alyssum
Lobularia maritima
Cushion; flowers white, pink, violet, June–Sept.; growth H: 2 to 6 in; location sunny.

Love-in-a-mist
Nigella damascena
Country garden plant; flowers white, blue, pink, June–Sept., balloonlike, spurred fruits; growth H: 16 to 20 in; location sunny.

Castor bean ☠
Ricinus communis
Shrublike; flowers red, male and female flowers separate, Sept.; Growth H: 7 to 10 ft; location sunny.

Texas or Scarlet salvia
Salvia coccinea
Scarlet labiate flowers, June–Sept.; growth H: 16 to 24 in; location sunny, warm.

Salvia; *Salvia viridis*
Ornamental-leaved plant; flowers insignificant, bracts blue, pink, or white; growth H: 16 in; location sunny.

Scarlet salvia
Salvia splendens
Classic for beds; fire red labiate flowers, June–Sept.; growth H: 8 to 20 in; location sunny, warm; fresh soil.

Vervain; *Verbena rigida*
Natural looking, winters over where seasons are mild; flowers lavender, small; growth H: 8 to 16 in; location sunny, warm. Z: 7–11.

Annual Climbing Plants

Mexican ivy; *Cobaea scandens*
Twining plant; flowers lavender-blue or white, bell shaped, Aug.–Oct.; H: 13 to 20 ft; location sunny to semishady, warm.

Glory flower
Eccremocarpus scaber
Fast-growing, twining; orange-red tubular flowers, July–Oct.; H: 5 to 13 ft; location sunny, protect from wind and rain.

Japanese hop
Humulus japonicus
Vigorous climber with decorative foliage; flowers insignificant, yellow-green, July–Oct.; H: 13 to 16 ft; location sunny to shady.

Morning-glory ☠
Ipomoea tricolor
Climbing plant; flowers depending on variety white, rose, blue; July–Oct.; H: up to 10 ft; location sunny, somewhat protected.

Sweet pea ☠
Lathyrus odoratus
Fragrant twining plant; flowers different according to variety, June–Sept.; H: 3 to 10 ft; location sunny. Before sowing, soak seeds in water overnight.

Scarlet runner bean ☠
Phaseolus coccineus
Undemanding twiner; flowers red or white, June–Sept.; H: 10 to 13 ft; location sunny to semishady. Important: Harvest beans as young as possible, or they become woody-stringy.

Black-eyed Susan vine
Thunbergia alata
Twining plant; flowers orange or white, depending on variety, with black eye, June–Oct.; H: 3 to 7 ft; location sunny.

Canary-bird vine
Tropaeolum peregrinum
Vigorous climber; flowers yellow, fringed, July–Oct.; H: 3 to 10 ft; location sunny, care only moderate fertilizing.

Biennials

Biennials, with their long period of bloom, are the ideal partners for spring-flowering bulbs: pansies (*Viola wittrockiana* hybrids) often flower from the fall, only interrupted by periods of frost, until the summer. There are only very few genera that come into consideration here, even with the inclusion of English daisies (*Bellis perennis*), forget-me-nots (*Myosotis sylvatica*), English primroses (*Primula vulgaris*), English wallflowers (*Cheiranthus cheiri*), and wallflowers (*Erysimum* x *allionii*). However, the large number of varieties permit innumerable variations.

The late-flowering biennials help to bridge the time between spring and summer flowers. They, thus, enter into a close partnership with the early-summer perennials and the complete the picture of a lushly flowering country garden (see pages 136–137). Examples of this are the hollyhocks (*Alcea rosea* hybrids), Canterbury bells (*Campanula medium*), and sweet Williams (*Dianthus barbatus*).

Once planted, many of these biennials re-seed themselves in the same spot, like the forget-me-not (*M. sylvaticus*), and, thus, provide for abundant offspring. Very natural-looking garden pictures develop in this fashion. Self-sown young plants should, however, be transplanted to other spots in the garden—best in the fall.

Overwintering of tender varieties of pansies (*V. wittrockiana* hybrids) and English daisies (*B. perennis*) can be facilitated in exposed situations with pine branches. The plants benefit from an application of complete fertilizer early in the spring.

Often pansies and English daisies can also be bought and planted in the fall with the bulbs. This is the only way to create a harmony of colors. Forget-me-nots don't begin flowering until May, but then they provide pretty combinations with late tulips.

However, you should proceed cautiously with the gay colors of the early cushion primulas if you plant them with intensely colored spring bulbs. English wallflowers (*Cheiranthus cheiri*) and wallflowers (*Erysimum* x *allionii*) are also suitable as clumps between shorter flowers and bulbs.

Canterbury bells.   *Hollyhock.*

Canterbury bells
Campanula medium
Large bell flowers. Flowers blue, pink, white, semidouble, in racemes; May–July. Foliage dull green, ovate. Growth H: 20 to 28 in (50–70 cm), leaf rosettes first year, upright inflorescence second year. Location sunny, warm; fresh, rich, loose soil. Z: 4–8.

Hollyhock
Alcea rosea
Country garden plant. Flowers white, yellow, pink, dark crimson, saucer shaped; July–Sept. Foliage flat green, textured, roundish, petiolate. Growth H: 24 to 87 in (60–220 cm), upright. Location sunny, warm; porous, nutrient-rich soil. Z: 3–9. Important: Fertilize well.

Sweet Williams flower for a long time and have a delicate fragrance.

Sweet William
Dianthus barbatus
Wonderfully colored, velvety shimmering flowers, country garden plants, also useful as cut flower. Flowers salmon to crimson, pink white, sometimes bicolored with white, densely packed in umbrella-like inflorescences; May–Aug. Foliage dark green, lanceolate. Growth H: 20 to 24 in (50–61cm), leaf rosette first year, clump second year, upright. Location sunny; moderately dry to fresh, porous, rich soil. Z: 4–9. Varieties "Albus" white; "Pink Beauty" pink; "Heimatland" red with white center; "Atrosanguineus" dark crimson
Important: Nice plant for front of borders.

English daisies with double, dainty little flower heads.

Pansies come in countless color combinations.

English daisies
Bellis perennis

Cultivated form of the daisy, flowering until early summer. Flowers white, pink, crimson to scarlet red, sometimes doubled into pompon, on short stems; Mar.–May. Foliage fresh-green, spatulate. Growth H: 6 to 8 in (15–20 cm), compact leaf rosettes. Location sunny to semishady; fresh to moist, nutrient-rich, loose soil. Varieties "Pomponette Weiss" white, and "Pomponette Rot" red, with long stems, also for cutting. Z: 3–7.

Pansies
Viola x wittrockiana hybrids

Widely distributed, robust spring bloomer with cheerful colors. Flowers all colors, sometimes with markings in second color, asymmetrical petals, large flowers; Mar.–May. Foliage grass green, ovate, crenated. Growth H: 6 to 10 in (15–25 cm), bushy, spreading. Location sunny to semishady; fresh to damp, loose, humus, rich soil. Varieties gigantic assortment, with new varieties coming to market every year. Important: Always plant in groups, cover with pine branches for winter protection. Most often grown as an annual.

Honesty.

Forget-me-nots with their adorable flowers.

Dame's rocket.

Honesty
Lunaria annua

Decorative seed pods. Flowers deep violet, white, 4-petaled, fragrant; Apr.–June, from Sept. silvery round seed pods. Foliage dark green, ovate, toothed. Growth H: 24 to 32 in (60–81 cm), single stemmed, upright. Location sunny to shady; fresh, porous soil. Grown as an annual Z: 3–11; perennial Z: 6–9.

Forget-me-not
Myosotis sylvatica

Ideal for beds that are cleared after spring blooming and must be replanted. Flowers brilliant blue to sky blue with yellowish or yellow-orange eyes, small flowers in dense, terminal, curved racemes; Apr.–June. Foliage dull-green, hairy, lanceolate. Growth H: 6 to 12 in (15–30 cm), bushy, spreading. Location sunny; moist, nutrient-rich, loose, well-drained humusy soil. Varieties "Amethyst" sky blue, H: 6 in (15 cm); "Indigo Compacta" intense blue, H: 12 in (30 cm). Important: Water in dry spells, even in winter; protect from frost with branches or straw. Z: 4–8.

Dame's rocket
Hesperis matronalis

Usually only biennial, wild perennial. Flowers whitish pink to violet, in dense racemes, fragrant; May–June. Foliage bright green, heart shaped. Growth H: 24 to 39 (60–99 cm), upright, branching. Location semishady to shady, warm; fresh, rich, chalky soil. Z: 3–9.

Fern fronds, with their geometric structures, are small works of graphic art.

GRASSES AND FERNS

Changes in garden design, with the trend toward getting closer to nature, have resulted in more attention to the grasses and ferns. The early proponent for this idea was Karl Foerster, the renowned perennial breeder and garden writer, who spoke out for their use in his book, *Introduction of Grasses and Ferns in the Garden* (*Einzug der Gräser und Farne in die Gärten*), published in 1957. He also called grass "the hair of Mother Earth" and at that time regretted that it mainly appeared in the garden in a shorn state. Now, fortunately, that has changed.
Grasses and ferns are not related to each other botanically, but both are used because of their attractive foliage:

• The flowers on grasses are inconspicuous or not showy. They form interesting clumps that look very elegant and graphic. Many take on very striking color in the fall.

• Ferns develop no flowers but have beautifully formed leaf fronds. Ferns only feel at home in the shady parts of the garden, where life for flowering plants is often difficult. In addition, there are shade-tolerant grasses, some of which are green in winter, which create a good effect when placed with ferns.

In the first place, grasses and ferns add to the natural character of a planting and the grasses, especially, create wonderful contrasts to lush arrays of flowers of the showy perennials, roses, and annuals and biennials. In the second place, grasses and ferns are ideal partners for wild perennials in natural areas.

Grass ensemble in widely varying shades of green, with dainty or stately clumps and often with feathery inflorescences.

Grasses

Grasses belong to the monocotyledonous plants and possess hollow, jointed, round stems, which are also called grass stalks. The elongated leaf blades firmly enclose the stem. The flowers are inconspicuous. They need not lure insects because they are pollinated by the wind. Grasses create effects with their form: Their clumps can be dwarf-size all the way up to gigantic, with the stalks and blades looking dainty to very compact. The species used in most gardens are usually perennials. However, there are also some annuals that can be combined very well with annual and biennial flowers (see pages 262–265).

Grasses for all occasions. There is a suitable grass for every location and every type of garden. But many grasses are so robust that they thrive in the most difficult places.

• Short and medium-tall grasses are suitable for dry locations, for edges of paths, and for interplanting in rock gardens, pebble beds, and heath gardens. These are mainly fescue species (*Festuca gautieri*, see photo) in shades of green, gray, and blue. They also go very well with roses and small shrubs, as does the somewhat taller blue oat grass (see table). Medium-tall grasses like fountain grass (*Pennisetum alopecuroides*, see photo) create a beautiful transition from low to tall plants. Delicate feather grasses like *Stipa barbata* (see table) go well in heath gardens and dry areas.

• Tall grasses like feather reed grass (see photo), switch grass (see table), and eulalia (*Miscanthus sinensis*)(see photo) are ideal green companions for showy perennials and are best suited for creating structure in the planting. Interestingly colored forms like the zebra eulalia (*Miscanthus sinensis* "Zebrinus") do well as specimen plantings. Taller winter green bamboos like *Sinarundinaria nitida* can replace a shrub.

• Shade grasses also thrive in front of or underneath trees and shrubs. The plantain sedge (*Carex plantaginea*) and the nodding melic grass (*Melica nutans*) function as ground covers. Tall grasses like *Carex pendula* (see table), ferns, and wild perennials are suitable for loosening up plantings.

• Sedges, rushes, and reed grasses as well as reed species mainly grow in and around water.

Dealing with grasses. Some grasses like the dwarf bamboos (*Pleioblastus pumilus*) have the habit of growing extremely vigorously to the point of being invasive. In small spaces, sucker-producing bamboos should be provided with a curb in the root region. To do this, line the planting hole with a thick, firm plastic mat so that the rhizomes of the bamboo can't find their way through it. Grasses are best planted and propagated (divided) in the spring (April to May). The dried, dead grass clumps are also only cut back at this time.

Blue fescue, here the variety "Pic Carlit,"grows like a lawn.

Blue fescue
Festuca gautieri

Low grass that forms dense cushions and can also spread sideways. Flowers yellow-brown, narrow, slightly arching panicles; July–Aug., H: 10 in (25 cm). Foliage lush green, filamentous, somewhat sharp, evergreen, H: 4 to 6 in (10–15 cm).

Growth flat, dense cushions, lawnlike. Location sun to semishade; moderately dry to fresh soil, porous, humusy, nutrient poor. Varieties "Pic Carlit" is a selection from a natural location that forms a particularly compact, dark green cushion; the blades are sharp.

Perennial Grasses

Mosquito grass
Bouteloua gracilis (N.)
Brown ears, July, H: 20 in (50 cm); foliage brown-green, arching, H: 8 in; location sunny, warm. Z: 5–9.

Quaking grass; *Briza media*
Violet ears, May–June, H: 16 to 24 in; foliage fresh green, H: 8 to 12 in; location sunny to semishady. Z: 5–9.

Sedge grass
Carex pendula (N.)
Evergreen; green-yellow ears, June–July, H: up to 47 in; foliage lush green, H: up to 36 in; location sunny to shady. Z: 5–9.

Tufted hair grass
Deschampsia caespitosa (N.)
Noninvasive; green-yellow panicles, June–July, H: 28 to 47 in; foliage green, arching, H: 8 to 36 in; location sunny to semishady, moist. Z: 5–9.

Blue oat grass
Helictotrichon sempervirens
Evergreen; flowers golden yellow, July–Aug., H: up to 47 in; foliage blue-green, H: 20 in; location sunny, no sogginess. Z: 4–9.

Greater wood rush
Luzula sylvatica
Wintergreen, offsets; beige panicles, Apr.–July, H: 16 in; foliage dark green, H: 8 to 12 in; location semishady to shady, humid. Z: 5–9.

Switch grass
Panicum virgatum
Brown panicles, July–Oct., H: up to 63 in; foliage grass green, yellow-red in fall, H: up to 47 in; location sunny. Z: 5–9.

Pheasant, Feather grass
Stipa barbata
Silvery ears, feathery awns up to 16 in, July; foliage gray-green, H: 12 to 16 in; location sunny, warm. Z: 5–11.

Fountain grass "Hameln."

Japanese sedge grass "Variegata."

Fountain grass
Pennisetum alopecuroides
Ornamental grass with decorative arrangement of fruits on the axis and many varieties; remains very attractive throughout the entire winter. Flowers light brown to red brown, cylindrical, terminal ears; Aug–Sept., dense, long awns on the individual flowers, H: 20 to 35 in (50–90 cm). Foliage sturdy green, narrow linear, arching, H: 16 in (40 cm), in fall golden yellow. Growth broad, clumping. Location sunny, warm; moderately dry to moist humus soil. Z: 6–9. Varieties "Hameln" (H: 24 in [60 cm]) blooms earlier and very lushly. All varieties go well with fall-flowering perennials like asters and chrysanthemums.

Japanese sedge grass
Carex morrowii
Wintergreen sedge for underplanting shrubs and trees. Flowers short, yellow ears; Apr. H: 16 in (40 cm). Foliage stiff, broad, pointed, arching, dark green, narrow white stripes on the blade edge, H: 12 in (30 cm). Growth low, very dense, widely spreading clumps. Location semishade to shade, moderately warm to cool; moist soil, humusy, avoid sogginess and dryness. Z: 5–9.

Pampas grass.

Moor grass.

Feather reed grass "Karl Foerster."

Japanese silver grass "Kleine Fontäne."

Pampas grass
Cortaderia selloana
Popular specimen grass. Flowers silver-white panicles; Sept.–Oct. H: up to 99 in (251 cm). Foliage gray-green, linear, arching; H: up to 59 in (150 cm). Growth clumping. Location sunny, no sogginess. Z: 8–10. Important: Tie the crown together and cover with leaves for the winter.

Tall purple moor grass
Molinia cacrula ssp. arundinacea
Decorative clumps. Flowers brown, finely sectioned, branched panicles; Aug. H: 71 in (180 cm), yellow in fall. Foliage linear, slightly overhanging, green, yellowish in fall, H: 20 in (50 cm). Growth clumping, loose. Location sun to semishade; fresh soil.

Feather grass
Calamagrostis x acutiflora
Rewarding ornamental grass. Flowers cream-colored, loose panicles, July–Aug., later beige; H: up to 71 in (180 cm). Foliage narrow linear, new growth early, H: 24 to 28 in (60–70 cm). Growth clumping, not vigorous. Location sun to semishade; soil partly dry to moist. Z: 5–9.

Japanese silver grass
Miscanthus sinensis
Clumping grass, many varieties. Flowers silvery or reddish to brown, feathery panicles; July; H: 39 to 79 in (99–201 cm). Foliage linear, showy, arching, H: 35 to 79 in (90 –201 cm), yellow to brown fall coloring. Growth upright. Location sunny; moderately dry. Z: 5–9.

Ferns

Ferns are often called "living fossils," for their relatives are among the oldest land plants—they developed long before flowering plants. The ferns in existence today are the remnants of a plant group of which many species became extinct 300 million years ago and only are preserved still as fossils.

In contrast to almost all other garden plants, the ferns have no flowers and also form no seeds. Spores and a complicated alteration of generations (metagenesis) take over the task of propagation. The brown spore cases are located on the tops or undersides of the fern leaves or a special, leaflike fruit stalk. The leaves of the fern, which arise from the center of the plant, are termed fronds. Their variety in size, form, and color makes them popular objects for collectors. The charm of the fern also lies in the unusual way it unfolds its fronds: At first, they are curled up like snails; then they unroll slowly from underneath to the end. Many ferns look especially interesting in this stage, such as the male fern (*Dryopteris filix-mas*) or the royal fern (*Osmunda regalis* "Purpurascens"), whose fronds are reddish when they are young. When ferns are fully developed, their form can be impressive: They can grow widespread, fan- or funnel-shaped. Some also develop dense, jungle-like stands. The colors change from delicate, bright spring green to fresh summer green to yellow and brown fall colors or deep winter green. Among the evergreen ferns are the Japanese shield fern (*Dryopteris erythrosora*) and the European polypody (*Polypodium vulgare*). However, they only thrive in places that are also protected from the sun in winter.

Most garden ferns grow in the company of trees and shrubs in their natural habitat and often in the vicinity of water. Therefore, they also love rather shady, damp places in the garden and a humus soil and, thus, they find outstanding conditions in older gardens with well-established shrubbery and tall, shadow-casting deciduous trees. To display ferns to the best advantage, use them primarily as partners for shade-tolerant wild perennials (see pages 246–247), but small bulbs (see pages 250–251) and narcissi (see pages 254–255) are also good neighbors in spring.

A popular combination is of tall, finely segmented ferns like *Polystichum setiferum* (see photo) with Japanese anemones and astilbes under deciduous trees. However, not every fern can cope with the root strength of large trees—an exception is the ostrich fern (see photo), which proliferates vigorously and soon overruns such locations. Because ferns are at home in the woods, you can let the fallen leaves lie on them without any worries. They are also grateful for an occasional application of leaf compost. Ferns tolerate dryness poorly, but there is no rule without its exception: The charming little evergreen rusty-back fern (*Ceterach officinarum*) even grows in sunny crevices of walls.

Regal fern
Osmunda regalis
(see photo above)
Long-lived, native fern, under environmental protection as wild plant. <u>Foliage</u> light to yellow-green, bipinnate, leatherlike, sturdy fronds, arranged in funnel shape toward outside, golden brown spore frond stiffly upright in the center; beautiful fall color.

<u>Growth</u> H: 4 to 7 ft (1.2–2 m), S: up to 10 ft (3 m) in optimal location, clumping, slow growing. <u>Location</u> semishady to shady, in damp location also sunny, humid; moist, or soggy soil, loose, humus, preferably acid. Z: 3–9.
<u>Important:</u> Particularly effective on most pond and brook banks.

In general, ferns are in the right place if it is where they might have appeared naturally and natively—and even if it is only a small spot at the foot of the wall or a tree. They never belong in ornamental borders.

Northern maidenhair or five-finger fern.

Bulblet bladder fern.

Northern maidenhair fern
Adiantum pedatum (N.)
Also called five-fingers fern. Foliage light green, palmate, pinnulate fronds, on wiry stems, golden yellow fall coloring. Growth H: 16 to 24 in (40–60 cm), broad clumps, weakly spreading. Location semishady to shady, cool, humid; fresh to moist, porous, humus soil.

Varieties "Imbricatum" (dwarf maidenhair fern) grows only 8 in (20 cm) high and has bluish green foliage. The evergreen maidenhair fern (*Adiantum venustum*) has finely divided fronds that arch over elegantly and are wintergreen. H: 10 in (25 cm) Z: 3–8.
Important: Cover with branches; fern is at risk of late frosts.

Bulblet bladder fern
Cystopteris bulbifera (N.)
Suckering. Foliage light green, slender, pinnate, stems and ribs reddish, pea-sized bulblets on undersides of upper fronds that drop off in the fall and quickly spread. Growth H: 16 to 20 in (40–50 cm), clumping. Location semishady, moderately damp. Z: 3–7.

Ostrich fern.

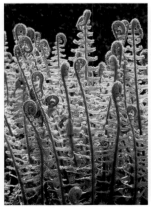

Golden-scaled male fern.

Hart's-tongue fern.

Soft shield fern.

Ostrich fern
Matteuccia struthiopteris (N.)
Impressive fern, but only for large areas, because it spreads by suckers. Foliage bright green, bipinnate, spore-bearing frond olive green, later light brown. Growth H: 2.5 to 3 ft (0.8–0.9 m), funnel shaped. Location semishady, cool, humid; humus soil. Z: 2–8.

Golden-scaled male fern
Dryopteris affinis
Wintergreen. Foliage golden brown when new, then dark green, dully glossy, leatherlike, pinnate, S: 8 in (20 cm), stems densely scaled with golden brown. Growth H: up to 3 ft (0.9 m), funnel shaped. Location semishady to shady, plants love evening or morning sun. Z: 4–8.

Hart's-tongue fern
Phyllitis scolopendrium (*Asplenium*) (N.)
Wintergreen, many varieties. Foliage shining green, tongue shaped, undivided, leathery, wavy edges, strong middle rib. Growth H: 12 to 20 in (30–50 cm), broadly clumping. Location shady, cool, humid, protected from wind; lime-tolerant. Z: 4–8.

Soft shield fern
Polystichum setiferum (N.)
Wintergreen, many varieites. Foliage delicate green, large, bipinnate, finely divided, loosely arching. Growth H: 1.5 to 3 ft (0.5–0.9 m), S: 2 to 4 ft (0.6–1.2 m), arching. Location semishady to shady, cool, humid. Varieties "Proliferum," "Dahlem," and "Herrenhausen." Z: 5–8.

Animals soon establish themselves
in even a small garden pond.

WATER AND MARSH PLANTS

For planting areas around ponds and stream banks, only plants that are naturally adapted for these environments can be considered. This group also includes many species plants that have not been manipulated by the hybridizers. Many natural wetlands plants are protected by law from being dug up in the wild; however, there are numerous other species from new crossings to be had in the garden trade. They are divided into the following three groups according to their requirements:

<u>Plants for the riverbank.</u> They live in damp to wet soil but do not depend on constant moisture, such as the globeflower (*Trollius europaeus*) and the purple loosestrife (*Lythrum salicaria*).

Note: In the United States, *Lythrum* has been banned for planting in wetlands; It becomes too invasive and chokes out other vegetation.

<u>Plants for marsh and shallow water areas.</u> They need constant "wet feet" and settle in areas with a water level of up to about 6 in (15 cm). Here many attractive plants are comfortable, such as the yellow flag (*Iris pseudacorus*), the cattail (*Typha* species), and the cowslip (*Caltha palustris*).

<u>Plants for the open water.</u> These environments are divided into floating and floating-leaved plants. The lowest possible water level here is 8 to 12 in (20–30 cm), but many plants prefer greater depths, up to about 3 ft (0.9 m).

• Floating plants live either completely underwater, like the bladderwort (*Utricularia vulgaris*), which is therefore classified as an underwater plant, or they float on the water surface like the duckweed (*Lemna* species). Some have no roots at all; others only scantily developed ones.

• Floating-leaved plants, on the other hand, are rooted in the ground, usually with their leaves lying on the surface of the water. Among these are the water lilies (*Nymphaea* species), the most popular pond plants.

*Water lilies (*Nymphaea *species and varieties, here "Perfecta") cast a spell over every garden pond with their bewitchingly beautiful flowers.*

Water Lilies and Other Water Plants

The water plants have adapted well to their environment: Their submerged leaves and stems are able to take carbon dioxide and nutrients directly from the water—therefore, many floating plants never have roots. Their outer membranes are particularly thin and sensitive for better nutrient uptake. To achieve a good substance exchange over an especially large surface, their leaves are often greatly slit (laciniated), sometimes even feathered (filamentose). Air canals in the leaves provide for the necessary buoyancy. Underwater plants are the "cleaning crew" of bodies of water. Among them are the hornwort (*Ceratophyllum demersum*), bladderwort (*Utricularia vulgaris*), featherfoil (*Hottonia palustris*), and milfoil (*Myriophyllum* species). They compete for food with the disagreeable algae, which make the water cloudy. Besides, underwater plants are important sources of oxygen (see pages 16–17). They ensure that the water quality is constantly improved. Therefore, you should always use underwater plants in your pond and see to it that there is enough light under the surface of the water for their metabolic processes. Also for aesthetic reasons, at most only half the water surface should be covered with plants. Some underwater plants are tiny, so that they are often introduced with other plants or are easily propagated by division. Many of them have a powerful capacity to spread and must therefore regularly be thinned. Fish out a portion of them. Exotic floating plants like the water hyacinth (*Eichhornia crassipes*), water lettuce (*Pistia stratiotes*), water aloe (*Stratiotes aloides*), and trapa nut (*Trapa natans*) require higher water temperatures to thrive and survive only in mild regions or must be taken indoors for the winter. Floating-leaved plants either root directly in the bottom of the pond or pool or in baskets that must be set at the proper depth for the particular species and variety. There are even pygmy water lilies for the smallest pools. The water lily (*Nymphaea alba*) is very adaptable, but in deeper ponds and nutrient-rich water and soil it develops too vigorously by means of runners and can quickly cover the entire water surface. The colored water lily hybrids are also mostly very vigorous. However, they can be kept in check to some degree if the planting medium is lean and they are only able to spread a little in their container. Beyond this, it is possible to regularly remove the outer circle of leaves—a simple method of controlling growth. Conservation in the garden pond. Pesticides, herbicides, and fertilizers must not be used, because they spread in the water and are poisonous to pond animals. Even biological controls disturb the symbiotic relationships in the water.

Featherfoil.

Milfoil.

Featherfoil
Hottonia palustris
Underwater plant. Flowers delicate pink, primula-like, inflorescence up to 12 in (30 cm) above the water; May–June. Foliage comblike pinnate. Growth sends out runners, partly rooted in soil. Location water level of 4 to 8 in (10–20 cm), poor in lime, nutrients, sunny. Z: 5–9.

Milfoil
Myriophyllum species
An underwater plant. Flowers pink spikes; June–July Foliage comblike divided, in whorls, delicate green. Growth offsets form dense lawns over the water, trailing runners. Location water levels of 8 to 16 in (20–40 cm), nutrient- and lime-rich water. Depending upon species. Z: 4–11.

Yellow floating heart.

Water knotweed.

Yellow floating heart
Nymphoides peltata
Floating-leaved perennial for larger ponds. Flowers yellow, on stems above water; July–Aug. Foliage water lily-like, circular, lying on surface of water. Growth floating runners, fast growing. Location water depth 12 to 20 in (30–50 cm), sunny to semishady. Z: 7–11.

Water knotweed
Polygonum amphibium
Beautiful floating-leaved perennial. Flowers pink, spikes above the water; June–Sept. Foliage lanceolate, elliptical, leathery, lying on the water surface on long stems. Growth forms runners. Location water depths 1 to 39 in (2.5–99 cm), sunny to semishady, open surfaces.

Fragrant water lily "Chromatella."

Pink water lily hybrid.

White water lily hybrid.

Fragrant water lily
Nymphaea odorata

Wild form, along with hybrids. Flowers white, depending on variety also yellow and pink, diameter 5 to 6 in (13–15 cm), hybrids larger; June–Sept. Foliage large, shining, green, ovate. Growth vigorous, creeping. Location nutrient-rich, standing water, depth 12 to 24 in (30–61 cm) and more, sunny to semishady.
Important: There are about 100 winter-hardy water lily species and varieties; if possible, research and consider more than the color of the flowers. Z: 5–11.

Rose-pink
Nymphaea hybrid

Water lilies are the queens of the garden pond. Flowers water lily colors range from white to yellow and copper to light salmon, pink, and red and to very dark shades, with blue only appearing in tropical forms, diameter 6 to 8 in (15–20 cm). Depending upon species/cultivars. Z: 5–11.

Pure white
Nymphaea hybrid

The pure white forms are the quintessence of a water lily. The point of departure for many hybrids is *Nymphaea alba*, which is protected by law. White water lilies glow with particular intensity over dark water surfaces. Z: 5–11, by species/cultivar. *Nymphaea alba* is hardy from Z: 5–11.

Yellow pond lily.

Pygmy water lily "Indiana."

White pygmy water lilies ornament the smallest pond.

Yellow pond lily
Nuphar advena

Floating-leaved plant. Flowers hemispherical, yellow, fragrant, on sturdy stems above the water, 2 in (5 cm) in diameter; June–July. Foliage water lily-like. Growth creeping, rampant. Location from 24 in (61 cm) water level, nutrient rich, muddy, sunny to semishady. Z: 4–9.

Pygmy water lily
Nymphaea tetragona

One of the water lily species that stay small, several varieties. Flowers orange-copper, globular form, diameter 4 in (10 cm); June–Sept. Foliage diameter 7 in (18 cm), in young stage very spotted. Growth dwarf form for small pools and tubs. Location 10 to 12 in (25–30 cm) water depth. Z: 4–10.

White pygmy water lily
Nymphaea hybrid

A suitable water lily for small ornamental pools and low water levels. Flowers many different varieties in all water lily colors; in the pygmy water lilies the number of petals is less, i.e., 12 to 14 instead of 25 to 30 in *Nymphaea odorata;* the flower diameter is about 4 in (10 cm); blooming time June–Sept. Foliage in many varieties is reddish in young stage, later green; especially in the Laydekeri varieties, the most important pygmy water lily hybrids, it remains dark flecked even later. Growth creeping. Location water depths 6 to 12 in (15–30 cm). Depending upon species/cultivar. Z: 5–11.

Plants for the Water's Edge

The environment along the water's edge is one of the most varied of all. Many plants that thrive in shallow water (a water level of at least 4 in [10 cm]) grow invasively. Among them are the mare's-tail (*Hippuris vulgaris*) and many cattails (*Typha* species). If you want to prevent this, the plants should be set in containers.

Marsh plants. Among these there are many beautiful flowering perennials like the water gladiolus (*Butomus umbellatus*), cowslip (*Caltha palustris*), and marsh trifoil (*Menyanthes trifoliata*). With these, the water level may fall to zero, as long as the subsoil remains marshy. A little space is enough to create a small marsh bed. To make this somewhat more active and interesting, you should create shallow hollows and little hillocks lying above the water level. The bank-edge plants, such as the Siberian iris (*Iris siberica*) or the queen-of-the-meadow (*Filipendula ulmaria*), can be placed there, because they tolerate an occasional flooding.

Bank perennials. They also grow well in normal garden soil as long as it is damp enough. The transition from water's edge to garden can be designed the most beautifully with these and the biotope harmoniously inserted into the land on its border. In this transitional area from water to land, charming situations result when plants with a meadow character, like the daylilies (*Hemerocallis* species), the Jacob's-ladder (*Polemonium caeruleum*), hemp agrimony (*Eupatorium cannabium*), ligularia (*Ligularia* species), but also cranesbill (*Geranium* species), and many grasses create a community. Mainly it is the plants with narrow, grasslike foliage or with ornamental leaves that fit the character here at the water's edge.

Planting instructions for marsh and water plants (see pages 142–143).

• Water plants must never dry out and should not be left unprotected from sun and wind before they are planted.

• The substrate should not be too rich and humus. Therefore, mix good garden soil up to half with sand. In the pond, the soil layer will be covered with sand or gravel, so that no particles of humus can float up. The ready-mixed pond soil available in trade consists mainly of loam and sand.

• Vigorously growing plants are best set in wire baskets or closed containers where their growth is more securely kept within bounds.

• If a place in the pond is too deep, you can place the container on bricks and so achieve the proper planting depth.

Japanese iris variety "Royal Pageant."

Japanese iris
Iris kaempferi, I. ensata
Old Japanese cultivated plant with many varieties. Flowers abundant, in many color nuances from pink, blue to violet, richly marked, wavy or curled, the standards weakly developed; May–June. Foliage long and narrow, green with dark center rib, decorative into fall. Growth H: 32 to 39 in (81–99 cm). Location in areas bordering ponds, wet only in spring and summer, drying after flowering, loamy garden soil, poor in lime, sunny. Z: 4–8.

Important: Older plants can be divided well; the wild species is also propagated by seed.

Yellow flag.

Yellow flag
Iris pseudacorus
Wild. Flowers yellow with dark brown markings; June–July. Foliage strong, smooth, sword like leaves. Growth H: 32 to 39 in (81–99 cm), upright. Location wet bank areas to shallow water, maximum water level 8 in (20 cm), sunny to semishady. Z: 5–8.

Siberian iris "Superba."

Siberian iris
Iris sibirica
Long-lived. Flowers blue and violet shades; June. Foliage narrow, long leaves, last a long time. Growth H: 32 to 47 in (81–120 cm), dense clumps. Location water's edge with alternating soil moisture, also drier places, sunny. Z: 3–8.

Plants for Shallow-Water Areas

Mad-dog weed
Alisma plantago-aquatica
Also growing wild; flowers whitish pink, dainty panicles; June–Sept.; foliage spatular; growth H: 28 in; location wet bank areas, sunny to semi-shady. Z: 5–8.

Golden-club
Orontium aquaticum
Water to edge of bank plant; brilliant yellow flowers May–June; dark green 1 ft long leaves; location semishady.

Pond bulrush
Scirpus lacustris
Invasive, only for large ponds; small, red-brown ears; July–Aug.; foliage chive-like; growth 39 to 59 in; location sunny to semishady. Z: 6–9.

Buttercup ☠
Ranunculus lingua
Invasive, only for large ponds; flowers yellow, large, sturdy, saucer shaped; June–Aug.; foliage gray-green, tongue shaped; growth H: 28 to 39 in; location sunny to semishady. Z: 4–9.

Old world arrowhead
Sagittaria sagittifolia
Very decorative leaves; flowers white with red base; June–July; foliage arrow shaped; growth H: 20 in, forming runners; location sunny to semishady. Z: 5–11.

European brooklime
Veronica beccabunga
Salad and medicinal plant; blue flowers in racemes; May–Sept; foliage roundish, ovate; growth H: 16 in, fast spreading; location sunny to semishady. Z: 4–9.

Marsh trefoil
Menyanthes trifoliata
Medicinal plant; flowers white in dense racemes; May–June; foliage trifid, clover-like; growth H: 12 in, forming runners; location sunny to semishady. Z: 3–9.

Plants for Border Zones with Changing Moisture

Monkey flower; *Mimulus luteus*
Self-seeding; flowers yellow, large; May–Aug.; foliage ovate, sturdy green; growth H: 16 in, bushy; location marshy moist soil. Z: 9–11.

Purple loosestrife
Lythrum salicaria
Medicinal plant, many varieties; flowers brilliant rose to violet, 12 in long inflorescence; July–Sept.; foliage heart shaped; growth H: up to 59 in, bushy; location wet, heavy soil. Z: 4–9.
Caution: Very invasive. Some states have banned this plant in nursery trade to prevent choking of natural wetland areas.

Globeflower ☠
Trollius europaeus
Cutting plant; flowers yellow, globular; May–June; foliage palmate, lush green; growth H: 20 in, bushy; location damp, humus soil. Z: 3–8.

Swamp forget-me-not
Myosotis palustris
Ground cover; flowers light blue, lush; May–Sept.; foliage lanceolate, fresh green; growth H: up to 20 in, creeping; location moist, sunny. Z: 4–8.

Queen-of-the-meadow
Filipendula ulmaria
Robust; flowers white or pink, panicle-like; July–Aug.; foliage pinnate, green; growth H: up to 39 in; location sunny, loamy soil. Z: 3–9.

Moneywort
Lysimachia nummularia
Ground cover; flowers penny size, egg yolk yellow; May–July. Foliage roundish, light green; growth flat, creeping; location moist loamy soil. Z: 3–9.

Joe-pye weed
Eupatorium purpureum (N.)
Long-lived; flowers dull pink; umbel-like racemes; July–Sept.; foliage lanceolate; growth H: up to 6 ft; location full sun, moist loamy soil. Z: 5–11.

Cowslip.

Pickerel weed.

Cowslip ☠
Caltha palustris
Wild perennial. Flowers single, golden yellow; Apr.–June. Foliage roundish, kidney shaped, glossy green. Growth bushy, up to 12 in (30 cm) high. Location rich, damp to wet places, also with occasional flooding, sunny to semishady. Z: 4–9.

Pickerel weed
Pontederia cordata
Lushly blooming but delicate. Flowers blue spikes; June–Aug. Foliage on long stems, shining green, heart shaped, particularly pretty leaves. Growth H: 24 to 32 in (60–81 cm). Location damp bank areas with standing shallow water levels, sunny, warm. Z: 4–9.

Water gladiolus.

Cattail.

Water gladiolus
Butomus umbellatus
Valuable flowering perennial. Flowers rose-pink umbel-like inflorescences; June–Aug. Foliage very narrow, rushlike, trigonal. Growth H: 20 to 39 in (50–99 cm). Location wet bank areas with shallow water, up to 8 in (20 cm) deep, sunny to semishady. Z: 6–11.

Cattail
Typha angustifolia
Stately wild perennial in reed banks. Flowers rust brown, cylindrical fruit spadix, in June–Aug. Foliage grass green, long, narrow leaves. Growth H: up to 7 ft (2 m), suckers. Location wet bank areas, shallow water, sunny. Important: *Typha minima* is a smaller species. Z: 2–10.

Slow-growing pears can be trained against the house
as space-saving and decorative espaliers.

FRUIT

Even in the smallest garden there is still room for fruit. There are dwarf apple trees, and sour cherries, plums, and quinces also remain relatively small. Berry bushes need only a little space and can be integrated into the ornamental garden outstandingly well. Flowers will still thrive under the crown of a small standard; herbs or vegetables and strawberries can serve as bed enclosures.

Planning points.

• In larger gardens there should be different fruit species, which make it possible to have fresh fruit at staggered times.

• Also, by choosing early, mid-season, or late varieties, a "fruit glut" can be avoided.

• Small tree forms such as dwarfs and bushes (see pages 172–175) are easy to inspect, care for, and harvest.

• A large standard can, however, be planted as a decorative shade tree.

• Before buying in a good nursery, ask about the fruiting conditions of the individual species and varieties. Many are dependent on pollination from other species and won't set fruit without a suitable pollinator nearby. But even with self-fertilizing varieties, pollination from another plant leads to better quality fruit.

• When selecting species and variety, consider the climatic requirements and the soil conditions in your garden.

• Many fruit species produce so-called "tired soil." You should, therefore, not plant the same species in the same place again.

•Choose the healthiest possible varieties so that you can avoid using chemical plant sprays.

Important: The health value of the fruit should not be underrated, for it contains many vitamins and minerals.

The apricot (Prunus armeniaca) *can be grown where peaches thrive. Their fruits taste pleasantly spicy and produce a marvelous jam.*

Pome Fruit

The pome fruits comprise the apple (*Malus domestica*), pear (*Pyrus communis*), and common quince (*Cydonia oblonga*). They form pips as seeds. Botanically speaking, these are pseudo-fruits, for only the ovule, the five-chambered core, develops as usual out of the ovary. The fleshy covering that one eats develops from the flower receptacle.

Pollination. Apples and pears, in contrast to quinces, are dependent on cross-pollination. For each apple and pear variety, there are good and bad pollinators. Get advice in the nursery and ask your neighbors what varieties are growing in their gardens. Also, it's important to remember that the flowering times must always overlap. If you haven't space in the garden for any other varieties and there aren't any nearby in the community, plant a tree on which two or three compatible varieties are grafted.

Location. Apples and pears bloom somewhat later than the stone fruit, pears even earlier than apples, from the middle to the end of mid-spring. Early varieties also flower earlier. Normally the late- and long-flowering varieties are less threatened by frost. An apple blossom can hold for up to a week; a whole tree remains in flower for about a month long. Pears achieve only half the time; they need warmer locations altogether than the more tolerant apple varieties. With apples the average annual temperature should be around 43° to 46° F (6°–8°C), for pears a few degrees higher.

Generally apples also prefer a higher humidity. In mild locations, the fruit quality is better. Also, they don't have any extraordinary requirements for soil. However, fruit quality and yield are increased through soil improvement.

Understock. The fancy fruits can only be propagated vegetatively, so the scion is grafted onto an understock. This can be an apple or pear seedling or a vegetatively propagated form with special growth characteristics. Today it is primarily slow growth that is desired. The understock is responsible for root development, anchoring, nutrient uptake and transport; the grafted variety develops trunk and crown and determines the fruit variety. The understock can strengthen the characteristics of the scion variety or suppress them. With apples, especially, the breadth of variations of the understock types is so great that fruit can be harvested even in the smallest gardens (dwarfs [slender spindles]) and on the terrace (ballerinas). Small trees also have the advantage over the standards of achieving their full yield capacity after very few years. Apples can be grown in zones 3–9. Certain cultivars have more limited range. Check each variety's zone before purchasing. Pears can grow in zones 4–9, check each variety.

Apple variety "Jonathan"

(see photo above)
A red-cheeked, sweet winter apple, it is also grown commercially in large scale. Fruit medium size, truncated cone shaped, slightly ribbed, dark red with lemon yellow, has a bloom (pruinose), medium vitamin C content, not easily bruised. Taste sweetly tart. Harvest end Sept–Oct. Storage until Mar. Growth slow to moderately vigorous, crown medium size, spherical, dense, branches trailing downward. Location warm, protected. Important: Not very susceptible to frost but subject to mildew.

Common quince.

Common quince
Cydonia oblonga
Largely self-pollinating, Fruit bright yellow, furry, very hard when raw. Taste mildly spicy. Harvest/storage Oct. not very keepable, Growth sturdy, upright, treelike, H: 5 to 16 ft (1.5–5 m). Location warm spot. Z: 5–9.

"Roter Berlepsch."

"Gravenstein."

"Roter Boskoop."

Apple variety
"Red Burlepsch"

More intensely colored than "Burlepsch" but contains little vitamin C. <u>Fruit</u> medium size, golden yellow, red cheeked. <u>Taste</u> flavorsome, quite tart. <u>Harvest/storage</u> Oct., until Feb. <u>Growth</u> less vigorous than parent form. <u>Location</u> moderately moist, little affected by late frost.

Apple variety
"Gravenstein"

Only moderately frost-hardy. <u>Fruit</u> large, yellow-green, sunny side flamed with red. <u>Taste</u> unique aroma, intense apple fragrance. <u>Harvest/storage</u> Aug., up to Jan. <u>Growth</u> strong, horizontal branches. <u>Location</u> evenly moist soil, protected from late frosts.

Apple variety
"Roter Boskoop"

Tastes milder than the parent form "Boskoop." <u>Fruit</u> large, yellow-green, with red cast. <u>Taste</u> flavorful, tart. <u>Harvest/storage</u> Oct., up to Feb. <u>Growth</u> very large, wide-spreading crown. <u>Location</u> moist soil, protected from late frost.

"Köstliche aus Charneux."

Pear variety "Gräfin von Paris."

"Alexander Lucas."

Pear variety
"Köstliche aus Charneux"

One of the most popular dessert pears. <u>Fruit</u> large, greenish yellow, red cheeked. <u>Taste</u> juicy, sweet, spicy. <u>Harvest/storage</u> Oct.–Nov., up to Jan. <u>Growth</u> moderately vigorous, suitable for espaliers or dwarf, branches vertical. <u>Location</u> warm and protected, dry, frost protected. <u>Important:</u> Susceptible to scab.

Pear variety
"Gräfin von Paris"

Good eating and cooking pear variety for the fancier's orchard. <u>Fruit</u> large to medium, regular pear shape, dull to straw yellow, faintly orange on the sunny side. <u>Taste</u> sweet, slightly spicy flavored. <u>Harvest/storage</u> middle to end of Oct., up to Jan. <u>Growth</u> moderately vigorous, dwarf tree.

<u>Location</u> sunny and warm, if possible wine-grape-growing climate, soil with no tendency to sogginess, avoid locations open to wind.
<u>Important:</u> Wood is frost-hardy, the flowers susceptible to late frosts; the pear is itself a good pollinating variety, a good pollinator for "Köstliche aus Charneux."

Pear variety
"Alexander Lucas"

Delicious dessert pear. <u>Fruit</u> large, yellow-green, red cheeked. <u>Taste</u> sweet, spicy. <u>Harvest/storage</u> Oct.–Nov., up to Jan. Growth moderately tall, for espalier, dwarf. <u>Location</u> warm, protected. <u>Important:</u> Not a self-pollinating variety; good pollinator "Charneux"

Stone Fruit

The stone fruits include plums and damsons (*Prunus domestica*), sour cherries (*Prunus cerasus*), sweet cherries (*Prunus avium*), peaches (*Prunus persica*), and apricots (*Prunus armeniaca*). Stone fruits form true fruits from the ovary: the innermost cell layer encloses the ovule, a hard kernel (stone); the outer layer forms the juicy flesh of the fruit. The stone is only edible in the almond (*Prunus dulcis*).

Pollination. In the stone fruits, all stages from self-fruitful to self-infertility can be found. Thus, good pollinators in the near vicinity are also the recipe here for successful, satisfactory yields.

Location. Plums will still thrive in harsh locations. Peaches, apricots, and nectarines, on the other hand, will only produce good harvests in grape-growing climates or on southern exposures that are protected from wind. Stone fruit blooms in mid-spring in some cases and is, thus, at risk for late frosts. In some species, the wood is also frost-sensitive; strong temperature fluctuations in winter are most unfavorable. All stone fruit wants a well-drained soil that warms easily. However, high humidity promotes fungus disease (see pages 192–193).

• A standard sweet cherry may grow to be about 50 years old and requires an area of at least 538 sq ft (54 m²). Even the dwarf sweet cherry still reaches a sizable crown breadth, though not such a great age. Sweet cherries are classified into two groups: the softer heart cherry and the snapping bigarreau cherry, which easily splits in rain.

• Sour cherries display a much slower growth pattern. They tend to lose leaves, and a weeping growth pattern regularly occurs, particularly in the morello. In order to avoid this, sour cherries should be regularly pruned after harvest. This dainty tree is outstandingly suitable for the smaller garden. Two types are also distinguished here; the morello with colored juice and the colorless amarelle.

• Plums are very different in fruit form, color, and taste. As well as the robust damson this group also includes Mirabelle and Reneklode—but they are more for enthusiasts. The fruit of the plums are roundish and have a distinct longitudinal suture. In the long firm damson, the stone is easily removed from the flesh—they are, therefore, especially good for baking.

Gummosis. Stone fruits tend to gummosis. It is traceable to poor climate, parasites, and environmental influences but also to incorrect cultivation measures and as a result, an exudation of sap leaks through the bark at various places. As a result, the tree or at least part of it can die back.

Sweet cherry
Prunus avium

(see photos above and right) Sweet cherries are usually self-sterile, thus, can only be pollinated by the pollen of other species; you can get information about this in textbooks or nurseries; either plant 2 trees or talk with your neighbors; for small gardens, there are also dwarfs on which 2 or 3 suitable varieties have been grafted. Fruit large, depending on variety dark violet, red, yellowish-red, yellow. Taste sweet, depending on variety flavorsome, spicy. Growth sweet cherries used to be extremely tall and only something for the large garden, but dwarf understocks can be selected for sweet cherries; the varieties grafted onto them grow considerably smaller and lower; the smallest being the English bred understock "Colt" and

Sweet cherry.

the understocks bred in Weihenstephan, Germany, which are all designated with "W" and a number. Location warm, protected from late frost. Z: 5–9.

Morello.

Apricots give pleasure with both flowers and fruit.

Peach.

Sour cherry
Prunus cerasus

The morello is a popular sour cherry variety, very good for preserves. Fruit large, dark red, color remains when cooked. Taste sour, strong. Harvest May–Aug. Growth moderately tall, arching. Location sunny, protected from late frost. Z: 4–8.

Apricot
Prunus armeniaca

In early spring, the very beautiful but very frost-sensitive delicate rose-pink flowers appear; apricots are self-pollinating. The fruits are a delicacy eaten fresh or preserved. Fruit yellow to yellow-orange, red cheeked, depending on variety smooth or fuzzy, stone is easily removed from flesh. Taste sweet and flavorful. Harvest July–Aug., pick carefully, fruits bruise easily. Growth short to medium-tall, depending on understock, well suited for espaliers. Location sunny, frost protected, rich soil. Variety "Aprikose von Nancy." Z: 3–8.

Peach
Prunus persica

Dark pink flowers starting in March. Fruit depending on variety yellow-green, yellow, pink, red, skin fuzzy, early varieties with white flesh, late with yellow. Taste sweet-sour to sweet. Harvest July–Sept. Growth medium tall, also for espaliers. Location like apricots. Z: 5–9.

Damson.

Mirabelles are sweet and juicy.

Reneklode.

Damson
Prunus domestica

A variety of the European plum. Fruit oblong-ovate, color depending on variety blue, blue-violet, or yellow, fruit flesh yellow to orange. Taste sweet-sour, flavorful. Harvest Aug.–Oct. Growth moderately tall, round crown. Location protected, sunny. Z: 4–9.

Mirabelle plum
Prunus domestica

Pure white small flowers in early to mid-spring; mirabelles are self-pollinating, yield only begins after 6 to 8 years; good harvests only possible in regions with mild climate. Fruit round, plum size, yellow, with red spots when fully ripe, much vitamin C. Taste sweet and flavorful. Harvest Aug. Growth moderately tall, small trees, suitable as specimens. Location full sun, protected from wind, warm sandy-humus soil, not too dry. Important: Regular pruning to thin increases the yield of fruit. Z: 4–9.

Greengage
"Althans Reneklode"

For home gardens only on dwarf understock, self-sterile. Fruit round, violet, also yellow-green and red varieties. Taste sweet-sour, flavorful. Harvest Aug.–Sept. Growth moderately tall to tall. Location protected, sunny.

Berries

Berries are easy to grow, usually very undemanding as to climate and soil, and also sure to bear. Therefore, you need not do without them, even in the smallest garden. In the small garden, choose standards, which go very nicely in a flower bed. Berry bushes are also suitable for hedges and trellises.

Berry fruits include the currants (*Ribes rubrum* and *nigrum*), gooseberries (*Ribes uva-crispa*), and red raspberries (*Rubus idaeus*). Jostaberries are a cross between black currants and gooseberries. The vitamin C content is much greater than that of apples and pears; most outstanding of all are the black currants. Also berries hold first place for their carotene (precursor of vitamin A) value. They are an ideal addition to the menu and can be used in a number of ways; besides being served fresh they are good for compotes, jams and jellies, and for juice, fruit wines, and desserts.

Almost all species are self-fertile, but the fruit yield is better with cross-pollination. Therefore, plant several varieties if possible.

Location. Berry bushes need full sun and a wind-sheltered place for good harvests. Many also thrive in semishade, but the fruit remains small and the sweetness is missing.

Planting and care. The berry species have arisen through many crosses and selections. These garden hybrids are somewhat more demanding than the original wild forms. The better the conditions, the more the plants will yield. The culture of berry bushes is somewhat similar to that of the shallow-rooted shrubs (see pages 168–171). Fertilize in the fall and/or in the spring with organic or complete fertilizers (see pages 156–159). It is also important that the ground be covered by a low plant carpet or a layer of mulch all year round (see pages 172–173).

Selection of variety. In general, the harvest season for berries begins in early summer to fall and lasts until October. There are early-, mid-season-, and late-ripening varieties of all berry species, so that you can lengthen the harvest season at the start and the end by choosing the appropriate varieties. There are also once- and ever-bearing varieties of raspberries and strawberries. The once-bearing ones yield much more—ideal if one needs a large quantity for jam. On the other hand, the ever-bearing varieties are appropriate for a constant supply of fresh fruit for serving; those like the ever-bearing strawberries bear and ripen over an extended period.

Red raspberries are a pleasure to the eye and the palate.

Raspberries
Rubus idaeus
The once-bearing varieties form canes in summer that need support; in the second year, they fruit; the harvested canes are cut back to the ground; the new twice-bearing varieties need no supports; they bear fruit in the fall of the first year and again in early summer the followiing year. Fruit dark to light red. Taste sweet, flavorful. Harvest June–July. Growth H: 3 to 7 ft (0.9–2 m). Location sunny to semishady.

Important: Raspberries are self-fertile, but cross-pollination improves the yield. Z: 3–9.

Yellow raspberries are uncommon and very flavorful.

Yellow raspberries
Rubus idaeus
Whereas red raspberries are good for processing into jam, juice, alcoholic beverages, or even cakes, the yellow fruits are primarily suitable for serving fresh; their relatively short canes need no supports; in regions with very severe winters, it is recommended to add leaf compost in late fall so that the root buds don't freeze. Fruit medium size, yellow. Taste sweet, savory. Harvest June. Growth 4 ft (1.2 m). Location sunny to semishady, protected from wind. Varieties "Golden Queen," "Goldtraube," "Hauensteins Gelbe." Z: 3–9.

Black currants contain many vitamins.

Red currants.

Black currants
Ribes nigrum

Black currants really serve to extend the garden: They are undemanding and their fruit has an especially large quantity of vitamin C; they can be processed into a healthy juice, which is supposed to relieve gout and rheumatism, detoxify, and promote digestion. Fruit black, medium size to large, juice intensely colored, depending on variety short or long clusters. Taste tart flavorful to sweet flavorful. Harvest June–July. Growth sturdy upright shrubs, depending on variety H: up to 6 ft (1.8 m). Location sunny, protected from late frosts, all soils. Important: Cross-pollination increases the yield. Z: 3–6.

Red currants
Ribes rubrum

Well ripened, the slightly sour fruit can be served fresh or be preserved; newer varieties form long bunches with large berries and small seeds; they are often more robust and less disease-prone in addition; red currants are self-fertile, but cross-pollination with other varieties produces higher yields. Fruit size depends on variety, in long clusters, dark to bright red. Taste sweet-sour. Harvest June–Aug. Growth shrubby, H: 5 to 7 ft (1.5–2 m). Location sunny, protect from late frosts. Z: 3–6.

Gooseberries.

Jostaberries.

Gooseberries
Ribes uva-crispa

Gooseberries are self-pollinating, but larger berries are produced with cross-pollination; if you plant early-, mid-season-, and late-ripening varieties you increase the harvesting time. Fruit large, depending on variety yellow-green, yellow, or red. Taste sweet-sour, flavorful. Harvest June–July. Growth shrubby, H: 5 to 7 ft (1.5–2 m), also as standard. Location sunny to semishady, protected from late frosts. Z: 3–7. Important: Don't fail to choose new, mildew-resistant varieties. Note: Gooseberries can cause disease problems for white pine trees so do not plant near.

Jostaberries
Ribes x nidigrolaria

Cross between black currants and gooseberries, which first succeeded in our century after a breeder's decade-long experimental attempts. The new species resembles the currant in its growth habit, the lack of prickles on the fruit, and the leaf form, but the size of the fruit corresponds to a small-fruited gooseberry. Jostaberries survive late frosts even better than their parents. Fruit black and large. Taste tart, flavorsome. Harvest July. Growth sturdy, shrubby, also twiggy, H: 7 to 8 ft (2–2.5 m). Location sunny. Z: 3–7.

Berries

A garden without strawberries is almost unthinkable. The cultivated strawberry (*Fragaria x ananassa*) stems from the small alpine strawberry (*Fragaria vesca*). It offers the first fruit of the year and therefore represents a delicacy—and, besides, strawberries are very healthy.

Strawberries are slightly nonconforming in every respect. They are perennials and according to the strict rules of the botanists, they do not develop berries but receptacles with collections of seeds. The outer surface of their pseudo-fruit is covered with tiny seeds.

Worldwide there are about 1,000 cultivated strawberry varieties of differing quality. New hybrids for the trade are usually large-fruited and very firm-fleshed in order to guarantee good transportability. In your own garden, however, you should cultivate juicier and more flavorful varieties. For home use also the small but intensely flavored ever-bearing woodland strawberries (*Fragaria vesca* var. *semperflorens*) are recommended. They are also good as ground covers and still thrive in light shade. Ideal for small gardens are the so-called climbing strawberries, which need little space because they can be grown vertically on frames, but they will also thrive in containers—like hanging plants.

The chief harvest time is from the beginning of June to the beginning of July (early to mid-summer), with ever-bearing varieties producing fruit until late summer. The harvest can be hastened by about a week if the plants are protected with plastic or straw from the beginning of new growth to the first flower formation; under a floating row cover, they will fruit even earlier. Strawberries should always be picked dry and with the hulls left on.

After 3 years, cultivated strawberries bear poorly. You should, thus, bring on new young plants in a 3- to 4-year rhythm (see page 155). Planting time is in August (late summer). But so-called cold-tolerant plants can be planted all year round. Recommended, but somewhat more expensive, are virus-free strawberry varieties. As descendants of forest plants, strawberries especially like the soil covered with a layer of mulch. It prevents evaporation, suppresses weeds, promotes growth, and protects the fruit.

Grapevines and kiwis. Grapevines (*Vitis vinifera*) and the kiwi (*Actinidia chinensis*), (see page 221) only thrive in the more southern or moderate climates. The kiwis are dioecious, so for production of fruit there must be 1 male for every 5 female plants.

Blackberries (*Rubus* species) can be grown well on walls or on freestanding supports. The robust plants are also excellent as space dividers within the garden

Blueberries (*Vaccinium corymbosum*) develop very large fruits and in the fall turn a magnificent, brilliant red. But like their wild forms, they need acidic soil to thrive. On a chalky soil, they can only be maintained over a long period with a large quantity of special soil and acidifying fertilizer.

Sallow thorn, Common sea buckthorn
Hippophae rhamnoides
(see photo above)
Planted in hedges, it can repel unwanted intruders with its sturdy thorns; also it looks quite attractive as a specimen planting with is twiggy growth habit and silver-gray branches; it is frost-hardy and also tolerates windy locations; the sallow thorn is dioecious, so a male and a female must be planted for fruit production; the ripe fruits contain a great deal of vitamin C. Fruit diameter 0.25 to 0.33 in (6–8 mm), oval, orange-red; juice is yellow. Taste bitter, sour. Harvest Aug–Sept. Growth H: 7 to 13 ft (2–4 m). Location sunny, also salty soil.

Cultivated cranberries (*Vaccinium macrocarpon*) have similar requirements to the mountain cranberry but want drier locations. With their attractive red berries and beautiful fall coloring, they look especially good in a heath garden.

Wild fruit. Many wild fruit species also thrive in the garden. In natural hedges, there is a place for shrubs that offer food for people and birds, like elderberry (*Sambucus nigra*) and sallow thorn (*Hippophae rhamnoides*), (see photos above).

Black elderberries grow wild.

Blackberries.

European elder
Sambucus nigra
Can be found growing wild at the woods edge, from June–July its white to yellow, sweetly fragrant umbel-like racemes appear; they reach diameters of up to 8 in (20 cm); in trade, however, are the large-fruited varieties, which are even juicier. Fruit round, black single fruits in large panicles, edible cooked, rich in vitamins, the deep red juice makes stubborn spots. Taste herbal-sour. Harvest Aug–Sept. Growth shrub or small tree, H: 13 to 23 ft (4–7 m). Location sunny to semishady, any soil. Z: 2–9.

Blackberries
Rubus species
Thornless varieties are often less sweet and flavorful. Fruit black, about 0.75 in (19 mm) in diameter. Taste sour to sweetly flavorsome. Harvest June–Sept. Growth canes, up to 26 ft (8 m) long. Location sunny to semishady, protected from wind. Z: 5–11.

Strawberries are very popular in home gardens.

Cultivated blueberries.

Cultivated cranberries.

Cultivated strawberry
Fragaria x ananassa
Numerous once- and twice-bearing varieties have been bred from the large-fruited cultivated strawberry; breeders' goals are the largest possible flavorful fruit; there are also trailing varieties, which can be tied up as "climbing strawberries." Fruit dark to bright red, round to broadly heart shaped. Taste sweet, flavorful. Harvest May–Aug. Growth leaf rosettes with numerous runners, H: up to 8 in (20 cm). Location warm, sunny, sheltered from wind. Important: Woodland strawberries are very small and flavorful and fruit all season long. Z: 3–11.

Cultivated blueberries
Vaccinium corymbosum
Cultivated varieties produced from the large-fruited American blueberry. Fruit round, blue frosted, diameter up to 0.75 in (19 mm). Taste refreshingly flavorsome. Harvest July–Sept. Growth small shrub, H: up to 12 in (30 cm). Location sunny, protected from wind, acidic soil. Z: 2–9.

Cultivated cranberries
Vaccinium macrocarpon
Native to bog areas of the United States, evergreen, self-pollinating, cross-pollination promotes yields. Fruit reddish, almost cherry size. Taste astringent-sour. Harvest Aug–Oct. Growth dwarf shrub, H: 2 to 12 in (5–30 cm). Location sunny, humus, acid soil. Z: 3.

*Vegetables and herbs fresh from the garden—
the very essence of gardening pleasure.*

VEGETABLES AND HERBS

Vegetable is a collective term for a multitude of herbaceous plants or parts of them that serve as food for humans. In order to bring a certain order into this vegetable multitude, they are usually classified according to botanical criteria. In contrast to the vegetables, the so-called herbs (see page 302) have scarcely any nutrititional value; however, they essentially support the functions of the body.

<u>Content.</u> Vegetables and herbs are essential for a well-balanced diet. Fresh from the home garden they are especially valuable, because the nutrient value can be considerably diminished during transport and storage. Vegetables contain minerals, vitamins, fiber/roughage, protein, carbohydrates, and only a little fat. In herbs, there are aromatic substances that can stimulate appetite and digestion. When you grow vegetables and herbs organically in sunny, warm locations, you are guaranteed to be eating food that is low in pollutants.

<u>Construction of a garden.</u> Usually there isn't enough space for complete vegetable self-sufficiency, but you should at least grow your favorite kinds. How pretty the useful plants can be and how attractively they can be combined can be seen on pages 116–117 and 138–139. The care of vegetables that are planted between flowers is somewhat more difficult, however. Just as pretty and easier to care for is a separate vegetable garden enclosed by small shrubs like boxwood (*Buxus sempervirens*), herbs, or flowers. In the ideal situation, there is a special vegetable area in the garden where systematic crop rotation and mixed culture can be practiced (see pages 182–185). Hill beds and raised beds are alternatives for growing vegetables in small gardens or on poor soil.

Artichokes (Cynara scolymus) *are beautiful to look at but somewhat tricky; because of their sensitivity to frost they only really thrive well in warmer climates.*

Fruit Vegetables

The fruit vegetables offer a wealth of diversity in color, form, and taste. They are sometimes used raw and sometimes cooked with many tasting marvelous in both kinds of preparation. Through hybridization, the fruit, which originally only represented the "packaging" of the seeds, has become ever more strongly adapted to the human taste. Thus, the flesh of the fruit has gained the greatest importance, whereas to some extent the seeds are neglected. The fruit vegetables come from very different plant families, to which the legumes (see page 294) basically also belong; however, these burst their pods and scatter the seeds. The nightshade family, which includes the tomatoes (*Lycopersicon esculentum*), peppers (*Capsicum annuum*), and eggplant (*Solanum melongen*a), have distinctive flowers; their fruits are especially low in calories and rich in vitamins. Again, cucumbers (*Cucumis sativus*) and zucchini (*Cucurbita pepo*) are members of the gourd family and develop conspicuous large flowers. Cucumbers are among the oldest cultivated vegetables in central Europe, prized even by the Romans. Besides the numerous outdoor species, there are also the special hothouse species (such as the English cucumber), which can only be grown in a greenhouse.

Cultivation outdoors. All species come from tropical and subtropical regions. Because these plants are frost-tender in most climates, they must be started indoors and may only be placed outside after all danger of frost is past. Many gardeners, therefore, buy already started plants at the end of May (in late spring). About 2–4 months pass until harvest. Almost all fruit vegetables are heavy feeders and need much fertilizer and water. The location should be protected from the wind and sunny, for only thus will the vegetables develop their flavor and full vitamin content.

Cultivation under plastic. Because the fruit vegetables are sensitive to cold, their culture under plastic gains special importance. It guarantees earlier and more certain harvests.

• Recommended is black plastic mulch, with which the bed can be covered. The early started young plants are placed in the ground through a cross-shaped cut in the mulch. The soil warms especially well under the mulch. The moisture is retained and no weeds can get started. Additional water is only necessary in exceptional cases. The controlled conditions have a positive effect on the quality of plants and fruits.

• Floating row covers that are perforated (for tomatoes there are individual caps) offer additional protection from the wind and weather, but like cold frames, they must be ventilated in strong sunshine.

Pumpkins need rich fertilizer applications and lots of space.

Pumpkin
Cucurbita maxima
The food pumpkin is one of the heavy feeders and is, therefore, happy planted at the foot of the compost heap; it grows rampant and, therefore needs much space in the garden; one plant can provide for several households. Sowing April in pots, from middle of May outside. Planting May, planting distance 7 ft (2 m). Growth yard long (meter long), severally branching runners with thick, large leaves. Fruit white, yellow, or green, weighing up to 110 lb (50 kg). Harvest Pumpkins are ripe when they sound hollow when thumped; the plants then begin to yellow, Aug.–Sept. Location sunny; rich soil.

Sweet corn.

Cucumber.

Sweet corn
Zea mays var. *saccharata*
You should plant at least 2 rows so that wind pollination is ensured. Sowing Apr. in pots or beginning May outdoors, 16 in (40 cm) apart. Planting end of Apr. Growth H: up to 7 ft (2 m). Fruit yellow-kerneled ears. Harvest Aug. Location sunny; rich soil.

Cucumber
Cucumis sativus
Buy mildew-resistant and non-bitter outdoor varieties. Sowing Apr. in pots, from middle May outdoors. Planting middle of May. Growth creeping (pickling cucumbers) or climbing (salad cucumbers). Fruit green, 6 to 16 in (15–40 cm). Harvest June–Sept. Location sunny; nutrient-rich soil.

Zucchini.

Yellow squash, a light-feeding variety.

Peppers.

Zucchini
Cucurbita pepo

Zucchini forms male and female flowers; only the female ones bear fruit. <u>Sowing</u> Apr. in pots, middle May outdoors. <u>Planting</u> middle of May. <u>Growth</u> also climbing varieties. <u>Fruit</u> green, cucumber-like, weighing up to 11 lb (5 kg). <u>Harvest</u> June–Sept. <u>Location</u> sunny; rich soil.

Yellow squash and other squashes
Curcurbita pepo

The yellow squash is cultivated just like zucchini, but modern varieties don't bear such gigantic fruits; there are also yellow-green and black-green varieties. <u>Use</u> harvest squashes as early as possible, for they are at their best then; those filled with a stuffing of flowers are a delicacy. <u>More</u> <u>squashes</u> "Pattipan" whose fruits resemble white flying saucers; they are sliced and braised or dipped in egg and bread crumbs and fried; "Spaghetti Squash," which is cooked whole and then halved; during cooking, the meat collapses into pastalike ribbons.

Pepper
Capsicum annuum

The fruits are high in vitamin C. <u>Sowing</u> Mar. under glass. Planting from middle May. <u>Growth</u> bushy, H: up to 24 in (61 cm). <u>Fruit</u> green, yellow, red, or purple. <u>Harvest</u> from July. <u>Location</u> sunny, warm; rich soil. <u>Important:</u> In harsh climates, grow in greenhouse.

Early tomato variety "First in the Field."

Cherry tomato "Mikado."

Eggplant.

Tomato
Lycopersicon lycopersicum

Well-ripened and fresh from one's own garden, tomatoes are a delicacy; don't serve small green tomatoes, which contain the poison solanine. <u>Sowing</u> from Mar. under glass. <u>Planting</u> from middle May outdoors, 24 in (61 cm) apart. <u>Growth</u> depending on variety bushy or staked, H: up to 6 ft (1.8 m). <u>Fruit</u> depending on variety cherry to apple size, round, oval, or pear shaped, smooth or ribbed, red or yellow, always several in a cluster. <u>Harvest</u> from July. <u>Location</u> sunny, warm; rich soil. <u>Important:</u> Constantly thin out, letting only 5–6 flower clusters develop.

Cherry tomato
Lycopersicon esculentum var. cerasiforme

These smaller-size tomatoes are sown and planted like the large forms. <u>Growth</u> up to 39 in (99 cm). <u>Fruit</u> cherry size, taste sweeter and more flavorful than the large varieties; up to 50 fruits on 1 cluster.

Eggplant
Solanum melongena

Only fruit in mild regions outdoors. <u>Sowing</u> Mar. under glass. <u>Planting</u> end May. <u>Growth</u> bushy, H: up to 39 in (99 cm). <u>Fruit</u> dark purple, oval, up to 8 in (20 cm). <u>Harvest</u> Aug.–Sept. <u>Location</u> sunny, warm, protected; nutrient-rich soil. <u>Important:</u> Only let 5 fruits ripen.

VEGETABLES AND HERBS

Legumes, Onions, and Leeks

Legumes are members of the pea or pulse family. These plants are able to bind nitrogen in nodes on their roots with the help of nitrogen-fixing bacteria. In this way, they provide themselves with most of their own chief nutrients and are, thus, weak feeders. At the same time, they contribute to soil improvement, for the nitrogen from the roots that are left is made available for the succeeding plants.

The pods in which the seeds are formed are characteristic of the legumes. Because pod vegetables contain relatively high amounts of protein, starch, fat, vitamins, and minerals, they guarantee a well-balanced diet. Some of them, like peas (*Pisum sativum*) and pole beans (*Phaseolus vulgaris* var. *vulgaris*) are climbing plants that are grown on stakes or frames and can provide screening with their lush foliage.

Peas are among the oldest produce plants; they are served with and without pods:

• Wrinkled shelling peas have wrinkled seeds, contain more sugar and taste sweetish.

• Smooth shelling peas have round, smooth-skinned seeds that can also be dried.

• Sugar peas have delicate, fleshy, sweet pods, which are harvested and eaten when the seeds are still unripe.

Beans have a good sodium:potassium ratio, expel fluid, and relieve heart and circulation disturbances. With us, it is primarily the pole and bush beans (*Phaseolus vulgaris* var. *nanus*) that are the important ones.

Onions and leeks. These all belong to the lily family and develop interesting flowers. This vegetable group possesses more or less highly developed bulbs, which botanically are classed as storage stems. Onions and leeks have especially good dietetic characteristics. Their typical odor and taste is produced by their content of sugar and sulfur-containing ethereal oils (leek oil). Leek oil protects plants from being eaten by animals and is also used medicinally. The onion (*Allium cepa*) is indispensable in the kitchen. Leek (*Allium porrum*) has a favorable influence on the digestive processes and blood circulation, and its high potassium content supports kidney function. Garlic (*Allium sativum*) is often processed into medical preparations—they are effective against intestinal diseases, circulatory disturbances, and hardening of the arteries. It is a good partner in mixed culture and is frost-hardy and can also be planted in fall or early spring.

Scarlet runner bean
Phaseolus coccineus
(see photo above)

Scarlet runner beans develop decorative red or white flowers; they need poles or fences to climb on; they also form attractive shields from sight or wind. Sowing Mar. in pots (3 seeds per pot) or May outdoors (5 seeds per pole). Planting with pot ball at end of Apr. beginning May. Growth rampant. Fruit rough, long pods with large seeds, which depending on variety are green, white, or mottled. Harvest Aug, for serving fresh, pick twice a week; old beans become woody. Location sunny, warm, soil not freshly fertilized. Use for cooking, for freezing, or as dried beans.

Pole bean "Blauhilde."

Pole beans
Phaseolus vulgaris var. *vulgaris*

Need poles for climbing support. Sowing from middle of May, 6–8 seeds per pole. Growth rampant, H: up to 10 ft (3 m). Fruit depending on variety, pods green, yellow, blue, or marbled. Harvest July–Aug. Location Sunny, warm, soil not freshly fertilized.

Bush beans.

Sugar peas.

Wrinkled peas.

Bush beans
Phaseolus vulgaris var. *nanus*

Lowest-growing variety of beans. <u>Sowing</u> from middle May in rows outdoors. <u>Growth</u> bushy, H: 6 to 8 in (15–20 cm). <u>Fruit</u> pods, by variety, thin or broad, green, yellow, or blue. <u>Harvest</u> July–Aug. <u>Location</u> warm, loose soil. <u>Use</u> cooking, freezing.

Sugar peas
Pisum sativum convar. *axiphium*

Need support for climbing. <u>Sowing</u> middle of Apr. in rows outdoors. <u>Growth</u> rampant, H: up to 24 in (61 cm). <u>Fruit</u> flat, tender, sweet pods with small seeds. <u>Harvest</u> July–Aug. <u>Location</u> warm, porous soil. <u>Use</u> harvest young pods, cook, freeze.

Wrinkled peas
Pisum sativum convar. *medullare*

Can't be dried; stick large branches in soil for them to climb on. <u>Sowing</u> end Apr. in rows outside. <u>Growth</u> rampant, H: up to 24 in (61 cm). <u>Fruit</u> bright green pods, wrinkled, sweet seeds; sweeter than smooth seeded. <u>Harvest</u> July. <u>Location</u> warm, chalky soil.

Garlic.

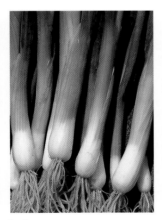

Leeks.

Shallots.

Onions "Gelbe Zittauer."

Garlic
Allium sativum

Healthy, but linked with odor. <u>Planting</u> Mar.–Apr. or Sept., stick single cloves in ground at distance of 6 in (15 cm) apart. <u>Plant</u> bulb with numerous white cloves, leek-like shoots and leaves. <u>Harvest</u> Aug.–Sept. <u>Location</u> warm, light soil.

Leek
Allium porrum

Very good soil enhancer because of its deep-reaching root system. <u>Sowing</u> depending on variety Mar.–Apr., earlier under glass. <u>Planting</u> May–June. <u>Plants</u> white shaft of rolled leaves, with greenish foliage over it, H: 12 in (30 cm). <u>Harvest</u> Oct. <u>Location</u> rich soil, no manure.

Shallots
Allium cepa var. *ascalonicum*

Very delicate taste; better keeping than cooking onions. <u>Planting</u> Mar., place bulbs 6 in (15 cm) apart. <u>Plant</u> develops lateral bulbs around the bulb, which grow together at the very bottom. <u>Harvest</u> June–July. <u>Location</u> light soil, no manure.

Onions
Allium cepa

Many different varieties as seeds or sets. <u>Sowing</u> end Mar. or Aug. <u>Planting</u> Mar.–Apr. <u>Plant</u> onions depending on variety round or oval, white, yellow, or red; tubular, hollow foliage. <u>Harvest</u> Aug.–Sept., store well dried. <u>Location</u> warm, deeply cultivated soil, no fresh manure.

Lettuces and Leaf Vegetables

Lettuces are mostly eaten raw, whereas leaf vegetables, mostly cooked. The flower formation in lettuces and leaf vegetables is controlled by the length of the day; they are either long-day plants or short-day plants. The flowers are, thus, stimulated by daylight under or over 12 hours. In practice, this means that the plants "bolt": The stem begins to stretch and flower buds form. It is, therefore, especially important to sow or plant a variety at the right season. With head lettuce (*Latuca sativa* var. *capitata*), for example, the winter, hothouse, early outdoor, and late outdoor varieties form shoots during the long days; the summer varieties, on the other hand, form shoots in the short days. Iceberg lettuce is less sensitive and is boltproof.

<u>Lettuces.</u> The important varieties stem from garden lettuce (*Lactuca sativa*). When lettuce is served fresh from the garden, its content of vitamins, minerals, and trace elements are available for the body undiminished. Citric and malic acids as well as latucin, a bitter principle, give the leaves their refreshing taste. There are many varieties of leaf lettuce (*Lactuca sativa* var. *crispa*). Loose leaf lettuce can be picked repeatedly, whereas with the "picking lettuces," the oldest leaves are picked first and the heart of the plant continues to grow, with the lettuce growing ever taller. Loose leaf lettuce holds a middle position between the head-forming and the headless lettuces. In the "Lollo" varieties, for example, the heads are half-round and compact half-round rather than loose. You can either pick single leaves or the entire head.

Corn salad, or Feldsalat (*Valerianella locusta*) is a frosthardy winter lettuce. Chicory greens (*Chichorium intybus* var. *foliosum*) like radicchio and endive contain many bitter principles and from them derive their inimitable tastes. It is the sprouts that are eaten, which develop after the cutting off of the summer growth. Endive will produce growth all winter long.

<u>Leaf vegetables.</u> The most important ones are the leaf and stem Swiss chard (*Beta vulgaris* var. *cicla*) and spinach (*Spinacea oleracea*). Spinach is extraordinarily sensitive to the period of daylight—it begins to flower when the days become longer. Therefore spinach is sown in late March or August, and in September for early and late harvests. Swiss chard can be harvested in about 50–60 days; and another harvest in spring is possible when it is wintered over.

Equally boltproof, but rather less known, is the New Zealand spinach (*Tetragonia tetragonoides*). It is not frosthardy and is only set outdoors after all danger of frost is past. The plants form creeping vines and fleshy leaves, which are picked and prepared like spinach.

There are many varieties of head lettuce.

Head lettuce
Lactuca sativa var. *capitata*
Head lettuce is a good gap filler in the vegetable bed. <u>Sowing</u> Feb. to Mar. under glass, from Apr. outdoors, sown in dense rows, it can also be used as looseleaf lettuce. <u>Planting</u> May–Aug. outdoors, 10 in (25 cm) apart; seedlings that droop after planting soon straighten up again. <u>Plant</u> depending on variety firm to loose heads, more or less curled, with green or reddish leaves. <u>Harvest</u> 2 months after planting. <u>Location</u> sunny; fresh, chalky soil.
<u>Important:</u> When heads begin to form, fertilize with nettle "tea"; protect young plants from snails.

Corn salad, Feldsalat.

Dandelion.

Corn salad, Feldsalat
Valerianella locusta
Only grow from Aug. to Mar.; otherwise begins to flower. <u>Sowing</u> broadcast or in rows, Aug.–Sept. Plant upright leaf rosettes. <u>Harvest</u> Oct.–Mar. <u>Location</u> loose, humus soil. <u>Important:</u> Cover with brush before severe frost.

Dandelion
Taraxacum offinale
Hybrid varieties are larger than wild form. <u>Sowing</u> from Mar. outdoors, distance between rows 10 in (25 cm). <u>Plant</u> rosettes of toothed leaves. <u>Harvest</u> Feb.–Mar., bleach (cover with black plastic mulch) lessens the proportion of bitter principles. <u>Location</u> loose, chalky soil.

Endive.

Radicchio.

Iceberg lettuce.

"Amerikanischer Brauner."

Endive
Cichorium endivia
Pleasantly bitter tasting. Sowing June–July outdoors. Planting from end of Aug., 10 in (25 cm) apart. Plant leaves loosely arranged; smooth, curly (Frisée), and slit-leaved varieties. Harvest 2 months after planting. Location fresh, chalky soil.

Radicchio
Cichorium intybus var. *foliosum*
Don't grow after other members of Composite family. Sowing by variety June–Aug. Plant loose rosette of reddish brown leaves. Harvest Sept.–Mar. Location moist, deeply cultivated soil. Important: Cut late varieties in Oct.; small heads grow from stalk.

Iceberg lettuce
Lactuca sativa var. *capitata*
Keeps better than other head lettuces. Sowing Apr. under glass, from May outdoors. Planting from May. Plant firm, large heads, crisp leaves, green and red varieties. Harvest 6–8 weeks after planting. Location sunny; nutrient-rich, moist soil.

Loose leaf lettuce
Lactuca sativa var. *crispa*
Constant harvesting possible. Sowing from Jan. under glass, from Apr. outdoors in rows, 8 in (20 cm) apart. Plant delicate leaves on stems up to 8 in (20 cm) tall, green and red varieties. Harvest 6 weeks after sowing, pluck outer leaves. Location warm, nutrient-rich.

Spinach—ideal for early and late crops.

Red stem Swiss chard.

White stem Swiss chard.

Spinach
Spinacia oleracea
Spinach bolts when days are long; thus, there are varieties for growing in spring and fall. Late varieties can also be wintered over under covers. Spinach can store nitrates, so avoid fertilizing with nitrogen. Sowing depending on variety Mar.–Apr. or Aug.–Sept. Plant dark green to bright green leaves. Harvest 6 weeks–2 months after sowing, continually cutting leaves. Location humus, not too sandy soil. Important: Let the roots rot in the ground, which improves the soil.

Swiss chard
Beta vulgaris var. *cicla*
It is also called ribbed Swiss chard. Sowing Apr.–June, in rows, distance between rows 12 in (30 cm); after the necessary thinning, the pulled plants can be transplanted. Plant leaves H: up to 20 in (50 cm), depending on variety, fleshy, white, or red stems. Harvest first time 3 months after sowing, constantly cut off outer stems; the plants continue to make new growth from the center. Location all soils possible. Important: Cover with branches for overwintering; another harvest in spring is then possible. As soon as the plant begins to flower, it is no longer useful.

Cabbage Vegetables

All the cabbage species are botanically classified as crucifers (members of the Cruciferae family). The parent form is the wild cabbage (*Brassica oleracea*), which today still grows on the coasts of western Europe and the Mediterranean regions. Earlier, cabbage was also used as a medicinal plant, for all species contain vitamin C and other vitamins and minerals. Most cabbages are heavy feeders, but they should not be fertilized with manure because this affects their odor and taste unpleasantly. Also, crucifers may only be planted in the same area every 4 years. Otherwise soil exhaustion results, along with an increased incidence of pests and diseases such as clubroot, a fungus disease that produces proliferations of the root. Affected plants wilt and must be destroyed. Clubroot can affect all cabbage species. Cabbage vegetables are broken down into classifications as follows:

Head In this group, the leaves do not unfold but are firmly attached to a compressed stem and form dense heads. The best-known species are in this group:

• White and red cabbage (*B. oleracea* var. *capitata*); both are very healthy and no longer a cheap vegetable. The heads keep well, and canned sauerkraut is an important supplier of vitamins during the winter.

• Savoy cabbage (*B. oleracea* var. *sabauda*) with curly leaves. It is served fresh; late varieties also keep well.

• Chinese cabbage (*B. pekinensis*), which also tolerates frost and is distinguished by a short growing period of 8 weeks. Its heads store very well.

• Mustard cabbage or pak-Choi (*B. chinensis*), which only forms loose heads of shining dark green leaves with thick, white ribs and is harvested in fall. Its taste is reminiscent of Swiss chard.

Kale (*B. oleracea* var. *sabellica*) does not form heads. Its curly leaves, which taste better after the first frost, are harvested from bottom to top.

Broccoli and cauliflower. With these the fleshy, swollen inflorescence is served before the buds open. Broccoli (*B. oleracea* var. *italica*) is somewhat easier to grow than cauliflower (*B. oleracea* var. *botrytis*).

Kohlrabi (*B. oleracea* var. *gongylodes*), whose thickened stem bulb is served. There are pale green and violet varieties; all are frost-tender.

Brussels sprouts (*B. oleracea* var. *gemmifera*) form tiny cabbage heads in the leaf axils, the so-called "sprouts." These also are better after the first frost.

Important: With all the cabbage vegetables, do not use fresh manure in preparing the beds or for fertilization. Do not use any crucifer (such as mustard) as green manure before planting a bed of cabbage—risk of clubroot!

White cabbage develops sturdy heads.

White cabbage
Brassica oleracea var. *capitata*

Cabbage is a heavy feeder and is therefore planted directly in the garden in spring with early starting; there are early, medium-early, and late varieties. Sowing early varieties end of Jan. under glass, medium-early and late Mar.–Apr. under glass.

Planting early varieties end of Mar., medium-early and late from May outdoors, apply algae chalk in planting hole to prevent clubroot, 16 in (40 cm) between rows. Plant firm, large, pale green heads. Harvest early varieties after 6 weeks, late ones after 8–10 weeks. Location heavy, rich soil, no fresh manure.

Red cabbage adds color to the bed.

Red cabbage
Brassica oleracea var. *capitata*

There are also early, medium-early, and late varieties of red cabbage. Sowing and planting see white cabbage. Plant firm, large heads with red-purple leaves and light ribs. Harvest and location see white cabbage. Important: Corn salad or spinach are good succeeding crops for early cabbage varieties. With late varieties, the heads store very well if they are harvested before the first frost. White cabbage is processed in large quantities into sauerkraut. It is especially healthy raw because of its vitamin C content. Red cabbage is primarily conserved as pickled red cabbage.

Cauliflower.

Blue kohlrabi.

Brussels sprouts.

Pak-choi.

Cauliflower
Brassica oleracea* var *botrytis

There are early, medium-early, and late and mini varieties. Nurturing is needed, so buy young plants. Planting May–July. Plant white "flowers" sit in a wreath of leaves. Harvest 2–2½ months after planting. Location nutrient-rich, chalky soil.

Kohlrabi
Brassica oleracea* var. *gongylodes

Blue varieties are less woody than the green ones. Sowing from Feb. under glass. Planting middle of May, don't set too deep. Plant pale green or blue-violet stem bulbs close above the soil. Harvest 6 weeks–2 months after planting. Location nutrient-rich and chalky soil.

Brussels sprouts
Brassica oleacea* var. *gemmifera

Harvest continues all winter. Sowing Apr.–May outdoors. Planting May–July, intervals of 20 in (50 cm). Plant H: up to 39 in (99 cm), little "sprouts" in the leaf axils, green and red varieties. Harvest in about 95 days or after the first frost. Location nutrient-rich, chalky soil.

Pak-choi
Brassica chinensis

Also called mustard cabbage because of its taste; use raw or cooked. Sowing June. Planting Aug., 12 in (30 cm) apart. Plant loose heads of dark green leaves with white ribs. Harvest end of Sept. Location nutrient-rich, chalky soil.

Broccoli.

Savoy cabbage.

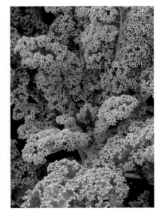

Kale.

Broccoli
Brassica oleracea* var. *italica

Less demanding than cauliflower. Sowing Feb.–Apr. under glass. Planting Apr.–July, distance 16 in (40 cm). Plant depending on variety green or purple "flowers" among a loose wreath of leaves. Harvest about 6 weeks to 2 months after planting, as soon as the flowers are completely developed. But the yellow flowers should not be open yet. At first, harvest the center flowers then later, the smaller ones growing in the leaf axils. Location nutrient-rich, chalky soil, no manure, which changes the taste of the broccoli.

Savoy cabbage
Brassica oleracea* var. *sabauda

Early, mid-season, and late varieties. Sowing early Jan., midseason Mar. under glass, late May outdoors. Planting early Apr., mid-season May, late June. Plant dense heads, curly leaves. Harvest 2–3 months after planting. Location loose, nutrient-rich soil.

Kale
Brassica oleracea* var. *sabellica

Decorative winter vegetable. Sowing May–June outdoors. Planting June–Aug., 24 in (60 cm) apart. Plant H: up to 39 in (99 cm), dark green, curly leaves. Harvest begins after first frost, pick leaves from bottom to top. Location heavy, nutrient-rich soil.

Root, Tuber, and Stem Vegetables

Root, tuber, and stem vegetables belong to different families. All have great importance for human nutrition.
Root and tuber vegetables have developed enlarged root or stem parts in which they store nutrients. They are generally rich in vitamins, minerals, and ethereal oils. The carrot develops especially large amounts of carotene and vitamin C.

Root and tuber vegetables need a deeply cultivated, loose soil. Fluctuations in water supply should be avoided, because roots and tubers split easily. Do not fertilize these vegetables with manure, which can attract pests.

• Potatoes (*Solanum tuberosum*) are first-class soil improvers.

Important: Green places on potatoes should not be eaten; they contain the poisonous solanine.

• Black salsify (*Scorzonera hispanica*) forms long, black, thickened taproots up to 16 in (40 cm) long.

• Horseradish (*Amoracia rusticana*) has brown, thickened, branching roots.

• Radish (*Raphanus sativus* var. *niger*) and the more familiar salad radishes come in many long and round varieties, in white and red, as well as black winter radish.

• Carrots (*Daucus carota* ssp. *sativus*) form long, stubby, or rounded roots.

• Red beets (*Beta vulgaris* var. *conditiva*) are round, red roots that are very good keepers.

• Celeriac (*Apium graveolens* var. *rapaceum*) has greenish brown tubers and spicy leaves.

Important: Radishes and parsnips, like the cabbages, are members of the crucifer family. Don't plant them after each other in the same bed in order not to give diseases like clubroot any encouragement.

Stem vegetables. Sometimes these species develop tasty, tender stems on their own; other times they are bleached. The bleaching process either involves tying up the aboveground parts, wrapping, or as with asparagus, hilling around it. Among the stem vegetables are:

• Rhubarb (*Rheum rhabarbarum*), whose thick stems are primarily used stewed and in pies. Its leaves are said to be poisonous.

• Fennel (*Foeniculum vulgare* var. *azoricum*), whose pseudo-tuber is formed of flat stem parts.

• Bleached stalk celery (*Apium graveolens* var. *dulce*), which is bleached by tying it together.

• Asparagus (*Asparagus officinalis*); to make the bleached asparagus so popular in Europe, it is grown in embankments and the soil heaped up around it.

• Cardoon (*Cynara cardunculus*), whose bleached stems are served.

Celery.

Celery
Apium graveolens var. *dulce*

In contrast to its relative celeriac, celery does not develop a tuber. Sowing Apr. in cold frame. Planting end of May. Plant depending on variety green or white fleshy stem, leaves lush green. Harvest before frost. Location heavy, nutrient-rich soil.

Celeriac.

Celeriac
Apium graveolens var. *rapaceum*

Stores well. Sowing Feb. under glass. Planting middle of May, 20 in (50 cm) apart; don't set too deep. Plant brown-green tubers, dark green leaves on thick stems. Harvest Oct. Location moist, nutrient-rich soil. Important: Leaves suitable for seasoning.

Potatoes.

Potato ☠
Solanum tuberosum

First-class soil improver; there are early, medium-early, and late varieties. Planting middle of Apr. Plants bush H: up to 20 in (50 cm), tubers brown, yellow, or reddish. Harvest after 3 to 4 months, as soon as foliage yellows. Location light to moderately heavy soil, no manure.

Fennel.

Fennel
Foeniculum vulgare var. *azoricum*

Strange looking. Sowing according to variety May–July outdoors, 16 in (40 cm) between rows, later thin out. Plant flat pseudo-tuber of stem parts, delicately pinnate leaves. Harvest as soon as the tuber is fat, but before the first frost. Location nutrient-rich, chalky soil.

Salad radishes.

Black winter radish.

Carrots.

Beet.

Salad radish
Raphanus sativus var. *sativus*

Typical early crop but not before crucifers. <u>Sowing</u> beginning in March outdoors, new sowings weekly. <u>Plant</u> roots round or icicle shaped, red, red-white, or white. <u>Harvest</u> 4 weeks after sowing, continuous. <u>Location</u> loose, humus soil.

Radish
Raphanus sativus var. *niger*

Many varieties. <u>Sowing</u> summer varieties from Apr. outdoors, fall and winter radishes from Aug. <u>Plant</u> roots spherical or stubby, white or red, also long-keeping black winter varieties. <u>Harvest</u> depending on species Aug.–Oct. <u>Location</u> no heavy soil.

Carrot
Daucus carota ssp. *sativus*

Up to 4 weeks germination time. <u>Sowing</u> from Mar. in rows outdoors, 8 in (20 cm) apart. <u>Plant</u> depending on variety bright to dark orange, long, short, fat, thin roots. <u>Harvest</u> after 4 to 5 months, late varieties can be stored. <u>Location</u> sandy soils are ideal.

Beet
Beta vulgaris var. *conditiva*

Don't plant near potatoes. <u>Sowing</u> from May outdoors, rows 12 in (30 cm) apart, thin. <u>Plant</u> red beet, by variety round or elongated, juice intensely colored, green-red leaves. <u>Harvest</u> July to first frost, store well. <u>Location</u> well-drained soil.

Horseradish.

Black salsify.

Rhubarb.

Horseradish
Armoracia rusticana

Horseradish grows invasively but you can limit it with barriers. <u>Planting</u> set out roots (offshoots) early spring. Mar.–Apr. <u>Plants</u> very long, brown, branching roots with sharp odor, large, lanceolate leaves. <u>Harvest</u> Oct.–Mar., dig out roots. <u>Location</u> sandy, nutrient-rich soil.

Black salsify
Scorzonera hispanica

Don't cultivate where nightshade family (Solonaceae) has been. <u>Sowing</u> Mar. or Aug. in rows 8 in (20 cm) apart. <u>Plant</u> black root, up to 16 in (40 cm) long, very narrow, long leaves. <u>Harvest</u> from Oct. to spring, roots break easily. <u>Location</u> loose, sandy, nutrient-rich soil.

Rhubarb
Rheum rhabarbarum

Continuing culture, only the stems are edible; the leaves are said to be poisonous. <u>Planting</u> Sept.–Oct., set rhizome about 2 in (5 cm) deep. <u>Plant</u> depending on variety thick red or green stem, up to 20 in (50 cm) long, large, green leaves. Red-stemmed rhubarb is somewhat milder than green-stemmed. <u>Harvest</u> do not for first 2 years after planting; after that until middle of July, once a week pull out the thick stems; harvest no more than two-thirds of the stems; break off inflorescences immediately. <u>Location</u> deeply cultivated, nutrient-rich soil <u>Important:</u> Cover with compost or rotted manure for the winter.

Herbs

Herbs belong in simply every garden; homegrown and freshly picked, they possess an unforgettable aroma. Not only are they healthy, they improve the taste of many dishes, and many are also attractive garden plants, thus, combining usefulness with beauty. In general usage, the term herbs connotes aromatic plants. This term includes annuals, biennials, and perennial plants but also half-shrubs with spicy, fragrant, and healing qualities. Besides essential oils that one can taste and smell, herbs also contain important minerals and bitter principles like alkaloids, which occur in concentration in poisonous plants. Therefore, it is important to proceed carefully with this plant group and to research for recipes and dosages that have been proven over time.

Location. Most herbs love sunny, warm places. Many come from southern countries. Only a few are decidedly shade-tolerant and love dampness, like the horseradish (*Armoracia rusticana*) and the peppermint (*Mentha piperita*). An herb bed near the kitchen that can also be reached quickly and with dry feet in bad weather is ideal.

Propagation and care. Almost all herbs can be sown from seed, but there are also young plants available commercially. With the perennials, buying a plant pays overall; usually it can be further propagated by division. Herbs are easily satisfied, but organic fertilizer or 1–2 additions of compost per year are recommended. Liquid manures are added now and then, and the perennials are mulched for winter protection. Plants that are not frost-hardy must be wintered over in the house. You can also pot up chives (*Allium schoenoprasum*) and parsley (*Petroselinum crispum*) in the fall and keep them growing on the kitchen windowsill.

Herbs are seldom affected by diseases, because the special substances they contain offer natural protection. Herb extracts are also applied as a preventive and healing measure for pests and disease symptoms (see page 189). If aphids actually ever appear, you can treat them with a soft soap solution.

Harvesting and use. The best time for a harvest is morning, when the night dampness has evaporated and the sun has not yet warmed the plants. Harvest herbs before they flower, if possible, because the content of essential oils and other substances is highest then. There are several possiblities for preserving them. Air drying is a tried-and-true method. Herbs that quickly lose their aroma, like basil (*Ocimum basilicum*), can be frozen. But preserving in vinegar or oil is also possible.

Chives develop beautiful little flower heads.

Chives
Allium schoenoprasum

Perennial member of onion family, flowers very ornamental and also suitable for enclosing a bed. Flower pink-violet head; June–July. Leaf tube shaped, narrow, aromatically fragrant. Growth up to 12 in (30 cm). Location sunny to semishady, nutrient-rich, fresh soil; pot up in the fall and take into the house. Z: 3. Use don't cut leaf tubules too short, use fresh; very versatile for salads, soups, cottage cheese, herb butter, green sauce, with eggs, vegetables, and potatoes as well as sandwich filling.

Lovage can grow very tall.

Lovage
Levisticum officinale

Perennial, vigorous plant, its taste is reminiscent of soup seasoning. Flower yellow-green umbels; June–July. Leaf large, pinnate, and shining. Growth H: up to 5 ft (1.5 m). Location sunny to semishady, nutrient-rich, fresh. Use the tender young leaves are harvested but because of the intense aroma, use only sparingly; for stews, meat, sauces, and soups. Z: 5–7. Important: The plant needs much space and is best planted at the edge or in the background of a bed.

Parsley with decorative leaves.

Summer savory.

Chervil.

Parsley
Petroselinum crispum
Biennial; curly form also very decorative as enclosure for bed. Flower inconspicuous, yellow-brown umbel in second year; June–July. Leaf dark green, smooth or curly. Growth H: up to 16 in (40 cm). Location sunny to semishady, nutrient-rich, fresh soil.

Use cut sturdy stems, leave heart, use fresh, then very high in vitamin C, for green sauce, soup, salads, and roasts, also edible decoration. Biennial; Z: 3.

Important: Smooth-leaved varieties are more aromatic than curly parsley; the roots of this are also usable and store well.

Summer savory
Satureja hortensis
Annual species; Satureja montana is the perennial species. Flowers lavender, Aug. Leaf linear, aromatically fragrant. Growth H: 12 to 20 in (30 to 50 cm). Location sunny, warm. Use fresh or dried.

Important: Ideal companion plant for beets, repels aphids.

Chervil
Anthriscus cerefolium
Annual, undemanding. Flower white umbel; May. Leaf parsley-like, smooth. Growth H: 12 to 24 in (30–60 cm). Location semishady. Use fresh leaves and branches for sauces, soups, fish, eggs.

Important: Length of culture only 6 weeks.

Dill.

Borage with brilliant blue stars of flowers.

Tarragon.

Dill
Anethum graveolens var. hortorum
Annual, fennel-like herb. Flower yellow-green umbels; June–Aug. Leaf pinnulate. Growth H: up to 4 ft (1.2 m) Location sunny, shady feet, protected. Use fresh leaves for salads, fish, raw vegetables, seeds for pickling cucumbers.

Borage
Borago officinalis
Annual plant with very decorative flowers; it is also called talewort and cool tankard. Flower brilliant blue, star shaped, also rose-pink forms; June–Aug. Leaf oval, soft, very hairy and rough, as is the stem. Growth H: up to 24 in (60 cm), bushy and branching.

Location sunny to semishady; nutrient-rich but porous soil. Use the flowers are both edible and used for decoration, the fresh leaves taste like cucumbers; with cucumbers, salads, egg dishes, for green sauce, fish dishes.

Important: Easily self-sows.

Tarragon
Artemisia dracunculus
var. sativa
Perennial plant with many varieties. Flower insignificant, yellow-green. Leaf small and narrow. Growth H: up to 3 ft (0.9 m), loosely bushy. Location sunny to semishady. Z: 5–9. Use fresh leaflets and stem tips for fish, poultry, salads.

Herbs

Because herbs smell and look beautiful, you can use them in the garden like ornamental plants. You have opportunities to create some very pretty designs with them:

Herb gardens. Traditional herb gardens are laid out in severely formal style (see pages 132–133 and 136–137). But a free-form design—perhaps only a straight border—can also be considered. Don't plant annual and biennial herbs with perennials, because they need entirely different work cycles. Tall plants like common wormwood (*Artemisia absinthium*) and fennel (*Foeniculum vulgare*) are planted in the middle or the background, so that they don't shadow the small ones. Herbs that like dryness are placed at the edge and run rampant in segregated areas.

Herbs in the ornamental garden. But herbs can also be planted in the perennial garden or pebble bed and in the rock garden. This kind of mixed culture even has a health-promoting effect on the other plants. The gray-leaved herbs find ideal conditions in dry beds or path edges and sitting areas. Green, variegated, and beautifully flowered herbs like blue borage (*Borago officinalis*), orange pot marigold (*Calendula officinalis*), and violet marjoram (*Majorana hortensis*) look pretty in country colorful perennial borders.

Herbs as enclosures. Parsley (*Petroselinum crispum*), chives (*Allium schoenoprasum*), lavender (*Lavandula officinalis*), or lavender cotton (*Santolina chamaecyparissus*), which all grow the same size and tolerate cutting, are wonderfully suitable for bordering formal beds.

Herb carpets. Many warmth-loving herbs find ideal conditions in walls and stone crevices or between stepping-stones in pathways and terraces. When walked on, this living carpet gives off a pleasant fragrance.

Herbs in pots. Individual plants—especially Mediterranean, non-winter-hardy ones like rosemary (*Rosemarinus officinalis*) or bay (*Laurus nobilis*)—become beautiful focal points in decorative containers. They can be grouped into small mobile gardens. In the fall, the frost-tender plants can be that much more easily transported into their winter quarters.

Basil.

Oregano.

Basil
Ocimum basilicum
Annual, warmth-loving herb. Flower inconspicuous; June–Aug. Leaf lanceolate oval, green and red varieties. Growth H: up to 20 in (50 cm). Location sunny, warm, protected, humus. Use fresh leaflets and stem tips, for salads, tomatoes, and fish.

Oregano
Origanum vulgare
Perennial, undemanding. Flower pink, pretty, attracts bees; July–Sept. Leaf ovate. Growth H: up to 20 in (50 cm). Location sunny, warm, porous, rather dry. Use leaves and stem tips, for meat and pasta dishes, pizza, vegetables. Z: 5–11.

Thyme.

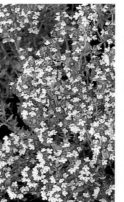

Marjoram.

Thyme
Thymus vulgaris
Perennial, evergreen, somewhat frost-tender. Flower small, rose-lavender; May–Sept. Leaf small and narrow. Growth H: 4 to 12 in (10–30 cm). Location sunny, warm, and dry. Z: 4–9. Use leaflets and stem tips cooked in stews, meat and tomato dishes, and pizza.

Marjoram
Origanum majorana
Frost-tender, only annual. Flower small, white, pink, or violet; June. Leaf ovate. Growth H: up to 20 in (50 cm). Location sunny, warm, porous. Use fresh leaves and stems only briefly cooked, for stews, roasts, soups, sauces, and sausage.

Rosemary.

Sage with interesting flowers.

Garden cress.

Rosemary
Rosmarinus officinalis
Perennial, small, non-frost-hardy shrub. <u>Flower</u> light blue; May–June. <u>Leaf</u> needle-like, evergreen. <u>Growth</u> H: about 39 in (1 m). <u>Location</u> sunny, warm, protected, porous. <u>Use</u> cook in leaflets and stems for all Mediterranean dishes. Z: 7–9.

Sage
Salvia officinalis
Perennial, decorative half-shrub. <u>Flower</u> whitish to violet; June–Aug. <u>Leaf</u> gray-green, lanceolate oval, winter-green. <u>Growth</u> H: up to 36 in (91 cm). <u>Location</u> sunny, warm, protected, porous. Z: 4–9. <u>Use</u> leaves and stem tips cooked in, use sparingly, for stews, meat and fish dishes, tomatoes. <u>Varieties</u> "Ictarine" with yellow marking; "Tricolor" with white-lilac leaf edges; both only winter-hardy in mild winters.
<u>Important:</u> Give light winter protection and cut back annually so that the plants don't get bare and will form fresh growth.

Garden cress, Pepper cress
Lepidium sativum
Very short-lived little herb. <u>Flower</u> inconspicuous, crucifer. <u>Leaf</u> pinnate, small. <u>Growth</u> H: up to 16 in (40 cm), but is primarily used in seedling stage. <u>Location</u> sunny to shady. <u>Use</u> fresh.
<u>Important:</u> Also can be grown on windowsill.

Lemon balm with aromatically fragrant leaves.

Peppermint.

Salad burnet.

Lemon balm
Melissa officinalis
Perennial, very vigorously growing and robust plant. <u>Flower</u> inconspicuous; June–Aug. <u>Leaf</u> green, also yellowish green with toothed edge, smelling of lemon. <u>Growth</u> H: up to 24 in (60 cm), bushy, forming runners. <u>Location</u> sunny to semishady, fresh and humus. <u>Use</u> fresh young leaves and stem tips for salads and other food, also for desserts and as edible decoration; teas from fresh and dried herb. <u>Variety</u> "Aurea" with golden yellow leaves. Z: 4–8.
<u>Important:</u> Flowering is tied to pruning at correct time.

Peppermint
Mentha x piperita
Perennial, very invasive plant. <u>Flower</u> pink-violet; July–Aug. <u>Leaf</u> lanceolate oval, green to reddish. <u>Growth</u> H: up to 32 in (81 cm), bushy. <u>Location</u> sunny to semishady, moist. Z: 3–9. <u>Use</u> young fresh leaflets, for lamb, sauces, sweet dishes, teas.

Salad burnet
Sanguisorba minor
Perennial pretty and unde-manding plant. <u>Flower</u> rose-green heads. <u>Leaf</u> pinnulate. <u>Growth</u> H: up to 24 in (61 cm). <u>Location</u> sunny to semishady, porous soil. <u>Use</u> fresh young leaves, for salads, cottage cheese, green sauce. Z: 4–8.

"Why should the warmth, the sun, the joy, and the fragrance of a wondrous season go to waste? Why shouldn't something of it, in the flowers or something else, be concentrated and kept back, available so that we could fetch it, take it home, and later derive comfort from it once more?"

Hermann Hesse

Index and Register of Species

Index and Register of Species

Index and Register of Species

Index and Register of Species

Index and Register of Species

Literature, Addresses, Photo Credits, Acknowledgments

Additional Reading

The Anderson Horticultural Library's Source List of Plants and Seeds, 4th ed. Compiled and edited by Richard T. Isaacson, et al. University of Minnesota, 1996.

Archer-Wills, A., *The Water Gardener.* Hauppauge, NY: Barron's, 1993.

Barton, B. J., *Gardening by Mail.* New York: Houghton Mifflin, 1994.

Bunemann, and Becker, *Roses.* Hauppauge, NY: Barron's, 1994.

Catterall, E., *Growing Begonias.* Portland, OR: Timber Press, 1984.

Clarkson, R. E., *Magic Gardens.* New York: Macmillan, 1992.

Clarkson, R. E., *Herbs: Their Culture and Uses.* New York: Macmillan, 1990.

Damerow, G., *Fences for Pasture & Garden.* Storey Communications, 1992.

Darden, J., *Great American Azaleas: A Guide to the Finest Azalea Varieties.* North Carolina: Greenhouse Press, 1986.

Ellis, B. and F. M. Bradley, eds., *The Organic Gardener's Handbook of Natural Insect and Disease Control.* Emmaus, PA: Rodale Press, 1992.

Fell, D., *Essential Bulbs: The 100 Best for Design and Cultivation.* New Jersey: Outlet Book Co., 1989.

Foster, F. G., *Ferns to Know and Grow.* Portland, OR: Timber Press, 1984.

Freeman, S., *Herbs for All Seasons: Growing and Gathering Herbs for Flavor, Health, and Beauty.* New York: NAL/Dutton, 1991.

Gibson, M., *Growing Roses for Small Gardens.* Portland, OR: Timber Press, 1991.

Greer, H. E., *Greer's Guidebook to Available Rhododendrons.* Eugene, OR: Offshoot Publications, 1987.

Heitz, H., G. Jankovics, and U. Dorner. *Container Plants.* Consulting Ed. Dennis W. Stevenson. Hauppauge, NY: Barron's, 1992.

Hertle, Kiermeier, Nickig, *Garden Flowers.* Hauppauge, NY: Barron's, 1994.

Hobhouse, P., *Flower Gardens.* Boston: Little, Brown, 1991.

Jefferson-Brown, M., *The Lily: For Garden, Patio and Display.* Vermont: Trafalgar Square, 1982.

Kourick, R. *Designing and Maintaining Your Edible Landscape Naturally.* Metamorphic Press, 1986.

Kremer, B.P. *Shrubs in the Wild and in Gardens.* Consulting Ed. Dennis W. Stevenson. Hauppauge, NY: Barron's, 1995.

Muckle, M. E., *Basic Hydroponics for the Do-It-Yourselfer: A Cultural Handbook.* Growers Press, 1994.

Pahlow, M. *The Healing Plants.* Hauppauge, NY: Barron's, 1993.

Riotte, L., *Successful Small Food Gardens.* Storey Communications, 1993.

Skeen, B., *Growing Chrysanthemums.* Portland, OR: International Specialized Book Services, 1985.

Stadelmann, P. *Water Gardens.* Hauppauge, NY: Barron's, 1992.

Taylor's Master Guide to Gardening. Boston: Houghton Mifflin, 1994.

Verey, R., *The Art of Planting.* Boston: Little, Brown, 1990.

Vriends, M., *Feeding and Sheltering Backyard Birds.* Hauppauge, NY: Barron's, 1990.

Williams, R. *The Garden Planner.* Hauppauge, NY: Barron's, 1990.

Yeo, P. F., *Hardy Geraniums.* Portland, OR: Timber Press, 1985.

Zeigler, C., *The Harmonious Garden.* Portland, OR: Timber Press, 1996.

Magazines/Newsletters

American Horticulturalist. American Horticultural Society. (bimonthly; free with membership)

The Avant Gardner. Horticultural Data Processors, P.O. Box 489, New York, NY 10028.

Beautiful Gardens. CMK Publishing, P.O. Box 2971, Dublin, CA 94568.

Fine Gardening Magazine. Taunton Press, Inc., 63 South Main St., P.O. Box 355, Newtown, CT 06470.

Garden Design. Evergreen Publishing Co., 4401 Connecticut Ave., NW, Ste. 500, Washington, D.C. 20008-2302

The Landscape Architect Specifier News. 2138 South Wright St., Santa Ana, CA 92705.

Organic Gardening. Rodale Press, 33 East Minor St., Emmaus, PA 18098.

Organic Gardening TLC...for plants. (Canada)

E-Mail

Agropolis, The Texas A&M University System Agriculture Program: http://agcomwww.tama.edu/agcom/agrotext/visitor.html

America On-line: The Garden Spot. Access through AOL's hobby files.

Garden Gate on Prairienet: http://www.prairienet.org/ag/garden/homepage.htm

Gardening Sites: http://www.ag.uiuc.edu/%7Edwardt/garden.htm

GardenNet: http://www.olympus.net/gardens/welcome.htlm

The National Gardening Association: http://www.wowpages.com/nga/

Ohio State University's WebGarden: http://hortwww-2.ag.ohio-state.edu/hvp/webgarden/webgarden.html

Organizations/Societies

American Horticultural Society. 7931 E. Boulevard Dr., Alexandria, VA 22308. (800/777-7931; 703/768-5700)

American Society of Landscape Architects. 4401 Connecticut Ave., NW, 5th Fl., Washington, D.C. 20008-2302. (202/686-2752)

Canadian Plant Conservation Program, c/o Devonian Botanic Garden, University of Alberta, Edmonton, Alberta, Canada T6G 2E1.

Garden Club of America. 598 Madison Ave., New York, NY 10022.

The Gardeners of America. 5560 Merle Hay Rd., Johnston, IA 50131-0241. (515/278-0255)

National Council of State Garden Clubs. 4401 Magnolia Ave., St. Louis, MO 63110-3492. (314/776-7574)

National Gardening Association. 180 Flynn Ave., Burlington, VT 05401. (802/863-1308)

National Junior Horticultural Assoc. 1424 N. 8th Ave., Durant, OK 74701-2602. (405/924-0771)

Ontario Horticultural Association. RR #3, Englehart, Ontario, Canada P0J 1H0 (705/544-2474)

United States Department of Agriculture (USDA). 6303 Ivy Lane, Room 400. Greenbelt, MD 20770 (301/344-2956)

Mail Order

Abracadata, Ltd. P.O. Box 2440, Eugene, OR 97402 (503/342-3030; 800/451-4871) *computer programs: landscape design, vegetable gardens, garden railway.*

Adirondack Designs. 350 Cypress Street, Fort Bragg, CA 95437 (707/964-4940; 800/222-0343) *furniture.*

Andy Brinkley Studio. P.O. Box 10282, Hickory, NC 28603 (704/462-1137; F: 462-4647) *garden sculptures, fountains.*

Alberta Nurseries & Seed Company. P.O. Box 20, Bowden, Alberta, Canada T0M 0K0 (403/224-3544; F: 224-2455) *plants, seeds, supplies.*

Bear Creek Nursery. P.O. Box 411, Northport, WA 99157-0411. *plants, tools.*

Bow House, Inc. P.O. Box 900, 92 Randall Road, Bolton, MA 01740 (508/779-6464 or 2271; F: 587-0223) *gazebos, garden structures.*

D.V. Burrell Seed Growers Co. P.O. Box 150, Rocky Ford, CO 81067-0150 (719/254-3318; F: 254-3319) *seeds, books, supplies, tools.*

W. Atlee Burpee Company. 300 Park Ave., Warminster, PA 18974 (215/674-4900; 800/888-1447) *plants, seeds, bulbs, books, supplies, tools.*

Carroll Gardens. P.O. Box 310, 444 E. Main St., Westminster, MD 21158 (410/848-5422; 800/638-6334) *plants, books, tools.*

Creative Playgrounds, Ltd. P.O. Box 10, McFarland, WI 53558 (608/838-3326; 800/338-0522; F: 838-9595)

Environmental Concepts. 710 N.W. 57th St., Ft. Lauderdale, FL 33309 (305/491-4490) *meters to measure pH, etc.*

Heritage Garden Furniture. 1209 E. Island Highway, #6, Parksville, British Columbia, Canada V9P 1R5 (605/248-9598, also FAX) *cedar furniture.*

International Irrigation Systems. P.O. Box 360, Niagara Falls, NY 14304 (416/688-4090; F: 688-4093)

Plants of the Southwest. Route 6, Box 11A, Agua Fria, Santa Fe, NM 87501 (505/471-2212; 438-8888) *plants, seeds, books.*

Pomona Book Exchange. Highway 52, Rockton, Ontario, Canada L0R1X0 *horticulture, agriculture*

Popovitch Associates, Inc. 346 Ashland Ave., Pittsburgh, PA 15228 (412/344-6097) *light fixtures.*

Solarcone, Inc. P.O. Box 67, Seward, IL 61077-0067 (815/247-8454; F: 247-8443) *composting containers.*

Taylor Ridge Farm. P.O. Box 222, Saluda, NC 28773 (704/749-4756) *arbors, trellises.*

Cooperative Extension State Offices

Alabama
Cooperative Extension Service, Auburn U., Duncan Hall, Auburn, AL 36849, P: (205) 844-4444

Alaska
Cooperative Extension Service, U. of Alaska, Fairbanks, AK 99775-6180, P: (907) 474-4746, F: (907) 474-6567

Arizona
Cooperative Extension, U. of Arizona, College of Argiculture, Forbes Bldg., Tucson, AZ 85721, P: (602) 621-7205, F: (602) 621-1314

Arkansas
Cooperative Extension Service, U. of Arkansas, 2201 Brookwood Dr., PO Box 391, Little Rock, AR 72203, P: (501) 671-2000

California
Cooperative Extension Service, U. of California, Kaiser Bldg., 300 Lakeside Dr., 6th Fl., Oakland, CA 94612-3560, P: (510) 987-0505

Colorado
Cooperative Extension, 1 Administration Building, Colorado State Univ., Fort Collins, CO 80523, P: (303) 491-6281

YOU JUST NEED TO KNOW HOW

Organizations, institutions, magazines, books provide information, ideas, and addresses on all horticultural subjects. These local institutions will refer you further or give you direct help if you have questions:

• *Department of environmental protection*

• *Agricultural experiment station or extension service*

• *Conservation groups Addresses are in your telephone book.*